Lecture Notes in Computer Science 12586

More information about this subseries at http://www.springer.com/series/7410

Lejla Batina · Stjepan Picek ·
Mainack Mondal (Eds.)

Security, Privacy, and Applied Cryptography Engineering

10th International Conference, SPACE 2020
Kolkata, India, December 17–21, 2020
Proceedings

 Springer

Editors
Lejla Batina 🆔
Faculty of Science
Radboud University
Nijmegen, Gelderland, The Netherlands

Stjepan Picek 🆔
Delft University of Technology
Delft, Zuid-Holland, The Netherlands

Mainack Mondal 🆔
Indian Institute of Technology
Kharagpur, India

ISSN 0302-9743   ISSN 1611-3349   (electronic)
Lecture Notes in Computer Science
ISBN 978-3-030-66625-5   ISBN 978-3-030-66626-2   (eBook)
https://doi.org/10.1007/978-3-030-66626-2

LNCS Sublibrary: SL4 – Security and Cryptology

This Springer imprint is published by the registered company Springer Nature Switzerland AG
The registered company address is: Gewerbestrasse 11, 6330 Cham, Switzerland

Preface

The 10th International Conference on Security, Privacy and Applied Cryptography Engineering 2020 (SPACE 2020) was held on December 17–20, 2020. This annual event is devoted to various aspects of security, privacy, applied cryptography, and cryptographic engineering. This is a challenging field, requiring expertise from diverse domains, ranging from mathematics and computer science to circuit design. It was first planned to host the conference at IIT Kharagpur, India, but it took place online due to the worldwide pandemic crisis.

This year we received 48 submissions from many different countries, mainly from Asia and Europe. The submissions were evaluated based on their significance, novelty, technical quality, and relevance to the SPACE conference. The submissions were reviewed in a double-blind mode by at least three members of the Program Committee, which consisted of 52 members from all over the world. After an extensive review process, 13 papers were accepted for presentation at the conference, leading to the acceptance rate of 27%.

The program also included two invited talks and four tutorials on various aspects of applied cryptology, security, and privacy, delivered by world-renowned researchers: Joan Daemen, Patrick Longa, Ahmad-Reza Sadeghi, Peter Schwabe, Ingrid Verbauwhede, and Yuval Yarom. Two of the program chairs also offered a tutorial on side-channel attacks. We sincerely thank the invited speakers for accepting our invitations in spite of their busy schedules. As in previous editions, SPACE 2020 was organized in cooperation with the International Association for Cryptologic Research (IACR). We are grateful to general chairs Indranil Sengupta and Debdeep Mukhopadhyay for their willingness to host the conference physically at IIT Kharagpur and their assistance with turning it into an online event.

There is a long list of volunteers who invested their time and energy to put together the conference. We are grateful to all the members of the Program Committee and their sub-reviewers for all their hard work in the evaluation of the submitted papers. We thank our publisher Springer for agreeing to continue to publish the SPACE proceedings as a volume in the Lecture Notes in Computer Science (LNCS) series. We are grateful to the local Organizing Committee, especially to the general chairs, Debdeep Mukhopadhyay and Indranil Sengupta, who invested a lot of time and effort in order for the conference to run smoothly. We would like to thank Antriksh Shah and his team from Payatu Technologies for not only partially sponsoring the event, but also being a partner in the organization.

Last, but not least, our sincere thanks go to all the authors who submitted papers to SPACE 2020, and to all of you who attended it virtually. At least due to the COVID-19 virus crisis we were able to have so many of you attending it online and registering for free. We sincerely hope to meet some of you in person next year.

November 2020

Lejla Batina
Mainack Mondal
Stjepan Picek

Organization

General Chairs

Debdeep Mukhopadhyay	Indian Institute of Technology Kharagpur, India
Indranil Sengupta	Indian Institute of Technology Kharagpur, India

Program Committee Chairs

Lejla Batina	Radboud University, The Netherlands
Mainack Mondal	Indian Institute of Technology Kharagpur, India
Stjepan Picek	TU Delft, The Netherlands

Program Committee

Subidh Ali	Indian Institute of Technology Bhilai, India
Lejla Batina	Radboud University, The Netherlands
Shivam Bhasin	Temasek Laboratories @ NTU, Singapore
Sukanta Bhattacharya	Indian Institute of Technology Guwahati, India
Ileana Buhan	Radboud University, The Netherlands
Claude Carlet	The University of Bergen, Norway and Université Paris 8 Vincennes-Saint-Denis, France
Rajat Subhra Chakraborty	Indian Institute of Technology Kharagpur, India
Sandip Chakraborty	Indian Institute of Technology Kharagpur, India
Rahul Chatterjee	University of Wisconsin-Madison, USA
Anupam Chattopadhyay	Nanyang Technological University, Singapore
Lukasz Chmielewski	Riscure, The Netherlands
Chitchanok Chuengsatiansup	University of Adelaide, Australia
Jean-Luc Danger	ENST, France
Soumyajit Dey	Indian Institute of Technology Kharagpur, India
Christian Doerr	Hasso Plattner Institute, Germany
Domenic Forte	University of Florida, USA
Fatemeh Ganji	Worcester Polytechnic Institute, USA
Annelie Heuser	IRISA, France
Naofumi Homma	Tohoku University, Japan
Dirmanto Jap	Nanyang Technological University, Singapore
Salil Kanhere	UNSW Sydney, Australia
Jean Peter Kapps	George Mason University, USA
Ramesh Karri	New York University, USA
Aniket Kate	Purdue University, USA
Marc Manzano	Technology Innovation Institute, Abu Dhabi
Luca Mariot	TU Delft, The Netherlands
Pedro Maat Massolino	PQShield, UK

Bodhisatwa Mazumdar	Indian Institute of Technology Indore, India
Nele Mentens	KU Leuven, Belgium
Mainack Mondal	Indian Institute of Technology Kharagpur, India
Debdeep Mukhopadhyay	Indian Institute of Technology Kharagpur, India
Sikhar Patranabis	ETH Zurich, Switzerland
Guilherme Perin	TU Delft, The Netherlands
Stjepan Picek	TU Delft, The Netherlands
Ilai Polian	University of Stuttgart, Germany
Chester Rebeiro	Indian Institute of Technology Madras, India
Sujoy Sinha Roy	University of Birmingham, UK
Dipanwita Roychowdhury	Indian Institute of Technology Kharagpur, India
Kazuo Sakiyama	The University of Electro-Communications, Japan
Somitra Sanadhya	Indian Institute of Technology Ropar, India
Vishal Saraswat	Robert Bosch Engineering and Business Solutions, India
Peter Schwabe	Radboud University, The Netherlands
Rijurekha Sen	Indian Institute of Technology Delhi, India
Johanna Sepulveda	Airbus, Germany
Sandeep Shukla	Indian Institute of Technology Kanpur, India
Eran Toch	Tel Aviv University, Israel
Christine van Vredendaal	NXP Semiconductors, The Netherlands
Jason Xue	University of Adelaide, Australia
Bohan Yang	Tsinghua University, China
Yuval Yarom	University of Adelaide, Australia; Data61
Amr Youssef	Concordia University, Canada
Fan Zhang	Zhejiang University, China

Additional Reviewers

Ayantika Chatterjee
Durba Chatterjee
Nandish Chattopadhyay
Siddhartha Chowdhury
Soumyadyuti Ghosh
Aritra Hazra
Jiaji He
Matthias J. Kannwischer
Chandan Karfa
Samuel Karumba
Mustafa Khairallah
Manas Khatua
Ipsita Koley
Anushree Mahapatra
Regio Michelin
Debasis Mitra

Shayan Mohammed
Rijoy Mukherjee
Ruchira Naskar
Hammond Pearce
Duy-Phuc Pham
Romain Poussier
Prasanna Ravi
Rajat Sadhukhan
Pranesh Santikellur
Deepraj Soni
Benjamin Tan
Imdad Ullah
Léo Weissbart
Yoo-Seung Won
Wanli Xue
Wenping Zhu

Contents

Systems Security

tPAKE: Typo-Tolerant
Password-Authenticated Key Exchange

Thitikorn Pongmorrakot[(⊠)] and Rahul Chatterjee

University of Wisconsin–Madison, Madison, USA
pongmorrakot@wisc.edu, chatterjee@cs.wisc.edu

Abstract. Password-authenticated key exchange (PAKE) enables a user to authenticate to a server by proving the knowledge of the password without actually revealing their password to the server. PAKE protects user passwords from being revealed to an adversary who compromises the server (or a disgruntled employee). Existing PAKE protocols, however, do not allow even a small typographical mistake in the submitted password, such as accidentally adding a character at the beginning or at the end of the password. Logins are rejected for such password submissions; the user has to retype their password and reengage in the PAKE protocol with the server. Prior works have shown that users often make typographical mistakes while typing their passwords. Allowing users to log in with small typographical mistakes would improve the usability of passwords and help users log in faster. Towards this, we introduce tPAKE: a typo-tolerant PAKE, that allows users to authenticate (or exchange high-entropy keys) using a password while tolerating small typographical mistakes. tPAKEallows edit-distance-based errors, but only those that are frequently made by users. This benefits security, while still improving usability. We discuss the security considerations and challenges in designing tPAKE. We implement tPAKE and show that it is computationally feasible to be used in place of traditional PAKEs while providing improved usability. We also provide an extension to tPAKE, called adaptive-tPAKE, that will enable the server to allow a user to log in with their frequent mistakes (without ever learning those mistakes).

Keywords: Passwords · Authentication · Password-authenticated key exchange (PAKE) · Typo-tolerant password checking

1 Introduction

Authenticating users on the Internet is still primarily done using passwords. Passwords are user-chosen short secrets. A user picks a password during registering an account with a service, and then the user has to reproduce the same secret exactly during the login process to get access to their account.

Passwords, ideally, should not be stored in plaintext on the server; they are hashed using a slow cryptographic hash function, such as scrpyt [30], bcrypt [32], Argon2 [9]. The communication channel between the server and the user device

© Springer Nature Switzerland AG 2020
L. Batina et al. (Eds.): SPACE 2020, LNCS 12586, pp. 3–24, 2020.
https://doi.org/10.1007/978-3-030-66626-2_1

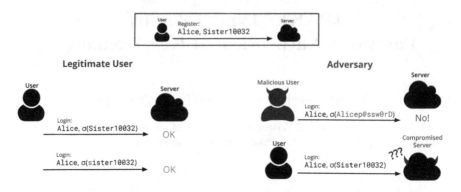

Fig. 1. Overview of how tPAKE operates. σ is a pseudo-random function that obscure the password. See Sect. 4 for more details.

is normally secured from network adversaries using SSL/HTTPS. Nevertheless, user passwords are still exposed to the server in plaintext format every time a user tries to log in. Therefore, an attacker with persistent access to the login server can learn users' plaintext passwords as they log in. Such persistent adversarial (or sometime accidental) access to the login server is not a rare incident. For example, due to poor security practices, certain Facebook server-side applications stored plaintext user passwords on disk for several years (between 2012 and 2019), and Facebook employees could view those stored passwords [24]. In 2018, Twitter had to ask its users to change their passwords after an incident that revealed millions of user passwords in the error log [4]. Therefore, in our current setting, an adversary with persistent access to the server can learn the passwords of the users who log in during the period when the adversary has access to the login server.

Password-authenticated key exchange (PAKE) [8] is proposed to protect user passwords from getting exposed to the service during login.[1] PAKE allows a user to prove their knowledge of the password without revealing it to the server during login. Thereby, an adversary that compromises the server would not learn the user passwords even if the user logs in during the time adversary controls the server: The adversary has to crack the stored computationally expensive hash digests of the passwords.

Several PAKE protocols [6–8, 11] have been proposed over the years. However, none of them allows even small typographical errors in the entered password by the user. A PAKE protocol will result in an error if the user, for example, accidentally switches the case of the first character of their password. Previous studies [12, 13] have shown that users often make mistakes while typing their

---

[1] It was originally designed for exchanging secret keys between two parties with knowledge of the same password over an untrusted network connection. Nonetheless, the same protocol can be used to protect passwords from being exposed to persistent adversaries who compromised the server as well. The later usage gained more interest over the years, especially as TLS can be used to exchange secrets.

passwords, especially while typing long and complex passwords. A key challenge in encouraging users to use long and complex passwords is their usability. And if PAKE is going to be used as a de-facto protocol for future authentication, it must overcome this usability challenge and allow users to complete a PAKE protocol despite making small typographical mistakes.

To enable small error tolerance in PAKE protocols, prior work [17] has proposed a modified PAKE protocol, called *Fuzzy-PAKE*, that draws from some ideas of secure sketches [16]. However, Fuzzy-PAKE tolerates Hamming errors—the protocol succeeds if the password entered by the user is withing a small Hamming distance from the registered password. However, this error model is not realistic as typographical mistakes are better represented as edit-distance errors—the protocol should succeed if the entered password is within some *small edit-distance* from the registered password. There is no straight forward way to extend Fuzzy-PAKE to allow edit distance-based errors. Also, allowing *any* error within certain Hamming or edit distance could degrade security [12].

In this paper, we propose a new protocol, called tPAKE (short for typo-tolerant password-authenticated key exchange), that can tolerate a fixed (configurable) number of typos that are frequently made by users while typing their passwords. The core idea behind the protocol for tPAKE is simple and elegant, allowing us to provide a simple argument for its security. Intuitively, the server stores a fixed number of possible variations of the password submitted during registration. During login, the client and the server engage in a private set intersection (PSI) protocol. (The variations to allow the user to log in can be chosen by the user or the server during registration).

Although, simple, this basic protocol has some key limitations in terms of security and efficiency. A secure PAKE must protect the user passwords from phishing attacks[2] or typo-squatting attacks[3]. That is to say, even if an adversary tricks the user into running the PAKE protocol with them, the adversary should not learn the user passwords. Similarly, the adversary also should not be able to impersonate the user as long as they don't know the user passwords (or any of the typos of that password). Therefore, the client and the server in our setting can act maliciously in the protocol (during login)[4] A schematic diagram of the functionality and threats of tPAKE is shown in Fig. 1. To protect the confidentiality of the user passwords, we have to use malicious-secure PSI protocols, which are yet to be efficient (see for example [31]). For designing tPAKE, we show how to extend a known PAKE protocol to enable typo-tolerance without degrading security.

We provide two protocols for allowing typo-tolerance. In the first case, the protocol picks the set of variations to tolerate during the registration process. In the second protocol, the server adaptively learns about the mistakes that a particular user frequently makes and let the user login with those passwords,

---

[2] https://en.wikipedia.org/wiki/Phishing.

[3] https://en.wikipedia.org/wiki/Typosquatting.

[4] We assume the registration process is done in a secure manner.

without ever learning user password or typos. The two modes of typo-tolerance are motivated by the two variations proposed in [12] and [13], respectively.

The protocol tPAKE utilizes oblivious pseudo-random functions (OPRF) to hide the user-entered passwords from the server. Along with the OPRF protocol, tPAKE ensures an implicit authentication so that at the end of the protocol, the server and the client learns the legitimacy of each other. During (trusted) registration, the server obtains the OPRF output of the user's password and its variations. During (untrusted) login procedure, the server only obtains proof that the user has the knowledge of the password, without obtaining the password in plaintext. We describe this protocol in Sect. 4. Adaptive-tPAKE extends on this protocol to enable secure storage of user's typos and other password submissions (some of which might not qualify as a typo) using a public key encryptions scheme. We describe this protocol and its security in Sect. 5. We prototype these protocols and measure their efficacy and computational performance in Sect. 6.

The main contributions of this work are the following:

(1) We design tPAKE, a PAKE protocol that allows a user to log in despite making small typographical mistakes.
(2) We analyze the security of tPAKE. We implement tPAKE, and show that the computational overhead of tPAKE is acceptable.
(3) We provide another variants of tPAKE, which we call adaptive-tPAKE, that can learn a user's typos over time (without ever seeing the typos themselves) and allow the user to log in with frequent but safe typos.

2　Background and Related Works

Despite several usability challenges, passwords are still used as the primary method for user authentication. The key challenges with passwords are: (a) they are easy to guess—low entropy secrets; and (b) hard to remember or type. In this section we discuss some background on password usability, tolerating password typos, and how to protect passwords from being revealed to a malicious server that tries to steal user passwords.

Usability Challenge in Password-Based Authentication. Users are more inclined to use simple, easily guessable passwords [10,19,29]. Mazurek et al. [28] hypothesize that one of the reasons for that is due to the increased difficulty in memorizing and typing more complex passwords. These simple passwords make these systems susceptible to various forms of guessing attacks, thus, greatly impacting the security of said systems. The increased effort required to type a more complex password can be one of the many factors that persuade users to resort to using more vulnerable passwords, especially when users mistype their passwords and redo the authentication process again. Moreover, a research [33] has found a correlation between the length of a password and the rate in which typo would occur, suggesting that longer passwords might lead to reduced usability due to mistyped passwords. Studies by Keith et al [22,23] showed that up to 2.2% of entries of user-chosen passwords had a typo (dened by thresholding via

Levenshtein distance), and the rate of typos roughly doubles for more complex passwords (at least length 7, one upper-case, one lower-case, one non-letter). A study found that up to 10% of failed login attempts fail due to a handful of simple, easily correctable typos [12]. The study also shows that out of all the typos made by users, a significant proportion of the typos are simple mistakes that can be fixed through simple operations, and fixing these typos can help reduce the frustration of mistyping their password for a significant fraction of users.

Typo-Tolerant Password Checking. Users often make mistakes while typing their passwords. Previous studies [12,13] have shown that this causes a huge usability burden on users. Allowing legitimate users to login with small mistakes improves user experience with a platform and saves unnecessary time wasted in retyping the password. Chatterjee et al. [12] employed typo correction functions by attempting to correct a typo using a number of preset functions (e.g., changing the capitalization of the first character, removing tailing character) when the first attempt at login fails. It is stated that by just correcting a handful of easily correctable typos, it allows a significant portion of users to achieve successful login. The TypTop system [13] is a personalized password checking protocol that allows the authentication system to learns over time the typos made by a specific user from failed login attempts. The TypTop system is able to provide an authentication system with minimal security loss that benefits 45% of users as a result of personalization. tPAKE works by having the server generate a set of typos from the password during registration. Different from traditional PAKE, the key exchange procedure would be performed multiple times during each round of communication to find the value that matches the user's input. If a match is found, a shared key will be established between the client and the server. Timestamp is also used during the authentication process for verification purposes. The server would be able to customize the set of accepted typos by adjusting the typo generation function used during registration.

Password-Authenticated Key Exchange. (PAKE) [6,11] is a key exchange protocol that allows a user to convince a server that the user possesses the password without revealing the password to the server. This prevents unnecessary exposure of the password and prevents server compromise. PAKE is a cryptographic method that allows two or more parties to safely establish a shared key through the knowledge of a shared secret, in this case, a password, such that an unauthorized party would not be able to participate. The protocol only reveals whether or not the shared secret matches and not the secret itself. PAKE is also safe against interception as plain text password is not sent during login. Boyko et al. implement PAKE protocol using Diffie-Hellman, which are secure against both passive and active adversaries. PAKE works by obscuring the shared secret through exponentiation and modulo operation, in which an attacker would not be able to extract any extra information from the communication after the one-way operation.

Fuzzy PAKE. [17] is a protocol based on PAKE that share a similar motivation with tPAKE. fPAKE aims to allow 2 parties to agree on a high-entropy cryptographic key without leaking information to man-in-the-middle attack. The leniency built into this protocol allows authentication to be done using a mistyped password. One of the fPAKE protocol is constructed using PAKE and Robust Secret Sharing (RSS) to allow agreement on similar passwords. However, this fPAKE protocol is limited in terms of how similarity is defined. This construction of fPAKE only allows comparison using hamming distances, which severely limits the options in how passwords can be compared as hamming distances requires two strings to be equal in length, making it impossible for fPAKE to account for password typos resulting from accidentally inserting or deleting a character. Hamming distance cannot be calculated between 'asdf1234' and 'asdf123', even though the 2 strings may very well be a typo of one another. Moreover, fPAKE is not modeled after user behavior. Typos with the same hamming distances might not have the same likelihood to happen in real-world usage as any character is more likely to be mistyped as only a certain few characters and not others, which is not a distinction that can be made using hamming distance. For instance, 'asdc1234' and 'asdp1234' would both be 1 hamming distance away from 'asdf1234', however, 'asdc1234' would be a more likely typo of 'asdf1234' assuming the user uses a QWERTY keyboard. Using Hamming distance as the metric does not account for the difference in the likelihood of one typo over another. We believe a more flexible protocol that allows the fine-tuning of typo acceptance could be helpful in modeling typo-tolerant password checking after real-world usage.

2.1   Threat Model

In PAKE (and tPAKE), the user stores information about their passwords and typos during registration, which we will refer to as server state. The registration process is secure and free from adversarial interference. However, it might be possible that the user passwords are exposed during registration (or password reset) on a compromised server, but for this paper, we will ignore that threat. This is because registration (and password reset) is a rare event compared to password login events. We will discuss in Sect. 4 how we can modify the protocol to protect against such attacks as well.

A secure PAKE protocol must protect the user passwords from a compromised server. The goal of the attacker is to learn user passwords. There are two kinds of compromise we will consider. In the first setting, a legitimate server is compromised, and the attacker has persistent access to the server. In this case, the attacker learns all the state stored on the server as well as all the transcripts of the login protocols ran during the malicious access. The attacker can also deviate arbitrarily from the protocol. Note the attacker can do an offline brute-force attack to uncover user passwords by simulating the login protocol with the stored state. Ideally, we would like to have this as the best attack for an adversary.

The second type of compromise is where the user accidentally engages in a PAKE protocol with the adversary—due to being a victim of phishing attack or typo-squatting attack. In this case, the attacker does not have access to the server state. Therefore, the attacker should not learn anything about the user password despite actively manipulating the protocol.

Given this threat model, the passwords of the registered users should not be stored in plaintext. Currently, without a PAKE protocol, the user's password is sent to the server in plaintext. (TLS protects the password in transit, but the server has plaintext access to the password.) That means an attacker would learn the password of the user when they try to log in to the compromised server.

Another threat model we have to consider is that if a malicious user tries to learn the password of another user. A malicious user can try to use an offline dictionary-based attack on the values shared by the server across multiple sessions to learn the user password. In a secure PAKE, the attacker should not be able to do any better than online password guessing (against the server).

3   The Problem Setting and Naive Solutions

Preliminaries. Let S be set of all strings from alphabet Σ (e.g., printable ASCII characters) of size no more than l (e.g., 50). Though Σ is typically printable ASCII characters, in modern authentication systems, users can pick any UTF-8 characters in their passwords. Let $W \subseteq S$ be the set of strings that are chosen as passwords by users; we associate a probability distribution p to W, such that $p(w)$ denotes the probability that a random password w is chosen by a user.

Users often mistype while typing their passwords. We assume $\tau_w(\tilde{w})$ denotes the probability that a user whose real password is $w \in W$ types $\tilde{w} \in S$. Of course, $\tau_w(\cdot)$ is a probability distribution over S, and $\sum_{\tilde{w} \in S} \tau_w(\tilde{w}) = 1$. Note, following the prior work [12], we assume that mistyping a password solely depends on the password, and not on the user who is typing. Our solution, however, can be extended to other scenarios where the typo-distributions τ also depends on the user who types the password. We only require a way to enumerate the points in the distribution in decreasing probabilities in an efficient manner. Let $T_l(w)$ be an enumerator of τ_w that outputs $l+1$ most probable typos of w, including w.

For our construction, we will use a prime-order group $\mathbb{G}$ of size q where the discrete log problem is hard. We will also assume that there exists a cryptographic hash function $H_{\mathbb{G}} : \{0,1\}^* \mapsto \mathbb{G}$ that can hash an arbitrary string onto the group. See [18,21] for details on how to do so.

Let H_{sl} and H_{fa} are two cryptographic hash functions that are oneway and collision-resistant. Moreover, H_{sl} is a slow and computationally expensive hash function (such as Bcrypt [32] or Scrypt [30]) ideal to be used for hashing password. The parameter for the computational overhead of this hash function can be tuned as necessary by the system engineers who deploy tPAKE. The hash function H_{fa} is a fast hash function such as SHA-256 or SHA-512. Also, we have a semantically secure and robust symmetric encryption scheme $\mathbf{SE} = (\mathsf{E}, \mathsf{D})$. Let the security parameter be ℓ. For simplicity, we will assume the ranges of both H_{sl} and H_{fa} are $\{0,1\}^\ell$, and the domain of keys required for $\mathbf{SE}$ is also $\{0,1\}^\ell$.

3.1 Naive Proposals for Making PAKE Typo-Tolerant

Typos are typically modeled using edit distance, also known as Levenshtein distance [26]. Therefore, to tolerate typos, one could envision accepting any variations of passwords within a certain edit distance. There are multiple issues with this approach. Firstly, any mechanism for computing edit distance coupled with PAKE will not work as the server learns nothing about the user password except it being equal to the one used during registration or not; the client obscures the original value of the password before sending to the server, making it impossible for calculating correct edit distance between the submitted password and the stored password. To overcome this challenge, we could employ secure multiparty computation technique to allow for computation of edit distance during key exchange protocol without each party revealing their secrets. However, implementation of this scheme would compromise security as it requires both parties to have the password in its plaintext form in order for the computation to be possible, which violates our security requirements. Moreover, SMC protocols secure against malicious adversaries—as required in our threat model—are slow and computationally expensive.

Besides the technical challenges, as shown in [12], allowing any typo within certain edit distance (such as ≥ 2) can degrade the security of the scheme significantly; a malicious client can try to impersonate a legitimate user by guessing their password or a variant within the given edit distance threshold. Chatterjee et al. proposed using a fixed set of variations instead of any typos within an edit-distance. The variations can be chosen based on population-wide or personal statistics and allow those that degrade security minimally. The method of finding such a list is empirical, and we refer the reader to [12] for more details.

Given a fixed number of possible variations of the user password, we could enable typo-tolerance by running multiple copies of an existing PAKE protocol—one for each variations (or corrections, as called in [12])—albeit in parallel. However, this is not secure if the client picks the variations during login. Because in PAKE there is no way for the server to learn anything about the submitted password, a malicious client can send multiple password guesses, instead of variations of the same password. This will effectively give an attacker lx more online guesses if the protocol allows l variations of the user password. Therefore, the password variations that will be accepted must be picked by the server, and it has to be during the registration.

Finally, private set intersection (PSI) protocols can be used for building typo-tolerant PAKE (or PAKE in general): The server has a list of password variations for a user, and the user has a singleton set of the input password. The protocol attempts to determine if the intersection between the two sets is non-empty without revealing anything beyond that.[5] The biggest challenge in using off-the-shelf PSI/PSI-CA protocol is that in most of those protocols one of the parties will learn the outcome, and it is hard to ensure the other party does not lie. For example, if the client gets to learn the final result that the intersection is

---

[5] This problem is more formally known as cardinality private set intersection (PSI-CA) [15].

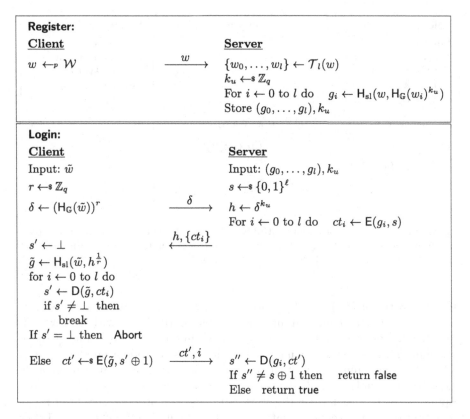

Fig. 2. Protocol for tPAKE. The client and the server are aware of the symmetric encryption scheme $\mathbf{SE} = (\mathsf{E}, \mathsf{D})$, the slow hash function $\mathsf{H_{sl}}$ and the (fast) hash function $\mathsf{H_G}$, and the group (G, q). The hash function $\mathsf{H_G}$ is used to hash any string onto a group element in G.

non-zero (or zero), the client can lie to the server. A PSI protocol is not an effective solution as we need security against malicious parties, and the goal of the client and the server is slightly different in a simple PSI setting. But we take some ideas from PSI and build our tPAKE protocol that we present in details in the next section.

4   tAKEtPAKE Protocol

To enable typo-tolerance, tPAKE uses oblivious pseudo-random functions (OPRF) [20] and implicit authentication to provide a secure PAKE protocol that can tolerate a set of typos in the user-entered password. Our protocol is different from prior PAKE protocols. Recall that we use a group $\mathbb{G}$ of size q, where discrete log problem is hard. At its core, tPAKE uses an OPRF, F_k, which we describe below.

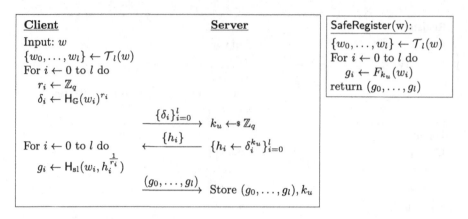

Fig. 3. Safe registration protocol for tPAKE. The server never sees the plaintext password from the user. On the **right** we show a short-hand notation that utilizes OPRF queries $F_{k_u}(\cdot)$ to the server holding the OPRF key k_u.

OPRF Protocol (F_k). OPRF protocols allows a client to obtain the pseudo-random output of a string x from a server holding the key k without revealing the value x. This is done by the client first sending a "blinded" value of the x, by computing $y \leftarrow H_G(x)^r$, where is a freshly chosen random number $r \leftarrow_\$ \mathbb{Z}_q$ and H_G is a hash function that maps any binary string onto an element in $\mathbb{G}$. The server responds with y^k. The client then "deblind", by raising the server's response with $1/r$; that is $(y^k)^{1/r} = H_G(x)^k$. We also apply a slow hash H_{sl} to the output of the final exponentiation. Together we have, OPRF $F_k : \{0,1\}^* \mapsto \{0,1\}^\ell$, where $F_k(x) = H_{sl}(x, H_G(x)^k)$.

In tPAKE, during registration, the server picks a random key k_u for user u, and use that to evaluate the PRF F_{k_u} (locally) on each of the variations of the input password w (sent by the user). The server stores the PRF outputs along with the key and the username. The registration process for user u is shown at the top protocol in Fig. 2. Note, we assume the registration process is done in a safe environment, which is to say that the user and the server act honestly during registration. This is a standard assumption given that registration is done only once, while login protocol is executed multiple times. For added security to prevent giving away user password to the server, we can tweak the protocol so that the server only learns hash of the password variations chosen by the client. We show this safe registration protocol in Fig. 3, which will ensure that the server doesn't see the actual password in plaintext, ever.

During Login, the client masks the password $\tilde{w}$ given by the user by raising the hash $H_G(\tilde{w})$ of it to a freshly generated random value r. Then the client forwards that value $\delta = H_G(\tilde{w})^r$ to the server, which raises δ to the power k_u, the secret value for the user u, selected during registration. The server also encrypts a freshly chosen random bitstring s using all the stored PRF outputs g_i for user u. The server sends back δ^{k_u} and the ciphertexts $\{ct_i\}$ to the client.

The client unmasks δ^{k_u} by raising it to the power $\frac{1}{r}$ and then computes $\tilde{g} = F_{k_u}(\tilde{w})$. With $\tilde{g}$, the client tries to decrypt each of the ciphertexts ct_i received from the server, and if any of the decryption succeeds, it learns that the entered password $\tilde{w}$ is either the correct password or one of its variations. One important design decision we made is to let the client know early whether the login is going succeed. Alternative options that reveal this decision to the server first could reveal the user password to a malicious or compromised server.

Finally, to prove to the server that the user successfully decrypted one of the ciphertexts, the user encrypt the modified value $s \oplus 1$ using its PRF output $\tilde{g}$. The server tries to decrypt that ciphertext using its knowledge of the stored PRF values, and if the decryption succeeds and $s'' = s \oplus 1$, the login succeeds, else the login fails.

The benefit of using encryption (instead of just hash functions, as used in prior works, such as [11]) is that we obtain implicit client and server authentication. We will expand on this next.

4.1 Security of tPAKE Protocol

The OPRF protocol we use is based on Chaum's blind signature [14]. This ensures that the server learns nothing about the user password through this OPRF call. We also assume that the hash functions are one-way and collision-resistant. The secret-key encryption scheme is semantically secure and robust, that is to say without the key, an attacker cannot learn anything about the plaintext.

As noted in our threat model (see Sect. 2.1), there are three threats we need to defend against. The first threat is about malicious client attacker who wants to learn about the password (or any non-trivial information about the password) of a legitimate user. The only values that are revealed to the client in the protocol are $h := \mathsf{H}_{\mathbb{G}}(\tilde{w})^{rk_u}$ and $\{ct_i := \mathsf{E}(g_i, s)\}$. Here, h does not contain any information about the passwords stored on the server; and ct_i is equivalent of random string unless the attacker can learn one of the $\{g_i\}$'s, for which the attacker has to be able to make OPRF queries on behalf of the user. This is equivalent of online guessing attack, which is the base case of any attack against authentication services. Thus a malicious client obtains no advantage over an attacker attempting to log in to a server that just allows typo-tolerant passwords.

Next threat is about a compromised server learning the user password. Ideally, a compromised server should not learn anything about the user password beyond what it already knows. There are two types of malicious server attacker. In the first case, where the attacker compromised the server, it already knows the PRF outputs $\{g_i\}$ of the user passwords. Therefore, from the interaction with the client, the attacker should not learn any information about the user password that can be used to recover the password faster than mounting dictionary attack against the g_i values. For the second case, where the attacker pretends to be a server via, say a phishing campaign, the server does not have g_i values. In this case the server should not learn *anything* about the password. Our protocol achieves both the security goals.

First, if a server does not have correct $\{g_i\}$ values and k_u, then the client will always end up aborting the protocol. This is because, given the server does not know the input password $\tilde{w}$, it is impossible for the server to guess $\tilde{g}$ without guessing the password $\tilde{w}$—a guarantee provided by the OPRF protocol we use. Without the knowledge of $\tilde{g}$ the server cannot construct ciphertexts ct_i, such that the decryption by the client $D(\tilde{g}, ct_i)$ succeeds—a guarantee we get from the robustness of the symmetric-key encryption scheme we use. Therefore, the attempt by the client to decrypt ct_i will always fail, the client will abort, and it will not send any further communication. The only value that the serve receives from the client is $H_G(\tilde{w})^r$, which is indistinguishable from a random value in G—from the obliviousness guarantee provided by the OPRF. It is important to note that the abort is necessary, otherwise, the malicious server will learn the encryption of $s \oplus 1$ under $\tilde{g}$, which the server can now use to mount offline dictionary attack.

In the second case, where the server that knows g_i, the only inputs are δ, ct', i. Here, δ is indistinguishable from as a random value in G, without the knowledge of the random exponent r; i has no information about the input password besides which typo is entered.[6] Finally, given g_i's, ct' contains no new information beyond if the login is successful or not. Therefore, the attackers best strategy is to mount guessing attack against g_i's. Therefore, the attacker who compromises the server learns no new information from the Login protocol, that can be used to learn user passwords faster. This concludes our security argument.

5   Adaptive-tPAKE Protocol

In Sect. 4, we give a protocol for allowing a fixed, predefined set of typos. By allowing population-wide popular typos, the previous solution limit its applicability to only those users who make "popular" typos, leaving out other users who make frequent but rather "unpopular" typos. Therefore, in this section we show how to build a typo-tolerant PAKE that can allow dynamically learned, personalized set of typos. We propose adaptive-tPAKE for the same. Adaptive-tPAKE employs a system similar to TypTop [13] that works by caching failed login attempts to let the system learn user's typos over time. PAKE's design prevents revealing the typos to the server, and, therefore, we do the testing for typo on the client-side after every successful login.

The pseudocode is shown in Fig. 5. The protocol uses a secure public-key encryption scheme **PKE** $= (\mathcal{K}, \mathcal{E}, \mathcal{D})$, where $\mathcal{K}$ is a key generation algorithm, $\mathcal{E}$ is a (randomized) encryption algorithm that uses the public key, and $\mathcal{D}$ is the decryption function that uses the secret key. So, for any message m, $\mathcal{D}(sk, \mathcal{E}(pk, m)) = m$ if $(sk, pk) \leftarrow_{\$} \mathcal{K}$. We also assume the this public-key encryption scheme can be also used for signing messages. We assume there is a function

---

[6] The server might be able to use this information to find out the most frequently entered password among $(g_0, \ldots, g_l)$. We can protect against such leakage by not sending the i, but that will require the server to try to decrypt ct' using every g_i, which is inefficient.

Register(w):	CacheUpdate(T, W):
$W \leftarrow \{(w, 1) \mid w \in \mathcal{T}_l(w)\}$	For $i \leftarrow 0$ to l_c do $T'[i] \leftarrow T[i]$
$k_u \leftarrow_\$ \mathbb{Z}_q$	For $(w, n) \in W$
$(sk_u, pk_u) \leftarrow_\$ \mathcal{K}$	For $i \leftarrow 0$ to l do
For $i \leftarrow 0$ to l_c do $T \leftarrow (\bot, 0)$	$w', n' \leftarrow T[i]$
$W \leftarrow \emptyset$	If CachePick(n', n) = true
$T \leftarrow$ CacheUpdate(T, W)	$g \leftarrow F_{k_u}(w_i)$
$ct_w \leftarrow_\$ \mathcal{E}(sk_u, w)$	$ct \leftarrow E(g_i, sk)$
Store pk_u on a trusted server	$T'[i] \leftarrow (w, n)$
return T, W, k_u, ct_w	return T

Fig. 4. (Left) ServerRegister protocol for adaptive-tPAKE. Here T is the typo-cache that keeps track of the typos the user is allowed to log in with; W is the wait list which stores the submitted passwords that are not yet checked for typo by the user. We also use a public key encryption scheme where, $\mathcal{K}$ is the key generation method. It is security critical that the public key pk_u is stored on a trusted server that the user can verify during login. (Right) CacheUpdate Protocol; CachePick is a function that would pick the cache line to be replaced following the caching policy (e.g. LFU, LRU, etc.). F_{k_u} is a OPRF call to the server holding the key k_u. Multiple queries to the server can be combined for network efficiency.

valid(sk, pk) that verifies if the sk and pk pairs are generated together from $\mathcal{K}$. So, let sign and verify are the functions for signing and verifying functions such that for any message m, verify(pk, sign(sk, m)) = true, if valid(sk, pk) = true.

The main idea behind adaptive-tPAKE is similar to that of tPAKE: use OPRF and implicit authentication. But adaptive-tPAKE has to store some more data for each user. The additional data includes a typo-cache T, and a "wait-list" W. The typo-cache holds the passwords that the user is allowed to log in with, and the wait-list holds the set of typos that are not yet verified by the legitimate user. Of course, none of these data is in plaintext. The typo-cache stores encryption of a secret key sk_u under different allowed typos. Only the legitimate user with the access to the real password or a typo of it can obtain the secret key sk_u. The secret and public keys are generated during registration (see left figure of Fig. 4). The corresponding public key pk_u is uploaded to a public key repositories, such as MIT PGP public key server[7]. This is important to ensure the user can reliably obtain the public key from a trusted server for security. If the public key is compromised (changed in a way that the user cannot verify), the security of this protocol is violated. We are not sure if adaptive-tPAKE can be created without the requirement of a trusted server to hold the public key.

Note that the registration makes OPRF call to the server which holds the OPRF key k_u, similar to what we did in SafeRegister. Thereby, the registration ensures that the server does not learn the plaintext passwords. The registration fills the typo-cache T with potential typos of the password (based on population-wide statistics) and the waitlist W. In addition to these, the server also stores

---

[7] https://pgp.mit.edu/.

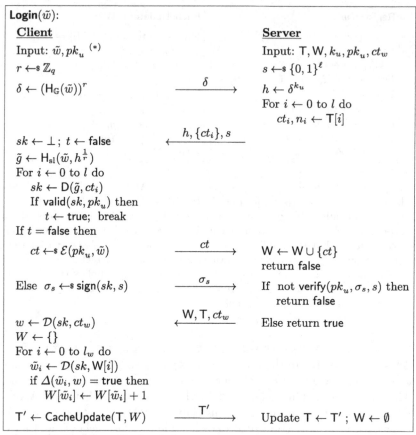

Login($\tilde{w}$):

Client	**Server**
Input: $\tilde{w}, pk_u$ (*)	Input: $\mathsf{T}, \mathsf{W}, k_u, pk_u, ct_w$
$r \leftarrow_{\$} \mathbb{Z}_q$	$s \leftarrow_{\$} \{0,1\}^\ell$
$\delta \leftarrow (\mathsf{H_G}(\tilde{w}))^r$	

$\delta \longrightarrow$

On server: $h \leftarrow \delta^{k_u}$

For $i \leftarrow 0$ to l do
    $ct_i, n_i \leftarrow \mathsf{T}[i]$

$\xleftarrow{\quad h, \{ct_i\}, s \quad}$

$sk \leftarrow \perp$; $t \leftarrow$ false
$\tilde{g} \leftarrow \mathsf{H_{sl}}(\tilde{w}, h^{\frac{1}{r}})$
For $i \leftarrow 0$ to l do
    $sk \leftarrow \mathsf{D}(\tilde{g}, ct_i)$
    If valid(sk, pk_u) then
        $t \leftarrow$ true; break
If $t =$ false then
    $ct \leftarrow_{\$} \mathcal{E}(pk_u, \tilde{w})$

$\xrightarrow{\quad ct \quad}$ $\mathsf{W} \leftarrow \mathsf{W} \cup \{ct\}$
return false

Else $\sigma_s \leftarrow_{\$} \text{sign}(sk, s)$

$\xrightarrow{\quad \sigma_s \quad}$ If not verify(pk_u, σ_s, s) then
return false

$\xleftarrow{\quad \mathsf{W}, \mathsf{T}, ct_w \quad}$ Else return true

$w \leftarrow \mathcal{D}(sk, ct_w)$
$\mathsf{W} \leftarrow \{\}$
For $i \leftarrow 0$ to l_w do
    $\tilde{w}_i \leftarrow \mathcal{D}(sk, \mathsf{W}[i])$
    if $\Delta(\tilde{w}_i, w) =$ true then
        $\mathsf{W}[\tilde{w}_i] \leftarrow \mathsf{W}[\tilde{w}_i] + 1$
$\mathsf{T}' \leftarrow \mathsf{CacheUpdate}(\mathsf{T}, \mathsf{W})$

$\xrightarrow{\quad \mathsf{T}' \quad}$ Update $\mathsf{T} \leftarrow \mathsf{T}'$; $\mathsf{W} \leftarrow \emptyset$

(*) pk_u is obtained from the trusted server.

Fig. 5. Pseudocode for the adaptive-tPAKE protocol. Here we use a public-key encryption scheme **PKE** $= (\mathcal{K}, \mathcal{E}, \mathcal{D})$. The typo-cache T holds the set of passwords that the user is allowed to log in with; and the waitlist W holds not-yet-verified typos. The function Δ is a function comparing two strings that return true when the two are deemed similar enough to be typo of one another.

the encryption of the real password w under the secret key sk. This password is used later to help a user identify valid typos present in the waitlist.

The first part of the protocol is similar to tPAKE (see Fig. 2), with the following difference. In adaptive-tPAKE, the server does not encrypt random value s, instead it forwards the encryption of the secret key sk to the user. Note the user can only decrypt after obtaining the OPRF output from the server. This ensures a malicious client cannot mount offline guessing attack against the user password (or typos). The server also sends challenge s in plaintext to the client, so that if the client is able to decrypt the secret key, it must sign the random value s with the sk, which the server verifies with the stored public key pk_u. If the client successfully obtains the secret key and convinces the server it is the legitimate user, then the server hands the client the waitlist W, typo-cache T, and the ciphertext of the plain text ct_w. At this point, the client has proven its legitimacy and it is warranted to obtain these information.

The client decrypts the waitlist and checks for the typos that are valid (within small edit distance, and matches other security requirements, e.g. difficult to guess). The valid typos are then inserted into the cache. The cache update procedure is shown in the right figure of Fig. 4. Interestingly, we use the same CacheUpdate function during registration to update the typo-cache T.

In case the user fails to obtain the secret key, it will encrypt the input password $\tilde{w}$, and submits that to the server to store it in the waitlist W.

Security of Adaptive-tPAKE. The security of adaptive-tPAKE relies on the legitimacy of the public key pk_u generated during registration. If the client relies on the server to obtain pk_u, then a malicious server can hand over a pk_u for which the server knows the secret key. In that case, when the client sends the encryption of the input password due to failing to obtain the secret key, the server will learn the input password. Therefore, we use a remote trusted server for this, and leave it as a open question whether we can have a secure PAKE protocol that adaptively learns users typos over time.

Assuming the pk_u is not tampered with, we can argue adaptive-tPAKE maintains the required security. When the client fails to obtain the secret key, the only values the client learns are $h := H_G(\tilde{w})^{rk_u}$, $\{ct_i := E(g_i, sk_u)\}$, and s. The client is not given the frequencies of each password, as that information can be misused for guessing attack. Following the same argument we used for tPAKE, the client learns nothing about the password in adaptive-tPAKE as well. The best the client can do is mounting online guessing attack by repeatedly calling the server to obtain the $F_{k_u}(\cdot)$. Only after the client successfully learns the secret key can the client learn the typo-cache T, the waitlist W, and ct_w.

Finally, a malicious server can try to learn about the user password. In adaptive-tPAKE, if the server does not have valid T, the client will not be able to decrypt and obtain the sk that is a valid pair of pk_u. Therefore, the client will abort after sending the encryption of the input password to the server. The input password $\tilde{w}$ is encrypted using the public key pk_u. If pk_u is legitimate, then the server cannot learn anything about $\tilde{w}$ from this.

If the server has a legitimate T, then the server will handover the typo-cache T and the waitlsit W to the client, and the client will respond with the updated T and W. During CacheUpdate, it is ensured the client never sends plaintext password to the server—it always use the OPRF protocol to obtain the $F_{k_u}(\cdot)$ of the waitlisted passwords that are to be inserted in the cache. Thus, the server does not obtain any information that it can use to mount guessing attack faster than what it already learns from the registration process.

	Register (ms)	Login (ms)
PAKE	37.85	65.16
tPAKE (5 passwords)	50.86	66.97
tPAKE (10 passwords)	64.94	67.56
Adaptive-tPAKE	109.50	174.54

Fig. 6. Total execution time (excluding network latency) for tPAKE registration and login.

6   Performance Evaluation tPAKE and Adaptive-tPAKE

Implementation and Test Setup. We prototype tPAKE and adaptive-tPAKE to measure their computational performance and efficacy of typo-tolerance. We measure the time to compute registration and login processes on the perspective of the client as well as compute some micro-benchmark on the server side. For instantiating the cryptographic primitives we use, SHA-256 as the hash function H_{fa} and H_{sl}, AES for symmetric-key encryption scheme, and brainpoolP256r1 [27] elliptic curve for the group G where discrete is known to be hard. The security parameter ℓ is chosen to be 128.

Both the server and the client are console-based Linux applications written in Python 3.6. We use Cryptography.io [5] for the symmetric-key and public-key encryption operations. For elliptic curve operations, we used `fastecdsa` library [25]. The server uses `flask` [1] for serving HTTP requests and `sqlite3` [3] for storage. On the other hand the client uses Python's `requests` [2] library for making requests. All experiments are run on Ubuntu 20.04 on an Intel Core i5 machine with 16 GB of RAM.

Performance testings are done using two separate machines in the same local network with minimal latency to avoid potential hardware and network bottleneck. The tests are done by setting up a server on one machine with the other machine acting as the client. The client would make HTTP POST requests to the server in order to log in. Server-side execution time is measured starting from when the client makes the request until the response is received. Client-side execution is measured by taking the time it takes to complete the whole protocol. Additionally, each user would not make consecutive login requests to avoid the impact of caching on the execution time.

For tPAKE, we first analyze the effect of the number of typos l on computational time and bandwidth. As shown in Fig. 6, tPAKE's performance overhead depends largely on the number of the passwords that the protocol would handle. Bandwidth required is linearly proportional to the number of acceptable passwords. On the other hand, there is no significant difference in execution time between PAKE and tPAKE in our testing. Adaptive-tPAKE, however, is considerably more expensive both in term of execution time and bandwidth. Noted that in our experiment, we assume that pk_u, the public key used to encrypt fail login attempts, is available locally on the client machine, thus, the performance overhead required to acquire pk_u isn't factored into our evaluation.

	Time (s)	Success (%)	attempts /success
PAKE	5.497	94.97	1.0529
tPAKE(5 passwords)	5.525	95.85	1.0432
tPAKE(10 passwords)	5.544	96.20	1.0394
Adaptive-tPAKE	5.815	96.40	1.0373

Fig. 7. Complete login test for PAKE, tPAKE, and Adaptive-tPAKE. The time column includes the time it takes for users to input the password (or passwords in case of reentry), the computation overhead on the client and the server side, and the network latency.

The set of typos we considered for this is taken from prior work. More details on the set of typo-correctors and their efficacy are noted in Appendix A.

Execution Time. Execution times for registration shown in the figure is measured on the safe registration protocol we introduced in Sect. 5 that ensures the security of the password during registration (Fig. 6).

To understand the total time spent in login and the benefit of allowing typo-tolerance, we simulate real world use cases by making use of actual user password input data collected in prior work [12] via an Amazon Mechanical Turk experiment. The dataset contains multiple login attempts of each user to their (hypothetical) accounts and the time taken to enter each password We simulate user input in the order it was collected to measure the time and the number of attempts it will take for successfully login should the password checking system employ tPAKE or adaptive-tPAKE. We also measure the average login success rate and the average number of login attempts required to successfully authenticate. The test shows that tPAKE and adaptive-tPAKE improves the login success rate and reduces the number of times the user has to attempt to log in. However, the rate of typos by the users of this experiment is low (<4%), therefore the benefit of typo-tolerance is reflected in the time saved in logging in. We expect the benefit to be more visible if users are more error prone, like while entering password through mobile touch pads [12].

Bandwidth. Next we measure the bandwidth overhead for our protocol. Bandwidth is measured as the total amount of data communicated between the server and the client. In our setting, the bandwidth is affected by the number of typos handled by the protocol. For our implementation, two rounds of communication are required during login, but only bandwidths of the first response from the server are affected by the number of typos. The size of the login request is 435 bytes. The response size is 345, 837, and 1,452 bytes for PAKE, tPAKE ($l = 5$), and tPAKE ($l = 10$), respectively.

Adaptive-tPAKE requires similar packet sizes to its tPAKE counterpart depending on the size of the typo-cache T. Additionally, adaptive-tPAKE, also requires an additional round of communication, essentially doubling the bandwidth. A verification round is needed for making sure that both agree on a session key and requires an additional 374 bytes. Packets measured in our tests only includes the minimal amount of data that are required to complete the protocols, thus, additional metadata could result in the increase of packet size.

Adaptive-tPAKE. Adaptive-tPAKE enables the personalization of typo-tolerant password-checking by incorporating a typo cache, which happens to adds several layers of complexity to the implementation of the protocol. An extra round of communication is required for every login, increasing the total execution time. While adaptive-tPAKE's execution cost might be considerably more expensive than PAKE or tPAKE, adaptive-tPAKE being able to reduce the number of attempts users are required to input their password not only make up for the lost time while also improving the usability of the login process. According to our test done using data collected via Amazon MTurk, adaptive-tPAKE shows a 1% increase in login success rate compared to conventional PAKE. It only requires an average of 1.0392 login attempts to successfully login with Adaptive-tPAKE compared to 1.0502 attempts using PAKE with no typo-tolerance. The simulation also shows that the time saved from reducing the average number of attempts make up for the more expensive execution time of adaptive-tPAKE. Furthermore, the performance of adaptive-tPAKE could potentially be even better in real-world use cases where the protocol would be better personalized to a user's input habit after an extended amount of login being made. Overall, the result shows that the adaptive-tPAKE improves the login success rate compared to tPAKE without having to increase the number of acceptable passwords.

7   Conclusion

We present typo-tolerant password-authenticated key exchange, or tPAKE, a communication protocol based on password-authenticated key exchange(PAKE) that allows PAKE to be tolerant to small typographical mistakes made by users securely. We provide a formal proof to demonstrate the security of tPAKE against man-in-the-middle and compromised server. We proposed the safe registration protocol that eliminates the need to assume that communication during registration is secure and not eavesdropped by making use of PAKE's security properties. Our safe registration protocol is not only computationally secure against eavesdropper but also compromised server. Furthermore, we also present a PAKE version of the TypTop system that allows the personalization of typo-tolerant password checking with PAKE's security properties. We measure execution time and bandwidth to gauge the performance overhead of our protocols. We also conduct simulations using data gathered via a study on Amazon MTurk to quantify the potential usability gain adaptive-tPAKE has over old-school PAKE.

A   Typo Analysis and Generation

Typo is handled in tPAKE by generating a preset number of typos from the password during registration, which will be used as the list of typos accepted

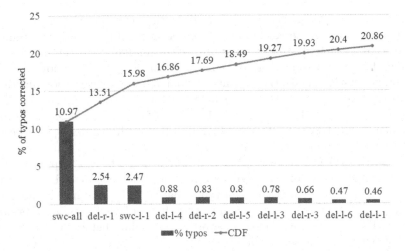

Fig. 8. Performance of different typo functions. First part (**swc**-l-1) of a function name refers to type of the operation. The second part of the name (swc-**l-1**) refers to the position that operations is applied on. E.g. swc-l-1 means substituting at the first character from the left with its shift-modified counterpart.

by tPAKE during login. Therefore, it is crucial that the typos generated would coincide with typos that users will make for tPAKE to be useful, so we analyzed typos data that was collected [12,13] and compiled a list of typo generation functions that can be implemented with tPAKE.

The type of typo generation functions implemented can greatly affect the effectiveness of tPAKE, thus, typo analysis is done on collected user data to determine suitable typo generation function (typo-gen). We found that 41.00% of all typos are within 1 edit distance. We analyzed different types of typos that users tend to make by categorizing typos into 4 types, insertion, deletion, substitution, and transposition. Insertion refers to adding a character at a position in the string. Deletion means removing a character from the string. Substitution refers to replacing a character in the string with another character. Transposition is done by swapping the location of 2 existing characters in the string. Out of all typos, insertion makes up of around 30%, whereas deletion and substitution make up of 17 and 28% respectively of all the typos within 1 edit. Contrary to our expectation, however, transposition makes up only a small fraction of the typos. Only around 4% of all typos fixed is from transposition operation.

The substitution of characters with its shift-modified counterpart is the most common type of substitution typos, especially at the first character where the character tends to be capitalized. We use `swc-1-1` typo-generator to handle this type of typos. We found `swc-1-1` can tolerate 2.47% of all typos. While other substitution typos (non-shift substitution) and insertion typos (typos that can be generated from substitution) are common, it is difficult to identify a consistent pattern to formulate a typo-gen. Transposition typos on the other hand are few and far between, which makes it ineffective to have a typo-gen for this type of typos. `swc-all` is typo-gen that switches all the characters in a string to its shift-modified counterpart. `swc-all` proves to be effective in typo generation and is able to account for 10.97% of all the typos. Other common typo-gen are function handling different variations of deletion typos that are both common and easy to program for which make them great candidates for typo generation functions. The 10 typo generation functions included in Fig. 8 account for 20.86% of all typos being made, in other words, 48.21% of all typos within one edit distance.

Similar to tPAKE, our adaptive-tPAKE protocol will only accept and cache typos that are within 1 edit away from the correct password. One advantage that Adaptive-tPAKE has over tPAKE is that it doesn't need to preemptively predict during registration what type of typos the user would make in the future, which means that it could account for typos that tPAKE could not, for instance, insertion typos that make up a significant portion of all typos. Furthermore, adaptive-tPAKE would adapt to password input habit that is unique to each user that our typo analysis could not capture.

References

1. Flask documentation. https://flask.palletsprojects.com/en/1.1.x/
2. Requests. https://requests.readthedocs.io/
3. Sqlite. https://www.sqlite.org/
4. Twitter advising all 330 million users to change passwords after bug exposed them in plain text (2018). https://www.theverge.com/2018/5/3/17316684/twitter-password-bug-security-flaw-exposed-change-now
5. Cryptography.io documentation (2019). https://cryptography.io/
6. Abdalla, M., Pointcheval, D.: Simple password-based encrypted key exchange protocols. In: Menezes, A. (ed.) CT-RSA 2005. LNCS, vol. 3376, pp. 191–208. Springer, Heidelberg (2005). https://doi.org/10.1007/978-3-540-30574-3_14
7. Bellare, M., Pointcheval, D., Rogaway, P.: Authenticated key exchange secure against dictionary attacks. In: Preneel, B. (ed.) EUROCRYPT 2000. LNCS, vol. 1807, pp. 139–155. Springer, Heidelberg (2000). https://doi.org/10.1007/3-540-45539-6_11
8. Bellovin, S.M., Merritt, M.: Encrypted key exchange: password-based protocols secure against dictionary attacks (1992)
9. Biryukov, A., Dinu, D., Khovratovich, D.: Argon and Argon2: password hashing scheme. Technical report (2015)
10. Bonneau, J., Schechter, S.: Towards reliable storage of 56-bit secrets in human memory. In: 23rd USENIX Security Symposium (USENIX Security 2014). USENIX (2014)
11. Boyko, V., MacKenzie, P., Patel, S.: Provably secure password-authenticated key exchange using Diffie-Hellman. In: Preneel, B. (ed.) EUROCRYPT 2000. LNCS, vol. 1807, pp. 156–171. Springer, Heidelberg (2000). https://doi.org/10.1007/3-540-45539-6_12
12. Chatterjee, R., Athalye, A., Akhawe, D., Juels, A., Ristenpart, T.: Password typos and how to correct them securely. In: IEEE Symposium on Security and Privacy (2016)

13. Chatterjee, R., Woodage, J., Pnueli, Y., Chowdhury, A., Ristenpart, T.: The typtop system: personalized typo-tolerant password checking. In: Proceedings of the 2017 ACM SIGSAC Conference on Computer and Communications Security, pp. 329–346. ACM (2017)
14. Chaum, D.: Blind signature system. In: Chaum, D. (ed.) Advances in Cryptology, p. 153. Springer, Boston (1984). https://doi.org/10.1007/978-1-4684-4730-9_14
15. De Cristofaro, E., Gasti, P., Tsudik, G.: Fast and private computation of cardinality of set intersection and union. In: Pieprzyk, J., Sadeghi, A.-R., Manulis, M. (eds.) CANS 2012. LNCS, vol. 7712, pp. 218–231. Springer, Heidelberg (2012). https://doi.org/10.1007/978-3-642-35404-5_17
16. Dodis, Y., Reyzin, L., Smith, A.: Fuzzy extractors: how to generate strong keys from biometrics and other noisy data. In: Cachin, C., Camenisch, J.L. (eds.) EUROCRYPT 2004. LNCS, vol. 3027, pp. 523–540. Springer, Heidelberg (2004). https://doi.org/10.1007/978-3-540-24676-3_31
17. Dupont, P.-A., Hesse, J., Pointcheval, D., Reyzin, L., Yakoubov, S.: Fuzzy password-authenticated key exchange. In: Nielsen, J.B., Rijmen, V. (eds.) EURO-CRYPT 2018. LNCS, vol. 10822, pp. 393–424. Springer, Cham (2018). https://doi.org/10.1007/978-3-319-78372-7_13
18. Farashahi, R.R., Shparlinski, I.E., Voloch, J.F.: On hashing into elliptic curves. J. Math. Cryptol. 3(4), 353–360 (2009)
19. Florencio, D., Herley, C.: A large-scale study of web password habits. In: Proceedings of the 16th International Conference on World Wide Web, WWW 2007, pp. 657–666. ACM, New York (2007). https://doi.org/10.1145/1242572.1242661
20. Freedman, M.J., Ishai, Y., Pinkas, B., Reingold, O.: Keyword search and oblivious pseudorandom functions (2005)
21. Icart, T.: How to hash into elliptic curves. In: Halevi, S. (ed.) CRYPTO 2009. LNCS, vol. 5677, pp. 303–316. Springer, Heidelberg (2009). https://doi.org/10.1007/978-3-642-03356-8_18
22. Keith, M., Shao, B., Steinbart, P.: A behavioral analysis of passphrase design and effectiveness. J. Assoc. Inf. Syst. 10(2), 2 (2009)
23. Keith, M., Shao, B., Steinbart, P.J.: The usability of passphrases for authentication: an empirical field study. Int. J. Hum. Comput. Stud. 65(1), 17–28 (2007)
24. Krebs, B.: Facebook stored hundreds of millions of user passwords in plain text for years (2020)
25. Kueltz, A.: Fastecdsa (2020). https://github.com/AntonKueltz/fastecdsa
26. Levenshtein, V.I.: Binary codes capable of correcting deletions, insertions, and reversals. In: Soviet Physics Doklady, vol. 10, pp. 707–710 (1966)
27. Lochter, M., Merkle, J.: Elliptic curve cryptography (ECC) Brainpool standard curves and curve generation, March 2010. https://tools.ietf.org/html/rfc5639
28. Mazurek, M.L., et al.: Measuring password guessability for an entire university. In: Proceedings of the 2013 ACM SIGSAC Conference on Computer & Communications Security, pp. 173–186. ACM (2013)
29. Morris, R., Thompson, K.: Password security: a case history. Commun. ACM 22(11), 594–597 (1979). https://doi.org/10.1145/359168.359172
30. Percival, C., Josefsson, S.: The scrypt password-based key derivation function (2015)
31. Pinkas, B., Rosulek, M., Trieu, N., Yanai, A.: PSI from PaXoS: fast, malicious private set intersection. In: Canteaut, A., Ishai, Y. (eds.) EUROCRYPT 2020. LNCS, vol. 12106, pp. 739–767. Springer, Cham (2020). https://doi.org/10.1007/978-3-030-45724-2_25

32. Provos, N., Mazieres, D.: Bcrypt algorithm. USENIX (1999)
33. Shay, R., et al.: Correct horse battery staple: exploring the usability of system-assigned passphrases. In: Proceedings of the Eighth Symposium on Usable Privacy and Security, p. 7. ACM (2012)

PAS-TA-U: PASsword-Based Threshold Authentication with Password Update

Rachit Rawat and Mahabir Prasad Jhanwar$^{(\boxtimes)}$ (iD)

Department of Computer Science, Ashoka University, Sonipat, India
rachit.rawat@alumni.ashoka.edu.in, mahavir.jhawar@gmail.com

Abstract. A single-sign-on (SSO) is an authentication system that allows a user to log in with a single identity and password to any of several related, yet independent, server applications. SSO solutions eliminate the need for users to repeatedly prove their identities to different applications and hold different credentials for each application. *Token-based authentication* is commonly used to enable a SSO experience on the web, and on enterprise networks. A large body of work considers distributed token generation which can protect the long term keys against a subset of breached servers. A recent work (CCS'18) introduced the notion of Password-based Threshold Authentication (PbTA) with the goal of making password-based token generation for SSO secure against server breaches that could compromise both long-term keys and user credentials. They also introduced a generic framework called PASTA that can instantiate a PbTA system.

The existing SSO systems built on distributed token generation techniques, including the PASTA framework, do not admit password-update functionality. In this work, we address this issue by proposing a password-update functionality into the PASTA framework. We call the modified framework PAS-TA-U.

As a concrete application, we instantiate PAS-TA-U to implement in Python a distributed SSH key manager for enterprise networks (ESKM) that also admits a password-update functionality for its clients. Our experiments show that the overhead of protecting secrets and credentials against breaches in our system compared to a traditional single server setup is low (average 119 ms in a 10-out-of-10 server setting on Internet with 80 ms round trip latency).

Keywords: Password-based authentication · Threshold cryptgography

1 Introduction

Password-Based Authentication (PbA): One of the primary purposes of authentication is to facilitate access control to a resource such as local or remote access to computer accounts; access to software applications, when an access privilege is linked to a particular identity. A typical scenario is when the remote

© Springer Nature Switzerland AG 2020
L. Batina et al. (Eds.): SPACE 2020, LNCS 12586, pp. 25–45, 2020.
https://doi.org/10.1007/978-3-030-66626-2_2

resource is a *application server*, and a user is using a *client application* to authenticate itself to the application server. Password-based techniques are a very popular choice underlying most authentication systems. In a password-based authentication (PbA) system, a user U creates its user credential record—a user identity id_U, and a hash of a secret password pwd, i.e. hash(pwd), with the application server through a one-time registration process. Later, in order to gain access (log in) to the application server, U provides (id_U, pwd) to its client which then computes hash(pwd), and sends $(id_U, hash(pwd))$ to the application server. The server compares this to the stored record for the stated id_U and gives access if it matches.

Token-Based Single-Sign-On (SSO): A single-sign-on is an authentication system that allows a user to log in with a single identity and password to any of several related, yet independent, server applications. SSO solutions eliminates the need for users to repeatedly prove their identities to different applications using different credentials for each application. We make a distinction by calling one of the application servers as the identity provider, i.e. IP, and the rest of the related application servers as AS. Token-based techniques are currently very common for the implementation of an SSO system. In such a system (see Fig. 1), an IP generates a one-time key pair of signing and verification keys (sk, vk), keeps the signing key sk with itself, and makes the verification key vk available to all ASs. A one-time registration phase allows a user U to create and store its credential (id_U, pwd) with the IP. In order to gain access to any AS, the user U must reach out to IP with its user credential $(id_U, hash(pwd))$, and a payload pld that contains the user's information/attributes, expiration time and a policy that would control the nature of access. The IP verifies U's credential by matching it against a stored record before issuing an authentication token tkn which is produced for the payload pld with the help of the secret singing key sk, i.e. tkn ← Sign(pld, sk). The token so obtained is stored by the user client in a cookie or the local storage, and can then be used for all future accesses to AS's without using the pwd, until it expires. In particular, when the user client presents the tkn to an AS requesting for an access, the tkn is verified by the AS which holds the verification key vk, i.e. $1/\perp$ ← Verify(tkn, vk). Popular token-based SSO systems include JSON Web Token (JWT), SAML, OAuth, and OpenID.

Password-Based Threshold Authentication (PbTA): The basic PbA systems, and the more advanced token-based SSO systems place greater responsibility on an identity provider IP of maintaining the confidentiality of a large number of users credentials. Such an IP is a single point of failure that if breached, enables an attacker to (1) recover the long term signing key sk and forge arbitrary tokens that enable access to all application servers and (2) obtain hashed passwords of users to use as part of an offline dictionary attack to recover their credentials. A large body of work considers distributed token generation through threshold digital signatures and threshold message authentication codes which can protect the long term signing key sk against a subset of breached servers [3–6, 12, 14]. A separate line of work on threshold password-authenticated key exchange (T-PAKE)

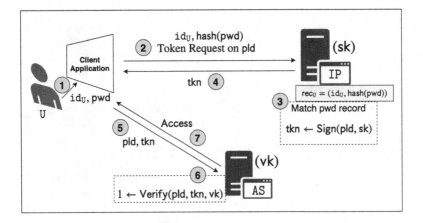

Fig. 1. SSO: Token-based

aims to prevent offline dictionary attacks in standard password-authenticated key exchange (PAKE) by employing multiple servers [1,9–11].

A recent work of Agrawal et al. [2] introduces the notion of Password-based Threshold Authentication (PbTA) for token-based SSO where they propose to distribute the role of identity provider IP among n identity servers $\{S_1, \ldots, S_n\}$ such that at any point a subset of these servers, any t of them, collectively verify users' passwords and generate authentication token for them (see Fig. 2). A PbTA system proposes a very strong *unforgeability* and *password-safety* properties with the goal of making password-based token generation secure against identity server breaches (up to $t - 1$ at a time) that could compromise both long-term keys and user credentials. This is enabled by requiring that any attacker who compromises at most $t - 1$ identity servers cannot forge valid tokens or mount offline dictionary attacks. In [2] a generic framework called PASTA which can instantiate a secure PbTA system was also proposed. The PASTA framework uses as building blocks any threshold oblivious pseudorandom function (TOPRF) and any threshold token generation (TTG) scheme, i.e., a threshold digital signature.

1.1 Our Contribution

The existing distributed token generation based SSO systems, including the PASTA framework, have so far not addressed the issue of password update functionality in their designs. The password update mechanism in a basic PbA is easy to implement and typically requires a user client to submit the hashes of both its current and a newly selected password. The current password hash is used for authentication by the identity provider before it replaces the current credentials with the updated credentials. Implementing password update mechanism in the setting of distributed token generation is not easy for the obvious reason that the identity provider is now split into several identity servers. This is particularly more problematic in the case of PASTA framework where no identity server holds

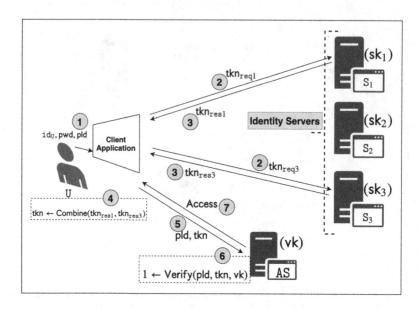

Fig. 2. PbTA: 2-out-of-3 Token Generation

the hashed user-passwords. In this work we propose to address this issue. The details are summarised as follows:

- We propose a password-update functionality to PASTA framework. The modified framework is now referred to as PAS-TA-U.
- We show how PASTA framework can be used to implement a distributed SSH key manager for enterprise networks (ESKM). The concept of an ESKM was first introduced by Harchol et al. in [7] and was instantiated therein using threshold cryptographic primitives. ESKM is a secure and fault-tolerant logically-centralised SSH key manager. The logically central key server of [7] was implemented in a distributed fashion using n key servers (also know as *control cluster* (CC) nodes) such that users in the enterprise network must interact with a subset of these CC nodes for a successful SSH connection. The problem of user authentication to CC nodes was also discussed in [7] and password-based variants were proposed for the same.
  The functionality of a password update mechanism for its users in an ESKM is an obvious requirement. As a concrete application, we implement PAS-TA-U to instantiate an ESKM that admits password update functionality for its users.
- The plain PASTA framework distributes the role of an identity provider IP among n identity servers $\{S_1, \ldots, S_n\}$. Consequently, the registration phase in PASTA involves a direct interaction between a user and the n identity servers. We propose to keep only a user and the identity provider IP as primary participants in the registration phase. It is during the registration phase that a user is provided with a set of identity servers $\{S_1, \ldots, S_n\}$ by the IP. The user consequently reaches out to all identity servers with necessary information.

In doing so we are keeping the identity provider in charge who may choose to select different identity servers for different users.

1.2 Organization

In Sect. 2, preliminaries required for PAS-TA-U framework are given. In Sect. 2.1 GapTOMDH problem is given; the details on secret sharing are given in Sect. 2.2; and the details on threshold token generation (TTG) and threshold oblivious pseudo-random function (TOPRF) are given in Sect. 2.3 and Sect. 2.4 respectively. The details on password-based threshold authentication (PbTA) are given in Sect. 3. The PAS-TA-U framework is given in Sect. 4. The security definitions for the underlying primitives make the basis for PbTA security definitions such as password-safety and unforgeability. As PAS-TA-U modifies PASTA frame directly to enhance it with a password functionality, we define password-update safety in Definition 8. The password-update safety of PAS-TA-U is directly reduced to the unforgeability requirement in Sect. 4.1. In Sect. 5 we use PAS-TA-U to construct a distributed SSH key manager for enterprise networks. The implementation details are given in Sect. 5.1.

2 Preliminaries

Notations. $\mathbb{N}$ denotes the set of natural numbers. $\mathbb{Z}_p$ denotes the finite field having elements $\{0, 1, \ldots, p - 1\}$ with addition and multiplication modulo the prime p. For a natural number n, we let $[n] = \{1, 2, \ldots, n\}$. For a set S, $a \xleftarrow{\$} S$ denotes that a is selected from S at random. We use PPT as a shorthand for probabilistic polynomial time and negl to denote negligible functions. The GroupGen be a PPT algorithm that on input a security parameter 1^λ, outputs $(p, g, \mathbb{G})$ where p is a λ bit prime, $\mathbb{G}$ is a multiplicative group of order p, and g is a generator of $\mathbb{G}$.

2.1 Hardness Assumption

For $q_1, \ldots, q_n \in \mathbb{N}$ and $t', t \in \mathbb{N}$ where $t' < t \leq n$, define $\mathsf{MAX}_{t',t} = \max\{\ell \mid \exists \; \hat{u}_1, \ldots, \hat{u}_\ell \in \{0, 1\}^n \text{ s.t. } \mathsf{HW}(\hat{u}_i) = t - t' \text{ and } \sum_{i=1}^{\ell} \hat{u}_i \leq (q_1, \ldots, q_n)\}$, where $\mathsf{HW}(\hat{u})$ denotes the number of 1's in the binary vector $\hat{u}$, and all operations on vectors are component-wise integer operations.

Definition 1 (GapTOMDH). *A cyclic group generator* GroupGen *satisfies the Gap Threshold One-More Diffie-Hellman (GapTOMDH) assumption if for all t', t, n, r where $t' < t \leq n$ and for all* PPT *adversary $\mathcal{A}$ in* $\mathsf{OneMore}_{\mathcal{A}}(1^\lambda, t', t, n, r)$ *game as defined in Fig. 3, there exists a negligible function* negl *s.t.*

$$\Pr[1 \leftarrow \mathsf{OneMore}_{\mathcal{A}}(1^\lambda, t', t, n, r)] \leq \mathsf{negl}(\lambda)$$

$\text{OneMore}_{\mathcal{A}}(1^{\lambda}, t', t, n, r)$

- $(p, g, \mathbb{G}) \xleftarrow{\$} \text{GroupGen}(1^{\lambda})$
- $g_1, \ldots, g_r \xleftarrow{\$} \mathbb{G}$
- $(\{(i, \alpha_i)\}_{i \in B}, \text{st}) \leftarrow \mathcal{A}(p, g, \mathbb{G}, g_1, \ldots, g_r)$, where $B \subseteq [n]$, $|B| = t'$
- $(k_0, k_1, \ldots, k_n) \xleftarrow{\$} \text{GenShare}(p, t, n, \{(i, \alpha_i)\}_{i \in B})$
- $q_i := 0$ for $i \in [n]$
- $((g'_1, h_1), \ldots, (g'_{\ell}, h_{\ell})) \leftarrow \mathcal{A}^{\langle \mathcal{O} \rangle}(\text{st})$
- output 1 $\iff$ $\begin{cases} \ell > \text{MAX}_{t', t}(q_1, \ldots, q_n) \\ g'_i \in \{g_1, \ldots, g_r\} \text{ and } h_i = g'^{k_0}_i \ \forall \ i \in [\ell] \\ g'_i \neq g'_j \ \forall \ 1 \leq i \neq j \leq \ell \end{cases}$

   – $\mathcal{O}(i, x)$
- Input: $i \in [n] \backslash B$, $x \in \mathbb{G}$
- $q_i := q_i + 1$
- Output: return x^{k_i}

   – $\mathcal{O}_{\text{DDH}}(x_1, x_2, y_1, y_2)$
- Input: $x_1, x_2, y_1, y_2 \in \mathbb{G}$
- Output: return 1 $\iff$ $\text{dlog}_{x_1} x_2 = \text{dlog}_{y_1} y_2$

Fig. 3. $\text{OneMore}_{\mathcal{A}}(1^{\lambda}, t', t, n, r)$

2.2 Shamir Secret Sharing

In the following we recall Shamir secret sharing scheme [13].

Definition 2 (Shamir Secret Sharing). *Let $t, n \in \mathbb{N}$ such that $1 < t \leq n$. A (t, n)-threshold Shamir secret sharing allows a dealer $\mathcal{D}$ to share a secret among n participants $\{P_1, \ldots, P_n\}$ such that at t least of them are required to reconstruct the secret back, and any set of less than t participants will have no information on the secret. In particular, the scheme has two algorithms (ShamirShare, ShamirRec) and they work as follows:*

– ShamirShare. *On input a secret* sk $\in \mathbb{F}_q$ *where $q > n$, the share generation algorithm* ShamirShare *outputs a list of n shares as follows.*
- $f(x) \xleftarrow{\$} \mathbb{F}_q[x]$ *s.t.* $f(0) = $ sk *and* $\text{degree}(f) \leq t - 1$.
- $\text{sk}_i = f(i) \mod p$, *for $i \in [n]$.*
- *Each P_i gets* sk_i, *the ith share of* sk
– ShamirRec: *The secret reconstruction algorithm* ShamirRec *requires any t shares for correct secret reconstruction.*
1. *Input:* $\{\text{sk}_i\}_{i \in S}$, *where $S \subseteq [n]$ and $|S| = t$*
2. *Output:* sk $= \sum_{i \in S} \text{sk}_i \lambda_i^S(0)$, *where* $\lambda_i^S(x) = \dfrac{\prod_{j \in S \backslash \{i\}} (x - j)}{\prod_{j \in S \backslash \{i\}} (i - j)}$ *(Lagrange Polynomials)*

2.3 Threshold Token Generation (TTG)

A threshold token generation scheme essentially refers to a threshold signature scheme. In a traditional public-key signature scheme, we have a signer who holds a secret signing key and a verifier who holds a public verification key. In a (t, n)-threshold signature scheme, where $t \leq n$, the secret key is split into n signers $\{P_1, \ldots, P_n\}$ such that at least t these parties must come together to sign a message. The collective signing is done in a way such that at no stage the secret key is revealed.

Definition 3 (Threshold Token Generation (TTG)). *A threshold token generation scheme Π is a tuple* (SetUp, PartSign, Combine, Verify) *of four* PPT *algorithms and they work as follows:*

- Setup($1^\lambda, t, n$) *The inputs to the setup algorithm are: a security parameter λ, n signing parties $P_1, \ldots, P_n$, and a number $t \leq n$. It proceeds as follows:*
  - *Generate a pair of singing and verification key* (sk, vk) *along with public parameters* pp
  - *Generate n shares* ($\mathsf{sk}_1, \ldots, \mathsf{sk}_n$) *of the signing key* sk
  - *Each signing party P_i receives* (sk_i, pp)
  - *The pair* (vk, pp) *is made publicly available.*
- PartSign(sk_i, x) *This algorithm is run by individual signers. The ith signer P_i takes as input a message x and its share sk_i. It returns a partial signature y_i on x.*
- Combine($\{y_i\}_{i \in S}$). *This algorithm puts together t part signatures $\{y_i\}_{i \in S}$ where $|S| = t$ and combine them to output a signature, also refer it as a token, tk on x.*
- Verify(vk, tk, x) *The verification algorithm takes as input the verification key vk, a token tk, and a message x. It outputs 1 if and only if tk is a valid signature on x.*

A TTG Construction. In the following we recall the famous TTG scheme due to Victor Shoup [14]. We begin by setting up a few notations. Let t, n be positive integers such that $1 < t \leq n$. Define $\Delta = n!$. In the following we now define modified Lagrange coefficients. The Lagrange coefficients are polynomials and the modified variants are defined as follows.

Definition 4 (Modified Lagrange Coefficients [14]). *Let $S \subset \{1, 2, \ldots, n\}$. For any $j \in \{1, 2, \ldots, n\} \backslash S$, define*

$$\tilde{\lambda}_j^S(x) = \Delta \lambda_j^S(x) = \Delta \cdot \frac{\prod_{k \in S \backslash \{j\}} (x - k)}{\prod_{k \in S \backslash \{j\}} (j - k)} \tag{1}$$

Clearly, $\tilde{\lambda}_j^S(x) \in \mathbb{Z}[x]$ for all $j \in \{1, 2, \ldots, n\} \backslash S$. In the following, we recall Lagrange interpolation over $\mathbb{Z}_N$ where N is an RSA modulus, i.e. $N = p \times q$ where p, q are distinct primes.

Theorem 1 ([14]). *Let* $f(x) = \sum_{k=0}^{t-1} a_k x^k \in \mathbb{Z}_N[X]$ *be of degree at most* $t - 1$, *where* $N > n$ *is an RSA modulus. Let* $\{(j, f(j))\}_{j \in S}$ *be* t *points over* $f(x)$, *where* $S \subseteq \{1, 2, \ldots, n\}$ *and* $\Delta = n!$. *Then,*

$$\Delta \cdot f(x) = \sum_{j \in S} f(j) \cdot \tilde{\lambda}_j^S(x) \bmod \phi(N) \tag{2}$$

In the following we now recall Shoup's [14] threshold signature, aka threshold token generation scheme.

- Setup$(1^\lambda, t, n)$: The setup algorithm generates necessary parameters for the n signers as follows:
  - Generate λ-bit primes p, q $(p \neq q)$
  - $N = pq$
  - $e, d \xleftarrow{\$} \mathbb{Z}_N$ s.t. $ed \equiv 1 \pmod{\phi(N)}$
  - $(\mathsf{sk}_1, \ldots, \mathsf{sk}_n) \longleftarrow \mathsf{ShamirShare}(d, t, n)$
  - Verification key $\mathsf{vk} = (e, N, H(\cdot))$, where $H : \{0,1\}^* \to \mathbb{Z}_N$ is a secure hash function.

  Each signer P_i receives sk_i.
- PartSign: A signer P_i runs this algorithm. It produces a partial signature on a message m using its secret share sk_i as follows:
  - Output: $y_i = H(m)^{2\Delta \mathsf{sk}_i} \bmod N$, where $\Delta = n!$
- Combine$(\{y_i\}_{i \in S})$: The input to these algorithms are partial signatures $\{y_i\}_{i \in S}$ received from t signers, i.e. $|S| = t$ where $S \subseteq \{P_1, \ldots, P_n\}$. This algorithm combines these partial signatures to obtain a full signature as follows.
  - Compute $w = \prod_{i \in S} y_i^{2\Delta \tilde{\lambda}_i^S(0)} \bmod N$
  - Find integers a, b such that $a4\Delta^2 + be = 1$
  - Compute $\sigma = w^a H(m)^b \bmod N$
  - Output (m, σ)
- Verify: The verification algorithm is used for checking signature validity. The input to this algorithm is a tuple (m, σ, vk) and it works as follows:
  - Output valid $\iff$ $H(m) \stackrel{?}{=} \sigma^e \pmod{N}$.

2.4 Threshold Oblivious Pseudo-Random Function (TOPRF)

A pseudo-random function (PRF) family is a keyed family of deterministic functions. A function chosen at random from the family is indistinguishable from a random function. Oblivious PRF (OPRF) is an extension of PRF to a two-party setting where a server S holds the key and a party P holds an input. S can help P in computing the PRF value on the input but in doing so P should not get any other information and S should not learn P's input. Jarecki et al. [8] extend OPRF to a multi-server setting so that a threshold number t of the servers are needed to compute the PRF on any input. Furthermore, a collusion of at most $t - 1$ servers learns no information about the input.

Definition 5 (Threshold Oblivious Pseudo-Random Function (TOPRF)). *A threshold oblivious pseudo-random function is a PRF* $\mathsf{TOP} : \mathcal{K} \times \mathcal{X} \rightarrow \mathcal{Y}$ *along with a tuple of four PPT algorithms* (Setup, Encode, Eval, Combine) *described below. The server S is split into n servers $S_1, \ldots, S_n$. The party P must reach out to a subset of these servers to compute a TOP value.*

- Setup($1^\lambda, t, n$) $\rightarrow$ (sk, $\{\mathsf{sk}_i\}_{i=1}^n$, pp). *It generates a secret key* sk, n *shares* $\mathsf{sk}_1, \ldots, \mathsf{sk}_n$ *of* sk, *and public parameters* pp. *Share* sk_i *is given to party* S_i. *The public parameters* pp *will be an implicit input in the algorithms below.*
- Encode(x, ρ). *It is run by the party P. It generates an encoding c of x using randomness ρ.*
- Eval(sk_i, c) *It is run by a server S_i. It uses sk_i to generate a share z_i of TOPRF value* TOP(sk, x) *from the encoding c.*
- Combine($x, \{(i, z_i)\}_{i \in S}, \rho$) *It is run by the party P. It combines the shares received from any set of t servers ($|S| = t$) using randomness ρ to generate a value h.*

Correctness. For all $\lambda \in \mathbb{N}$, and $t, n \in \mathbb{N}$ where $t \leq n$, all (sk, $\{\mathsf{sk}_i\}_{i=1}^n$, pp) $\xleftarrow{\$}$ Setup($1^\lambda, t, n$), any value $x \in \mathcal{X}$, any randomness ρ, ρ', and any two sets $S, S' \subseteq [n]$ where $|S| = |S'| \geq t$, if $c = \mathsf{Encode}(x.\rho)$, $c' = \mathsf{Encode}(x.\rho')$, $z_i = \mathsf{Eval}(\mathsf{sk}_i, c)$ for $i \in S$, and $z'_j = \mathsf{Eval}(\mathsf{sk}_j, c')$ for $j \in S'$, then Combine($x, \{(i, z_i)\}_{i \in S}, \rho$) = Combine($x, \{(i, z'_j)\}_{j \in S'}, \rho'$).

Security. For the details on TOPRF security, we refer the reader to [2].

A TOPRF Construction. In the following we recall a TOPRF construction called 2HashTDH [8] that PASTA uses. The underlying PRF for 2HashTDH is $H : \mathcal{X} \times \mathbb{Z}_p \rightarrow \{0,1\}^\lambda$, where $\mathcal{X}$ is the message space, and $\mathbb{Z}_p$ the key space. To define H, we require two hash functions: $H_1 : \mathcal{X} \times \mathbb{G} \rightarrow \{0,1\}^\lambda$, and $H_2 : \mathcal{X} \rightarrow \mathbb{G}$, where $(p, g, \mathbb{G}) \xleftarrow{\$} \mathsf{GroupGen}(1^\lambda)$. Finally, for $x \in \mathcal{X}$, and key sk $\in \mathbb{Z}_p$, define

$$H(x, \mathsf{sk}) = H_1(x, H_2(x)^{\mathsf{sk}}).$$

The TOPRF evaluation for H is described below, where P holds a message $x \in \mathcal{X}$, and the secret key sk is split between n servers.

- Setup($1^\lambda, t, n$).
  - $(p, g, \mathbb{G}) \xleftarrow{\$} \mathsf{GroupGen}(1^\lambda)$
  - sk $\xleftarrow{\$} \mathbb{Z}_p$
  - $(\mathsf{sk}_1, \ldots, \mathsf{sk}_n) \xleftarrow{\$} \mathsf{ShamirShare}(\mathsf{sk}, t, n)$
  - Set pp $= (p, g, \mathbb{G}, t, n, H_1, H_2)$.
  - Give $(\mathsf{sk}_i, \mathsf{pp})$ to each server S_i
- Encode(x). This is run by P
  - $\rho \xleftarrow{\$} \mathbb{Z}_p$

- Output $c = H_2(x)^\rho$
- Eval(sk_i, c). This is run by a server S_i
  - Output $z_i = c^{\mathsf{sk}_i}$
- Combine$(x, \{(i, z_i)\}_{i \in S}, \rho)$. This is run by P
  - Output $\perp$ if $|S| \leq t - 1$ where $S \subseteq [n]$
  - Compute $z = \prod_{i \in S} z_i^{\lambda_i}$, where λ_i are Lagrange coefficients computed over the set S $(|S| = t)$
  - Output $H_1(x, z^{\rho^{-1}})$

3   Password-Based Threshold Authentication with Password Update

A password-based threshold authentication scheme allows a set of related application servers to provide a seamless single sign-on (SSO) service to its users. The system components include: a primary identity provider IP; n identity servers $\{S_1, \ldots, S_n\}$ managing, between them, user's credentials; application servers AS's; users who want to gain access to all related yet independent applications servers ASs without the need for them to repeatedly prove their identities to these servers and hold different credentials for each of them; and a client application that facilitate user's interaction with the IP, identity servers S_i's, and application servers AS's. The algorithms for a PbTA system with password-update functionality are given below, along with their workflow.

- GlobalSetup(1^λ): In this phase the primary identity provider IP, on input a system wide security parameter λ, number of identity servers n, and a threshold parameter t $(1 < t \leq n)$, generates a pair of signing and verification key $(\mathsf{sk}, \mathsf{vk})$ along with system public parameters pp. The IP then chooses and initialises n identity servers $\{S_1, \ldots, S_n\}$ with the necessary parameters. In particular,
  - each identity server S_i is given a secret share sk_i of the signing secret key sk and the public parameters pp,
  - each application server AS is given the corresponding master verification key vk and the public parameters pp.
  The GlobalSetup phase also initialises user client application with the necessary public parameters.
- Registration: This one-time phase allows a user U to open an account and register its user credentials with the n identity servers $\{S_1, \ldots, S_n\}$ *by interacting with the identity provider* IP. It begins with the U choosing a pair of identity and password $(\mathsf{id}_U, \mathsf{pwd})$, and it ends with the each server S_i receiving and storing a distinct user record $\mathsf{rec}_{i,U}$ in its record database REC_i.
- TokenGeneration: The token generation algorithm is an interactive algorithm run between a user U's client application and a set of at t identity servers, say $\{S_1, \ldots, S_t\}$.
  - TG.Request. Run by a client application.
    - **Input** - $(\mathsf{id}_U, \mathsf{pwd}, \mathsf{pld}, \mathcal{T})$. As an input it takes a user identity id_U, a user password pwd, a payload pld, and a set $\mathcal{T} \subseteq [n]$.

    – **Output** - $(\mathsf{st}_{\mathsf{pld}}, \{(\mathsf{id}_U, \mathsf{pld}, \mathsf{req}_i)\}_{i \in \mathcal{T}})$. It outputs a secret state $\mathsf{st}_{\mathsf{pld}}$ and request messages $\{(\mathsf{req}_i)\}_{i \in \mathcal{T}}$. For $i \in \mathcal{T}$, $(\mathsf{id}_U, \mathsf{pld}, \mathsf{req}_i)$ is sent to S_i.

    • TG.Respond. Run by an identity server S_i.

    – **Input** - $(\mathsf{sk}_i, \mathsf{REC}_i, (\mathsf{id}_U, \mathsf{pld}, \mathsf{req}_i))$. As an input it takes a secret key share sk_i, a record set REC_i, a user identity id_U, a payload pld and a request message req_i.

    – **Output** - res_i. The output is a response message res_i which is sent back to the connecting client.

    • TG.Finalize. Run by a client application.

    – **Input** - $(\mathsf{st}_{\mathsf{pld}}, \{\mathsf{res}_i\}_{i \in \mathcal{T}})$. As input it takes a secret state $\mathsf{st}_{\mathsf{pld}}$ and response messages $\{\mathsf{res}_i\}_{i \in \mathcal{T}}$.

    – **Output** - $(\mathsf{tk}_{\mathsf{pld}})$. The output is a token $(\mathsf{tk}_{\mathsf{pld}})$ for the payload pld. The token will be used by U to gain access to AS services.

– Verification: The verification algorithm checks the validity of a tk. The inputs to the verification algorithm are: the master verification key vk, a payload pld, and a token $\mathsf{tk}_{\mathsf{pld}}$. The verification algorithm is run by the AS services every time they receive a login request.

– PasswordUpdate It allows users to update their passwords. The interactive algorithm PasswordUpdate is run between a user U and all identity servers, $\{S_1, \ldots, S_n\}$. U's inputs are its current password pwd and a new password pwd$'$. The algorithm ends with the each server S_i updating their respective $\mathsf{rec}_{i,U}$ for U. The updated records are now valid against the new password pwd$'$. It is important to note that the PasswordUpdate is not run between U and the application server AS.

3.1   Security [2]

In the following we recall the security game $\mathsf{SecGame}_{\Pi, \mathcal{A}}(1^\lambda, t, n)$ for a password-based threshold authentication scheme Π with password update as given in [2].

$\mathsf{SecGame}_{\Pi, \mathcal{A}}(1^\lambda, t, n)$

    • $(\mathsf{pp}, \mathsf{vk}, (\mathsf{sk}_1, \ldots, \mathsf{sk}_n)) \xleftarrow{\$} \mathsf{GlobalSetup}(1^\lambda, t, n)$

    • $(\mathcal{C}, U^*, \mathsf{st}_\mathcal{A}) \xleftarrow{\$} \mathcal{A}(\mathsf{pp})$ *# $\mathcal{C}$: corrupt servers, U^*: target user*

    • $\mathcal{V} := \phi$ *# set of corrupt users*

    • $\mathsf{PwdList} := \phi$ *# list of $(\mathit{id}_U, \mathsf{pwd})$ pairs, indexed by id_U*

    • $\mathsf{ReqList}_{U,i} := \phi$ for $i \in [n]$ *# token requests U makes to S_i*

    • $\mathsf{ct} := 0$, $\mathsf{LiveSessions} = []$ *# LiveSessions is indexed by ct*

    • $\mathsf{TokList} := \phi$ *# list of tokens generated through $\mathcal{O}_{\mathsf{final}}$*

    • $Q_{U,i} := 0$ for all U and $i \in [n]$

    • $Q_{U,\mathsf{pld}} := 0$ for all U and pld

    • $\mathsf{out} \leftarrow \mathcal{A}^{\langle \mathcal{O} \rangle}(\{\mathsf{sk}_i\}_{i \in \mathcal{C}}, \mathsf{st}_\mathcal{A})$

$\mathcal{O}_{\mathsf{corrupt}}(U)$

    • Input: id_U

    • $\mathcal{V} := \mathcal{V} \cup \{\mathsf{id}_U\}$

    • Output: if $(\mathsf{id}_U, *) \in \mathsf{PwdList}$, **return** $\mathsf{PwdList}[\mathsf{id}_U]$

$\mathcal{O}_{\texttt{register}}(\texttt{U})$
- Input: $\texttt{id}_U$, such that $\mathsf{PwdList}[\texttt{id}_U] = \bot$
- $\mathsf{pwd} \xleftarrow{\$} \mathbb{P}$
- • $\mathsf{PwdList} := \mathsf{PwdList} \cup \{(\texttt{id}_U, \mathsf{pwd})\}$
- $(\mathsf{rec}_{1,U}, \ldots, \mathsf{rec}_{n,U}) \xleftarrow{\$} \mathsf{Register}(\texttt{id}_U, \mathsf{pwd})$
- $\mathsf{REC}_i := \mathsf{REC}_i \cup \{\mathsf{rec}_{i,U}\}$ for $i \in [n]$

$\mathcal{O}_{\texttt{req}}(\texttt{U}, \mathsf{pld}, \mathcal{T})$
- Input: User identity $\texttt{id}_U$ with $\mathsf{PwdList}[\texttt{id}_U] \neq \bot$, payload pld, and a set $\mathcal{T} \subseteq [n]$.
- $(\mathsf{st}_{\mathsf{pld}}, \{\mathsf{req}_i\}_{i \in \mathcal{T}}) \xleftarrow{\$} \mathsf{TG.Request}(\texttt{id}_U, \mathsf{PwdList}[\texttt{id}_U], \mathsf{pld}, \mathcal{T})$
- $\mathsf{LiveSessions}[\mathsf{ct}] := \mathsf{st}_{\mathsf{pld}}$
- $\mathsf{ReqList}_{U,i} = \mathsf{ReqList}_{U,i} \cup \{\mathsf{req}_i\}$ for $i \in \mathcal{T}$
- $\mathsf{ct} = \mathsf{ct} + 1$
Output: return $\{\mathsf{req}_i\}_{i \in \mathcal{T}}$

$\mathcal{O}_{\texttt{resp}}(i, \texttt{U}, \mathsf{pld}, \mathsf{req}_i)$
- Input: The ith identity server is provided with a user identity $\texttt{id}_U$, payload pld, and a req_i for token generation
- $\mathsf{res}_i \leftarrow \mathsf{TG.Respond}(\mathsf{sk}_i, \mathsf{REC}_i, (\texttt{id}_U, \mathsf{pld}, \mathsf{req}_i))$
- $Q_{U,i} := Q_{U,i} + 1$ if $\mathsf{req}_i \notin \mathsf{ReqList}_{U,i}$
- $Q_{U,\mathsf{pld}} := Q_{U,\mathsf{pld}} + 1$
- Output: return res_i

$\mathcal{O}_{\texttt{final}}(\mathsf{ct}, \{\mathsf{res}_i\}_S)$
- Input: It is presented with a counter leading to a specific state, and identity server partial responses to a token generation request
- $\mathsf{st}_{\mathsf{pld}} := \mathsf{LiveSessions}[\mathsf{ct}]$
- $\mathsf{tk} := \mathsf{TG.Finalize}(\mathsf{st}_{\mathsf{pld}}, \{\mathsf{res}_i\}_{i \in S})$
- $\mathsf{TokList} := \mathsf{TokList} \cup \{\mathsf{tk}\}$
- Output: return tk

Definition 6 (Password Safety [2]). *A PbTA scheme Π is password safe if all $t, n \in \mathbb{N}$, $(t \leq n)$, all password space $\mathbb{P}$ and all PPT adversary $\mathcal{A}$ in* $\mathrm{SecGame}_{\Pi,\mathcal{A}}(1^\lambda, t, n)$, *there exists a negligible function negl such that*

$$\Pr[(U^* \notin \mathcal{V}) \wedge (\mathsf{out} = \mathsf{PwdList}[id_{U^*}] \neq \bot)] \leq \frac{\mathsf{MAX}_{|\mathcal{C}|,t}(Q_{U^*,1}, \ldots, Q_{U^*,n}) + 1}{|\mathbb{P}|} + \mathsf{negl}(\lambda)$$

Definition 7 (Unforgeability [2]). *A PbTA scheme is unforgeable if for all $t, n \in \mathbb{N}$, $(t \leq n)$, all password space $\mathbb{P}$ and all PPT adversary $\mathcal{A}$ in* $\mathrm{SecGame}_{\Pi,\mathcal{A}}(1^\lambda, t, n)$, *there exists a negligible function negl such that*

- *if $Q_{U^*,\mathsf{pld}^*} < t - |\mathcal{C}|$ then $\Pr[\mathsf{Verify}(\mathsf{vk}, id_{U^*}, \mathsf{pld}^*, \mathsf{tk}^*) = 1] \leq \mathsf{negl}(\lambda)$, else*
- $\Pr[(U^* \notin \mathcal{V}) \wedge (\mathsf{tk}^* \notin \mathsf{TokList}) \wedge (\mathsf{Verify}(\mathsf{vk}, id_{U^*}, \mathsf{pld}^*, \mathsf{tk}^*) = 1)] \leq$
  $\frac{\mathsf{MAX}_{|\mathcal{C}|,t}(Q_{U^*,1}, \ldots, Q_{U^*,n})}{|\mathbb{P}|} + \mathsf{negl}(\lambda)$

where $\mathcal{A}$'s output "out" in the $\mathrm{SecGame}_{\Pi,\mathcal{A}}(1^\lambda, t, n)$ *is parsed as $(\mathsf{pld}^*, \mathsf{tk}^*)$.*

Definition 8 (Password Update Safety). *A PbTA scheme is password update safe if for all* $t, n \in \mathbb{N}$, $(t \leq n)$, *all password space* $\mathbb{P}$ *and all* PPT *adversary* $\mathcal{A}$ *in* $\mathsf{SecGame}_{\Pi,\mathcal{A}}(1^\lambda, t, n)$, *there exists a negligible function* negl *such that*

$$\Pr[(U^* \notin \mathcal{V}) \wedge (i \in [n] \backslash \mathcal{C}) \wedge (F_i \text{ is true})] \leq \mathsf{negl}(\lambda)$$

where $\mathcal{A}$*'s output "out" in the* $\mathsf{SecGame}_{\Pi,\mathcal{A}}(1^\lambda, t, n)$ *is parsed as* $(i, \mathsf{rec}^*_{i,U^*})$, *and* F_i *denotes the event that* S_i *updates the existing record* rec_{i,U^*} *by replacing it with* rec^*_{i,U^*}.

4   PAS-TA-U: PASTA with Password Update

In the following we present PAS-TA-U framework. It is obtained by providing a password update functionality to the PASTA framework of [2]. Additionally, the registration phase in PAS-TA-U proposes, unlike the registration phase in plain PASTA, to keep a user and an identity provider IP as the primary participants. It is during the registration phase that a user is provided with a set of identity servers $\{S_1, \ldots, S_n\}$ by the IP. The user consequently reaches out to all identity servers with the necessary information. In doing so we are keeping the identity provider in charge who may choose to select different identity servers for different users. The user uses a client application for all its interactions with the IP, identity servers and application servers.

The other algorithms in PAS-TA-U framework remain exactly as described in plain PASTA. The underlying cryptographic primitives used are:

1. a threshold token generation scheme:
   TTG = (TTG.Setup, TTG.PartSign, TTG.Combine, TTG.Verify),
2. a threshold oblivious pseudo-random function:
   TOP = (TOP.Setup, TOP.Encode, TOP.Eval, TOP.Combine),
3. a symmetric-key encryption scheme: SKE = (SKE.Enc, SKE.Dec), and a hash function H.

- GlobalSetup: Both servers and clients are initialised with their respective setup parameters in the GlobalSetup phase:
  - TTG.Setup: Each server S_i, $1 \leq i \leq n$, receives $(\mathsf{sk}_i, \mathsf{pp}_{\mathsf{ttg}})$, where

$$(\mathsf{pp}_{\mathsf{ttg}}, [[\mathsf{sk}]] = (\mathsf{sk}_1, \ldots, \mathsf{sk}_n), \mathsf{vk}, \mathsf{sk}) \xleftarrow{\$} \mathsf{TTG.Setup}(1^{\lambda_1}, n, t)$$

The verification key vk (along with $\mathsf{pp}_{\mathsf{ttg}}$) is made available to all services managed by the AS. The master signing key sk is discarded.
  - TOP.Setup: A client generates and saves $\mathsf{pp}_{\mathsf{top}}$, where

$$\mathsf{pp}_{\mathsf{top}} = (p, g, \mathbb{G}, \mathcal{P}, H_1 : \mathcal{P} \times \mathbb{G} \to \{0,1\}^{\lambda_2}, H_2 : \mathcal{P} \to \mathbb{G}) \xleftarrow{\$} \mathsf{TOP.Setup}(1^{\lambda_2})$$

- Registration: The registration phase is used by a user U to create its login credentials. This involves a user client, an identity provider IP and n identity servers selected by the IP. The registration is a three-step process: In step1, the user client reaches out to the identity provider IP; in step2, IP responds to the client and also reaches out to all identity servers; and finally in step3, the user client reaches out to all identity servers. The details for each of these steps are as follows:
  - **Step1.** (U → IP): The user credentials for a user client U is a pair of user identity and a password $(\mathsf{id}_U, \mathsf{pwd})$. The registration begins with U computing and sharing the following with the IP:
    * $r \xleftarrow{\$} \mathbb{Z}_p^*$.
    * $\mathsf{reg.id}_U = H_2(\mathsf{pwd})^r$
    * Send $(\mathsf{id}_U, \mathsf{reg.id}_U)$ to IP
  - **Step2.** (IP → $\{U, \{S_i\}_{i=1}^n\}$): Upon receiving $(\mathsf{id}_U, \mathsf{reg.id}_U)$ from U, the identity provider IP responds as follows:
    * IP → U
      . $k \xleftarrow{\$} \mathbb{Z}_p^*$
      . $\mathsf{res.id}_U = (H_2(\mathsf{pwd})^r)^k$
      . Sends back $\mathsf{res.id}_U$ to U
    * IP → $\{S_i\}_{i=1}^n$
      . $(k_1, \ldots, k_n) \xleftarrow{\$} \mathsf{ShamirShare}(k, t, n)$
      . Sends (id_U, k_i) to S_i, $1 \le i \le n$,
  - **Step3.** (U → $\{S_i\}_{i=1}^n$): Upon receiving the response $\mathsf{res.id}_U$ from IP, U reaches out to identity servers with the following to complete the registration.
    * $H_2(\mathsf{pwd})^k = (\mathsf{res.id}_U)^{r^{-1}}$
    * $h = \mathsf{TOP}_k(\mathsf{pwd}) = H_1(\mathsf{pwd}, H_2(\mathsf{pwd}^k))$
    * $h_i = H(h\|i)$, $1 \le i \le n$
    * Sends (id_U, h_i) to S_i, $1 \le i \le n$.
  - Each S_i, $1 \le i \le n$, make a record of U's registration credentials by storing $[\mathsf{id}_U, (h_i, k_i)]$.
- TokenGeneration: This is run is by a user U to generate tokens (signed messages) used for accessing application services. As an input it takes a payload pld on which a token (signature) will be generated eventually and U's pwd. Consequently, the user client reaches out to any t out of n identity servers with the token generation request. Upon receiving all t responses, they are combined to produce a valid token.
  - TG.Request (U → $\{S_i\}_{i \in \mathcal{T}}$):
    * $\rho \in \mathbb{Z}_p^*$
    * $\mathsf{req}_{ttg} = \mathsf{TOP.Encode}(\mathsf{pwd}, \rho) = H_2(\mathsf{pwd})^\rho$
    * Sends $(\mathsf{id}_U, \mathsf{pld}, \mathsf{req}_{ttg})$ to a set of t identity servers, without loss of generality, say $S_1, \ldots S_t$.
  - TG.Respond (S_i → U): Upon receiving $(\mathsf{id}_U, \mathsf{pld}, \mathsf{req}_{ttg})$, the ith identity server S_i retrieves the corresponding record $[\mathsf{id}_U, (h_i, k_i)]$ and responds as follows:

* $z_i = \mathsf{TOP.Eval}(k_i, \mathsf{req_{ttg}}) = (\mathsf{req_{ttg}})^{k_i} = H_2(\mathsf{pwd})^{\rho k_i}$
* $y_i = \mathsf{TTG.PartSign}(\mathsf{sk}_i, \mathsf{pld}\|\mathsf{id_U})$
* $v_i = \mathsf{SKE.Enc}(h_i, y_i)$
* Return $\mathsf{ttg.res}_i = (z_i, v_i)$ to U

- **TG.Finalize:** The received responses $\{\mathsf{ttg.res}_i = (z_i, v_i) \mid 1 \le i \le t\}$ are combined by the user client to produce a token on the payload pld as follows:
  * $\theta = H_2(\mathsf{pwd})^{k\rho} = \prod_{i=1}^{t} z_i^{\lambda_i}$
  * $h = \mathsf{TOP}_k(\mathsf{pwd}) = H_1(\mathsf{pwd}, H_2(\mathsf{pwd}^k)) = H_1(\mathsf{pwd}, \theta^{\rho^{-1}})$
  * $h_i = H(h\|i), 1 \le i \le t$
  * $y_i = \mathsf{SKE.Dec}(h_i, v_i), 1 \le i \le t$
  * $\mathsf{tk_{pld}} = \mathsf{TTG.Combine}(\{y_i\}_{i=1}^{t})$

- Verification: The token verification algorithm is run by application services every time they receive a token $\mathsf{tk_{pld}}$ on a payload pld. The access to the service is allowed only if $1 \xleftarrow{\$} \mathsf{TTG.Verify}(\mathsf{pld}, \mathsf{tk_{pld}}, \mathsf{vk})$.

- PasswordUpdate: This is run by a user U, every time it wants to update its current password pwd and set it to a new password pwd'. The process requires U to run TOP evaluations twice: once on the input pwd and later on pwd'. As TOP is implicitly built into the TokenGeneration algorithm, U therefore runs the later twice (note that payload is not important here). In the final step U runs the TokenGeneration algorithm for the third time on a special payload. This token is finally shared with all identity servers, who then use it to update their respective records associated with U. The details are as follows:

  • **Step1:**
    - $\{\mathsf{ttg.res}_i = (z_i, v_i) \mid 1 \le i \le t\} \xleftarrow{\$} \mathsf{TG.Respond}(\mathsf{TG.Request}(\mathsf{pwd}, \mathsf{pld}_1))$
    - Use $\{z_i\}_{i=1}^{t}$ to compute $h = H_1(\mathsf{pwd}, H_2(\mathsf{pwd})^k)$
    - Compute $h_i = H(h\|i), 1 \le i \le n$

  • **Step2:**
    - $\{\mathsf{ttg.res}_i = (z_i', v_i') \mid 1 \le i \le t\} \xleftarrow{\$} \mathsf{TG.Respond}(\mathsf{TG.Request}(\mathsf{pwd}', \mathsf{pld}_2))$
    - Use $\{z_i'\}_{i=1}^{t}$ to compute $h' = H_1(\mathsf{pwd}', H_2(\mathsf{pwd}')^k)$
    - Compute $h_i' = H(h'\|i), 1 \le i \le n$

  • **Step3:**
    - Set $\mathsf{pld}_3 = \mathsf{SKE.Enc}(h_1, h_1\|h_1')\| \cdots \|\mathsf{SKE.Enc}(h_n, h_n\|h_n')\|\mathsf{id_U}$
    - Compute $\mathsf{tk_{pld_3}} \xleftarrow{\$} \mathsf{TokenGeneration}(\mathsf{pwd}, \mathsf{pld}_3)$ (the current password is used)

  • **Step4:** The user client for U finally sends $(\mathsf{pld}_3, \mathsf{tk_{pld_3}})$ to all identity servers for password update.

  PasswordUpdate: Upon receiving a token $(\mathsf{pld}_3, \mathsf{tk_{pld_3}})$ requesting password update, each identity server S_i proceeds as follows:
    * S_i ensures that $\mathsf{TTG.Verify}(\mathsf{pld}_3, \mathsf{tk_{pld_3}}, \mathsf{vk})$ returns 1
    * Extract $L_i = \mathsf{SKE.Enc}(h_i, h_i\|h_i')$ from pld_3
    * Compute $h_i\|h_i' = \mathsf{SKE.Dec}(h_i, L_i)$
    * Update the record for $\mathsf{id_U}$ as $[\mathsf{id_U}, h_i', k_i]$ (replacing h_i by h_i')

4.1 Security: Password Update

In the following we discuss password update security for PAS-TA-U as per the Definition 8. A successful password update in PAS-TA-U requires a user to obtain a valid token using the existing credentials. Consequently, an unauthorised password update is directly reduced to token forgery. The following theorem provides the necessary details.

Theorem 2. *For all $t, n \in \mathbb{N}$, $(t \leq n)$, all password space $\mathbb{P}$ and all* PPT *adversary $\mathcal{A}$ in* $\mathsf{SecGame}_{\Pi,\mathcal{A}}(1^\lambda, t, n)$ *(as given in Sect. 3.1), there exists a* PPT *adversary B in* $\mathsf{SecGame}_{\Pi,\mathcal{A}}(1^\lambda, t, n)$ *such that*

$$\Pr[(U^* \notin \mathcal{V}) \wedge (i \in [n]\backslash\mathcal{C}) \wedge (F_i \text{ is true})] \leq \mathsf{Adv}^{\mathcal{B}}_{\mathsf{Unforgreability}}(\mathsf{SecGame}_{\Pi,\mathcal{B}}(1^\lambda, t, n)) \tag{3}$$

where Π denotes PAS-TA-U, $\mathcal{A}$'s output "out" in the $\mathsf{SecGame}_{\Pi,\mathcal{A}}(1^\lambda, t, n)$ is parsed as $(i, \mathsf{rec}^*_{i,U^*})$, and F_i denotes the event that S_i updates the existing record rec_{i,U^*} by replacing it with the new record rec^*_{i,U^*}. The $\mathsf{Adv}^{\mathcal{B}}_{\mathsf{Unforgreability}}(\mathsf{SecGame}_{\Pi,\mathcal{B}}(1^\lambda, t, n))$ denotes $\mathcal{B}$'s advantage in forging a token in the $\mathsf{SecGame}_{\Pi,\mathcal{B}}(1^\lambda, t, n)$.

Proof. Assume, $\mathcal{A} = \mathcal{A}_{\mathsf{pu}}$ be a PPT adversary who can make any identity server S_i to update a target user U^*'s existing record rec_{i,U^*} by a record rec^*_{i,U^*}. We then construct a PPT adversary $\mathcal{B} = \mathcal{A}_{\mathsf{f}}$ who can forge token's for arbitrary users. The $\mathcal{A}_{\mathsf{f}}$ runs $\mathcal{A}_{\mathsf{pu}}$ as a subroutine. The details are as follows.

Let U^* be the target user for $\mathcal{A}_f$ in the $\mathsf{SecGame}_{\Pi,\mathcal{A}_f}(1^\lambda, t, n)$. Let $\mathcal{C} \subset [n]$ be the subset of identity servers that are corrupted by $\mathcal{A}_f$ such that $|\mathcal{C}| = t - 1$. Let $\mathsf{pwd}^e_{U^*}$ be the existing password for U^*. $\mathcal{A}_f$ chooses an identity server S_i such that $i \in [n]\backslash\mathcal{C}$ and a new password $\mathsf{pwd}^n_{U^*}$ for U^*. $\mathcal{A}_f$ then makes a call to $\mathcal{A}_{\mathsf{pu}}$ and present it with the input $(i, \mathsf{pwd}^n_{U^*}, h^*_i, \{\mathsf{rec}^e_{j,U^*}\}_{j \in \mathcal{C}})$ where $h^*_i = H(h^* \| i)$, $h^* = H_1(\mathsf{pwd}^n_{U^*}, H_2(\mathsf{pwd}^n_{U^*})^k)$. The h^* can be computed by $\mathcal{A}_f/\mathcal{A}_{\mathsf{pu}}$ by reaching out to any t identity servers on inputs id_{U^*}, $\mathsf{pwd}^n_{U^*}$.

The adversary $\mathcal{A}_{\mathsf{pu}}$ subsequently mounts an attack on the target identity server S_i. If successful, S_i would update its existing record $\mathsf{rec}_{i,U^*} = (\mathsf{id}_{U^*}, h_i, k_i)$ with the new record $\mathsf{rec}^*_{i,U^*} = (\mathsf{id}_{U^*}, h^*_i, k_i)$ where h^*_i is provided by $\mathcal{A}_{\mathsf{pu}}$.

On the other hand, $\mathcal{A}_f$ by itself could update the records of each of the $t - 1$ corrupted identity servers S_j's, $j \in \mathcal{C}$, with the respective h^*_j's where $h^*_j = H(h^* \| j)$, $h^* = H_1(\mathsf{pwd}^n_{U^*}, H_2(\mathsf{pwd}^n_{U^*})^k)$. Finally, let $\mathcal{C}' = \mathcal{C} \cup \{i\}$. As $|\mathcal{C}'| = t$, and as each identity server in $\mathcal{C}'$ now have the valid h^*_j's corresponding to the new password $\mathsf{pwd}^n_{U^*}$, $\mathcal{A}_f$ can obtain valid tokens issued on identity id_{U^*}. As we see a direct reduction here in terms of the problem instance for $\mathcal{A}_f$ being directly reduced to the problem instance for $\mathcal{A}_{\mathsf{pu}}$, this proves the claim of Eq. 3.

5 A Concrete Application of PAS-TA-U: Practical SSH key manager for enterprise networks

In the following We show how PAS-TA-U framework can be used to implement an SSH (Secure shell) key manager (ESKM) - an enterprise level solution for managing

SSH keys. The concept of an ESKM was first introduced by Harchol et al. in [7] and was instantiated therein using threshold cryptographic primitives. ESKM is a secure and fault-tolerant logically-centralised SSH key manager whose advantages include: (1) the ability to observe, approve and log all SSH connections origination from the home network, and (2) clients do not need to store secret keys and instead only need to authenticate themselves to the ESKM system (see Fig. 4). The ESKM central key server of [7] was implemented in a distributed fashion using n key servers (also know as *control cluster* (CC) nodes) such that users in the enterprise network must interact with a subset of these CC nodes for a successful SSH connection. The problem of user authentication to CC nodes was also discussed in [7] and password-based variants were proposed for the same. The functionality of a password update mechanism for its users in an ESKM is an obvious requirement. As a concrete application, we implement PAS-TA-U to instantiate an ESKM that admits password update functionality for its users. The different entities in PAS-TA-U are mapped to ESKM components as follows: (1) the key manager in ESKM play the role of an identity provider IP, and n control nodes represent the identity servers $\{S_1, \ldots, S_n\}$, (2) enterprise network has SSH key pairs (sk, vk) and SSH servers storing vk represent the application servers AS, and (3) users in the enterprise network must obtain valid tokens by connecting to a subset of t $(t \leq n)$ identity servers before they can gain access to these SSH servers. In the following we present a working flow of the system.

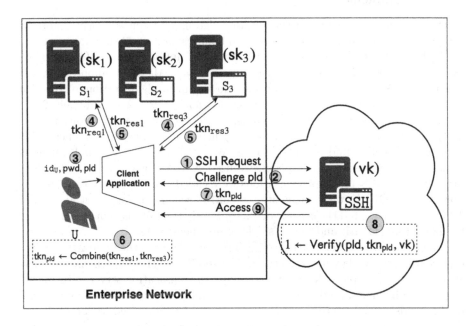

Fig. 4. Distributed SSH key manager for enterprise networks

- **Step 1.** The key manager (IP) runs the PAS-TA-U GlobalSetup to obtain (sk, vk) and n shares of $\{sk_1, \ldots, sk_n\}$ of sk. It submits vk with the application servers AS's (SSH servers). Finally, it sets up n identity servers $\{S_1, \ldots, S_n\}$ locally and initialises them with the respective shares: $S_i \leftarrow sk_i$.
- **Step 2.** Users in the enterprise network run PAS-TA-U Registration with the IP to create and store credentials with the identity servers $\{S_1, \ldots, S_n\}$.
- **Step 3.** This step shows how a registered user make an SSH connection into application servers. A user client initiates an SSH connection in to an application server AS. As part of user authentication, the SSH handshake phase presents to the client a challenge payload pld to be signed using the signing key sk. Consequently, the client runs the PAS-TA-U TokenGeneration on payload pld by reaching out to a set of t identity servers using U's password pwd. A set of t correct responses are combined to produce a signature token tk on the payload pld under the signing key sk. The generated tk is sent back to the application server which then verifies it using the stored verification key vk. A correctly generated token will give U an access to the application server.
- **Step 4.** Our password update mechanism allows any user to update its password by reaching out to a set of any t identity servers directly. The updated matching user credentials are then uploaded to all identity servers.

5.1   ESKM Implementation

In this section we provide implementation details and consequently report on the performance of our instantiation of an ESKM using PAS-TA-U under practical network scenarios. We developed separate client applications for (a) users (b) identity provider IP, and (c) identity servers S_i's. All client applications are developed in Python. The entire source code for our implementation is hosted at https://anonymous.4open.science/r/198222d4-a335-4b93-a219-5a0bf5a4ec23/.

The cryptographic algorithms implemented for client applications include a hash function, Shamir secret sharing scheme, a symmetric-key encryption scheme, a TOPRF, and a TTG scheme. We used SHA-256 as our hash function. For symmetric key encryption, we used AES-128 with OFB mode. Both SHA-256 and AES-128 implementations were called from Python Cryptography library. For TOPRF, we implemented 2HashTDH scheme of Jarecki et al. [8]. For TTG, we implemented the scheme of Victor Shoup [14]. We used openssl library for 2HashTDH TOPRF and Shoup's TTG implementations.

The user client authentication in the SSH connection to the application server is done using public-key based method. We used RSA signature scheme to generate a 2048 bits key-pair (sk, vk) and configure the application server with the vk. The openssh version used is 8.2p1 and it internally uses openssl version 1.1.1f. In the handshake phase of the SSH, the user client is presented with a challenge payload pld for it to be RSA signed using the secret signing key sk. The signing part is handled by the libcrypto library of openssl. In our case the secret key is not available with the client and instead it must reach out, using our python user client, to t identity servers for a threshold RSA signature generation (token) on the pld. To make this happen, we introduced a patch in `libcrypto` which can alter the usual signing flow. We replaced the secret key with an equivalent dummy key. If the `libcrypto`'s signing routine detects a dummy key, it calls our Python routine which computes signature by contacting t servers. Otherwise, the usual signing flow continues.

Experimental Setup: In order to evaluate the performance, we implemented various network settings described below. The experiments are run on a single laptop running Ubuntu 20.04 with 2-core 2.2 GHz Intel i5-5200U CPU and 8 GB of RAM. All identity providers are run on the same machine. We simulate the following network connections using the Linux `tc` command: (1) a local area network setting with 4 ms round-trip latency, and (2) an Internet setting with 80 ms round-trip latency.

Token Generation Time: Table 1 shows the total run-time for a user client to generate a single token in the `TokenGeneration` phase. We show experiments, both in the LAN and the Internet setting, for a different set of (t, n) parameters where n is the total number of identity servers and t $(t \leq n)$ is the threshold set of identity servers which are contacted by the user client. The reported time is an average of 100 token requests. The `Plain` setting in the table corresponds to the direct peer-to-peer client-server SSH connection (without the threshold token generation).

Password Update Time: Table 2 shows the total run-time for the client to update password in our `PbTA` protocol. The reported time is an average of 100 password change requests.

Table 1. Token Generation Time for User Clients in ESKM

Setting	(t, n)	Time (ms)
LAN	Plain	15.1
	(2, 3)	22.8
	(3, 6)	25.1
	(5, 10)	28.2
	(10, 10)	32.5
Internet	Plain	101.3
	(2, 3)	109.5
	(3, 6)	112.4
	(5, 10)	115.8
	(10, 10)	119.9

Table 2. Password Update Time for User Clients in ESKM

Setting	(t, n)	Time (ms)
Local	(2,3)	65.3
	(3, 6)	74.4
	(5, 10)	82.7
	(10, 10)	95.1
Internet	(2,3)	325.5
	(3, 6)	333.1
	(5, 10)	346.9
	(10, 10)	357.6

6   Conclusion

We presented PAS-TA-U to propose a password-update functionality into PASTA - a generic framework for password-based threshold authentication (PbTA) schemes. Secure password update is a practical requirement for PbTA applications such as single-sign-on systems. Existing PbTA schemes, including the PASTA framework, do not admit password update functionality.

As a concrete application, we instantiated PAS-TA-U to implement a distributed enterprise SSH key manager that features a secure password-update functionality for its clients. Our experiments show that the overhead of protecting secret credentials against breaches in our system compared to a traditional single server setup is low (average 119 ms in a 10-out-of-10 server setting on Internet with 80 ms round trip latency). The entire source code for our implementation is hosted at https://anonymous.4open.science/r/198222d4-a335-4b93-a219-5a0bf5a4ec23/.

References

1. Abdalla, M., Fouque, P.-A., Pointcheval, D.: Password-based authenticated key exchange in the three-party setting. In: Vaudenay, S. (ed.) PKC 2005. LNCS, vol. 3386, pp. 65–84. Springer, Heidelberg (2005). https://doi.org/10.1007/978-3-540-30580-4_6

2. Agrawal, S., Miao, P., Mohassel, P., Mukherjee, P.: PASTA: password-based threshold authentication. In: ACM CCS, pp. 2042–2059. ACM (2018)

3. Damgård, I., Koprowski, M.: Practical threshold RSA signatures without a trusted dealer. In: Pfitzmann, B. (ed.) EUROCRYPT 2001. LNCS, vol. 2045, pp. 152–165. Springer, Heidelberg (2001). https://doi.org/10.1007/3-540-44987-6_10

4. Desmedt, Y., Frankel, Y.: Threshold cryptosystems. In: Brassard, G. (ed.) CRYPTO 1989. LNCS, vol. 435, pp. 307–315. Springer, New York (1990). https://doi.org/10.1007/0-387-34805-0_28

5. Gennaro, R., Goldfeder, S., Narayanan, A.: Threshold-optimal DSA/ECDSA signatures and an application to bitcoin wallet security. In: Manulis, M., Sadeghi, A.-R., Schneider, S. (eds.) ACNS 2016. LNCS, vol. 9696, pp. 156–174. Springer, Cham (2016). https://doi.org/10.1007/978-3-319-39555-5_9

6. Gennaro, R., Halevi, S., Krawczyk, H., Rabin, T.: Threshold RSA for dynamic and ad-hoc groups. In: Smart, N. (ed.) EUROCRYPT 2008. LNCS, vol. 4965, pp. 88–107. Springer, Heidelberg (2008). https://doi.org/10.1007/978-3-540-78967-3_6

7. Harchol, Y., Abraham, I., Pinkas, B.: Distributed SSH key management with proactive RSA threshold signatures. In: Preneel, B., Vercauteren, F. (eds.) ACNS 2018. LNCS, vol. 10892, pp. 22–43. Springer, Cham (2018). https://doi.org/10.1007/978-3-319-93387-0_2

8. Jarecki, S., Kiayias, A., Krawczyk, H., Xu, J.: TOPPSS: cost-minimal password-protected secret sharing based on threshold OPRF. In: Gollmann, D., Miyaji, A., Kikuchi, H. (eds.) ACNS 2017. LNCS, vol. 10355, pp. 39–58. Springer, Cham (2017). https://doi.org/10.1007/978-3-319-61204-1_3

9. MacKenzie, P.D., Shrimpton, T., Jakobsson, M.: Threshold password-authenticated key exchange. In: Yung, M. (ed.) CRYPTO 2002. LNCS, vol. 2442, pp. 385–400. Springer, Heidelberg (2002). https://doi.org/10.1007/3-540-45708-9_25

10. Paterson, K.G., Stebila, D.: One-time-password-authenticated key exchange. In: Steinfeld, R., Hawkes, P. (eds.) ACISP 2010. LNCS, vol. 6168, pp. 264–281. Springer, Heidelberg (2010). https://doi.org/10.1007/978-3-642-14081-5_17

11. Di Raimondo, M., Gennaro, R.: Provably secure threshold password-authenticated key exchange. In: Biham, E. (ed.) EUROCRYPT 2003. LNCS, vol. 2656, pp. 507–523. Springer, Heidelberg (2003). https://doi.org/10.1007/3-540-39200-9_32

12. De Santis, A., Desmedt, Y., Frankel, Y., Yung, M.: How to share a function securely. In: ACM, pp. 522–533. ACM (1994)

13. Shamir, A.: How to share a secret. Commun. ACM **22**(11), 612–613 (1979)

14. Shoup, V.: Practical threshold signatures. In: Preneel, B. (ed.) EUROCRYPT 2000. LNCS, vol. 1807, pp. 207–220. Springer, Heidelberg (2000). https://doi.org/10.1007/3-540-45539-6_15

Re-markable: Stealing Watermarked Neural Networks Through Synthesis

Nandish Chattopadhyay$^{(\boxtimes)}$, Chua Sheng Yang Viroy,
and Anupam Chattopadhyay

School of Computer Science and Engineering, Nanyang Technological University,
Singapore, Singapore
nandish001@e.ntu.edu.sg

Abstract. With the advent of the deep learning paradigm, the state-of-the-art neural network models have achieved unprecedented success in a variety of tasks, particularly pertaining to image, text and speech processing. The key to their high performance involves efforts in systematic curation of relevant data, optimization of neural architectures and heavy investments in hardware infrastructure essential for training models. This necessitates the requirement of frameworks for establishing ownership on trained models by associated stakeholders. Watermarking neural networks have been used as a mechanism for establishing such Intellectual Property rights, verifiable when necessary, created with the goal of preventing theft and unauthorised use. In this paper, we explore the vulnerabilities of watermarking neural networks by backdooring, which spawned a wide range of variations around the same principle due to its potential robustness. We propose a model-modification attack to successfully extract the trained neural network and demonstrate the removal of watermarking signatures. We use synthesis with GANs to generate samples, which can be used to re-train the marked models and achieve comparable accuracies of performance (within about 3% of actual model). The proposed attack successfully removes verifiable watermarks, as tested on highly benchmarked datasets including MNIST, Fashion MNIST and CIFAR-10, thus jeopardizing the reliability of the state-of-the-art watermarking scheme.

Keywords: Watermarking neural networks · Backdooring · Model modification attack · Synthesis · Extraction

1 Introduction

Over the years, the unprecedented rise of attention towards research in the paradigm of machine learning can be much attributed towards the success of high-performance neural networks [1]. The realm of deep learning and its applications now touch upon almost every walk of life, from mobile apps to autonomous driving and Industry 4.0. The vast growth of data centers and the large amount

© Springer Nature Switzerland AG 2020
L. Batina et al. (Eds.): SPACE 2020, LNCS 12586, pp. 46–65, 2020.
https://doi.org/10.1007/978-3-030-66626-2_3

of big data repositories can be harvested using the most developed machine learning models to gain valuable insights that boost productivity and reduce dependence on human supervision. These technologies and associated mechanisms have been studied with great interests in the industry and academia alike. The flourishing use of AI took a major leap in 2012, when it was demonstrated for the first time that for a particular task, which was an image classification task, a trained model could out-perform the average human [2]. Historically, the statistical learning techniques made use of laborious data pre-processing, wherein the features were to be identified and extracted from the data by different techniques before being modelled for a specific task. This approach typically lacked generalization and also suffered from a saturation in performance, potentially due to poorly extracted hand-crafted features. With the proliferation of neural networks and the state-of-the-art in the field, end-to-end systems were feasible which would perform both feature extraction and thereafter classification or regression whatever be the task. This significantly reduced human involvement in modelling the abundance of data and laid the foundation of many AI applications [3,4].

Although the discussion on Deep Learning among researchers has been rather new, spiking about a decade back, neural networks have been in existence for over 60 years. The perceptron algorithm was introduced in 1958 [5] and modified thereafter. It did not gain the expected traction due to the lack of hardware infrastructure that is necessary towards unleashing the true potential of these learning systems. Some exceptional properties of neural networks like their highly parallelize-able operations owing to their inherent linearity of matrix multiplications for example, was majorly exploited by high-performance GPUs to train a network in relatively small amounts of time.

1.1 Background

There are three essential components towards the success of this system [6]. First and foremost is a large volume of curated data which is rich in information. Secondly, we need a neural network architecture comprising of the computational graph and the weight matrices. And finally, the hardware infrastructure is critical, that is able to train the network, that is to tune the weights or the parameters using the available data. Therefore, for accomplishing a particular machine learning task, the corresponding stakeholders need to invest heavily in:

- obtaining the necessary data, curating it and annotating it if that's necessary (especially for supervised machine learning tasks)
- optimizing the neural architecture best suited for the task
- heavily investing in powerful hardware infrastructure that is able to successfully train the neural network using the data so as to obtain the deploy-able trained model

Naturally, therefore anyone investing in any one or multiple of the aforementioned components would wish to establish some sort of authority and rights on their assets. It may be mentioned here that all of these tasks need not be accomplished in one place, and can be carried out separately by different parties mutually agreeing on a common goal. Whichever way, the trained model, which is the outcome of this entire exercise is a valuable asset for those involved.

Machine Learning as a Service (MLaaS): This is a highly evolving and naturally competitive market. Such sort of service providers claim to offer fully trained models to their customers at a cost, which in comparison to what the price would have been if they had to train the model from scratch using high-performing hardware resources, is almost negligible. Over and above that, the customers are provided the freedom to further fine-tune the model in order to improve its performance over time, whilst gathering further data from its sources, or perform some kind of transfer learning [7] thereafter to extract high-level features to accomplish similar tasks. Apart from this kind of open source models, MLaaS lets its customers create specific and often more personalized applications without having to delve deep into the training of the neural networks. While it looks quite simple apparently, this idea gives rise of a bunch of key questions pertaining to security and legality, particularly in the context of IP rights. A company that plays in the market of MLaaS may consider the eventualities that its customers who purchase a trained model from it, may indulge in malpractices. Typical examples of such breaches in contract may include redistribution of the model beyond what is legally permitted as per legal documentation, or even further selling of it, to other parties, thereby posing a threat to its business. Such scenarios of potential theft should be avoided at all costs. Therefore there is an imminent requirement of developing a robust procedure for authenticating a trained neural network model.

This issue has become prominent in the field of machine learning research as more and more solutions are being brought to the market, and thus giving rise to new associated problems. Being a rather new topic in the machine learning research community, some researchers are looking to borrow from the security community, particularly in the VLSI security research groups where this particular problem is well documented and studied as part of digital watermarking [8]. Digital Watermarking is formally defined as "the process of robustly concealing information in a signal (e.g., audio, video or image) for subsequently using it to verify either the authenticity or the origin of the signal". The idea of digital watermarking has found a lot of applications in many aspects of digital media including images, videos and audio signals. However, it must be noted that the literature in digital watermarking, although diverse, is not trivially applicable to the context of watermarking neural networks. This is specifically due to the challenge of embedding the watermarks within the neural network model, without bringing down its performance on its actual designated task. One needs to carefully map the techniques existing in the field of watermarking to machine learning models.

1.2   Related Works and Motivation

There have been multiple techniques proposed in the past for watermarking neural networks. Some prominent works include BlackMarks [9], which is a black-box watermarking scheme for Deep Neural Networks, later refined as DeepMarks [10], claiming to be a digital fingerprinting framework for Deep Neural Networks. Other approaches include DeepSigns [11], which is a generic watermarking framework for protecting the ownership of Deep Learning Models. Adversarial samples have also been used to implement watermarking schemes, like in DAWN [12], which is a dynamic adversarial watermarking of Neural Networks. However, they have not been reliable because of the simultaneous development in attacks on these models, by adversaries. These works include DeepInspect [13], which is a black-box Trojan detection and mitigation framework for Deep Neural Networks and TABOR [14] which claims to be a highly accurate approach to inspecting and restoring Trojan backdoors in AI systems etc.

Inspite of such competition among watermarking schemes and attacks, the most accepted and widely used mechanism, which is thought to be robust against attacks, is watermarking using backdooring [15]. This approach targets the over-parameterized nature of a neural network to implement a watermarking algorithm. Given its acceptance and prevalence, it is important to review its capabilities and vulnerabilities before it is used to practical deployment in the market. This approach uses backdooring, typically a flaw observed in neural networks, to its advantage to embed specific watermarks within the neural network model. These are planted by corresponding modifications of the weights. While being very effective in both embedding the watermarks and verification afterwards when necessary to prove ownership, it borrows caveats from the research into vulnerabilities of backdoors. While they may be of less adversity towards this novel approach, it is very crucial to study its own weaknesses against potential attacks by adversaries. Typical mechanisms of stealing watermarked models, primarily Evasion attacks like Ensemble attacks and Detector attacks don't work well against this scheme, as further discussed in Sect. 3.2. This watermarking mechanism is not robust against our proposition of a model modification attack nevertheless. This necessitates a detailed study in exploring and mitigating the associated vulnerabilities.

1.3   Contribution

In this paper, we explore the vulnerabilities of the watermarking scheme with backdooring and propose a model modification attack mechanism to extract or steal the trained model. Our contribution includes:

- proposition and demonstration of two kinds of model extraction mechanisms involving specific re-training the watermarked model to remove signatures
- use of synthesis by Generative Adversarial Networks to re-create samples which emulate samples derived from the same distribution as that of the training data (considering the adversary is aware of the data domain) to retrain the model.

1.4   Organization

In this paper, the Sect. 2 touches upon the key theoretical constructs and formulation that are necessary for understanding the scope and relevance of the task at hand. In particular we discuss the essentials of Watermarking in general, backdoors in neural networks, the state-of-the-art watermarking schemes using backdooring and finally, the key instrument of our mode of model modification attack: Synthesis using Generative Adversarial Networks. In Sect. 3, the various modes of attack on watermarking schemes are discussed, only to put into perspective our proposed method of attack and how it works in details. This is followed by the experimental design, with results and observations in Sect. 4. We conclude thereafter with some concluding remarks and scope of future progress in this area of research.

2   Theoretical Formulation

In order to arrive at the task of exploring potential vulnerabilities is digital watermarking schemes for neural networks, it is imperative to briefly look at the key components of the overall problem and its evolution. In this section, we discuss the idea of watermarking in general, the existence of backdoors in neural networks and how they can be utilised to watermark trained models and finally look at the process of synthesis whereby we get acquainted with the tools to attack the existing scheme. Throughout the description we have some standard nomenclature defined here. We make an assumption about the existence of a ground-truth function f that is always able to correctly classify inputs by assigning correct labels. A machine learning model attempts to approximate that function. The data in the context of the task belongs to the domain D. That way, the ground-truth function f maps $f : D \rightarrow L$, L being the set of correct labels for each sample in D. Naturally, it is not possible to realise all samples in D, and therefore we work with a dataset, which has two sets: $train\_data$ with its correspondingly mapped L_t and $test\_data$. The objective of approximating f is fulfilled by learning a neural network model M on the $train\_data$. Therefore, we have two functions, $Train(train\_data, L_t)$ and $Classify(M, test\_data)$. Having mentioned this, we can delve deeper into the formulation.

2.1   Watermarking

A typical watermarking scheme would consist of three major components. Let us assume we have a curated training dataset called $train\_data$ and a trained neural network model M. Firstly, there is a requirement of an algorithm to create a secret key m_k for the purpose of marking, which the marker will embed as the watermark, and its corresponding public key v_k for verification designed for detection and therefore verify the watermark at a later point of time to establish rights. Secondly, one needs another algorithm to place the watermark into the object, which in this particular case happens to be the neural network model. Thirdly, there needs to be another algorithm that involves both the secret key m_k for marking and the public key v_k for verification. These algorithms can therefore be stated as:

- *KeyGeneration*(): returns the pair of marking and corresponding verification keys (m_k, v_k)
- *Marking*(M, m_k): takes as parameter an input neural network model and a secret marking key m_k, returns a watermarked model $\hat{M}$
- *Verification*(m_k, v_k, M): takes as parameters the marking and verification key pair (m_k, v_k) and the watermarked model $\hat{M}$, returns the output bit $b \in \{0, 1\}$

The success of the watermarking scheme depends on the correct functioning of all the three aforementioned algorithms (*KeyGeneration, Marking, Verification*) together. The notion of correctness can be formally described as:

$$Pr_{(M,\hat{M},m_k,v_k) \leftarrow WM()}[Verify(m_k, v_k, \hat{M}) = 1] = 1 \qquad (1)$$

where, the watermarking algorithm $WM()$ is made up of the following:

1. Creating $M \leftarrow Train(train\_data)$
2. Sampling $(m_k, v_k) \leftarrow KeyGeneration()$
3. Computing $\hat{M} \leftarrow Marking(M, m_k)$
4. Return $(M, \hat{M}, m_k, v_k)$

There are some key properties that any particular watermarking scheme should satisfy. They are enlisted here:

- Functionality-preserving: The accuracy of the model in accomplishing the designated task doesn't change with the introduction of the watermarks.
- Non-triviality of ownership: The knowledge of the watermarking algorithm wouldn't disclose the key pairs to an adversary.
- Unremovability of watermarks: The adversary would not be successful in removing the watermark with the help of the knowledge of the algorithm and the existence of a watermark.
- Unforgeability of watermarks: Just the knowledge of the verification key is not sufficient to establish ownership.

Another key aspect of ensuring the proper functioning of the watermarking scheme is maintaining the sanctity and uncompromised privacy of the private key. Commitment schemes are used for this purpose as explained hereafter.

Commitments: Mechanisms of establishing commitment schemes are rather common in the field of cryptography. These algorithms make sure that the sender is able to lock some secret information into vault that can't be tampered with, before sharing it with the corresponding receiver. The receiver is unable to extract information from the vault single-handedly without the sender (hiding property). Similarly, the sender is also unable to modify the locked information once the receiver has received it (binding property).

Typically therefore, a formal definition of a commitment scheme would consist of two algorithms as listed here:

- $Commitment(x, r)$ takes as input a value $x \in S$ and a bitstring $r \in \{0,1\}^n$ and returns a bitstring c_x
- $Release(c_x, x, r)$ takes as input $x \in S, r \in \{0,1\}^n, c_x \in \{0,1\}^*$ and returns 0 or 1.

This holds good for the generic idea of watermarking, particularly watermarking neural networks. The exact details of the watermarking scheme and therefore the description of each of the aforementioned algorithms is presented later, after discussing some related key ideas that make it possible.

2.2 Backdoors in Neural Networks

Originally observed a flaw in neural networks, backdooring is a specifically designed technique to intentionally train a machine learning model to return erroneous (in comparison to the naturally occurring ground-truth function f and its labels L) labels T_L for a set of inputs T. Hence, we can define $T \subset D$ to be a subset of samples from domain D, which is called the Trigger Set. The labels corresponding to the samples present in the Trigger Set, which are different from what the ground truth function f would have returned, is captured by T_L. An explicitly trained model therefore is expected to associate these labels when tested with samples from the Trigger Set. The backdoor therefore is this pair of Trigger Set and its corresponding labels taken together, $b = (T, T_L)$. Defining the Trigger Set implies defining T_L as well.

Considering such a backdoor b, one can define a backdooring algorithm $Backdoor$ that takes as input a neural network model, and returns the model with the backdoor b embedded in it, such that the new model performs very poorly on the Trigger Set with respect to the ground-truth f, but is able to match the output labels with T_L, with high probabilities. The success of the backdooring depends on the extent of this match. It is worth mentioning here that this process of embedding a backdoor b in the model M to create the backdoored/watermarked model $\hat{M}$ can be carried out in two methods:

- The $Backdoor$ algorithm can use the existing trained neural network M and embed the backdoors in it, this mechanism of marking being referred to as backdooring a pre-trained model.
- Otherwise, the algorithm can also train the model $\hat{M}$ from scratch. This approach is similar to that of intentional data poisoning. This naturally is more time-consuming, and the original model M is just used to benchmark the accuracy required to make M and $\hat{M}$ comparable in performance.

Having touched upon the principles of Watermarking and Backdooring, we can now proceed to looking at the way backdoors can be used as watermarks. Thereafter, we shall demonstrate the attack by exposing its vulnerabilities.

2.3   Watermarking Using Backdooring

The method of implementing a watermarking scheme using backdooring has been well studied [15]. Essentially, there is an algorithm that embeds the backdoor in the neural network model, the backdoor itself being the secret marking key while the commitment works as the public verification key (Fig. 1).

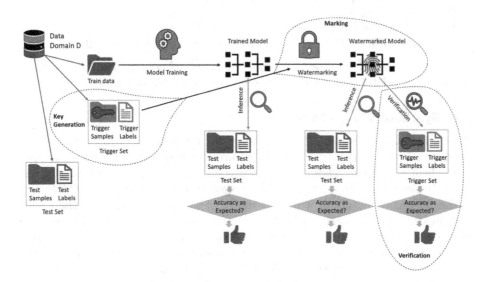

Fig. 1. Schematic diagram of watermarking using backdooring.

To formalise, the mechanism described by the authors proposing to use backdooring as a means of watermarking and keeping the formulation discussed earlier in place, we have:

$KeyGeneration()$:
1. Execute $(T, T_L) = b \leftarrow BackdoorSample(train_{data})$
   where $T = \{t^{(1)}, \ldots, t^{(n)}\}$ and $T_L = \{T_L^{(1)}, \ldots, T_L^{(n)}\}$.
2. Draw $2n$ random strings $r_t^{(i)}, r_L^{(i)} \leftarrow \{0,1\}^n$
   and create $2n$ commitments $\{c_t^{(i)}, c_L^{(i)}\}_{i \in [n]}$
   where $c_t^{(i)} \leftarrow Commitment(t^{(i)}, r_t^{(i)}), c_L^{(i)} \leftarrow Commitment(T_L^{(i)}, r_L^{(i)})$.
3. Set $m_k \leftarrow (b, \{r_t^{(i)}, r_L^{(i)}\}_{i \in [n]}, v_k \leftarrow \{c_t^{(i)}, c_L^{(i)}\}_{i \in [n]}$
   and return (m_k, v_k).

$Marking(M, m_k)$:

1. Consider $m_k = (b, \{r_t^{(i)}, r_L^{(i)}\}_{i \in [n]}$
2. Make the computation to return $\hat{M} \leftarrow Backdoor(train_{data}, b, M)$

$Verification(m_k, v_k, M)$:

1. Let $m_k = (b, \{r_t^{(i)}, r_L^{(i)}\}_{i \in [n]}, v_k = \{c_t^{(i)}, c_L^{(i)}\}_{i \in [n]}$.
   For $b = (T, T_L)$, test if $\forall t^{(i)} \in T : T_L^{(i)} \neq f(t^{(i)})$.
   If not then return 0.
2. For all $i \in [n]$, match for
   $Release(c_t^{(i)}, t^{(i)}, r_t^{(i)}) = 1$ and $Release(c_L^{(i)}, T_L^{(i)}, r_L^{(i)}) = 1$.
   Otherwise return 0.
3. For all $i \in [n]$, test that $Classify(t^{(i)}, M) = T_L^{(i)}$.
   If true for all but $\epsilon|T|$ elements of T, the return 1 or else return 0.

In the model modification attack proposed in this paper, we shall attempt to extract the model which has been watermarked using backdooring.

2.4 Synthesis Using GANs

Generative models are a nice way of leveraging the abilities of managing high-dimensional probability distributions, by learning means to represent and manipulate them as needed. These models are good for various kinds of simulation tasks. In situations like ours, wherein we need to perform synthesis of data by learning the distribution of it from a subset of samples belonging to the same domain, these models are a perfect tool. The state-of-the-art in this area of research would point to Generative Adversarial Networks (GANs) [16]. Some reasons for its success include their overall superiority in the subjective quality of the generated samples, their ability of successfully parallelize well, the design of the generator function which has lesser restrictions, the lack of variational bounds and that Markov chains are not necessary. Keeping these in mind, we chose the GANs as out choice of tool for performing the task of synthesis.

GANs work on a game theoretic approach. A game is set up between two entities, a Generator and a Discriminator. The Generator attempts to recreate samples from the distribution underlying the training dataset. The Discriminator classifies the samples thus generated into whether they are real or fake. It is much like a traditional supervised machine learning model, that splits the inputs into real/fake. The Generator on the other hand, is trained to fool the discriminator. Formally, the two players in this so-called game are represented by differentiable functions. These functions are differentiable with respect to inputs and parameters alike. The Discriminator function C takes x as its input along with parameters $\theta^{(C)}$. The Generator function G takes z as its input and its parameters $\theta^{(G)}$. The cost functions of both players are defined in terms of each other's parameters. The Discriminator has control only over its parameters $\theta^{(C)}$ and tries to minimize a certain cost function $J^{(C)}(\theta^{(C)}, \theta^{(G)})$. The Generator function has control only over its parameters $\theta^{(G)}$ and it attempts to minimize $J^{(G)}(\theta^{(C)}, \theta^{(G)})$. Since each player has leverage only on its own parameters, the solution to this kind of a game is a Nash equilibrium. For this particular situation, a Nash equilibrium is a tuple $(\theta^{(C)}, \theta^{(G)})$ which happens to be the local minimum of $J^{(C)}$ with respect to $\theta^{(C)}$ and also a local minimum of $J^{(G)}$ with respect to $\theta^{(G)}$.

DCGAN: The DCGAN (Deep Convolutional Generative Adversarial Network) architecture is the most widely accepted and used version of GANs [17]. The specifics of the DCGAN structure include, but are not limited to the following:

- The Generator and the Discriminator network both have layers for batch normalizing. The Discriminator has separate normalization. For the Generator, the last layer doesn't have normalization. The initial layer of the Discriminator also doesn't have normalization. This is aimed at making the synthesized samples in sync with the scale and mean of the data distribution which it tries to emulate.
- The structure of the network is quite similar to that of the all convolutional net [18], particularly lacking pooling and unpooling layers. If the Generator requires higher dimension for spatial representation, the stride is set to greater than unity.
- The optimizer of choice is the ADAM optimizer instead of the traditional batch Stochastic Gradient Descent with momentum.

3 Exposing Vulnerabilities

In order for stake-holder to make use of watermarking schemes based on backdooring in a reliable fashion, one needs to study the vulnerabilities of the mechanism. Primarily, what must be noted right at the onset is that the success of the watermarking scheme is dependant on three key aspects, simply put as follows:

- Effective embedding of the watermarks (using backdooring for example) within the trained neural network model
- Confidentiality of the key that is used to watermark (the Trigger set and its corresponding labels for example)
- Reliable verification of the watermark when needed to establish ownership.

3.1 Criteria for Model Extraction

An adversary aims to attack the watermarked model by negating the aforementioned requirements. Thereby, an issue created by exploiting vulnerabilities related to any one or more of the above, could potentially jeopardise the entire watermarking mechanism. In particular, an adversary would be able to steal a trained neural network model by such attacks. The criteria for an attack mechanism to be successful are:

1. The extracted model must be similar in performance with respect to the machine learning task for the particular domain of data, in this case on the Test Set.
2. The process of verification of the embedded watermarks must fail, i.e., the model must perform poorly on the Trigger Set here.

3.2 Modes of Attack

There are multiple modes of attack that can be used for exploiting the vulnerabilities of watermarking schemes and stealing models. We look at two common mechanisms available in the literature, which are Evasion attacks, and mention their shortcomings. While having their own advantages in being effective against certain watermarking schemes, they have not been successful against the state-of-the-art watermarking mechanism using backdooring. In order to overcome this, we introduce the model modification attack to expose vulnerabilities of this so called robust mechanism.

Failure of Evasion Attacks: There are two predominant modes of Evasion attack, Ensemble attacks and Detector attacks. In the Ensemble attack mechanism, the adversary leverages the capabilities of multiple trained neural network models simultaneously, by creating an ensemble of models which are all made to perform the same task [19]. Let us consider that all the models have their own watermarks, and would behave in particular ways when subjected to specific inputs. The key intuition behind this sort of an attack is that while each watermarked model is trained to respond to a sample from its Trigger set in a particular way, the probability of that particular sample belonging to all the Trigger Sets of all the models, is very low [20]. However, the provision of obtaining multiple trained models is costly, and the majority voting principle is not very reliable. Moreover, all the models should be able to work simultaneously in a synchronous fashion for this mechanism to work.

There is another kind of attack that an adversary may use to work against any particular watermarking scheme, known as Detector attacks [19]. This attack mechanism is aimed at training a special deep neural network that is able to distinguish between a clean input and an input which is part of the Trigger set. However, the accuracy of this network is difficult to improve, particularly due to the unbalanced nature of the distribution of clean samples and those belonging to Trigger sets. This attack fails when the trained classifier is unable to detect the Trigger samples from amongst clean ones.

Having touched upon the attacks and why they have not been successful against robust watermarking schemes, we introduce our proposition of a model modification attack using synthesis.

3.3 Proposed Solution - Model Modification Attack

It is worthwhile noticing that the aforementioned Ensemble attacks or Detector attacks, being both Evasion attacks, are not able to remove the watermarks from the marked models. This is a major reason for which these attacks are unable to extract models when the watermarks are embedded throughout the network amongst little modifications of the weights. Particularly, watermarking using backdooring proves to be quite robust against these attacks. However, in a model modification attack mode, one can actually employ techniques to remove the watermarks from the models altogether. The extracted model would no longer have the embedded weights sensitive to the Trigger inputs and the verification process would therefore fail. The adversary would obtain a high performing model without having to pay royalties to the true owner who curated the data and trained the model. The attack proposed in this paper is a model modification attack using synthesis and the details of it are discussed in the following sections.

3.4   Objective and Assumptions

The goal, as mentioned earlier, is to develop a mechanism wherein a watermarked neural model can be used by an adversary to successfully carry out the machine learning task (like classification), without having to deal with the consequences of the embedded watermarks that have been left behind by those who trained it in the first place. In the mechanism proposed in this paper, our white-box attack intends to use Transfer Learning [21] in order to effectively re-use the knowledge that has already been learnt by other involved parties in the business. For this attack, we will consider the following reasonable assumptions:

- This being a white-box attack, the adversary has access to the watermarked trained neural model (the computational graph and the weights). This is natural for customers who obtain services from MLaaS companies (suppliers) who let them use the model upon the belief that they would be able to establish ownership since it is watermarked.
- The adversary does not have access to, or any related information as well, about the Trigger Set and its corresponding labels. That private key rests with the supplier of the model.
- The adversary wants to successfully extract the model, whereby it would be able to use the model to achieve similar performance accuracies as the watermarked model, whilst doing poorly on the Trigger Set (thus de-establishing ownership by the supplier).
- The adversary and the supplier or owner of the model work on the same domain, aiming to fulfil the same machine learning task.

3.5   Methodology: Model Modification Attack with Synthesis

Considering the nomenclature discussed in Sect. 2, we have a watermarked neural network model $\hat{M}$, which has been created from a standard model M and a Trigger Set T and its corresponding labels T_L. The model M was trained on the data $train_{data} \subset D$ and the clean test set was $Test_{data} \subset D$. Typically, the watermarked model $\hat{m}$ would perform as well as M during inference, with high/full accuracy on the Trigger Set T. Since the adversary is acquainted with the domain D, it has its own dataset d, such that we have $d \subset D$. Now it not natural to have an overlap between d, $train_{data}$ and $Test_{data}$, although if it were to happen, the attack would only be more easier and successful. Keeping the aforementioned assumptions in mind, since the adversary has the white-box access to the watermarked model, it is able to retrain it. The retraining is essential here to remove the watermarks embedded in the model, so that is successfully extracted to obtain a model E and is usable without consequences of questionable ownership. The proof of removal of watermarks would lie in the performance of the extracted model on the Trigger Set; if the matches between the Trigger labels and the labels predicted by the extracted model E is low, then the adversary is prevailed. Now typically, retraining it would adversely affect the performance of the model on the actual machine learning task itself, which would render the extracted model E useless for further use. This specific issue is very well addressed by synthesis. The adversary can make use of the dataset d which it has at its disposal. To train a GAN that attempts to learn the distribution of the domain D, and is able to create many samples $\hat{d}$, which would be similar to actual samples that are in domain D. The quality of the samples generated by the GAN would impact the efficacy of the retraining (Fig. 2).

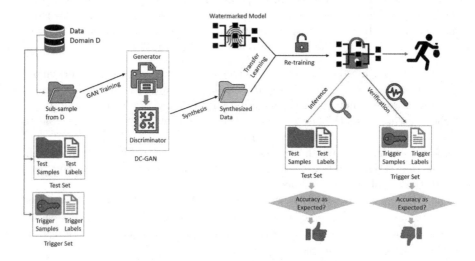

Fig. 2. Schematic diagram of model modification attack using synthesis.

One can affirm that if an adversary were to re-use the stolen model for its own purpose, which is a task very similar to the one for which the owner/supplier had trained it, then the GANs can be modified slightly and tuned as per the requirements of the re-use. This way, the adversary may be able to re-purpose a stolen model for its specific demands.

It is very important to note here, that for a specific task and a domain of data necessary to accomplish it, the exercise of synthesis using the GANs is a one-time process. Any adversary with some data d in its possession can train a GAN to generate the $\hat{d}$ beforehand, and may use it to retrain multiple/different watermarked models in order to steal them by removing the watermark. Also, the process of retraining just a few layers, as discussed hereafter, is comparatively way less time consuming and less demanding in terms of hardware resources, and therefore is a lucrative option for anyone with this sort of ill intention.

For converting the watermarked model into E, there are two approaches that we propose and study in this paper. In both cases, the re-training by Transfer Learning is carried out using the same set of GAN-generated samples $\hat{d}$. Although this attack mechanism is agnostic to the specifics of the neural network architecture, we only consider a Convolutional Neural Network (CNN) where there is a series of convolution-pooling layers followed by a densely connected multi-layer perceptron. The approaches are addressed as follows:

- *Mode 1:* The final convolutional layer is rich in extracted features. Resetting this layer ensures the new model learns refreshed features, while carrying forward the pre-tuned weights of the dense layered classifier. In this mode of retraining, we rest the last convolutional layer and retrain the whole model thereafter with the synthesized samples. This approach reduces the cost of retraining significantly.
- *Mode 2:* In addition to resetting the final convolutional layer which is rich in features, This mode of attack is designed to also reset the entire classifier, which is built of the densely connected layers. The rest of the convolutional layers are however frozen and the model is then retrained with the synthesized samples. While this approach involves higher cost of retraining (proportional to the size of the dense classifier layers), this improves the accuracy of retraining.

4   Implementation and Results

To experimentally demonstrate the performance of the proposed model modification attack through synthesis, we opted for the state-of-the-art watermarking scheme using backdooring [15] as our target model $\hat{M}$. This is essentially a VGG-16 model [22] and a ResNet model [23] with watermarks embedded in it. The Trigger Set T was constructed as in the original paper for comparing the results. Naturally, when studying the attacks, we considered that the adversary has no access to the Trigger Set T and its labels T_L, and it is only used for validating the successful extraction of the model having removed the watermarks. We varied the datasets over multiple well documented ones: MNIST [24], Fashion-MNIST [25] and CIFAR-10 [26] in order to ensure that the work is easily reproducible. The GAN used for synthesis of samples is a DC-GAN [17]. We implemented the watermarking scheme and built the attack on it in PyTorch [27], on a 7th generation Intel core i7 processor with an additional NVIDIA GeForce GTX 1080 Ti GPU support.

4.1   Experimental Design

In order to get into the specifics of the experiments, let us first set out the different variational aspects that are considered in this analysis. In terms of models, we have the VGG-16 used for the datasets MNIST and Fashion MNIST and the ResNet CNN used for CIFAR-10. The choice of models in keeping in mind the state-of-the-art performances of the neural networks on these datasets, for the task of image classification. The data belonging to all the datasets is split into parts, for training, for inference and for synthesis using GANs. These clean models are watermarked using backdooring using the mechanism described in Sect. 2. In particular, we have two modes of embedding the backdoors, one is training the model from scratch (referred to as From Scratch in the observations) which is akin to data-poisoning and the other is using a pre-trained model (referred to as Pre-trained in the observations). For both of these kinds of watermarked models, we implement the proposed model modification attack through Synthesis, using the two modes described in Sect. 3: *Mode 1* and *Mode 2*. The retraining of the models using the samples collected from the GANs is carried out with as many samples as in the test set. In order to study the performance of the setup, we have two metrics, which are very typical of such performance analysis tasks. We study the accuracy of classification of the different models (clean, watermarked, extracted etc) on the actual Test Set and the specific Trigger Set. The expectations from a successful extraction mechanism of the watermarked model would be two-fold. Firstly, there is a massive drop of accuracy of the model on the Trigger Set upon classification. Secondly, the change in the inference accuracy on the clean samples (Test Set) with respect to that of the watermarked model is not that significant, within an acceptable range (Fig. 3).

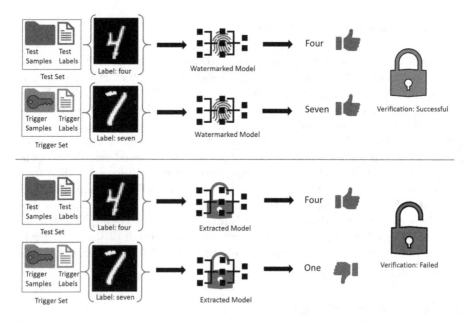

Fig. 3. Demonstration of successfully extracting models and their behaviour as opposed to a watermarked model, considering one sample from the MNIST dataset.

4.2   Observations and Findings

The performances of the different versions of the VGG-16 model trained on the MNIST dataset is presented in the Table 1. We observe that in general, from a watermarking perspective, the From Scratch method works better in matching up to the performance of the clean model without watermarks, while maintaining a full accuracy on the Trigger Set to establish ownership during verification. Among the extracted models, the attack *Mode 2* works better and is within about 3% range of accuracy (for the From Scratch version) when it comes to the actual classification task, whilst bringing the accuracy on the Trigger Set to a extremely low value, thus proving the removal of watermarks. The criteria for a successful attack has been met.

Table 1. Extracting model from watermarked neural network (VGG-16) on the dataset: MNIST

Model	Accuracy (test set)		Accuracy (trigger set)	
	From scratch	Pre-trained	From scratch	Pre-trained
Clean model	98.99%	–	10%	–
Watermarked model	98.96%	97.59%	100%	100%
Extracted model (*Mode 1*)	90.76%	84.15%	12%	14%
Extracted model (*Mode 2*)	95.40%	81.82%	14%	13%

The performances of the different versions of the VGG-16 model trained on the Fashion-MNIST dataset is presented in the Table 2. For the watermarked model, the difference between the two mechanisms From Scratch and Pre-trained in terms of performance is almost same, both being as good as a clean model. What is interesting is that, the mode used to extract the model and remove the watermarks is not very significant because they have almost identical performances, both within about 3% away from the accuracy of the watermarked model. The watermarks are successfully removed though, as evident from the Trigger set accuracies. The criteria for a successful attack has been met.

Table 2. Extracting model from watermarked neural network (VGG-16) on the dataset: Fashion-MNIST

Model	Accuracy (test set)		Accuracy (trigger set)	
	From scratch	Pre-trained	From scratch	Pre-trained
Clean model	90.41%	–	12%	–
Watermarked model	90.14%	90.95%	100%	94%
Extracted model (*Mode 1*)	87.13%	87.31%	13%	11%
Extracted model (*Mode 2*)	87.76%	87.97%	13%	11%

The performances of the different versions of the ResNet model trained on the CIFAR-10 dataset is presented in the Table 3. For the watermarked model, the difference between the two mechanisms From Scratch and Pre-trained in terms of performance is almost same, both being as good as a clean model. Among the extracted models, the attack *Mode 2* works better and is within about 3% range of accuracy (for both the From Scratch and Pre-trained versions) when it comes to the actual classification task, whilst bringing the accuracy on the Trigger Set to a extremely low value, thus proving the removal of watermarks. The criteria for a successful attack has been met.

Table 3. Extracting model from watermarked neural network (ResNet) on the dataset: CIFAR-10

Model	Accuracy (test set)		Accuracy (trigger set)	
	From scratch	Pre-trained	From scratch	Pre-trained
Clean model	88.49%	–	16%	–
Watermarked model	88.39%	88.06%	100%	100%
Extracted model (*Mode 1*)	81.80%	82.38%	19%	24%
Extracted model (*Mode 2*)	84.54%	84.72%	60%	24%

As mentioned at the outset, the success of extracting the model from the watermarked version retaining accuracy of classification, depends highly on the quality of samples being synthesized by the Generative Adversarial Networks. The GANs need training on a subset of data that is sampled from the same domain as the original training data of the model. The number of passes over the sampled data, that the GANs need to churn, determined by the epochs of the GAN training is critical towards achieving the necessary quality of synthesis. We have also studied how the performance of the GANs saturate after a certain number of epochs, indicating that the synthesis is up to the mark. The performance in this context is measured as expected exactly like the earlier results, that is the accuracies on the Test sets and the Trigger sets. For each epoch, the reported result is the average of the performance obtained for multiple 'seeds', which is the element that introduces the randomness in the training of the GANs.

In Table 4, we present the study on the MNIST dataset, with our DC-GAN and the VGG network. The performance of the GAN saturates at around 40 epochs and thereafter the increment is rather small.

Table 4. Training the GANs with varying epochs (dataset: MNIST)

Model	GAN training	Accuracy (test set)		Accuracy (trigger set)	
		From scratch	Pre-trained	From scratch	Pre-trained
Extracted model (*Mode 1*)	Epochs: 30	86.78%	68.91%	7%	8%
	Epochs: 35	88.28%	84.17%	6%	10%
	Epochs: 40	94.36%	91.28%	13%	12%
Extracted model (*Mode 2*)	Epochs: 30	95.26%	86.25%	8%	9%
	Epochs: 35	95.25%	87.12%	8%	13%
	Epochs: 40	96.48%	93.72%	12%	10%

In Table 5, we present the study on the Fashion MNIST dataset, with our DC-GAN and the VGG network. The performance of the GAN saturates at around 45 epochs and thereafter the increment is not very significant.

Table 5. Training the GANs with varying epochs (dataset: Fashion MNIST)

Model	GAN training	Accuracy (test set)		Accuracy (trigger set)	
		From scratch	Pre-trained	From scratch	Pre-trained
Extracted model (*Mode 1*)	Epochs: 35	83.68%	83.82%	13%	12%
	Epochs: 40	83.38%	83.66%	12%	8%
	Epochs: 45	87.52%	87.16%	8%	12%
Extracted model (*Mode 2*)	Epochs: 35	84.08%	83.87%	13%	11%
	Epochs: 40	84.26%	84.60%	8%	7%
	Epochs: 45	87.42%	87.30%	8%	12%

As evident from the results presented here, the watermarks are successfully removed because the re-training with the synthesized samples from the GAN works well. This is particularly due to its ability to tweak the specific weights distributed within the network, which would be responsible for being sensitive towards the Trigger inputs. Any potential counter-measure to this attack should therefore target to distribute the embedded watermarks well and evenly, so that model modification attacks involving re-training are not able to remove them while maintaining classification accuracy on the actual task.

5 Concluding Remarks

Acknowledging the necessity of robust watermarking schemes for properly verifiable ownership and establishment of IP rights of high-performing trained neural networks, a study of their vulnerabilities is crucial. Before deploying such models on public platforms or being offered to customers of companies who provide Machine Learning as a Service (MLaaS), the stakeholders must ascertain that adversaries would not be able to steal their proprietary material. Their faith in watermarking schemes is based on the assurance that these are hard to break, and the guarantees originate from cryptographic primitives.

There have been many such schemes which have been proved to be futile, as and when a new attack exposed their weaknesses. The state-of-the-art watermarking scheme by embedding backdoors in the weights of the neural network has gained attention due to its claimed robustness towards attacks. In this paper, we proposed a model modification attack, which is able to successfully extract the model by eliminating such embedded backdoors. This approach is not based on the typical attempts to identify the backdoors and reverse-engineer the Trigger Set at all. We make the reasonable assumption that being an interested party in the business, the adversary has access to some data in the same domain as that of the training data of the model, and uses synthesis to generate samples which can be used to retrain the model. The objective would therefore be to ensure that the extracted model has an accuracy comparable to that of the watermarked model on the test data, given the machine learning task. At the same time, as proof of elimination of the backdoors, and thereby the watermarks, the extracted model should perform poorly on the Trigger Set.

We have demonstrated this mechanism works well, on multiple image classification tasks on highly benchmarked datasets including MNIST, Fashion MNIST and CIFAR-10. We have been able to achieve classification accuracies nearly about 3% to what the watermarked model could get to, whilst steeply dropping the performance on Trigger Set, thus successfully failing the verification process. This way of stealing the model could severely jeopardise the interests of the stakeholders investing in the development of these machine learning models. It is worth noting that although we demonstrated the attack on the state-of-the-art watermarking mechanism, our approach of breaking watermarking is not limited to just this particular method of marking through backdooring and works for other mechanisms as well. This work puts into perspective the serious requirement of reconsidering the way we watermark models and develop more robust mechanisms in order to safeguard IP rights of the trained neural networks and defend the investment of the associated stakeholders better.

References

1. Goodfellow, I., Bengio, Y., Courville, A., Bengio, Y.: Deep Learning, vol. 1. MIT Press, Cambridge (2016)
2. Deng, J., Dong, W., Socher, R., Li, L.-J., Li, K., Fei-Fei, L.: ImageNet: a large-scale hierarchical image database. In: IEEE Conference on Computer Vision and Pattern Recognition, CVPR 2009, pp. 248–255. IEEE (2009)
3. Stephenson, N., et al.: Survey of machine learning techniques in drug discovery. Curr. Drug Metab. **20**(3), 185–193 (2019)
4. Mohseni, S., Zarei, N., Ragan, E.D.: A survey of evaluation methods and measures for interpretable machine learning. arXiv preprint arXiv:1811.11839 (2018)
5. Rosenblatt, F.: The perceptron: a probabilistic model for information storage and organization in the brain. Psychol. Rev. **65**(6), 386 (1958)
6. Friedman, J., Hastie, T., Tibshirani, R.: The Elements of Statistical Learning. Springer Series in Statistics, vol. 1. Springer, New York (2001)
7. Pan, S.J., Yang, Q.: A survey on transfer learning. IEEE Trans. Knowl. Data Eng. **22**(10), 1345–1359 (2009)
8. Qu, G., Potkonjak, M.: Intellectual Property Protection in VLSI Designs: Theory and Practice. Springer, Heidelberg (2007). https://doi.org/10.1007/b105846
9. Chen, H., Rouhani, B.D., Koushanfar, F.: Blackmarks: blackbox multibit watermarking for deep neural networks. arXiv preprint arXiv:1904.00344 (2019)
10. Chen, H., Rohani, B.D., Koushanfar, F.: DeepMarks: a digital fingerprinting framework for deep neural networks. arXiv preprint arXiv:1804.03648 (2018)
11. Rouhani, B.D., Chen, H., Koushanfar, F.: DeepSigns: a generic watermarking framework for protecting the ownership of deep learning models
12. Szyller, S., Atli, B.G., Marchal, S., Asokan, N.: DAWN: dynamic adversarial watermarking of neural networks. arXiv preprint arXiv:1906.00830 (2019)

13. Chen, H., Fu, C., Zhao, J., Koushanfar, F.: DeepInspect: a black-box trojan detection and mitigation framework for deep neural networks. In: IJCAI, pp. 4658–4664 (2019)
14. Guo, W., Wang, L., Xing, X., Du, M., Song, D.: TABOR: a highly accurate approach to inspecting and restoring trojan backdoors in AI systems. arXiv preprint arXiv:1908.01763 (2019)
15. Adi, Y., Baum, C., Cisse, M., Pinkas, B., Keshet, J.: Turning your weakness into a strength: watermarking deep neural networks by backdooring. In: 27th {USENIX} Security Symposium ({USENIX} Security 18), pp. 1615–1631 (2018)
16. Goodfellow, I.: NIPS 2016 tutorial: generative adversarial networks. arXiv preprint arXiv:1701.00160 (2016)
17. Radford, A., Metz, L., Chintala, S.: Unsupervised representation learning with deep convolutional generative adversarial networks. arXiv preprint arXiv:1511.06434 (2015)
18. Springenberg, J.T., Dosovitskiy, A., Brox, T., Riedmiller, M.: Striving for simplicity: the all convolutional net. arXiv preprint arXiv:1412.6806 (2014)
19. Hitaj, D., Hitaj, B., Mancini, L.V.: Evasion attacks against watermarking techniques found in MLaaS systems. In: 2019 Sixth International Conference on Software Defined Systems (SDS), pp. 55–63. IEEE (2019)
20. Tramèr, F., Zhang, F., Juels, A., Reiter, M.K., Ristenpart, T.: Stealing machine learning models via prediction APIs. In: 25th {USENIX} Security Symposium ({USENIX} Security 16), pp. 601–618 (2016)
21. Torrey, L., Shavlik, J.: Transfer learning. In: Handbook of Research on Machine Learning Applications and Trends: Algorithms, Methods, and Techniques, pp. 242–264. IGI global (2010)
22. Simonyan, K., Zisserman, A.: Very deep convolutional networks for large-scale image recognition. arXiv preprint arXiv:1409.1556 (2014)
23. Targ, S., Almeida, D., Lyman, K.: Resnet in resnet: generalizing residual architectures. arXiv preprint arXiv:1603.08029 (2016)
24. LeCun, Y., Cortes, C., Burges, C.J.: Mnist handwritten digit database. AT&T Labs, 2 (2010). http://yann.lecun.com/exdb/mnist
25. Xiao, H., Rasul, K., Vollgraf, R.: Fashion-MNIST: a novel image dataset for benchmarking machine learning algorithms. arXiv preprint arXiv:1708.07747 (2017)
26. Krizhevsky, A., Nair, V., Hinton, G.: The CIFAR-10 dataset (2014). http://www.cs.toronto.edu/kriz/cifar.html
27. Paszke, A., et al. Pytorch: an imperative style, high-performance deep learning library. In: Advances in Neural Information Processing Systems, pp. 8026–8037 (2019)

Robust Adaptive Cloud Intrusion Detection System Using Advanced Deep Reinforcement Learning

Kamalakanta Sethi[(⊠)], Rahul Kumar, Dinesh Mohanty, and Padmalochan Bera

Indian Institute of Technology, Bhubaneswar, India
{ks23,rk36,dm22,plb}@iitbbs.ac.in

Abstract. Intrusion Detection System (IDS) is a vital security solution for cloud network in providing defense against cyber attacks. However, existing IDSs suffer from various limitations that include the inability to adapt to changing attack patterns, identify novel attacks, requirements of significant computational resources, and absence of balance between accuracy and false-positive rates (FPR). These shortcomings in current IDSs reduce their effectiveness for deploying in cloud-based application systems. Moreover, most of the cloud IDS researches use conventional network benchmark datasets like NSL-KDD for evaluation, which do not provide the actual picture of their performance in real-world cloud systems. To address these challenges, we propose a Double Deep Q-Network (DDQN) and prioritized experience replay based adaptive IDS model built for accurate detection of new and complex attacks in cloud platforms. We evaluated our proposed model using a practical cloud-specific intrusion dataset, namely, ISOT-CID and a conventional network-based benchmark dataset (NSL-KDD). The experimental results show better performance than state-of-the-art IDSs along with novel attack detection capabilities. Further, We have used flow-based analysis in our model to ensure low computing resource requirements. Besides, we evaluated the robustness of our model against a black-box adversarial attack resembling a real-life scenario and observed a marginal decrease in the performance. Finally, we demonstrated our model's usability in a practical use case with frequent changes in the attack pattern.

Keywords: Intrusion Detection System · Double Deep Q-Network · Cyber attacks · ISOT-CID · NSL-KDD · False positive rate · Black-box adversarial attack

1 Introduction

Cloud Computing is an effective application design and implementation platform that allows on-demand access to a shared pool of configurable resources (e.g., servers, applications, storage, networks, computation) through networks. These

© Springer Nature Switzerland AG 2020
L. Batina et al. (Eds.): SPACE 2020, LNCS 12586, pp. 66–85, 2020.
https://doi.org/10.1007/978-3-030-66626-2_4

resources are easily scalable and swiftly provisioned with the least management effort or interaction with the service provider. However, the open, distributed, and multi-tenant architecture of cloud makes it vulnerable to various network attacks (such as IP spoofing, Distributed Denial of Service (DDoS), etc) as well as some cloud platform-specific attacks (such as insider attack, cloud malware injection, etc) [6]. In the last decade, network industries have developed various tools like firewalls, access control mechanisms to control unauthorized access to data and resources. However, these techniques are not resilient to insider attacks. Subsequently, researchers have proposed cloud intrusion detection systems as the second line of defense to protect the organizational assets from intruders. IDS monitors network traffic and system-level activities to detect intrusions. IDS can be classified into two categories based on the target environment it is operating, i.e. (1) host-based (installed and deployed in a host to monitor the behavior of a single system [5]) and (2) network-based (captures traffic of the entire network and systematically analyses to detect any attack on the hosts of that network for possible intrusions). There are two methods based on the data source to be analyzed in network-based IDSs (NIDSs): packet-based NIDSs and flow-based NIDSs. Packet-based NIDSs have to scan all the individual packets that pass through the network connection and inspect their content beyond the protocol header, which requires much computation. On the other hand, the flow-based NIDSs looks at aggregated information of related packets of network traffic in the form of flow and consume fewer resources.

Researchers also classified IDS based on the detection technique as (1) signature-based systems, and (2) anomaly-based systems [5]. Signature-based systems use a repository of signatures of already identified malicious patterns to detect an attack. They are efficient in detecting known attacks but fail in case of unforeseen attacks. In contrast, anomaly-based IDS detects intrusions when the activity of any user deviates from its normal functionality. Although these systems detect zero-day attacks, they tend to generate a lot of false alerts leading to a high false-positive rate (FPR).

In the last decade, many researchers proposed traditional machine learning and deep learning-based cloud IDS system that show excellent performance [1, 22]. However, they also have several limitations that include: 1) lack of proper adaptivity towards novel and changing attack patterns in the cloud environment and inability to identify them with high accuracy and low False Positive Rate (FPR), 2) require frequent human intervention for training which introduces more vulnerabilities and, thereby, affects the model's performance, 3) use datasets (such as NSLKDD, UNSW, and AWID) that are obtained by simulating a conventional network environment and thus, do not reflect a real cloud environment.

Machine learning classifiers are vulnerable to adversarial scenarios where the attacker introduces small perturbations in the input and attempts to bypass the security system. Adversarial machine learning is the study of such techniques where attackers exploit vulnerabilities of ML models and attempts to dupe them with perturbed inputs. In paper [27], the author shows that slight perturbations to the raw input can easily fool DNNs into misclassification. Therefore, it is essential to understand the performance against adversarial scenarios and ensure a robust security system design. Several properties of cloud computing including multi-tenancy, open access, and involvement of large business firms capture the attention of adversarial attackers. This is mainly because of its potential to cause serious economic and reputational damage. These attacks have become more sophisticated in recent times due to better computation resources and algorithms. There is very little research done towards understanding the performance degradation of an IDS that occurs in adversarial scenarios.

Therefore, we aim at designing a robust and adaptive IDS suitable for cloud platforms using advanced deep reinforcement learning techniques. Here, we present significant contributions and novelty of our proposed IDS.

(1) Implementation of a Double Deep-Q Learning-based Cloud IDS: We use DDQN, which is an advanced deep reinforcement learning algorithm for building an adaptive cloud IDS. Our proposed IDS can detect and adapt to novel cloud-specific attack patterns with minimal human interaction.

(2) Integration of prioritized learning: Online reinforcement learning agents use experience replay to retain and reuse experiences from the past. Instead of random or uniform selection, we used a concept of prioritizing experiences to call on significant transitions (with higher learning values) more often that ensures more effective and efficient learning.

(3) Experimentation on a realistic cloud-specific intrusion dataset (ISOT-CID): We have evaluated our model on the first publicly available cloud-specific dataset (ISOT-CID) whose features were obtained by applications running on Openstack based cloud environment. We have also obtained the model's performance on a very well-known conventional network-based NSL-KDD dataset for comparison with state-of-the-art-works.

(4) Durability against adversarial attacks: Adversarial attackers exploit the vulnerabilities of the machine and deep learning models and trick them for misclassification. We employed the concept of DDQN that eliminates the overestimation problems faced by other Q-learning techniques and shows high robustness with only marginal performance degradation when exposed to adversarial samples produced by a practical black box attack.

The rest of the paper is organized as follows. Background on DDQN, and prioritized experience replay is presented in Sect. 2. In Sect. 3, we discuss the related work. Section 4 presents a brief overview of datasets and their preprocessing steps. Our proposed IDS model is presented in Sect. 5. The robustness of our IDS model is presented in Sect. 6. The experimental results and conclusions are discussed in Sect. 7 and Sect. 8 respectively.

2 Background

In this section, we discuss a brief introduction of two key concepts used in this paper, including DDQN and prioritized experience replay.

2.1   Double Deep Q Learning (DDQN)

Double Deep Q Learning algorithm is based on the Double Q Learning and Deep Q Learning algorithms. These algorithms are themselves derived from Q Learning algorithm. Q Learning algorithm is a popular model-free reinforcement learning algorithm used in FMDP (Finite Markov Decision Process), where an agent explores the environment and figures out the strategy to maximize the cumulative reward. Agent takes actions that make it, move from the current state to a new state generating a reward alongside. For the specific FMDP, it identifies an optimal action selection policy to maximize the expected value of the total reward that can be obtained in the successive steps (provided that it is given infinite exploration time and a partly-random policy) [12].

A significant limitation of Q-learning is that it works only in environments with discrete and finite state-action spaces. To extend Q-learning to richer environments (where storing the full state-action table is often infeasible), we use Deep Neural Networks as function approximators that can learn the value function by taking just the state as input. Deep-Q Learning is one such solution. Deep Q Learning was tested against classic Atari 2600 games [31], where it outperformed other Machine Learning methods in most of the games and performed at a level comparable with or superior to a professional human games tester. However, in the paper [7], Hado et al. explain the frequent overestimation problem found in Deep Q Learning due to the inherent estimated errors of learning. Such overestimation related errors are also seen in the Q Learning algorithm and were first investigated by Thrun and Schwartz [12]. They proposed Double Q-learning as a solution, in which there is a decoupling of action selection and action evaluation procedures that help lessen the overestimation problem significantly. Later, Hado et al. [7] proposed a Double Deep Q Learning architecture that uses the existing architecture and DQN algorithm to find better policies, thereby improving the performance [7]. They tested their model on six Atari games by running DQN and Double DQN with six different random seeds. The results showed that the over-optimistic estimation in Deep Q Learning was more frequent and severe than previously acknowledged. The results also showed that Double Deep Q Learning gave the state of the art results on the Atari 2600 domain.

2.2   Prioritized Experience Replay

Many Reinforcement Learning algorithms involve storing past samples and retraining the model with such samples to help the agents memorize and reuse past experiences. In the simple experience replay algorithm, the samples are chosen randomly. However, Schaul et al. [12] pointed out that selecting the samples based on their capacity to improve the learning of RL agent would lead to much better learning from past experiences. This gave rise to the concept of prioritized experience replay wherein the samples are assigned priorities based on metrics similar to Temporal Difference, which represent the scope of improvement that lies for the agent to be able to correctly predict the outcomes for the sample under consideration. In particular, the priority for i^{th} sample is given by $P(i) = \frac{p_i^\alpha}{\sum_k p_k^\alpha}$, where $p_i = |\delta_i| + \epsilon$, α is the prioritization factor which determines the importance that is to be given to priorities while sampling past experiences. Here, δ_i is the Temporal Difference error function on which the Huber Loss Function [30] is applied. The frequency of selection of samples is made to be directly proportional to such priority values. Retraining RL models with samples selected based on the principles of prioritized experience replay gives much faster learning speeds and significant improvements in performance when tested on the Atari Dataset [12]. We have briefly described the implementation details in Sect. 5.

3   Related Work

In this section, we presents some network-based IDS works for cloud environment that use machine learning techniques.

In [10], Lopez-Martin *et al.* proposed a advanced IDS based on several deep reinforcement learning (DRL) algorithms using NSL-KDD and AWID datasets. They replaced the requirement of conventional DRL technique for real-time interaction with environment by the concept of pseudo-environment, which uses a sampling function over the dataset records. They analyse the performance of their technique on four different DRL models that includes Deep-Q-Network (DQN), Double Deep-Q-Network (DDQN), Policy Gradient (PG), and Actor-Critic (AC). It has been observed that the DDQN algorithm gives the best results. However, this IDS work limited to enterprise environment rather than the cloud architecture.

Sethi *et al.* [2] presented a cloud NIDS using reinforcement learning. Their IDS can detect new attacks in the cloud and also adaptive to attack pattern changes in the cloud. They validated the efficacy of their model using a conventional network dataset (UNSW) instead of cloud network datasets. However, this work uses UNSW dataset which is not derived from any cloud environment.

Kholidy *et al.* [4] created a new dataset called cloud intrusion detection dataset (CIDD) for cloud IDS evaluation. The dataset includes both knowledge and behavior-based audit data. To build the dataset, the authors implemented a log analyzer and correlator system (LACS) that extracts and correlates user audits from a set of log files from the DARPA dataset. The main issue with this dataset is that its main focus is on detecting a masquerade attack. Also, it does not consider network flows involving hypervisor. Moreover, the dataset is not publicly available.

However, none of the above-mentioned works considers the effectiveness of the IDS system against smart adversarial attackers, which is more frequent in the cloud platform. Szegedy *et al.* [29] first observed the exposure of the DL-based approach to adversarial attacks. Wang [28] proposed a DL-based IDS system in 2018, considering the adversary's effect.

In summary, state-of-the-art works don't apply DRL for Cloud intrusion detection systems though a few recent attempts are present on conventional network applications. Also, the existing works do not use cloud-specific datasets

and, thereby, are not capable of representing a real cloud environment. Aldribi
et al. [3] introduced the first publicly available cloud dataset called ISOT-CID,
which is derived from a real cloud computing environment. The dataset consists of a wide variety of traditional network attacks as well as cloud-specific
attacks. The author discusses a hypervisor-based cloud IDS involving novel feature extraction, which obtains an accuracy (best performance) of 95.95% with an
FPR of 5.77% for phase 2 and hypervisor-B portion of the dataset. Our proposed
IDS employs an advanced DRL technique, involving the concepts of DDQN and
prioritized experience replay, for accurate detection of intrusions in the cloud.
We have used the ISOT-CID dataset for testing the effectiveness of our model on
real-world cloud platforms along with the benchmark NSL-KDD dataset. The
experimentation shows that the proposed model is adaptive to changes in attack
patterns as well as robust to the adversarial scenarios.

4   Dataset Description and Prepossessing

Our proposed intrusion detection system is evaluated on benchmark NSL-KDD
and cloud-specific ISOT-CID dataset. In this section, we will present a brief
overview of both datasets as well as their preprocessing to obtain relevant features.

4.1   NSL-KDD Dataset

Here, we discuss about the overview and preprocessing steps on the benchmark
NSL-KDD dataset.

1. **Overview of the dataset:** We evaluated our proposed IDS model on NSL-
   KDD dataset [13,14]. NSL-KDD is one of the most widely used dataset for
   evaluating any network intrusion detection system. The dataset consists of
   a total of 1,48,517 records. The total records are divided into a training
   dataset and a testing dataset. The training dataset consists of 1,25,973 records
   whereas the testing dataset consists of 22,544 records. Each record in training and testing dataset consists of 41 attributes. The training dataset consists
   of 23 attack types. Similarly testing dataset consists of 37 attack types out
   of which 16 are novel attacks that not present in the training dataset. The
   attack types are grouped into four types. namely DoS (Denial-of-Service),
   Probe, U2L, and R2L. The distribution of labeled data in the training and
   testing dataset is Table 1.

Table 1. NSL-KDD dataset classes
distribution

Dataset	Total	Normal	Attack
Training	125973	67343	58630
Testing	22544	9711	12883

Table 2. ISOT-CID dataset classes
distribution

Dataset	Total	Normal	Attack
Training	17296	10377	6919
Testing	7411	4447	2964

2. **Preprocessing of the dataset:** As the NSL-KDD dataset contained categorical features, we used one-hot encoding as part of the preprocessing of the dataset to encode all such categorical features. This process increased the count of features from 41 to 122. The next operating step is feature normalization. Many classifiers use distance as a normalization tool. The train and test datasets of NSL-KDD were normalized to values between 0 and 1 by L2 normalization [15]. Further, we modified the category column into binary types for binary classification. The sample's label value is 1 in the presence of some form of attack while it is 0 if the label value is normal.

4.2   ISOT-CID Dataset

Here, we discuss about the overview and preprocessing steps on the ISOT-CID dataset.

1. **Overview of the dataset:** To evaluate our model we have used the ISOT Cloud Intrusion Dataset (ISOT-CID) [8], which is the first publicly available cloud-specific dataset. The data was collected in the cloud for several days with time slots of 1–2 h per day with the help of special collectors at different layers of the OpenStack based production environment (hypervisor layer, guest hosts layer and the network layer), that forwarded the collected data (network traffic, system logs, CPU performance measures, memory dumps, etc) to the ISOT lab log server for storage and analysis. Malicious activities includes both outsider and insider attacks. For our purpose, we have used only the network traffic data portion of the ISOT-CID. The entire ISOT-CID dataset of size 8 TB consists of 55.2 GB of network traffic data. The collected network traffic data was stored in a packet capture (pcap) format. In phase 1, a total of 22,372,418 packets were captured out of which 15,649 (0.07%) were malicious, whereas in phase 2, a total of 11,509,254 packets were captured out of which 2,006,382 (17.43%) were malicious.

2. **Preprocessing with Tranalyzer:** Since packet payload processing involves huge amount of data that have to be processed at very fast rate, flow-based analysis for intrusion detection is considered better for high-speed networks due to lower processing loads [11]. To obtain flow-based data from packet-based data, we have used this open-source tool called Tranalyzer which is a lightweight flow generator and packet analyzer designed for practitioners and researchers [9]. With the help of Tranalyzer, we were able to get about 1.8GB of flow based data in JSON format from about 32.2 GB of packet-based data in pcap format.

3. **Analysis of Tranalyzer output:** All the 37 JSON object files which were output by Tranalyzer, were converted into a single CSV file. This CSV file was further processed to deal with lists of numbers (replaced by mean value) and lists of strings (replaced with first string). Finally, all the strings and hexadecimal values (representing particular characteristics of flow) were one-hot encoded for further improvement of the training data. Further, the values that are not integers or floating-point numbers, were converted to 'Nan' values

and later removed in such a way that can make the dataset compatible for the machine learning analysis. We then labeled the dataset based on the list of malicious IP addresses that were provided along with the ISOT-CID documentation [3].

Finally, we apply feature selection process that helps in removing irreverent features avoiding over-fitting and achieving better accuracy of the model at low computational ability. In our model, we have used chi-square feature selection algorithm [26]. The number of selected features becomes 36 and 164 after applying feature selection on the NSL-KDD dataset and ISOT-CID respectively. For both dataset, feature vector refers to any record consisting the same features as obtained from the feature selection process. Feature set refers to the collection of all such feature vectors for a particular dataset. Further in case of ISOT-CID post preprocessing, we found out that the dataset was highly skewed, i.e, the number of non attack samples was much higher than that of the number of attack samples. Hence, to prevent biased learning, we selected a portion of the dataset which had a more balanced distribution having 9883 attack samples and 14,824 normal samples. Table 2 shows the distribution of the dataset in the training and testing phase.

5   Proposed Intrusion Detection System

Here, we present our proposed cloud IDS that uses concepts of DDQN and prioritized learning. Figure 1 show the deployment architecture of our proposed IDS. It mainly consists of three sub-components: (i) host network, (ii) agent network, and (iii) cloud administrator network. The host network has the running virtual machines (VMs), hypervisors, and host machines. The agent network consists of three modules namely Log Processor, Feature Extractor, and Agent. Agent network is connected to host network through VPN (Virtual Private Network). The use of VPN is to prevent the agent network from being compromised by external attackers and to ensure fast sharing of attack related information or abnormal activities in the network. To identify the potential intrusions, it is essential to obtain the audit logs of the target machine. Hence, our model uses system call traces to communicate audit log information that may include VM instance specification, CPU utilization, and memory usage in the host machine.

The agent network obtains audit logs from the host network and performs preprocessing and feature selection on these data to extract the feature vectors. Finally, it identifies the state of the host network and shares the same with the Cloud Administrator. In general the state of a host can be "attacked" and "not attacked". Depending upon the capacity of the host network, the agent network logic can be deployed on a single VM (for a small number of host VMs) or as a Virtual Cluster (VCs) (for a large number of host VMs) in a separate physical machine in the cloud infrastructure. Next, we discuss the three major functional components in the agent network.

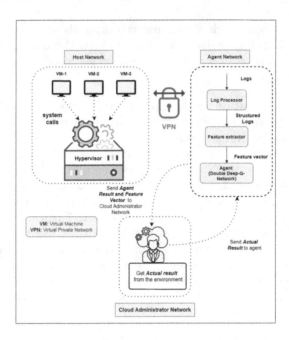

Fig. 1. Cloud IDS deployment architecture

(1) **Log Processor module:** This module receives logs (in an unstructured format) as input from the hypervisor via VPN channel. It processes logs and converts it into a structured format. The communication between the hypervisor and this module is generally realized with high bandwidth links so that necessary logs are shared before there is any intervention from the attacker.

(2) **Feature Extractor module:** This module first applies preprocessing on data collected from log processor module. This step is mainly used for input data validation such as removal of NULL values, data-types conversion, string data removal, one-hot encoding, etc. Subsequently, it performs feature extraction and feature selection to obtain essential feature values. Further, these feature values are combined to obtain a $feature\_vector$, which is fed as input to the current DQN in agent module.

(3) **Agent module:** This module executes an algorithm (i.e., Algorithm 1) that includes a combination of trained advanced machine learning classifiers and a Double-Deep-Q-Network (DDQN). It takes $feature\_vector$ as input and obtains classifier predictions. The concatenation of feature vector and the corresponding classifier prediction results forms a state vector. This state vector is fed to the Current DQN which produces $agent\_result$. Then, the agent result (i.e., $agent\_result$) is shared with the cloud administrator, and the final decision (i.e., $actual\_result$) is obtained based on a voting mechanism by cloud administrator. Subsequently, the agent calculates the reward using the actual result and continuously improves its learning over the time.

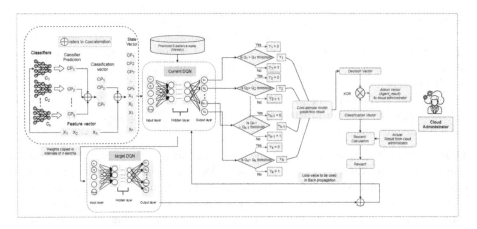

Fig. 2. Agent result calculation workflow using DDQN and prioritised learning. CP_1, CP_2,...CP_k denotes the prediction in form of 1 (for attack) and 0 (for normal) for classifier C_1, C_2,...C_k respectively

Next, we derive important reinforcement learning (RL) parameters including the state vector, action, and rewards.

State: State in RL describes the input by the environment to an agent for taking actions. In cloud environment, system logs parameters ($feature\_vector$) are used for state parameters as it reflects its current running status. Also, we run the combination of trained classifiers with $feature\_vector$ as input to extract prediction values as $classification\_vector$. These two vectors are concatenated to obtain $state\_vector$. Experimentally, the integration of advanced classifiers with DDQN logic has shown good performance in obtaining higher accuracy along with low FPR values. The dotted part in blue color of Fig. 2 presents a workflow on the calculation of state vector estimation process.

Action: An action refers to the agent's decision after monitoring the state of the cloud system during a given time window. The Agent network produces an $action\_vector$ for a given input feature vector, which is the basis for the final judgment about the attack. It uses three essential steps: a) Obtaining the state vector using the $feature\_vector$ and the classifier prediction on these feature vectors, b) Feeding the $state\_vector$ to the Current DQN, c) Thresholding the output of the Current DQN (i.e., the Q-values) against predetermined threshold values, also known as Q-threshold value, for classifying the decision as an attack or normal, d) Combining the classifications to form a vector called the $decision\_vector$. e) Obtaining $action\_vector$ as logical XOR between the $decision\_vector$ and the $classification\_vector$. We perform the steps c) to e) to ensure that the action vector should include output same as the classifier prediction if the corresponding Q-value exceeds the Q-threshold value. Otherwise, it should include output that is against the classifier prediction. Also, in our algorithm, the term $action\_vector$ and $agent\_result$ refers to same. Figure 2 shows the entire workflow on the calculation of $agent\_result$.

Reward: A reward indicates the feedback from the environment about the action by an agent. A reward vector r is dependent on the confidence vector of individual agent and thus it varies from agent to agent. A positive reward is obtained by a classifier when the classification result[1] matches the *actual_result* else it obtains a negative reward. The magnitude of reward is directly proportional to the probability of prediction by the classifier. Our model ultimately discovers rules to give appropriate Q-values based on the classifier's performance for a particular state vector.

DDQN Architecture. In DDQN, the major advantage is handling the overestimation of action values that takes place in DQN. One of the important principles of DDQN is the decoupling of action selection and action valuation components. This is achieved in our case by using two different neural networks. One neural network is used for computing current Q values while other neural network is used to compute target Q values. Here, back-propagation takes place in the current DQN and its weights are copied to the target DQN with delayed synchronization which helps stabilize the target Q values. This copying is done after regular intervals of a fixed number of epochs. In experimentation, we have used the epoch interval as 32 as it was found to give optimal results in most of the cases. The actions (raising appropriate alarms) are taken as per the current Q function, but the current Q_{new} values are estimated using the target Q function. This is done to avoid the moving target effect when doing gradient descent. A similar approach has been used by Manuel Lopez-Martin et al. in paper [10]. This method of delayed synchronization between two neural networks ensures the required decoupling and thereby handling the moving target effect of DQN.

Here, we present our algorithms for intrusion detection. Algorithm 1 shows the learning process executed by an agent. In Algorithm 1, *transition* comprises of *state_vector* and updated Q-values. We use memory M to store these transitions for prioritized experience replay concept of DQN using the sum tree implementation proposed by Schaul *et al.* [12]. The value of epoch interval, i.e., m is set to 32 in Algorithm 1.

Administrator network executes Algorithm 2 based on output of Algorithm 1 (refer step 13). In step 25 of Algorithm 1, the parameters s, r, w, and γ indicate *state_vector*, *reward_vector*, *weights* and *learning_rate* respectively. The parameter γ is taken as 0.01 (found by performing grid search on a logarithmic scale for values between 1 and 10^{-6}). The function of the administrator network is shown in Algorithm 2. It uses a voting system to identify the presence or absence of an attack.

Functional Task of Cloud Administrator: The cloud administrator runs Algorithm 2 where it monitors the activities of the cloud system constantly and detect its state. On receiving agent results, it checks for the intrusion and accordingly shares the actual result to the agent. It also identifies the location of the intrusion, including entry doors and target VMs.

---

[1] Each value of the classification vector denotes the classification result of a particular classifier.

Algorithm 1: Agent Logic

---

1 Initialize memory M;
2 Get the *feature_set* using the network parameters;
3 k=1;
4 **for** *each feature_vector in feature_set* **do**
5   Input the *feature_vector* to different classifiers $C_1, C_2 ... C_n$ and store the output as *confidence_vector*;
6   Run thresholding on *confidence_vector* and generate *classification_vector*;
7   Form the *state_vector* using *feature_vector* and *classification_vector*;
8   Input the *state_vector* to the Target Deep Q-network and store the output as Q'_value_vector;
9   Again input the *state_vector* to the Current Deep Q-network and store the output as Q_value_vector;
10 Run thresholding on Q_value_vector and generate *decision_vector*;
11 $action\_vector = decision\_vector \wedge classification\_vector$;
12 $agent\_result = action\_vector$;
13 Send *agent_result* along with *feature_vector* to the Administrator Network;
14 Get the *actual_result* from the Cloud Administrator Network;
15 Extend the *actual_result* to the length of the *classification_vector* by repeating the *actual_result* in every position;
16 $sign\_vector = actual\_result \oplus classification\_vector$;
17 Initialize *reward_vector*;
18 **for** *i in range(len(sign_vector))* **do**
19   **if** *(sign_vector[i] == 0)* **then**
20    $reward\_vector[i] = confidence\_vector[i]/2$;
21   **else**
22    $reward\_vector[i] = -1 \times (confidence\_vector[i]/2)$;
23   **end**
24 **end**
25 Update Q values in current Deep Q Network using the following equation:
  $Q_{new(current)}(s, a, r, w) = r + \gamma * Q'_{(target)}(s, a, r, w)$;
26 Store the transition in memory M;
27 Update the weights (w) of the current DQN with the latest transition in memory M;
28 **if** *(k == m)* **then**
29   Copy the weights of current Deep Q Network into the Target Deep Q Network;
30   $k = k + 1$;
31 **end**
32 **for** *j in range(n)* **do**
33   Update current Deep Q-network weights (w) using prioritized learning based selection of transitions from M;
34 **end**
35 **end**

Algorithm 2: Cloud Administrator Logic

---

1 Obtain *agent_result* and *feature_vector* from the host network;
2 **for** *each agent* **do**
3   p = Count of digit 1 in *agent_result*;
4   k = Count of digit 0 in *agent_result*;
5   **if** $p \leq k$ **then**
6    $status \leftarrow$ "normal";
7   **else**
8    $status \leftarrow$ "attack";
9   **end**
10 Obtain the *actual_result* from the cloud environment;
11 Send the *actual_result* to the host network for reward calculation;
12 **end**

---

6 Robustness of the Model

In this section, we discuss the procedure for generating adversarial samples for evaluating the performance of the model against adversarial attacks. This experiment highlights our proposed model's robustness against the vulnerabilities of intentional and small perturbations in the input data that can lead to misclassification. Subsect. 7.4 describes the experimental results that show the high durability of the model against a practical adversarial attack.

6.1 Adversarial Attack Synthesis

During intrusions, the attacker often wants to create adversarial inputs thoughtfully with minimum perturbations in order to escape any threat detection tool like IDS. Thus in our experimentation, we use an efficient and practical black-box adversarial attack as described in the paper [18]. It involves a two-step procedure for obtaining adversarial samples [19]:

1. **Creation of a Substitute Model:** The attacker aims to create a model F, which clones the target model's decision abilities. For this, they use results for synthetic inputs obtained by a Jacobian based heuristic method. It primarily includes five sub-steps including a) Collection of training dataset, b) Selection of substitute DDQN architecture, c) Labeling of substitute dataset, d) Training of substitute model, and e) Augmentation of the dataset using Jacobian-based method.

2. **Generation of Adversarial Samples:** The attacker uses the substitute model F obtained from step 1 to generate adversarial samples. Due to the transferability principle, the target model gets duped by the perturbed input sample and thus misclassify it. There are two prominent methods for this step, including (1) Fast Gradient Sign Method (FGSM) and (2) Jacobian-based Saliency Map Attack (JSMA) [16]. Although the FGSM method is capable of generating many adversarial samples in less computation time, their perturbations are high, making them susceptible to detection. In contrast, the JSMA method produces smaller perturbations, and it is also more suitable for misclassification attacks. Thus, in this paper, we use the JSMA method for generating the adversarial samples.

Jacobian-Based Saliency Map Attack (JSMA) [17]: It is a simple iterative method to introduce perturbation in the samples, resulting in the target model classifying incorrectly. It identifies the most critical feature in every iteration and adds noise to them. In our paper, we use a DDQN model to implement the stated adversarial method.

To implement step 1, we used a ten layered DDQN model and trained this model using the training samples of ISOT-CID dataset (refer Table 1) to obtain the substitute model. Later, we augment data as per the procedure described in the paper [18] to perform the sub-step e) i.e, augmentation of data. In addition, for step 2, we implement a five layered deep sequential neural network with same size input-output labels as the number of features in the dataset. The *generate_np* function of the *Saliency_Map_Method* class in the *cleverhans.attacks* package of *cleverhans* [20] library in Python language implements the above adversarial method. We iteratively fed unperturbed feature vectors and *jsma_parameter* as input to this function as it returns an adversarial sample as output. Algorithm 3 briefly discusses the related steps to obtain adversarial dataset from the clean dataset.

Algorithm 3: Practical black box adversarial sample creation

---

1 Let $V = \emptyset$;
2 Define the Oracle L as the IDS model;
3 ∀ classes in the dataset, collect samples from each of them into V;
4 Select and initialize the architecture for substitute model S;
5 Fix the number of iterations δ_{max};
6 **for** δ *in range* 1 *to* δ_{max} **do**
7   ∀ $v \in V$, label it using the Oracle L denoted by T;
8   Convert the labels to binary form i.e benign (0) label remains same but any non-benign label (1 to number of classes) becomes 1;
9   Train and update the parameters θ_S of the substitute model S with (V, T);
10   Carry out Jacobian based data augmentation to the set V;
11 **end**
12 Craft adversarial samples either by using Saliency Map Attack (JSMA);

---

7 Experimental Results and Discussion

We implemented the model on the Google Colaboratory[2] and used Keras and Tensorflow library for building the DDQN model. We analyzed the performance of the model using two datasets, including the ISOT-CID and NSL-KDD. The ISOT-CID dataset is the first publicly available cloud intrusion dataset consisting of raw data collected at various components of a real-world cloud infrastructure hosted on the OpenStack platform. On the other hand, NSL-KDD is a renowned benchmark dataset for IDS, derived from a conventional network environment. The experimental results include three standard machine learning performance metrics, i.e., FPR (False Positive Rate), ACC (Accuracy), and AUC (Area under ROC Curve).

7.1 Classifiers in Model

We obtain the performance on the ISOT-CID and NSL-KDD dataset of five best and most advanced classifiers for IDS, namely, AdaBoost (ADB), Gaussian Naive Bayes (GNB), K-Nearest Neighbours (KNN), Quadratic Discriminant Analysis (QDA), and Random Forest (RF). Table 1 and Table 2 show the distribution of labeled data of the training and the testing phase that is used for evaluation in NSL-KDD and ISOT-CID dataset respectively. Later, we group these classifiers into Low-FPR classifiers and High-Accuracy classifiers. We then integrate some sets of suitable combinations of these classifiers in our model and conduct evaluation. Finally, we select the most suitable combination that ensures the best balance between high accuracy and low FPR. The next section presents the evaluation results of the individual classifiers.

7.2 Evaluation of Individual Classifiers on NSL-KDD and ISOT Dataset

Table 3 presents the performance of individual classifiers on the NSL-KDD and ISOT-CID dataset. For the ISOT-CID dataset, Table 3 shows that RF, ADB, and KNN obtain better accuracy than other classifiers, and we group them as

---

[2] An online cloud-based platform specially designed for ML and deep learning applications based on the Jupyter Notebook framework.

High-Accuracy classifiers. On the other hand, the classifiers like QDA and GNB give relatively lower FPR values, and we group them as a Low-FPR classifier. Further from Table 3, we obtain the same group of High-Accuracy and Low-FPR classifiers for the NSL-KDD dataset. Next, we create suitable combinations by choosing appropriate classifiers from each group. We employ such combinations in our model and obtain the corresponding evaluation matrices.

Table 3. Individual classifier performance on NSL-KDD and ISOT-CID Dataset

Classifier	NSL-KDD			ISOT-CID		
	Accuracy	FPR	Auc	Accuracy	FPR	AUC
RF	77.95	2.66	0.8054	94.95	5.66	0.792
ADB	78.65	7.009	0.7763	93.65	6.009	0.705
GNB	66	1.688	0.705	85.51	1.78	0.672
KNN	75.67	2.801	0.8087	91.67	4.801	0.7
QDA	69.71	1.59	0.7299	87.71	1.6	0.709

7.3   Evaluation of Proposed IDS Having Combination of Classifiers

The output layer of the current DQN (refer Fig. 2) contains Q-values for a given feature vector. We observed that the accuracy of Low-Accuracy classifiers (including GNB and QDA) can be improved by varying the threshold on Q-values. To get the optimal accuracy, we have tried several threshold values on Q-values corresponding to these classifier in the final output layer. On the other hand, we fix the threshold on Q-values for the other High-Accuracy classifiers to a constant value of 0.5 as it is found to produce the optimal results during experimentation.

Table 4. Performance of our system with classifiers, on NSL-KDD, **C1:** *RF, ADB, GNB* **C2:** *RF, ADB, QDA* **C3:** *RF, KNN, ADB, QDA* **C4:** *RF, KNN, ADB, GNB*

Threshold	C1		C2		C3		C4	
	Accuracy	FPR	Accuracy	FPR	Accuracy	FPR	Accuracy	FPR
0.5	78.87%	1.44%	77.1%	1.96%	79.16%	1.6%	79.16%	1.1%
0.2	78.89%	1.47%	83.08%	1.6%	83.24%	1.89%	80.04%	1.17%
0.7	82.88%	1.81%	83.16%	1.6%	83.25%	1.96%	83.40%	1.44%
0.8	83.11%	1.80%	83.24%	1.64%	83.32%	2.00%	**83.40 %**	**1.48%**

Table 5. Performance of our system with classifiers on ISOT-CID, **C1:** *RF, ADB, GNB* **C2:** *RF, ADB, QDA* **C3:** *RF, KNN, ADB, QDA* **C4:** *RF, KNN, ADB, GNB*

Threshold	C1		C2		C3		C4	
	Accuracy	FPR	Accuracy	FPR	Accuracy	FPR	Accuracy	FPR
0.5	89.17%	4.43%	90.6%	4.06%	92.2%	3.86%	91.5%	3.96
0.6	91.23%	3.42%	92.7%	2.71%	93.23%	2.42	93.06%	2.53
0.7	93.5%	2.61%	95.87%	2.05%	**96.87%**	**1.57%**	96.12%	1.81%
0.8	93.2%	2.59%	95.17%	2.5%	95.6%	1.59%	95.3%	1.7%

We choose a combination of three classifiers that includes two classifiers from High-Accuracy class and one from Low-FPR classifiers. This selection strategy is found to give optimal performance in the direction of reducing FPR and increasing accuracy. Two combinations can be formed including C1 (GNB, ADB, RF) and C2 (QDA, ADB, RF). To further improve the accuracy, we included an additional High-Accuracy classifier (KNN) with each combination of C1 and C2 to create combination C3 and C4. Next, we evaluated the model against combinations with four classifiers. Table 4 and Table 5 present the evaluation results on varying the Q-threshold values of the model using these four combinations of classifiers on NSL-KDD and ISOT-CID dataset respectively. The outcomes show that the combination C3 (KNN, QDA, ADB, RF) obtains the optimal balance (i.e., the accuracy of 96.87% and FPR of 1.57%) at the Q-threshold value of 0.7 for ISOT-CID dataset. The combination C4 (KNN, GNB, ADB, RF) gives the best performance (i.e., the accuracy of 83.40% and FPR of 1.48%) for the NSL-KDD dataset at the Q-threshold value of 0.8. The evaluation results show that our models' performance improves marginally after addition of KNN classifier. Thus, we use combination C3 and C4 for further experimentation on ISOT-CID and NSL-KDD dataset respectively as they give the highest accuracy and least FPR.

The experimentation shows that our proposed model obtains significantly better evaluation results than individual classifiers. Further, we evaluated the DQN model described in the paper [25] on both the datasets to compare with the DDQN model that we have proposed in this paper.

7.4   Experimental Analysis of Proposed IDS on Black-Box Adversarial Attack

We emulated an adversarial attack on the proposed DDQN based model. Adversarial attacks on the machine and deep learning models is a widespread problem. The design of such adversarial models to test the robustness of designed models is a thriving research topic. However, very little work has been done to conduct adversarial analysis in the context of cloud IDS. We evaluated the robustness of our model based on the practical black-box adversarial attack proposed in [27]. We observed a substantial change in the feature vector after applying the adversarial model, i.e., nearly one-third of the feature values were found to be perturbed after applying the adversarial method on the datasets. Then we evaluated the performance of our model using the black box implementation. The Tables 6 show the test set evaluation of our model on the ISOT-CID and NSL-KDD dataset respectively. As can be seen from the Tables, the average accuracy fell down by about 3.5% and the FPR value increased by 1.5 times in case of NSL-KDD dataset. On the other hand, in the case of ISOT-CID dataset, there was a marginal decrease in the performance with nearly 4% fall in accuracy and 2% rise in FPR.

Table 6. Measuring robustness of our system against adversarial attacks based on NSL-KDD and ISOT-CID Data set

Action	NSL-KDD			ISOT-CID		
	Accuracy	FPR	Auc	Accuracy	FPR	AUC
Model before adversarial attack	83.40	1.48	0.8432	96.87	1.5	0.861
Model after adversarial attack	79.77	3.7	0.7980	92.17	3.3	0.8112

7.5 Performance of Model on Continuously Changing Attack Types

In this section, we evaluate our model performance when targeted by a continuously changing attack types. The key highlight of this experiment is to understand the adaptive and dynamic behaviour of the model towards novel attacks. Here, the model faces a zero-day attack scenario, and it is expected to adapt and detect the newer attack type with improving performance as the number of such attack samples increases. We have emulated this by deriving a new dataset using the different attack types of ISOT-CID dataset. ISOT-CID dataset collects the logs in a span of eighteen days where each day has new attack types. However, the majority of the volume belongs to first six days and each of these days has new attack type. We leveraged this property of the data set to find out the efficacy of model regarding adaptiveness towards novel attacks. We conducted experiments which involved making our model face new attacks constantly and noting down its accuracy, FPR and AUC (refer Table 7). The performance of any i^{th} day is obtained by training the model to dataset belonging from day 1 to day $i - 1$ and evaluating it on the ith day dataset. This is similar to situation in the real-world where model would face novel threats on almost every new day and its prediction would depend on the learning from past. As it can be seen from Table 7, our model performs fairly well even if it is trained for a few days and tested on unknown attack types. The consistent improvements in metrics like Accuracy, FPR and AUC, in subsequent days, suggest high adaptability and robustness in long term use.

Table 7. Performance of model on daily changing attack type

Day	Attack type	Number of samples	ACC	FPR	AUC
1	DTA and UCM	24622	–	–	–
2	NS	66124	82.23%	2.81%	0.8211
3	SQLI, CSS, PT, S-DOS	36517	87.16%	0.88%	0.8801
4	BFLA (failed)	43489	89.11%	0.16%	0.9030
5	UCM, DNSADOS, HTTPFDOS	48716	92.80%	0.10%	0.9381

ACC: Accuracy, DTM: Dictionary Traversal Attack, UCM: Unauthorized Crypto-mining, NS: Network scanning, SQLI: SQL Injection, CSS: Cross-site Scripting(XSS), PT: Path Traversal, S-DOS: Slowloris DOS, BFLA: Brute Force login attack, UCM: Unauthorized Crypto-mining, DNSADOS: DNS amplification DOS, HTTPFDOS: HTTP flood DOS

7.6 Comparison of Proposed IDS with State-of-the-Art Works

We compared our proposed model to existing intrusion detection models using NSL-KDD, and ISOT-CID datasets. We evaluated the performance with parameters such as Design, Adaptiveness, Dataset, Robustness, suitability for Cloud platform, Accuracy, FPR. The comparative study is presented in Table 8.

Most state-of-the-art IDS models [3, 21–25] use deep learning or reinforcement learning. In contrast, our proposed IDS implements a DDQN logic, which is an advanced deep reinforcement learning algorithm. Although the model described in paper [10] uses DDQN based IDS, the architecture of the model is suited for conventional networks and not for the cloud environment. Also, in contrast to [10], we evaluate our proposed IDS using ISOT-CID (which is a practical cloud-specific intrusion dataset) along with NSL-KDD. The paper [3] presented a cloud IDS and did an evaluation using the ISOT-CID dataset. However, the model in paper [3] lacks adaptiveness towards novel attacks and provides no study about the impact of the adversarial attack. Both of these two parameters are an essential security requirement for the current cloud environment. In contrast to [3], our work is adaptive, robust against adversarial attacks, and maintains a good balance between accuracy and FPR.

Table 8. Comparison of performance: our model vs. state-of-the-art works

Reference	Model	Adaptive	Robustness	Cloud suitability	Dataset	Accuracy (%)	FPR (%)
[21]	RNN	✗	✗	✗	NSL-KDD	83.28	3.06
[10]	DDQN	✓	✗	✗	NSL-KDD	89.78	–
[22]	DNN	✗	✓	✗	NSL-KDD	78.5	6.94
[23]	AE-RL	✗	✓	✗	NSL-KDD	80.16	–
[25]	DQN	✓	✓	✗	NSL-KDD	81.80	2.6
[24]	DL H2O	✓	✗	✓	NSL-KDD	83	–
[3]	OMSCA	✗	✗	✓	ISOT-CID	96.93	7.56
Our model	DDQN	✓	✓	✓	NSL-KDD	83.40	1.48
					ISOT-CID	96.87	1.5

* RNN: Recurrent Neural Network, DDQN: Double Deep-Q-Network, DNN: Deep Neural Network, DQN: Deep-Q-Network, GAN: Generative Adversarial Network, AE-RL: Adversarial Environment Reinforcement Learning, DL H2O: Deep Learning H2O, OMSCA: Online Multivariate Statistical Change Analysis

8 Conclusion

In this paper, we present an advanced deep reinforcement learning based cloud intrusion detection system that provides high accuracy and low FPR when evaluated using ISOT-CID and NSL-KDD dataset. Our models aim to meet the real-world constraints of limited processing resources and adaptability towards novel attacks and changing attack patterns. For this, we did experimentation on the dataset with a flow-based technique that is computationally lighter. We introduced DDQN based IDS to handle the overestimation of action values in the Deep Q Learning-based model. The Experimental results show significant improvements in evaluation metrics as compared to individual classifiers. In

Sect. 7.4, we verified the robustness of the proposed IDS against a practical black-box adversarial attack. Further, Sect. 7.5 shows our system's ability to handle newer attack types (even with very little training data). Overall, the evaluation of the model shows a better performance compared to state-of-the-art works and its effectiveness for deploying in the cloud platforms. In the future, we intend for the deployment, implementation and evaluation of the proposed IDS on a practical cloud infrastructure.

References

1. Li, Z., Sun, W., Wang, L.: A neural network based distributed intrusion detection system on cloud platform. In: 2012 IEEE 2nd International Conference on Cloud Computing and Intelligence Systems, Hangzhou, pp. 75–79 (2012). https://doi.org/10.1109/CCIS.2012.6664371
2. Sethi, K., Kumar, R., Prajapati, N., Bera, P.: Deep reinforcement learning based intrusion detection system for cloud infrastructure. In: 2020 International Conference on COMmunication Systems & NETworkS (COMSNETS), Bengaluru, India, pp. 1–6 (2020). https://doi.org/10.1109/COMSNETS48256.2020.9027452
3. Aldribi, A., Traoré, I., Moa, B., Nwamuo, O.: Hypervisor-based cloud intrusion detection through online multivariate statistical change tracking. Comput. Secur. **88**, 101646 (2020). https://doi.org/10.1016/j.cose.2019.101646. ISSN 0167-4048
4. Kholidy, H.A., Baiardi, F.: CIDD: a cloud intrusion detection dataset for cloud computing and masquerade attacks. In: 2012 Ninth International Conference on Information Technology - New Generations, Las Vegas, NV, pp. 397–402 (2012). https://doi.org/10.1109/ITNG.2012.97
5. Parampottupadam, S., Moldovann, A.: Cloud-based real-time network intrusion detection using deep learning. In: 2018 International Conference on Cyber Security and Protection of Digital Services (Cyber Security), Glasgow, pp. 1–8 (2018). https://doi.org/10.1109/CyberSecPODS.2018.8560674
6. Patil, R., Dudeja, H., Modi, C.: Designing an efficient security framework for detecting intrusions in virtual network of cloud computing. Comput. Secur. **85**, 402–422 (2019). https://doi.org/10.1016/j.cose.2019.05.016. ISSN 0167–4048
7. van Hasselt, H., Guez, A., Silver, D.: Deep reinforcement learning with double Q-learning. arXiv:1509.06461 (2015)
8. Aldribi, A., Traore, I., Moa, B.: Data sources and datasets for cloud intrusion detection modeling and evaluation. In: Mishra, B.S.P., Das, H., Dehuri, S., Jagadev, A.K. (eds.) Cloud Computing for Optimization: Foundations, Applications, and Challenges. SBD, vol. 39, pp. 333–366. Springer, Cham (2018). https://doi.org/10.1007/978-3-319-73676-1_13
9. Tranalyzer documentation (2020). https://tranalyzer.com/documentation
10. Lopez-Martin, M., Carro, B., Sanchez-Esguevillas, A.: Application of deep reinforcement learning to intrusion detection for supervised problems. Expert Syst. Appl. **141**, 112963 (2020). https://doi.org/10.1016/j.eswa.2019.112963. ISSN 0957-4174
11. Gogoi, P., Bhuyan, M.H., Bhattacharyya, D.K., Kalita, J.K.: Packet and flow based network intrusion dataset. In: Parashar, M., Kaushik, D., Rana, O.F., Samtaney, R., Yang, Y., Zomaya, A. (eds.) IC3 2012. CCIS, vol. 306, pp. 322–334. Springer, Heidelberg (2012). https://doi.org/10.1007/978-3-642-32129-0_34

12. Schaul, T., Quan, J., Antonoglou, I., Silver, D.: Prioritized experience replay. arXiv:1511.05952 (2015)

13. Meena, G., Choudhary, R.R.: A review paper on IDS classification using KDD 99 and NSL KDD dataset in WEKA. In: International Conference on Computer Communications and Electronics, Jaipur, pp. 553–558 (2017)

14. Shone, N., Ngoc, T.N., Phai, V.D., Shi, Q.: A deep learning approach to network intrusion detection. IEEE Trans. Emerg. Top. Comput. Intell. **2**(1), 41–50 (2018). https://doi.org/10.1109/TETCI.2017.2772792

15. scikit-learn user guide, scikit-learn Developers, Release 0.21.dev0 [User Guide] (2015). http://scikit-learn.org/dev/_downloads/scikit-learn-docs.pdf

16. Goodfellow, I.J., Papernot, N., McDaniel, P.D.: Cleverhans v0.1: an adversarial machine learning library. CoRR, abs/1610.00768 (2016)

17. Papernot, N., McDaniel, P., Jhay, S., Fredriksonz, M., Berkay Celik, Z., Swamix, A.: The limitations of deep learning in adversarial setting. In: 1st IEEE European Symposium on Security & Privacy, Saarbrucken, Germany (2016). https://doi.org/10.1109/EuroSP.2016.36

18. Papernot, N., McDaniel, P., Goodfellow, I., Jha, S., Berkay Celik, Z., Swami, A.: Practical black-box attacks against machine learning. arXiv preprint arXiv:1602.02697v4 (2016)

19. Biggio, B., et al.: Security evaluation of support vector machines in adversarial environments. In: Ma, Y., Guo, G. (eds.) Support Vector Machines Applications, pp. 105–153. Springer, Cham (2014). https://doi.org/10.1007/978-3-319-02300-7_4

20. Google Inc.: OpenAI and Pennsylvania State University, a repository for *cleverhans* library [Github Repository] (2016). https://github.com/tensorflow/cleverhans

21. Yin, C., Zhu, Y., Fei, J., He, X.: A deep learning approach for intrusion detection using recurrent neural networks. IEEE Access **5**, 21954–21961 (2017)

22. Vinayakumar, R., Alazab, M., Soman, K.P., Poornachandran, P., Al-Nemrat, A., Venkatraman, S.: Deep learning approach for intelligent intrusion detection system. IEEE Access **7**, 41525–41550 (2019). https://doi.org/10.1109/ACCESS.2019.2895334

23. Caminero, G., Lopez-Marti, M., Carro, B.: Adversarial environment reinforcement learning algorithm for intrusion detection. Comput. Netw. **159**, 96–109 (2019)

24. Parampottupadam, S., Moldovann, A.: Cloud-based real-time network intrusion detection using deep learning. In: 2018 International Conference on Cyber Security and Protection of Digital Services (Cyber Security), Glasgow, pp. 1–8 (2018)

25. Sethi, K., Rupesh, S., Kumar, R., Bera, P.L., Madhav, V.: A context-aware robust intrusion detection system: a reinforcement learning-based approach. Int. J. Inf. Secur. (2019). https://doi.org/10.1007/s10207-019-00482-7

26. Pedregosa, F., Varoquaux, G., Gramfort, A., et al.: Scikit-learn: machine learning in Python. J. Mach. Learn. Res. **12**, 2825–2830 (2011)

27. Papernot, N., McDaniel, P., Jhay, S., Fredriksonz, M., Berkay Celik, Z., Swamix, A.: The limitations of deep learning in adversarial setting. In: 1st IEEE European Symposium on Security and Privacy, Saarbrucken, Germany (2016)

28. Wang, Z.: Deep learning-based intrusion detection with adversaries. IEEE Access **6**, 38367–38384 (2018)

29. Szegedy, C., et al.: Intriguing properties of neural networks (2013). arXiv:1312

30. Huber, P.J.: Robust estimation of a location parameter. Ann. Math. Stat. **35**(1), 73–101 (1964). JSTOR. www.jstor.org/stable/2238020. Accessed 6 July 2020

31. Mnih, V., Kavukcuoglu, K., Silver, D., et al.: Human-level control through deep reinforcement learning. Nature **518**, 529–533 (2015)

A Forensic Technique to Detect Copy-Move Forgery Based on Image Statistics

Ayush Nirwal[✉], Raghav Khandelwal[✉], Smit Patel[✉],
and Priyanka Singh[✉]

Dhirubhai Ambani Institute of Information and Communication Technology,
Gandhinagar, India
{201701091,201701015,201701071,priyanka_singh}@daiict.ac.in

Abstract. The proliferation of easy multimedia editing tools has ruined the trust in what we see. Forensic techniques are proposed to detect forgeries unnoticeable by naked human eyes. In this paper, we focus on a specific copy-move forgery attack that happens to alter portions within an image. It may be aimed to hide any sensitive information contained in a particular image portion or misguide the facts. Here, we propose to exploit the image's statistical properties, specifically, mean and variance, to detect the forged portions. A block-wise comparison is made based on these properties to localize the forged region called a prediction mask. Post-processing methods have been proposed to reduce false positives and improve the accuracy(F-score) of the prediction mask. This decrease in FPR in the final result is comes from post processing method of overlaying multiple masks with different values of threshold and block_size of the sliding window.

Keywords: Copy move forgery · Statistical properties · Mean

1 Introduction

The readily accessible, easy-to-use, and potent digital image editing tools such as Photoshop have made it easy to manipulate and tamper with digital images without leaving any visible clues. As a result, there is a massive rise in digitally produced forgeries in mass media and on the Internet. This pattern suggests vulnerabilities issues and reduces the integrity of digital images. Developing techniques for checking the validity and authenticity of digital images has become very necessary, mainly since the images displayed are evidence in a courtroom, as news reports, as a financial document. In this context, image tamper identification has become one of the critical objectives of image forensics.

We focus here on a particular form of image manipulation where a part of the image is usually copied and pasted on to another section, typically to cover unwanted parts of the image, named as copy-move forgery. An example of copy-move forgery is shown in Fig. 1, where image (a) is the original image and shows

© Springer Nature Switzerland AG 2020
L. Batina et al. (Eds.): SPACE 2020, LNCS 12586, pp. 86–98, 2020.
https://doi.org/10.1007/978-3-030-66626-2_5

three missiles, whereas image (b) is the forged image in which one missile is copy pasted at a different location on the image to show that there were four missiles launched instead of 3. From this example, it becomes clear that it is quite possible that forgeries may not leave any perceptual clues of tampering. Thus, it becomes quite challenging to identify such cases and ensure that the integrity of the image is intact. They may be crucial to applications at times.

(a) Original Image   (b) Forged Image

Fig. 1. An example of copy-move forgery

To detect copy-move forgeries, many schemes have already been proposed in the literature. Some schemes propose solutions that are too computation intensive while others lack at accurate region localization for the forged portions and result in high false positive rate (FPR). FPR values for various copy move forgery detection (CMFD) schemes has been enlisted in Table 1.

Table 1. Approximate FPR of various CMFD techniques

Algorithms	False positive rate
PCA [15]	9.04
DCT [2]	11.33
IDCT [14]	9.81
DyWT [9]	12.91
DWT [17]	10.11
DyWT_zernike [16]	8.08
SVD [11]	7.87
Dixit et al. [3]	2.55
Proposed SCMFD	0.051

In this paper, we propose a copy-move forgery detection algorithm for images. The baseline idea is to utilize the statistical image properties, specifically, mean and variance to detect the duplicate regions. The image is partitioned into blocks and comparison based on the block properties is done to categorize it as tampered or authentic region. We achieve a detection accuracy (F-score) of 97.05% with FPR as low as 0.051%. Rest of the paper is organized as follows: The related work is discussed in Sect. 2. Detailed steps of the proposed Statistical Copy Move Forgery Detection (SCMFD) algorithm are presented in Sect. 3. In Sect. 4, we present the results and the analysis and Sect. 5 concludes the work along with the future directions.

2   Related Work

The area of copy-move forgery is well researched and many methods have already been proposed to detect copy-move forgery. One of the most straightforward and obvious technique is comparing each pixel of an image with other pixels to detect manipulation [2]. Though the idea seems pretty simple, but it has a lot of computational complexity. The computation would be of order $O(P^2)$, where P is the total number of pixels in the image. The number of computations can be reduced by lexicographically sorting the pixels according to their values and only comparing the values in the near vicinity to find copy-move pixels [1]. However, this method has its shortfalls even after optimizing the computations. This method can be tricked by slightly changing the values of the pixel or rotating it during copy-move forgery. And perpetrators often change this value by color corrections and smoothing. This often results in disconnected pixels being detected as shown in Fig. 2. This method is also not robust against JPEG compression [2].

(a) Copy-move forgery on a image   (b) Disconnected pixels in simple block based detection

Fig. 2. Shortfalls of a simple block based copy-move forgery detection technique [2]

A simple block based approach to detect copy-move forgery would be to compare the mean and standard deviation of blocks [3]. However, this approach alone is not resilient to images where background looks similar or have similar pixels properties. This background creates a high number of false positives, which increases the false positive rate (FPR) and decreases the accuracy. Another standard method for copy-move forgery detection is auto-correlation. Most of the 'information' in an image is stored in the low-frequency range, so we cannot directly apply auto-correlation on the image; otherwise, we will have spikes on the edges [2]. We first pass it through a high pass filter, which will remove all the high frequency from the image. Then we compute the auto-correlation of the image to detect copy-move forgery. This method is not computationally intensive, but it has a hard time detecting copy-move forgeries, which are relatively smaller to the size of the image [2].

A popular method for copy-move detection is using Discrete Cosine Transform (DCT) [1]. The image is divided into a number of consecutive blocks usually 8×8, then DCT is applied on that block, and low-frequency data is extracted using zig-zag traversal. Then this block is sorted lexicographically to find similar blocks within a user-defined threshold [1]. Another similar method for copy-move forgery detection is using Principal component analysis (PCA) instead of DCT [13]. PCA is used to represent higher dimension data into lower dimensions, and in this case, PCA will extract data from the blocks and then compare that said data to find similar blocks that are copy-moved. DCT is a better approach in comparison to PCA to find copy-move forgery [1].

Similarly, many more approaches have been proposed in the field of copy-move forgery detection. In [4], the authors proposed a sorted neighborhood technique based on a discrete wavelet transform (DWT). Then Singular Value Decomposition (SVD) is applied on the image's low frequency information, this method is robust against JPEG compression. In [5], the authors proposed an approach based on Fourier-Mellin Transform (FMT) along with bloom filters for CMFD. This approach is also resilient to post processing techniques like Gaussian Noise and blur. In [6], the authors proposed an approach based on DCT and singular value decomposition (SVD). Although the approach is not robust against rotation but it gives good results in case of noise, blurring, and compression.

In [7], the authors proposed an approach based circular block extraction and Local Binary Patterns (LBP). This approach is robust against compression, rotation, blurring and noise. In [8], the authors used an approach based on circular blocks and Polar Harmonic Transform (PHT). In [9], the authors proposed a technique based on Dyadic Wavelet Transform (DyWT). In [10], an approach based on Histogram of Oriented Gradients (HOG) is used to detect the copy-move forge regions. High false positive rate (FPR) was the bottleneck for most of the approaches which the proposed approach is successful at drastically decreasing as tabulated in Table 1.

3   The Proposed Statistical Copy Move Forgery Detection (SCMFD) Approach

In this section, we present the proposed Statistical Copy Move Forgery Detection (SCMFD) approach. It aims to accurately localize the forged portions within an image exploiting it's statistical properties. An overview of the proposed SCMFD approach is shown in Fig. 3. Some optimizations are proposed to improve the overall accuracy of the final prediction mask.

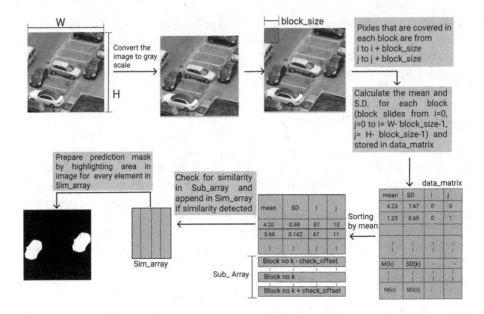

Fig. 3. An overview of proposed SCMFD approach

3.1 SCMFD

Here, we present a region duplication detection method for images. It utilizes the statistical image features viz., mean, and variance to detect forgery on a block-basis. The image is first converted to a gray-scale (if input image is a color image) to reduce computational cost and further analysis for forgery detection is done with just one channel. A filter of a particular block size is slid across the image and then mean and standard deviation (SD) is calculated for all the pixel in it. Each of these values are appended to a matrix *data_array* along with the coordinates of the top left pixel of that image block. Thus, this matrix has four columns as mean, SD, x and y co-ordinates respectively.The matrix is sorted row-wise based on the mean values to arrange in order (either descending or ascending). Traverse the resulting matrix row-wise and for every element in sorted matrix *sorted_array*, generate a *Sub_array* with *check_offset* as number of neighbors on both of its side. Compute absolute mean difference, absolute SD difference and euclidean distance between the element and its neighbors (elements of *Sub_array*).

Algorithm 1. SCMFD

INPUT: Image I of size $W \times H$, Mean_Ths, SD_Ths, Dist_Ths, SD_block,block_size

OUTPUT: Prediction Mask Bit Matrix PM of size $W \times H$

Define: 1. Mean_Ths is threshold for maximum threshold for absolute minimum difference between two image blocks to be identified as similar

2. SD_Ths is threshold for maximum threshold for absolute Standard deviation difference between two image blocks to be identified as similar

3. Dist_Ths is threshold for minimum threshold for euclidean distance between two image blocks to be identified as similar

4. SD_block is threshold for minimum threshold for image block to be considered for detection

5. block_size is block size for image blocks

6. PM is the output prediction mask of size $W \times H$. It is initialized with zeros

```
 1: procedure SCMFD(I, Mean_Ths, SD_Ths, Dist_Ths, SD_block, block_size)
 2:     Convert image to gray-scale
 3:     data_matrix = Empty array
 4:     for i = 0; i < H − block_size; i = i + 1 do
 5:         data_array = Empty array
 6:         for j = 0; j¡W − block_size; j = j + 1 do
 7:             block = I [i:i+block_size][j:j+block_size]
 8:             data_array[0] = mean(block)
 9:             data_array[1] = SD(block)
10:             data_array[2] = i
11:             data_array[3] = j
12:             append data_array to data_matrix
13:         end for
14:     end for
15:     Sort the data_matrix row-wise according to the mean value(key at j=0)
16:     Traverse in the resulting matrix row-wise
17:     Sim_array = Empty array
18:     for i = 0; i < len(sorted_array); i = i + 1 do
19:         Sub_array = sorted_array[max(0,i-check_offset) : min(len(sorted_array),
            i+check_offset)]
20:         Calculate abs(mean difference), abs(SD difference) and distance between
            the element and its neighbors (elements of sub_array)
21:         if abs(mean difference) < Mean_Ths and SD of element > SD_block and,
            abs(SD difference) < SD_Ths and euclidean distance > Dist_Ths then
22:             append element to Sim_array
23:         end if
24:     end for
25:     for each element in Sim_array do
26:         PM(i:i+block_size,j:j+block_size) = 1
27:     end for
28:     return PM
29: end procedure
```

If absolute mean difference < *Mean_Ths*, and absolute SD difference < *SD_Ths*, and euclidean distance > *Dist_Ths*, SD of element > *SD_block* then append element into a new array called *Sim_array*. The prediction mask *PM* is then created by highlighting blocks identified as similar.

3.2 Optimizations in SCMFD

We can reduce the false positives by comparing both mean value and SD of the blocks with a specified threshold. If the difference in mean value between two blocks is below this threshold *Mean_Ths* and if the standard deviation of these blocks is the same, then these blocks will be identified as similar by SCMFD algorithm. Image blocks that are physically closer in the image may also lead to false positives. Therefore we would only consider those block pairs where the sum of the number of similar blocks identified at a particular distance meets the minimum user-defined threshold *Dist_Ths*. This way, we discard anomalies that are often next to each other or are often a part of the same object and not the corresponding copy-moved object. We also use another user-defined threshold *SD_block* to ensure that block pairs whose distance from each other is below a threshold are discarded as shown in Fig. 4.

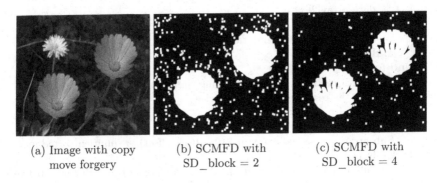

(a) Image with copy   (b) SCMFD with   (c) SCMFD with
    move forgery   SD_block = 2   SD_block = 4

Fig. 4. PM using threshold *SD_block* on SD of individual image blocks

The proposed SCMFD algorithm does provide accuracy of 76% with FPR of 1.38% that increases with increase in *block_size* and decrease in *SD_block* (*Mean_Ths*, *SD_Ths* and *Dist_Ths* kept as constant). It seems to be far less when compared to other statistical approaches for CMFD, but the big advantage of SCMFD is that it runs very fast as feature vector's length is just 2 containing only the mean value and SD value. This makes similarity check a lot easier among the blocks. Therefore, no PCA is needed. Also opposed to other statistical approaches, increasing block size increases performance (note that if the block size is large, there is a slight decrease in number of total blocks which slightly increases performance). To further increase the accuracy of the *PM*, we prepare the final *PM* by overlaying *PM's* iteratively from the previous pass of the

SCMFD algorithm varying the block sizes *block_size* and *SD_block* for every pass.

$$PM_{mul} = \frac{\sum_0^N PM_i}{N} \tag{1}$$

where, PM_i represents the prediction mask at the ith iteration and N as the total number of passes.

The final PM will have values ranging from 0 to 1. A simple filter is applied on this mask to change every value greater than a threshold to 1 and 0 otherwise (we used 0.4 in our study) as shown in Fig. 5. The resulting prediction mask gives us 97% accuracy on an average with 0.05% FPR.

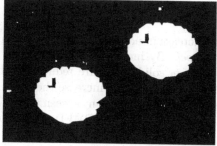

(a) Multiple passes of SCMFD overlayed   (b) Applying filter

Fig. 5. Overlayed prediction mask

4   Experimental Results and Analysis

To evaluate the performance of the proposed approach, we have used Copy-Move Forgery Dataset [12]. Exhaustive set of experiments were conducted using the images from this standard dataset and overall F-score and FPR presented in the results.

4.1   Dataset

The Dataset [12] is made of medium sized images (almost all 1000×700 or 700×1000) and it is subdivided into several datasets (D0, D1, D2). We have used the subdivided dataset - D0 for our experiments which contains uncompressed images and their translated copies.

4.2   Results

The base algorithm SCMFD provides accuracy up to 76% with a FPR of 1.38%. The F-score and FPR are shown in Table 2 and Table 3 respectively, which shows

Table 2. Average values for F-score for different block sizes and respective *SD_block*

	SD_block				
block_size	0	1	2	3	4
5		21.01	26.93	35.70	41.83	45.81
10		34.67	40.26	52.97	60.30	64.84
15		40.55	45.61	57.87	65.47	70.64
20		44.67	49.17	60.45	68.17	73.39
25		47.62	51.62	62.28	71.06	76.56
30		50.82	54.87	64.43	73.31	76.60

Table 3. Average values for FPR for different block sizes and respective *SD_block*

	SD_block				
block_size	0	1	2	3	4
5		19.35	10.72	4.65	2.56	1.68
10		16.04	11.52	4.09	2.21	1.51
15		15.68	12.06	4.52	2.38	1.73
20		14.74	11.63	4.77	2.60	1.72
25		12.99	12.03	5.48	2.52	1.44
30		10.40	8.74	5.01	2.25	1.37

the increase in accuracy and decrease in FPR as we increase the *block_size* and *SD_block*. By increasing the *SD_block*, we see that the areas having repeated pattern or solid colors are reduced in the PM as shown in Fig. 6 moving from (a) to (e). And as we increase the *block_size*, we see that the false positives are reduced greatly that can be seen if we move from Fig: 6, 7, 8, 9, 10 and 11. The accuracy obtained by SCMFD are further optimize.

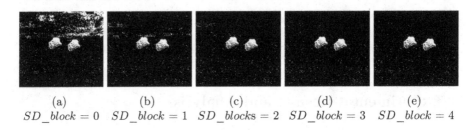

(a)   (b)   (c)   (d)   (e)
SD_block = 0   *SD_block* = 1   *SD_blocks* = 2   *SD_block* = 3   *SD_block* = 4

Fig. 6. Prediction mask for block_size = 5 with different *SD_block*

The results are further improved by doing multiple passes and overlaying different prediction mask from different passes of SCMFD with different block sizes and *SD_block*.

Table 4 shows how the accuracy is increased by overlapping prediction mask of different block-sizes and taking different standard deviations into consideration. By doing so, we get 5 different overlaying prediction masks which are shown in Fig. 12(a) prediction mask obtained by overlaying prediction mask of all block-sizes and all *SD_block* values. Figure 12(b) prediction mask obtained by overlaying prediction mask of all block-sizes with *SD_block* values = 1, 2, 3, 4. Figure 12(c) prediction mask obtained by overlaying prediction mask of all block-sizes with *SD_block* values = 2, 3, 4. Figure 12(d) prediction mask obtained by overlaying prediction mask of all block-sizes with *SD_block* values = 3, 4. Figure 12(e) prediction mask obtained by overlaying prediction mask of

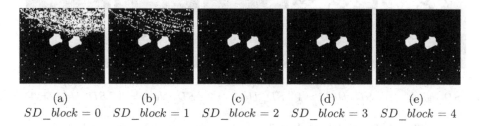

(a)   (b)   (c)   (d)   (e)

$SD\_block = 0$ $SD\_block = 1$ $SD\_block = 2$ $SD\_block = 3$ $SD\_block = 4$

Fig. 7. Prediction mask for block_size = 10 with different SD_block

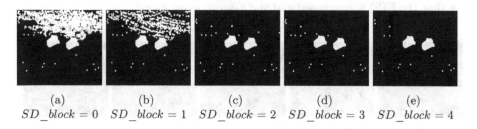

(a)   (b)   (c)   (d)   (e)

$SD\_block = 0$ $SD\_block = 1$ $SD\_block = 2$ $SD\_block = 3$ $SD\_block = 4$

Fig. 8. Prediction mask for block_size = 15 with different SD_block

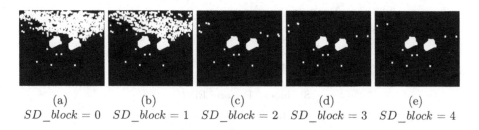

(a)   (b)   (c)   (d)   (e)

$SD\_block = 0$ $SD\_block = 1$ $SD\_block = 2$ $SD\_block = 3$ $SD\_block = 4$

Fig. 9. Prediction mask for block_size = 20 with different SD_block

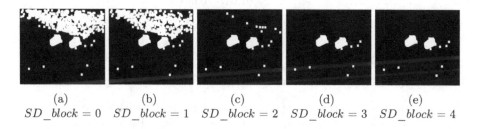

(a)   (b)   (c)   (d)   (e)

$SD\_block = 0$ $SD\_block = 1$ $SD\_block = 2$ $SD\_block = 3$ $SD\_block = 4$

Fig. 10. Prediction mask for block_size = 25 with different SD_block

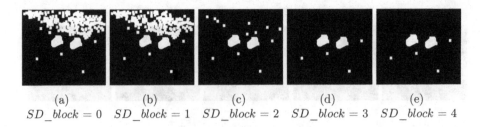

(a)	(b)	(c)	(d)	(e)
$SD\_block = 0$	$SD\_block = 1$	$SD\_block = 2$	$SD\_block = 3$	$SD\_block = 4$

Fig. 11. Prediction mask for block_size = 30 with different SD_block

all block-sizes with SD_block values = 4. From these prediction masks, we can see that the FPR is decreased and the F-score is increased.

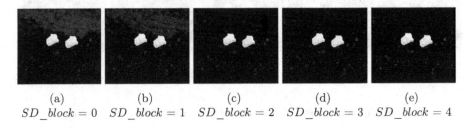

(a)	(b)	(c)	(d)	(e)
$SD\_block = 0$	$SD\_block = 1$	$SD\_block = 2$	$SD\_block = 3$	$SD\_block = 4$

Fig. 12. Prediction mask obtained after doing multiple passes of SCMFD

Table 4. F-score and FPR after optimization

SD_block	F-score	FPR
[0,1,2,3,4]	86.14	1.9
[1,2,3,4]	88.892	1.023
[2,3,4]	96.487	0.114
[3,4]	96.644	0.095
[4]	97.047	0.051

4.3 Comparative Performance with State-of-the-art Approaches

The comparative performance of the proposed approach with the other state-of-the-art schemes in tabulated in the Tables 5 and Table 6 based on F-score and FPR respectively. High F-score of approximately 98.38% in case of DyWT_zernike [16] and Dixit et al. [3] is achieved which is marginally higher

Table 5. Comparative performance based on F-score

Schemes	F-score [%]
PCA [15]	96.78
DCT [2]	97.24
IDCT [14]	97.84
DyWT [9]	98.02
DWT [17]	98.09
DyWT_zernike [16]	98.38
SVD [11]	97.62
Dixit et al. [3]	98.38
Proposed SCMFD	97.05

Table 6. Comparative performance based on FPR

Schemes	FPR
PCA [15]	9.04
DCT [2]	11.33
IDCT [14]	9.81
DyWT [9]	12.91
DWT [17]	10.11
DyWT_zernike [16]	8.08
SVD [11]	7.87
Dixit et al. [3]	2.55
Proposed SCMFD	0.051

than that achieved by the proposed approach. However, these methods have approximate FPR of 8.08% and 2.55% which is much higher when compared to the proposed approach that attains FPR as low as 0.051%.

5 Conclusion

In this paper, we propose SCMFD approach that aims to accurately localize the forged portions within an image exploiting it's statistical properties. It utilizes the statistical image features viz., mean, and variance to detect forgery on a block-basis. The accuracy is further improved by preparing new prediction mask by overlaying different prediction mask from different passes of SCMFD. As our future work, we would like to make the proposed method robust against various attacks of noise addition, scaling, jpeg compression, etc.

References

1. Gupta, A., Saxena, N., Vasistha, S.K.: Detecting copy move forgery using DCT. Int. J. Sci. Res. Publ. **3**(5), 1 (2013)
2. Fridrich, A.J., Soukal, B.D., Lukáš, A.J.: Detection of copy-move forgery in digital images. In: Proceedings of Digital Forensic Research Workshop (2003)
3. Roy, A., Dixit, R., Naskar, R., Chakraborty, R.S.: Copy-move forgery detection exploiting statistical image features. Digital Image Forensics. SCI, vol. 755, pp. 57–64. Springer, Singapore (2020). https://doi.org/10.1007/978-981-10-7644-2_4
4. Li, G., Wu, Q., Tu, D., Sun, S.: A sorted neighborhood approach for detecting duplicated regions in image forgeries based on DWT and SVD. In: 2007 IEEE International Conference on Multimedia and Expo, pp. 1750–1753. IEEE, July 2007

5. Bayram, S., Sencar, H.T., Memon, N.: An efficient and robust method for detecting copy-move forgery. In: 2009 IEEE International Conference on Acoustics, Speech and Signal Processing, pp. 1053–1056. IEEE, April 2009
6. Zhao, J., Guo, J.: Passive forensics for copy-move image forgery using a method based on DCT and SVD. Forensic Sci. Int. **233**(1–3), 158–166 (2013)
7. Li, L., Li, S., Zhu, H., Chu, S.C., Roddick, J.F., Pan, J.S.: An efficient scheme for detecting copy-move forged images by local binary patterns. J. Inf. Hiding Multimed. Signal Process. **4**(1), 46–56 (2013)
8. Li, L., Li, S., Zhu, H., Wu, X.: Detecting copy-move forgery under affine transforms for image forensics. Comput. Electr. Eng. **40**(6), 1951–1962 (2014)
9. Muhammad, G., Hussain, M., Bebis, G.: Passive copy move image forgery detection using undecimated dyadic wavelet transform. Digit. Invest. **9**(1), 49–57 (2012)
10. Lee, J.C., Chang, C.P., Chen, W.K.: Detection of copy-move image forgery using histogram of orientated gradients. Inf. Sci. **321**, 250–262 (2015)
11. Kang, X., Wei, S.: Identifying tampered regions using singular value decomposition in digital image forensics. In: 2008 International Conference on Computer Science And Software Engineering, vol. 3, pp. 926–930. IEEE, December 2008
12. Diid.unipa.it. n.d. Download — CVIP Group. http://www.diid.unipa.it/cvip/?page_id=48#CMFD. Accessed 1 Aug 2020
13. Sunil, K., Jagan, D., Shaktidev, M.: DCT-PCA based method for copy-move forgery detection. In: Satapathy, S., Avadhani, P., Udgata, S., Lakshminarayana, S. (eds.) ICT and Critical Infrastructure: Proceedings of the 48th Annual Convention of Computer Society of India-Vol II. Advances in Intelligent Systems and Computing, vol. 249, pp. 577–583. Springer, Cham (2014). https://doi.org/10.1007/978-3-319-03095-1_62
14. Huang, Y., Lu, W., Sun, W., Long, D.: Improved DCT-based detection of copy-move forgery in images. Forensic Sci. Int. **206**(1–3), 178–184 (2011)
15. Popescu, A.C., Farid, H.: Exposing digital forgeries by detecting duplicated image regions. Department of Computer Science, rtmouth College, Technical report TR2004-515, pp. 1–11 (2004)
16. Yang, J., Ran, P., Xiao, D., Tan, J.: Digital image forgery forensics by using undecimated dyadic wavelet transform and Zernike moments. J. Comput. Inf. Syst. **9**(16), 6399–6408 (2013)
17. Zhang, J., Feng, Z., Su, Y.: A new approach for detecting copy-move forgery in digital images. In: 2008 11th IEEE Singapore International Conference on Communication Systems, pp. 362–366. IEEE, November 2008

Cryptography

ExtPFA: Extended Persistent Fault Analysis for Deeper Rounds of Bit Permutation Based Ciphers with a Case Study on GIFT

Priyanka Joshi$^{(\boxtimes)}$ (ID) and Bodhisatwa Mazumdar (ID)

Indian Institute of Technology Indore, Khandwa Road Simrol,
Indore 453552, Madhya Pradesh, India
{phd1801201001,bodhisatwa}@iiti.ac.in

Abstract. Persistent fault analysis (PFA) has emerged as a potent fault analysis technique that can recover the secret key by influencing ciphertext distribution. PFA employs the persistent fault model that alters algorithm constants such as Sbox elements, and the fault endures until the system restarts. As the PFA fault model does not require high precision and controllability to carry out the attack, it has gained considerable attention from the cryptography research community. However, most of the research work highlights its application for investigating only the last round, albeit a persistent fault impacts all internal rounds too. In this work, we present an extension of the original PFA to recover deeper round keys of Substitution bit-Permutation Network (SbPN) based ciphers by leveraging its capability to affect every round. We use GIFT cipher as a case study and show the effectiveness of the proposed approach through simulation. We could recover the full master keys of both the GIFT cipher versions by retrieving the round keys up to the depth 2 and 4 for GIFT-128 and GIFT-64, respectively. We also analyzed the success rate of our approach on both the versions in two dimensions: *Depth-wise* and *Hamming distance-wise*. We observed that the number of ciphertexts required to recover the round key increases exponentially as we move deeper from the final round. Furthermore, the number of required ciphertexts to recover the key increases exponentially with Hamming distance between indexes of two identical elements in faulty Sbox. In GIFT-64, for Hamming distance of value 1 between the indexes, the round keys can be recovered in approximately 110, 290, and 750 ciphertexts for round number 28, 27, and 26, respectively, with a 100% success rate. For round 25, around 2000 ciphertexts are sufficient to recover the round key in 90% of the cases out of 1000 experiments. For GIFT-128, around 200 ciphertexts are enough to extract the last round key for the Hamming distance of value 1. For 39th round, the round key can be recovered with a 100% success rate in roughly 380, 575, and 1100 ciphertexts for the Hamming distance 1, 2, and 3, respectively. However, for the same round with Hamming distance of value 4, the success rate is 75% for around 2000 ciphertexts.

© Springer Nature Switzerland AG 2020
L. Batina et al. (Eds.): SPACE 2020, LNCS 12586, pp. 101–122, 2020.
https://doi.org/10.1007/978-3-030-66626-2_6

Keywords: Secret-key cryptography · Fault attacks · GIFT cipher · Persistent fault analysis · Lightweight encryption

1 Introduction

In the era of smart things, the usage of tiny embedded devices such as radio frequency identification devices (RFID), smart cards, wearable devices, medical sensing networks, sensor networks for military surveillance, etc. is growing exponentially. Often, these devices are shared by many users, so there is an ominous concern for the misuse of the information, and consequently, the security of these devices. The lightweight cryptographic primitives are designed to achieve the security goals of these embedded devices. These devices are often physically accessible by the adversaries, who can easily mount the most dangerous type of attacks called implementation attacks, including fault attacks, side-channel analysis, probing attacks, reverse engineering, etc.

The notion of Fault analysis and it's effectiveness on cryptographic implementations was first introduced by Boneh et al. [3] in 1996. The fault-based side-channel analysis comprises modification of instructions or data when a hardware/software platform is in execution. The device is forced to operate out of normal operating conditions through clock glitches, voltage spikes, laser beams, etc. Such device tampering can lead to corruption of memory contents, modifying instruction flows, or cause certain changes, thus revealing information about the algorithm's intermediate data. The resulting computational errors are used in *fault analysis* (FA) to reveal secret keys embedded in the targeted device. These keys are then used to breach the targeted system's security that comprises methods, such as key recovery, ePurse balance increase, false signature acceptation, PIN code recovery, etc.

Fault analysis attacks are a predominant threat to cryptographic implementations; a single faulty encryption may break even a mathematically proven to be secure cryptographic system [13,17]. *Differential fault analysis* (DFA) [2] is the most popular fault analysis technique that requires pairs of faulty and fault-free ciphertexts corresponding to the same plaintext. DFA is a *chosen-plaintext attack* (CPA) and assumes a strong adversary. Unlike the DFA and other classical fault analysis techniques, *persistent fault analysis* (PFA) introduced by Zhang et al. in [14], is a variant of *Statistical Fault Analysis* (SFA) [8] technique and based on ciphertext only attack. In PFA, the adversary manipulates ciphertext distribution through fault injection and later exploits this non-uniform distribution of ciphertext to extract the implementation secrets.

In the attacker's perspective, the main advantage of PFA is its relaxed fault model. In contrast to the classical fault analysis techniques, the persistent fault model employed in PFA does not require high precision and synchronization during fault injection. The fault once injected remains in the system until it is rebooted. Therefore, the collection of faulty ciphertexts requires less effort. These pros made PFA the most studied fault analysis technique in the recent past. However, the true potential of the PFA is still unexplored. Due to the persistent nature, the fault affects every round of an encryption; but most of the research works specifies the significance of PFA for analyzing the last round only.

In this paper, we propose an *Extended Persistent Fault Analysis* (ExtPFA) approach that can be used to analyze deeper rounds of a *Substitution bit-Permutation Network* (SbPN) cipher by leveraging the capabilities of persistent faults. To validate our approach we used GIFT cipher, which is among the most efficient lightweight ciphers.

1.1   State-of-the-Art

In [14], PFA was proposed and first applied on AES, in which the authors could successfully attack a *Dual Modular Redundancy* (DMR) countermeasure based implementation. Pan et al. [11] performed a study and demonstrated that using PFA, even higher-order masking countermeasures, could be circumvented with single fault injection. PFA was introduced to be applicable SPN based cryptographic implementations. Caforio et al. [4] showed that Feistel structure based ciphers could be vulnerable against PFA if the adversary can collect pairs of faulty and fault-free ciphertexts of the same plaintexts. Gruber et al. [9] proposed a PFA method tailored for authenticated encryption schemes and demonstrated on three CAESAR finalists. In [15], authors performed a detailed analysis of PFA's applicability to several implementations. Zhang et al. in [16] discuss many practical concerns related to PFA, such as how, where, and whether the persistent fault is injected. Carrè et al. [5] demonstrated how maximum likelihood estimation could be used to reduce the number of required ciphertexts. Chakraborty et al. [6] proposed a PFA based method to recover deeper round keys and demonstrated its application on 9th round of AES. The technique is based on a partial key guess, and complexity largely depends on the size of the guess.

1.2   Our Contributions

The contributions of this work are as follows:

1. The persistence of fault over several encryptions has much more potential to reveal the secrets hidden in the deeper rounds than explored to the date. In this work, We present an extension of PFA that can be used to recover deeper round keys of the Substitution bit-Permutation Networks (SbPN) class of ciphers such as GIFT, PRESENT, TRIFLE, HyENA, etc.
2. As a case study, we demonstrate the above mentioned approach to GIFT cipher and verify the proposed key-recovery attack through a set of simulations.

The remainder of this work is organized as follows. Section 2 proposes a modified version of PFA suitable for ciphers having permutation layer after substitution layer in the last round. Section 3 introduces and discusses the proposed approach. In Sect. 4, we provide a case study of our proposed attack on the GIFT cipher. Section 5 presents the results of the attack. In Sect. 7, we briefly discuss countermeasures, followed by the Conclusion in Sect. 8.

2   Persistent Fault Analysis

The classical fault analysis techniques such as Differential Fault Analysis (DFA), Algebraic Fault Analysis (AFA), and their variants primarily rely on injection of transient faults. Due to the temporary nature, the attacker needs to inject faults into registers within a specific round in each encryption operation, which often requires high precision and synchronization. In contrast, PFA employs persistent faults to attack cryptographic implementations. A persistent fault can be injected before the encryption starts and persists for all subsequent encryption operations until the device running the cryptographic algorithm restarts. Thus, it is relaxed in the context of required control over fault location and target round at the run time. This characteristic makes it easier for the PFA attacker, hence it has gained a lot of attention from the cryptographic research community.

In PFA, the algorithmic constants stored in memory, for example, Sbox values is/are modified through fault injection. This modification transforms the uniform distribution of ciphertexts to a biased distribution. Later, the biased distribution is analyzed to extract the implementation secrets, like recovering the secret key. A persistent fault can be induced in memory by flipping bits through a rowhammer fault injection technique [10].

2.1   Original PFA

Now, let us revisit the original PFA attack mechanism, as described in [14]. PFA comprises of three phases. In the first phase called the *fault injection phase*, persistent fault is injected in the cipher implementation even before the encryption starts. In the second phase, the encryption algorithm is executed multiple times, which generate non-uniformly distributed faulty ciphertexts. The third phase is referred to as *fault analysis phase* comprises analysis of the distribution of the collected faulty ciphertexts to recover the secret key.

(a) Structure considered in original PFA and last round in SPN ciphers like AES, COLM, etc.

(b) Structure of internal rounds in all SPN ciphers and last round in SPN ciphers like PRESENT, GIFT, etc.

Fig. 1. Variations in SPN round structures

Figure 1a depicts a structure used in last round of SPN ciphers such as AES, OCB, and COLM, etc. PFA considers an SPN round without a linear layer as shown in Figure 1a, for attack analysis and key recovery. The round input state consists of N words of b bits. The input of a b-bit wide Sbox S is x_j i.e. the jth word of the state. The output of the Sbox is y_j i.e. $y_j = S[x_j]$. The corresponding round key and the resulting ciphertext are k_j and c_j, respectively. The relation between y_j, k_j, and c_j can be expressed as $c_j = y_j \oplus k_j$. The probability distribution of ciphertexts is used for analysis to recover the round key. The probability distribution of the Sbox output, y_j, is denoted as $Pr[y_j]$. For fault-free cipher with $b \times b$ bijective Sbox, $Pr[y_j = i] = 2^{-b}, \forall i \in \{0, \ldots, 2^b - 1\}$. When a fault (bit-flip) is injected in an Sbox entry $S[i] = v$, the value of $S[i]$ changes to a different value v^*, i.e., $v \neq v^*$. Consequently, the probability of occurrence of v^* doubles whereas for v it becomes zero, $Pr[y_j = v^*] = 2^{1-b}$ and $Pr[y_j = v] = 0$. The probability of occurrence of all other values of y_j remains the same, $Pr[y_j] = 2^{-b}$. Due to the fixed round key k_j, the relation between probability distribution of y_j and c_j is as shown in Eq. (1).

$$Pr[c_j] = Pr[y_j \oplus (k_j)] \tag{1}$$

Suppose, $t \in \{0, \ldots, 2^b - 1\}$ represents a possible value of b-bit ciphertext word c_j. Then, the value of t that occurs maximum number of times is denoted as t_{max}, and the value that occurs minimum number of times is denoted as t_{min}. The key can be recovered using any of the three below mentioned attack strategies.

(i) **Strategy 1**: Assuming the faulty element's original value v is known, the key can be computed using the equation, $k_j = v \oplus t_{min}$.
(ii) **Strategy 2**: The values of $t \neq t_{min}$ can be used to prune out impossible key candidates, with the same assumption that the value of v is known. For these values of t, we apply, $k_j = v \oplus t$.
(iii) **Strategy 3**: If the adversary knows the value v^*, t_{max} can be used to determine k_j with the help of equation, $k_j = v^* \oplus t_{max}$.

Although all three strategies can recover the round key, the first and second strategies require lesser faulty ciphertexts than the third method because it requires sufficient faulty ciphertexts to ensure t_{max} approaches 2^{b-1}. Moreover, to apply the third strategy, the knowledge of v^* is essential. That implies the adversary must know the exact positions of bits flipped due to fault injection. Whereas in the first and second strategy, the knowledge of the faulty element's index is sufficient; for example, the value of i is all that is needed to be known if the element $S[i]$ experiences the fault regardless of the number of flipped bits and their locations.

It is important to notice that all the strategies are applicable to the round structure shown in Fig. 1a. In summary, PFA can recover the round key k, which is added immediately after the substitution layer. As the permutation layer, P is linear, it does not change the distribution. However, since it diffuses the bits, the distribution of a b-bit word y_j does not reflect in corresponding c_j. Therefore, the relation $c_j = y_j \oplus k_j$ is rendered invalid when there is a permutation layer in between Sbox and AddRoundKey. Hence, to apply PFA on a typical SPN round structure depicted in Fig. 1b, the permutation layer's effect requires to be neutralized. In the next section, we discuss how PFA can be used to recover the round key if there is a permutation layer in between Sbox and AddRoundKey.

2.2 Applying PFA on Typical SPN Round Structure

The original PFA can recover the round key k, which is added immediately after the substitution layer. This section demonstrates how the PFA attack can be employed to extract the round key of an SPN round that has a permutation layer between the substitution layer and AddRoundKey operations. Consider a typical SPN round shown in Fig. 1b, the relation between y_j and c_j can be expressed as Eq. (2).

$$c_j = P(y_j) \oplus k_j; \quad \Rightarrow y_j = P^{-1}(c_j \oplus k_j) \tag{2}$$

Now, since P^{-1} is a bit-wise operation it can be distributed over XOR. So, the relation in Eq. (2) can be expressed as:

$$y_j = P^{-1}(c_j) \oplus P^{-1}(k_j); \quad \Rightarrow P^{-1}(c_j) = y_j \oplus P^{-1}(k_j) \tag{3}$$

Now, the relation between the probability distribution of the Sbox output, y_j and ciphertext, c_j can be expressed as in Eq. (4).

$$Pr[P^{-1}(c_j)] = Pr[y_j \oplus P^{-1}(k_j)] \tag{4}$$

The obtained key bits resulting from PFA strategies would be $P^{-1}(k_j)$. That means strategy equation would become as follows:

(i) **Strategy 1:** $P^{-1}(k_j) = v \oplus t_{min}$.
(ii) **Strategy 2:** $P^{-1}(k_j) = v \oplus t$.
(iii) **Strategy 3:** $P^{-1}(k_j) = v^* \oplus t_{max}$.

Once $P^{-1}(k_j)$ is obtained, the value of k_j can be computed by applying permutation operation, P as $k_j = P(P^{-1}(k_j))$.

3 ExtPFA: Extended PFA

Due to the ease of mounting persistent faults and subsequent analysis, the PFA technique drew significant attention from cryptography researchers. The underlying fault model can influence every round of the targeted cryptographic implementation. However, until now, its usage has been limited to the last round analysis only in the existing literature. In this section, we present an extension of the PFA analysis method that can recover keys in deeper rounds of a cipher to recover the full master key. In this work, we propose *extended PFA* on Substitution-bitPermutation Network (SbPN) class of block ciphers, which we refer to as ExtPFA. Similar to the original PFA, the proposed ExtPFA attack is also a *Ciphertext-only Attack*, which is weakest threat model in terms of attacker's capabilities, and hence is the most practical in real applications.

3.1   Fault Model

In the fault model, the adversary can control the physical environment in which the cipher executes. In the proposed work, the fault model assumes a round-iterated (rolled) implementation of the targeted cipher. In this case, the same faulty Sbox is invoked in each substitution operation in the cipher's rolled implementation. The Sbox is implemented as Look Up Table (LUT). The attacker can inject bit-flip faults in a Sbox entry. The affected entry remains faulty unless refreshed. The adversary can inject fault before the encryption operation starts. All subsequent computational iterations are performed with faulty Sbox. The attacker can control the fault's location and compute the new value of the faulty entry. The attacker can collect a sufficient number of faulty ciphertexts, which she can later use for analysis.

3.2   Description of the Attack

Figure 2 shows a generic SbPN cipher with R rounds. K_r and I_r denote the rth round key and intermediate data input to the rth round, respectively. Assuming the LUT implementation of Sbox, we consider the threat model in which the adversary injects fault in only one entry of the Sbox, generating faulty ciphertext C'. As a result, the value of the ith element, $S[i]$ changes from v to v^*, i.e., $S[i] = v$ changes to $S'[i] = v^*$ under fault injection, where S and S' denote original and faulty Sbox mappings, respectively. Note that since all possible output values of S are equiprobable, the value v^* must be present in mapping of S before fault injection. Suppose it is element j, i.e., $S[j] = v^*$, so in faulty Sbox S', v^* appears twice, i.e., $S'[i] = S'[j] = v^*$. The faulty Sbox S' is invoked in the substitution operation of each round $r \in \{1, \ldots, R\}$.

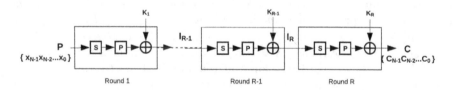

Fig. 2. A generic SPN cipher

To recover K_{R-1}, we first retrieve final round key K_R by using the method discussed in Sect. 2.2. We then partially decrypt (only the final round R) the faulty ciphertext C' using the recovered key K_R and obtain I_R as a result of decryption. Here I_R is the intermediate state between the rounds R and $(R-1)$. As we are using faulty ciphertext C' in decryption, the obtained intermediate state, I_R is also faulty, and so we denote it as I'_R.

As mentioned above, the value of $S[i]$ becomes v^* after fault injection, i.e., for faulty Sbox, $S'[i] = v^* = S[j]$. Thus, during the partial decryption (of last round R), the probability of occurrence of value v^* increases as compared to fault-free condition, and that of value v decreases to zero at the input of inverse

Sbox operation, S^{-1}. Consequently, the intermediate state, $I'_R = S^{-1}[P^{-1}(C' \oplus K_R)]$ has more occurrences of the value j and no occurrence of i. This leads to ambiguity or inexactness in deciding whether the value j is the actual value or a result due to the injected fault, $S'[i] = v^*$. Hence, a value j in I'_R may be a false value and so leads to *ambiguous words* during the analysis of penultimate round, $(R - 1)$. We call this false value j as **faulty word**.

A *b-bit word*, w is called **ambiguous** *if it involves an ambiguous bit coming from a faulty word j. Note that all the b bits in a faulty word are not ambiguous; only the bits in j differing from the corresponding bits in i are ambiguous.* Figure 4 illustrates the idea of *faulty word, ambiguous bit, ambiguous word*, and their effect during analysis with an example. In this example, values of i, j, v, and v^* are $0x2$, $0x3$, $0xD$, and $0x5$, respectively. This implies $S'[2] = S'[3] = S[3] = 5$. Consequently, during analysis, the value $0xD$ never occurs at the input of inverse substitution layer, S^{-1}. Henceforth, the value $0x2$ never appears at the output of S^{-1}; instead, the value $0x3$ appears more frequently than its actual frequency during encryption. In this case, every occurrence of the value $0x3$ in intermediate text I'_r between rounds $(r - 1)$ and r, is a *faulty word*.

Even though we need I'_R to be faulty so that we can obtain the biased distribution and analyze the penultimate round to recover K_{R-1}, the presence of *ambiguous words* is undesirable as it may influence the distribution and mislead in the key recovery process. Therefore, the hindrance due to the faulty substitution layer of round R needs to be overcome by discarding *ambiguous words* from the analysis of round $(R-1)$. In the next section, we present a method for locating ambiguous bits and the corresponding ambiguous words in round $(R - 1)$.

3.3   Identifying Locations of *ambiguous words*

Suppose, the faulty intermediate state between rounds R and $(R - 1)$, denoted as I'_R, can be expressed in w, b-bit words as: $I'_R = \{I'_{R_{w-1}}, I'_{R_{w-2}}, \ldots, I'_{R_0}\}$, where each word I'_{R_l}, $0 \le l \le w - 1$, can be expressed as, $I'_{R_l} = \{e_{b-1}, e_{b-2}, \ldots, e_0\}$. Assume, $M = \{m_{b-1}, m_{b-2}, \ldots, m_0\}$ is a b-bit word, and $Y = \{Y_{w-1}, Y_{w-2}, \ldots, Y_0\}$ is the input at the inverse of substitution layer, S^{-1} at round $(R - 1)$. The ambiguous bits and the corresponding *ambiguous words* during analysis of round $(R - 1)$ can be identified as follows. The value of M can be computed as,

$$M = i \oplus j ; \quad S'[i] = S'[j] = S[j] = v^* \tag{5}$$

For each pair (l, q), where $(I'_{R_l} = j)$ and $(m_q = 1)$ the index of an ambiguous bit in I'_R, denoted as $\mathcal{A}_{lq}$ can be computed as,

$$\mathcal{A}_{lq} = l \cdot b + q \tag{6}$$

This implies that a bit at position $\mathcal{A}_{lq}$ in I'_R is ambiguous and should be discarded during analysis of round $(R - 1)$. The position of the ambiguous bit in Y, represented as Ψ, is computed as follows,

$$\Psi = P^{-1}(\mathcal{A}_{lq}) \tag{7}$$

Hence, Y_Ψ is an ambiguous bit in Y. The location of the corresponding *ambiguous word* Y_w can be found as in Eq. (8). Similarly, of the *ambiguous words* in Y can be identified.

$$w = \Psi/b \tag{8}$$

3.4   Analysis

As mentioned above, Y is the input at the inverse of substitution layer, S^{-1} at round $(R-1)$, it can be expressed as

$$Y = P^{-1}(I'_R \oplus K_{R-1}) \tag{9}$$

Since Eq. (9) is similar to Eq. (2), the PFA analysis discussed in section 2.2 is applicable on Y as follows. In Eq. (9), as P^{-1} is a bit-wise operation; it distributes over XOR operation.

$$Y = P^{-1}(I'_R) \oplus P^{-1}(K_{R-1}); \quad \Rightarrow P^{-1}(I'_R) = Y \oplus P^{-1}(K_{R-1}) \tag{10}$$

The distribution probability of intermediate text is related to the probability of $(Y \oplus P^{-1}(K_{R-1}))$ as follows:

$$Pr[P^{-1}(I'_{R_j})] = Pr[Y_j \oplus P^{-1}(K_{R-1})] \tag{11}$$

The distribution probability of jth word of I'_R is denoted as $Pr[P^{-1}(I'_{R_j})]$, and can be computed statistically, similar to the computation of $Pr[P^{-1}(c_j)]$ for last round. But a it requires a modification that the identified *ambiguous words* in Y should not be considered while computing t_{min} and t_{max}. In this way, the penultimate round key K_{R-1} can be recovered using ExtPFA. The same procedure can be used to recover K_{R-2} with the help of recovered keys K_{R-1} and K_R.

3.5   An Example

In this section, we demonstrate the proposed ExtPFA approach through an example. Consider, a 16-bit SbPN cipher with R rounds, where each round performs following three operations in the same order:

- *SubNibble*: A non-linear substitution layer which divides the cipher state in w, 4 bit words. Then a bijective Sbox S is applied on each nibble. S is shown in Table 1.
- *Permute*: A linear layer that applies following P operation on each bit.
  $P(i) = (i \ggg 6) \, mod \, 16, \quad \forall i \in \{0, 1, \ldots, 15\}$.
- *AddKey*: A 16-bit round key is used in key whitening operation.

Table 1. Sbox S

x	0	1	2	3	4	5	6	7	8	9	A	B	C	D	E	F
$S(x)$	9	F	D	5	7	0	8	A	F	6	E	1	3	C	B	4

After injecting a persistent fault in Sbox S, suppose the value of the 3rd element of the Sbox changes from $0xD$ to $0x5$, i.e., $S[2] = D$ and $S'[2] = 5$, where S' denotes the faulty Sbox. Since fault is introduced in one element only, the other elements remain unaffected. This implies that value of $S'[3]$ is also $0x5$, thus resulting in two elements mapped to value $0x5$, and no element mapped to $0xD$ value, thereby disrupting the balancedness property of the Sbox. Therefore, for this example, values of i, and j, are $0x2$ and $0x3$, respectively, and so the value of M is "0001".

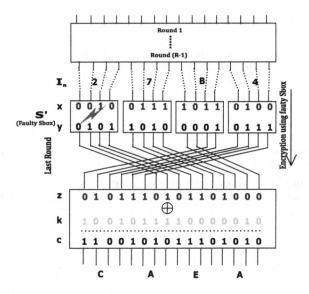

Fig. 3. Example to demonstrate the effect of faulty Sbox during last round of encryption

Figure 3 shows the operation of last round encryption with the faulty Sbox. For example, the 16-bit intermediate state (output of penultimate round) and round key are taken as $I_R = 0x27B4$, $K_R = 0x9782$, respectively, resulting in the faulty ciphertext $C' = 0xCAEA$. Figure 4 shows the effect of fault and identification of *ambiguous words* in penultimate and $(R-2)^{th}$ round analysis for the ciphertext $C' = 0xCAEA$, obtained as a result of faulty encryption in Fig. 3. The key addition layer is not considered in Fig. 4, as we need to compute $Pr[P^{-1}(I'_R)]$, or $Pr[P^{-1}(C)]$ for analysis, which does not involve XORing of the round key while collecting the statistics. In this example, the value of M is

"0001", which means the least significant bit (LSB) of every word with value $0x3$ in intermediate text I'_R, is *ambiguous*. These bits then propagate to certain words at the inverse substitution layer, S^{-1} of $(R-1)^{th}$ round, and therefore these words become *ambiguous words* in the analysis of $(R-1)^{th}$ round. It is apparent that the number of *ambiguous words* is directly proportional to the number of ambiguous bits. Hence, the Hamming weight of M, denoted by $HW(M)$, plays a vital role in the complexity analysis.

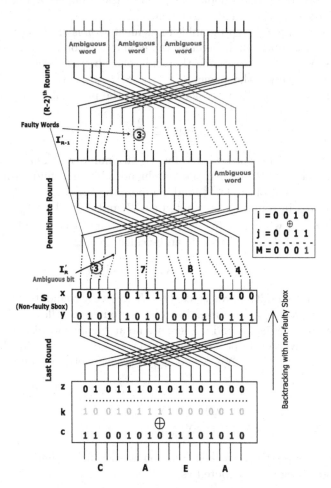

Fig. 4. Example to illustrate the process of locating faulty words, ambiguous bits, and corresponding ambiguous words along with propagation of fault during `ExtPFA` analysis of rounds $(R-1)$, and $(R-2)$. With the obtained ciphertext, the process involves backtracking through final round, penultimate round, and so on. Key whitening operations for rounds $(R-1)$ and $(R-2)$ are omitted in this figure as generation of faulty words and propagation of ambiguous bits remain unaffected.

3.6 Complexity Analysis

The complexity of the proposed ExtPFA has two components: *Computation complexity* and *number of ciphertexts required*. The *number of ciphertexts required* refers to the minimum number of ciphertexts needed during analysis to recover the round key. In this section, we discuss the relation between *number of ciphertexts required* (N_c), the number of ambiguous words (N_{aw}), the size of the Sbox (b), and the targeted round's depth (D_r), where the value of D_r is 1 for the last round, 2 for penultimate round, and so on.

Suppose the targeted cryptographic implementation is an N-bit block cipher, the size of Sbox is b-bits, and therefore the number of words N_w in cipher state is defined as $N_w = \frac{N}{b}$. We assume that only one Sbox element, $S'[i]$, is faulty and after fault injection the elements $S'[i] = S'[j] = v^*$, thus $M = (i \oplus j)$. In a faulty ciphertext or faulty intermediate state, the probability of a word to be faulty is,

$$Pr[W_f] = \frac{2}{2^b} \tag{12}$$

In a faulty word (a word with value j), the number of ambiguous bits is $h = HW(M)$. For a SbPN cipher, the h ambiguous bits in round r will influence h words in the analysis of $(r-1)^{th}$ round. Suppose the number of faulty words and ambiguous words in round r are denoted as N_f^r and N_{aw}^r. The N_{aw}^r ambiguous words of rth round will affect $(b \cdot N_{aw}^r)$ words in round $(r-1)$. The number of ambiguous words in $(r-1)^{th}$ round can be calculated as,

$$N_{aw}^{(r-1)} = (h \cdot N_f^r) + (b \cdot N_{aw}^r) \tag{13}$$

If the number of faulty words is fixed to N_f for every round, then the number of ambiguous words N_{aw}^r for a round can be computed as follows.

During analysis of last round r, there are no ambiguous words, i.e., $N_{aw}^r = 0$. However, for analysis of deeper rounds, $(r-1)$, $(r-2)$, and $(r-3)$, the number of ambiguous words, N_{aw}^{r-1}, N_{aw}^{r-2}, and N_{aw}^{r-3}, respectively, are computed as,

$$N_{aw}^{r-1} = (h \cdot N_f) + (b \cdot N_{aw}^r) = h \cdot N_f$$
$$N_{aw}^{r-2} = (h \cdot N_f) + (b \cdot N_{aw}^{r-1}) = (b+1) \cdot (h \cdot N_f)$$
$$N_{aw}^{r-3} = (h \cdot N_f) + (b \cdot N_{aw}^{r-2}) = (b^2 + b + 1) \cdot (h \cdot N_f)$$

Similarly, considering the recurrence relation for $(r-n)^{th}$ round, the number of ambiguous words can be computed as:

$$N_{aw}^{r-n} = (b^{n-1} + b^{n-2} + \cdots + b^2 + b + 1) \cdot (h \cdot N_f) = \left(\frac{b^n - 1}{b - 1}\right) \cdot (h \cdot N_f) \tag{14}$$

It can be observed that in the proposed ExtPFA approach, the same faulty ciphertexts can be reused for the analysis of different rounds and therefore, the total number of ciphertexts required to recover all round keys up-to the round $(r-n)$ is same as that required only for $(r-n)^{th}$ round. From Eq. (14), the number of ambiguous words, N_{aw}, grows exponentially on increasing the depth of the round, D_r. It can be deduced that the number of required ciphertexts, N_c, is directly proportional to the number of ambiguous words. Hence, *the required number of ciphertexts increases exponentially with round's depth*, i.e., $N_c \propto 2^{D_r}$.

Furthermore, as the number of ambiguous words is directly proportional to h, the Hamming distance between i and j, *the number of ciphertexts required increases exponentially with the Hamming distance between the indexes of the identical elements of the faulty Sbox*, i.e., $(N_c \propto 2^h)$. From attacker's perspective, the number of ambiguous words is dependent on two parameters: N_f and h. Therefore, to minimize the attack effort, i.e., for minimum value of N_c, the values of N_f and h should be minimum. In ciphertext-only attack setting, the attacker cannot change N_f, however, h is tunable. The minimum value of h is *one*, if i and j have a Hamming distance of 1, for example, $(i = 0100, j = 1100)$ and $(i = 0010, j = 0011)$. In this case, the number of ciphertexts required N_c, will be minimum.

3.7   Algorithm

Algorithm 1 describes a step-wise procedure of the proposed ExtPFA approach explained in the previous section.

3.8   Identifying Fault Location

The proposed ExtPFA approach assumes that the attacker knows the values of both v and v^*. The values of v and v^* can be determined through profiling due to the following fact: the PFA model targets altering entries in LUT implementation of Sbox. The fault is induced in a LUT entry through rowhammer technique [14]. Chakraborty et al. in [6] observed that the vulnerable locations within a page, are almost invariant.

Moreover, there are only 2^n possible fault locations, and for lightweight ciphers the value of $n \leq 8$. Hence, it is easy to mount divide-and-conquer analysis, and compute all 2^n keys while considering fault at each location with the assumption that only one LUT entry is faulty. Therefore, the identification of the fault location is not required.

4   ExtPFA: Case Study on GIFT Lightweight Cipher

In this section we show the working of ExtPFA on GIFT lightweight cipher. The GIFT cipher as described in [1] is provided below.

4.1   GIFT Cipher

GIFT is designed by Banik et al. and proposed in CHES 2017 [1]. It is one of the most energy-efficient lightweight ciphers. There are two variants of GIFT: GIFT-64 and GIFT-128, where 64 and 128 are block sizes with 28 and 40 rounds,

---

Algorithm 1: ExtPFA

Input:	C' - set of faulty ciphertexts
	N - size of the block cipher
	n - size of set C'
	b - size of Sbox is bXb
	v - original value of the faulty element
	v^* - faulty value of the faulty element
	d - depth of analysis; d=3 means compute upto $K_{(R-2)}$

Output: $K[d]$ - list of d keys

```
    /* Initialization                                                     */
 1  w ⟵ N/b ;                              // # words in a cipher state
 2  I' ⟵ φ ;                               // N-bit Intermediate state
 3  p ⟵ 2ᵇ ;                               // # possible values of a word
 4  Count[w][p] ⟵ {0} ;                            // Statistics
 5  K[d] ⟵ {0} ;                      // d round keys initialized to zero
 6  Aw ⟵ φ ;                              // set of ambiguous words
 7  Fw ⟵ φ ;                              // set of faulty words
 8  i ⟵ S⁻¹[v],     j ⟵ S⁻¹[v*],    M = i ⊕ j;
    /* Obtain keys in bottom-up order; starting from last round          */
 9  for r = 0 to (d − 1) do
10  |   for l = 0 to (n − 1) do
11  |   |   if (r == 0) then
12  |   |   |   I'[l] ⟵ C'[l] ;
13  |   |   end
14  |   |   else
15  |   |   |   I'[l] ⟵ S⁻¹[P⁻¹(C'[l] ⊕ K[r − 1])] ;
16  |   |   |   C'[l] ⟵ I'[l] ;                  // to be used in next round
17  |   |   |   IdentifyFaultyWords(Fw, I',v*) ;
18  |   |   |   IdentifyAmbiguousWords(Aw,Fw, b, M) ;
19  |   |   end
20  |   |   for k = 0 to (w − 1) do
21  |   |   |   if (j ∉ Aw) then
22  |   |   |   |   for q = 0 to (p − 1) do
23  |   |   |   |   |   if (I'[k] == q) then
24  |   |   |   |   |   |   Count[k][q] = Count[k][q] + 1 ;
25  |   |   |   |   |   |   break ;
26  |   |   |   |   |   end
27  |   |   |   |   end
28  |   |   |   end
29  |   |   end
30  |   |   if (exactly (p − 1) elements of Count[x] are nonzero, ∀x ∈ w) then
31  |   |   |   flag = 1 ;                  // No more ciphertexts are required
32  |   |   |   break ;
33  |   |   end
34  |   end
35  |   if ((flag == 0)) then
36  |   |   message("Insufficient data to obtain statistics") ;
37  |   |   return φ
38  |   end
39  |   K[r] ⟵ RecoverKey(Count,v, w, p) ;
40  |   return;
41  end
```

```
42  Function : IdentifyFaultyWords(F_w, I', v*)
43  |    j = S^{-1}[v*] ;
44  |    if (I' == j) then
45  |    |    F_w ⟵ F_w ∪ {j} ;
46  |    end
47  |    return;

48  Function : IdentifyAmbiguousWords(A_w, F_w, b, M)
49  |    T_{aw} ⟵ A_w ;
50  |    A_w ⟵ φ ;
51  |    for (f ∈ F_w) do
52  |    |    for m = 0 to (b − 1) do
53  |    |    |    if (M[m] == 1) then
54  |    |    |    |    Ψ ⟵ P^{-1}(f + m) ;
55  |    |    |    |    w ⟵ Ψ/b ;
56  |    |    |    |    A_w ⟵ A_w ∪ {w} ;
57  |    |    |    end
58  |    |    end
59  |    end
60  |    for (a ∈ T_{aw}) do
61  |    |    for m = 0 to (b − 1) do
62  |    |    |    Ψ ⟵ P^{-1}(a + m) ;
63  |    |    |    w ⟵ Ψ/b ;
64  |    |    |    A_w ⟵ A_w ∪ {w} ;
65  |    |    end
66  |    end
67  |    return;

68  Function : RecoverKey(Count, v, w, p)
       /* Find value of t_min and corresponding keyword in K          */
69  |    for j = 0 to (w − 1) do
70  |    |    for k = 0 to (p − 1) do
71  |    |    |    if (Count[j][k] == zero) then
72  |    |    |    |    t_min = k
73  |    |    |    |    break
74  |    |    |    end
75  |    |    end
76  |    |    K^{inv}[j] = v ⊕ t_min
77  |    end
78  |    K = P^{-1}(K^{inv}) ;          // invert permutation layer's effect
79  |    return K
```

respectively. Both variants use 128-bit key. The working of the cipher is as mentioned below.

Initialization: Input to the cipher is a tuple (S, K), where state S of the cipher is an n-bit plaintext $b_{n-1}b_{n-2} \ldots b_0$, where b_0 is the least significant bit. The cipher state S is divided into s 4-bit words $S = w_{s-1}\|w_{s-2}\| \ldots \|w_0$, where s $= 16, 32$. K is a 128-bit key expressed as $K = k_7\|k_6\| \ldots \|k_0$ as the key state, where k_i is 16-bit long keyword.

Round Function: A round of GIFT is an SPN structure with following operations:

1. **SubCells** - The operation SubCells transforms each nibble x of the cipher state using $GS(x)$ mapping shown in table 2. $GS(x)$ is a bijective 4-bit Sbox. Both the versions of GIFT use the same Sbox described in hexadecimal notation in Table 2.

Table 2. GIFT Sbox

x	0	1	2	3	4	5	6	7	8	9	A	B	C	D	E	F
$GS(x)$	1	A	4	C	6	F	3	9	2	D	B	7	5	0	8	E

2. **PermBits** - This transformation is applied at bit level. It re-positions the ith bit of cipher state to $P(i)$. The details of bit permutation specifications of GIFT-64 and GIFT-128 can be found in [1].
3. **AddRoundKey** - This transformation consists of two sub-transformations: *round key addition* and *round constants addition*. An $\frac{n}{2}$-bit round key RK is extracted from the key state, it is further partitioned into two s-bit words $RK = U\|V = u_{s-1} \ldots u_0\|v_{s-1} \ldots v_0$, where s = 16; 32 for GIFT-64 and GIFT-128 respectively.
   (a) Round Key addition: Round key bits are added as follows -
   GIFT-64: $b_{4i+1} \leftarrow b_{4i+1} \oplus u_i, \quad b_{4i} \leftarrow b_{4i} \oplus v_i, \quad \forall \in \{0, \ldots, 15\}$.
   GIFT-128: $b_{4i+2} \leftarrow b_{4i+2} \oplus u_i, \quad b_{4i+1} \leftarrow b_{4i+1} \oplus v_i, \quad \forall \in \{0, \ldots, 31\}$.
   (b) Round Constants addition: A single bit "1" and a 6-bit round constant $C = c_5 c_4 c_3 c_2 c_1 c_0$ are XORed into the cipher state using equations below[1].

$$b_{n-1} \leftarrow b_{n-1} \oplus 1;$$
$$b_{23} \leftarrow b_{23} \oplus c_5; b_{19} \leftarrow b_{19} \oplus c_4; b_{15} \leftarrow b_{15} \oplus c_3;$$
$$b_{11} \leftarrow b_{11} \oplus c_2; b_7 \leftarrow b_7 \oplus c_1; b_3 \leftarrow b_3 \oplus c_0 :$$

Key Schedule: For both variants of GIFT the key schedule is the same with a difference in round key extraction. For GIFT-64, two 16-bit words of the key state are extracted as the round key $RK = U\|V$, where, $U \leftarrow k_1$; $V \leftarrow k_0$. Similarly, In GIFT-128, four 16-bit words of the key state are extracted as round key as $RK = U\|V$, where, $U \leftarrow k_5\|k_4$; $V \leftarrow k_1\|k_0$. The key state is then updated as: $k_7\|k_6\| \ldots \|k_1\|k_0 \leftarrow k_1 \ggg 2\|k_0 \ggg 12\| \ldots \|k_3\|k_2$, where $\ggg i$ is an i bits right rotation within a 16-bit word.

4.2 Attack on GIFT Cipher

Both versions of GIFT lightweight cipher, GIFT-64 and GIFT-128, use 128-bit master key as an initial key-state, which is updated by a simple key schedule after every round. As a round key, GIFT-128 uses 64-bits out of the 128-bits

---

[1] For exhaustive list of round constants please refer [1].

of the updated key state. The attacker needs to recover last and penultimate round keys to retrieve the entire master key as these rounds use disjoint sets of the master key bits. Therefore, we apply `ExtPFA` with the goal of recovering round keys up to the depth 2, i.e., K_{40} and K_{39}. On the other hand, a round key in GIFT-64 is of size 32-bits. Similar to the GIFT-128, the last four round keys are disjoint. Thus, to extract the full master key, an attacker has to apply ExtPFA up to the depth 4. Hence, the goal here is to recover round keys up to the depth 4, i.e., K_{28}, K_{27}, K_{26}, K_{25}. We simulate our proposed ExtPFA attack on C-implementations of both of the GIFT versions.

As both versions of GIFT use the same Sbox, we discuss attacks on both versions simultaneously. For the experiments, we considered that the *fourth* element of the GIFT Sbox experiences a one bit-flip fault at MSB. This implies that the most significant bit of v is flipped from one to zero, i.e., $S[2] = S'[2] = S'[3] = 0x4$, thus $i = 0x3$, $j = 0x2$, $v = 0xC$ and $v^* = 0x4$. For recovering the key, we use the first strategy where, $Pr[y = v] = 0$; as mentioned in Sect. 2.2. To validate our approach, we run 1000 attacks using random plaintexts and keys, for each experiment. We conducted experiments on GIFT-64 to analyze the impact of *depth* on N_c (the required number of ciphertexts). We performed experiments on GIFT-128 to analyze the relationship between N_c and h, the *Hamming distance* between i and j, such that $S'[i] = S'[j]$.

5   Results

5.1   Success Rate

We performed experiments to verify the success rate of the proposed approach on deeper rounds of both GIFT versions.

GIFT-128: Figure 5 depicts the success rate of proposed ExtPFA approach on last and penultimate rounds of GIFT-128. Our approach could recover entire master key in at most 400 ciphertexts with 100% success rate, for Hamming distance of value *one* where, $i = 0x3$, $j = 0x2$.

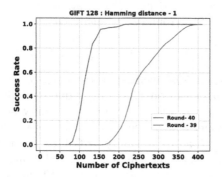

Fig. 5. Success rate of proposed ExtPFA approach on last two rounds of GIFT-128 cipher.

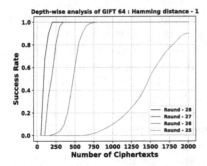

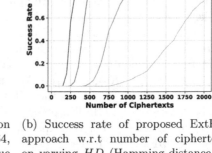

(a) Success rate of proposed approach on rounds 28, 27, 26, and 25 of GIFT-64, w.r.t number of ciphertexts when value of HD (Hamming-distance between indexes of two identical elements of faulty Sbox) is fixed to value 1.

(b) Success rate of proposed ExtPFA approach w.r.t number of ciphertexts on varying HD (Hamming-distance between indexes of two identical elements of faulty Sbox) for 39th round of GIFT-128.

Fig. 6. Success rate of proposed ExtPFA approach on GIFT-64 and GIFT-128

GIFT-64: Figure 6a shows the round-wise success rate of our approach on GIFT-64. For this experiment, we run 1000 attacks for each round with fixed value of *Hamming distance* to *one* where, $i = 0x3$, $j = 0x2$. The results report that the round keys of rounds 28, 27, and 26 can be recovered with a 100% success rate, in less than 110, 300, and 750 ciphertexts, respectively. For the 25th round, 90% of the attacks recovered the round key in 2000 ciphertexts. Hence, using ExtPFA approach the full master key of GIFT-64 can be recovered in less than 2000 ciphertexts with 90% success rate. This experiment also demonstrates the effect of round's depth on the required number of ciphertexts.

5.2 Relation Between Depth of Round and Number of Ciphertexts

Figure 6a also indicates that the required number of ciphertexts, N_c, grows exponentially with respect to depth. The relation can be expressed as in Eq. (15), where d is depth of the round to be analyzed.

$$N_c \propto 2^d \tag{15}$$

This is due to the exponential increase in the number of ambiguous words at each round. Since ambiguous words are a byproduct of faulty words, the underlying cause of exponential growth is the number of faulty words. Empirically, we observed that on average, 15% of the total number of words are faulty at each round, i.e., between 4 to 5 words are faulty for GIFT-128 and that of 2 to 3 words for GIFT-64. This empirical value can be formulated as in Eq. (16), where N_{fw}, $Pr[W_f]$, and W denote the approximate number of faulty words, probability of a word to be faulty, and total number of words in the cipher state, respectively.

The values of W are 16 and 32 for GIFT-64 and GIFT-128, respectively. The value of $Pr[W_f]$ using Eq. (12), is $(\frac{2}{16})$ for both versions.

$$N_{fw} \approx Pr[W_f] \cdot W \tag{16}$$

5.3 Relation Between Number of Ciphertexts and Hamming-Distance Between Indices of Two Identical Elements in Faulty Sbox

As discussed in Sect. 3.6, the Hamming distance $h = HD(i,j)$, where i is index of v and j is index of v^* in Sbox S, affects the number of ambiguous words according to the Eq. (14). The impact of h on N_c can be represented as:

$$N_c \propto 2^h \tag{17}$$

We performed 1000 attacks on the penultimate round of GIFT-128, with varying Hamming distance to determine the relation between the Hamming distance h and the required number of ciphertexts, N_c. We found that the empirical results validate the proposition in Eq. (14), which is shown in Fig. 6b.

The results are summarized in Tables 3a and 3b, where N_c is the required number of ciphertexts averaged over 1000 attacks, H is Hamming distance between indexes of identical elements in faulty Sbox, and D is depth of round; $D = 1$ indicates last round.

Table 3. Summary of experiments performed on GIFT-128 and GIFT-64

GIFT-128			
D	2	2	2	2
H	1	2	3	4
N_c	230	420	774	1765

GIFT-64			
D	1	2	3	4
H	1	1	1	1
N_c	85	190	480	1500

(a) Effect of **H** (Hamming-distance between indexes of two identical elements in faulty Sbox) on **N_c** (number of ciphertexts required) for 39th round of GIFT-128.

(b) Effect of **D** (round's depth) on **N_c** (number of ciphertexts required) in GIFT-64 when Hamming-distance is fixed to 1.

5.4 Comparison with Previous Attacks on GIFT

The comparisons of our results with existing fault-attacks on GIFT cipher are summarized in Table 4, where SCA stand for side-channel analysis.

Table 4. Comparison with existing fault-analysis on GIFT

Version	Analysis Type	Attack #round	Complexity	Key-bits recovered	Source
GIFT-64	ExtPFA	25, 26, 27, 28	1500 ciphertexts	128	Sect. 4
GIFT-128	SCA	40	6–9 faults	64	[12]
GIFT-128	ExtPFA	39, 40	1765 ciphertexts	128	Sect. 4

6   Applicability on AES-Like Constructions

The permutation layer in AES round operation consists of *ShiftRows* and *Mix-Columns* operations, instead of bit permutations. The *ShiftRows* operation does not affect the analysis but the *MixColumns* operation is based on diffusion matrix i.e. MDS matrix. The diffusion matrix-based permutation layer contributes to a higher diffusion rate than a bit-permutation based layer, which consequently increases attack efforts to recover the secret material. This holds true for the proposed approach as well. Moreover, it is also formally proved that the *Mix-Columns* operation cancels all biases created by *SubByte* operations [5]. However, the DRPFA method described in [6] employs partial decryption up to the inverse *MixColumns* of the target round to exploit bias at the S-Box outputs, which presents a future scope of work.

7   Countermeasures

The common countermeasures used against fault attacks such as redundant computation, randomization, etc. do not work on attacks based on persistent faults because it is persistent and targets Look-Up Table (LUT) implementation of Sbox. PFA class of attacks can be throttled if Sbox is not stored in memory and computed on demand. That means, to avoid PFA class of attacks, a bit-sliced implementation should be preferred over LUT implementation of the Sbox. Also, as per the analysis presented in [7] by Chakraborty et al., these types of fault attacks can be thwarted using Error-Correcting-Codes (ECC) enabled systems. However, the ECC has a limitation on the number of bits of error it can detect and correct. Since the number of bit-flips does not affect much the performance of PFA attacks, a higher number of bits of error can be introduced to bypass the ECC countermeasure.

8   Conclusion

In this paper, we proposed an extension of the PFA attack that can recover deeper round keys of SbPN block ciphers, wherein the last round key alone can not determine the entire master key. The proposed ExtPFA approach takes advantage of the persistent nature of fault that affects every round. We also analyzed the proposed approach over various parameters, such as relations of Hamming distance and depth of analysis with required number of ciphertexts. As a use-case, we demonstrate the attack on C-implementations of both versions of GIFT cipher to perform complete key recovery. We validated the proposed ExtPFA attack and recovered the round keys of the last four rounds of GIFT-64 and the last two rounds of GIFT-128 ciphers. We also analyzed the success rate of our approach on both the versions in two dimensions: *Depth-wise* and *Hamming distance-wise*. We observed that the number of ciphertexts required to recover the round key increases exponentially as we move deeper from the final round. Furthermore, the number of required ciphertexts to recover the key increases exponentially with Hamming distance between indexes of two identical elements in faulty Sbox. We expect that our work will contribute to a more comprehensive understanding of SPN-based lightweight cryptosystems' security against persistent fault analysis.

References

1. Banik, S., Pandey, S.K., Peyrin, T., Sasaki, Yu., Sim, S.M., Todo, Y.: GIFT: a small present. In: Fischer, W., Homma, N. (eds.) CHES 2017. LNCS, vol. 10529, pp. 321–345. Springer, Cham (2017). https://doi.org/10.1007/978-3-319-66787-4_16
2. Biham, E., Shamir, A.: Differential fault analysis of secret key cryptosystems. In: Kaliski, B.S. (ed.) CRYPTO 1997. LNCS, vol. 1294, pp. 513–525. Springer, Heidelberg (1997). https://doi.org/10.1007/BFb0052259
3. Boneh, D., DeMillo, R.A., Lipton, R.J.: On the importance of checking cryptographic protocols for faults. In: Fumy, W. (ed.) EUROCRYPT 1997. LNCS, vol. 1233, pp. 37–51. Springer, Heidelberg (1997). https://doi.org/10.1007/3-540-69053-0_4
4. Caforio, A., Banik, S.: A study of persistent fault analysis. In: Bhasin, S., Mendelson, A., Nandi, M. (eds.) SPACE 2019. LNCS, vol. 11947, pp. 13–33. Springer, Cham (2019). https://doi.org/10.1007/978-3-030-35869-3_4
5. Carré, S., Guilley, S., Rioul, O.: Persistent fault analysis with few encryptions. IACR Cryptol. ePrint Arch. **2020**, 671 (2020)
6. Chakraborty, A., Bhattacharya, S., Saha, S., Mukhopadhyay, D.: Explframe: exploiting page frame cache for fault analysis of block ciphers. In: 2020 Design, Automation & Test in Europe Conference & Exhibition, DATE 2020, Grenoble, France, 9–13 March 2020, pp. 1303–1306. IEEE (2020)
7. Chakraborty, A., Bhattacharya, S., Saha, S., Mukhopdhyay, D.: Rowhammer induced intermittent fault attack on ECC-hardened memory. Cryptology ePrint Archive, Report 2020/380 (2020)
8. Fuhr, T., Jaulmes, É., Lomné, V., Thillard, A.: Fault attacks on AES with faulty ciphertexts only. In: 2013 Workshop on Fault Diagnosis and Tolerance in Cryptography, Los Alamitos, CA, USA, 20 August 2013, pp. 108–118 (2013)
9. Gruber, M., Probst, M., Tempelmeier, M.: Persistent fault analysis of OCB, DEOXYS and COLM. In: 2019 Workshop on Fault Diagnosis and Tolerance in Cryptography, FDTC 2019, Atlanta, GA, USA, 24 August 2019, pp. 17–24. IEEE (2019)
10. Kim, Y., et al.: Flipping bits in memory without accessing them: an experimental study of DRAM disturbance errors. In: ACM/IEEE 41st International Symposium on Computer Architecture, ISCA 2014, Minneapolis, MN, USA, 14–18 June 2014, pp. 361–372. IEEE Computer Society (2014)
11. Pan, J., Zhang, F., Ren, K., Bhasin, S.: One fault is all it needs: breaking higher-order masking with persistent fault analysis. In: Teich, J., Fummi, F. (eds.) Design, Automation & Test in Europe Conference & Exhibition, DATE 2019, Florence, Italy, 25–29 March 2019, pp. 1–6. IEEE (2019)
12. Patranabis, S., Datta, N., Jap, D., Breier, J., Bhasin, S., Mukhopadhyay, D.: SCADFA: combined SCA+DFA attacks on block ciphers with practical validations. IEEE Trans. Comput. **68**(10), 1498–1510 (2019)

13. Tunstall, M., Mukhopadhyay, D., Ali, S.: Differential fault analysis of the advanced encryption standard using a single fault. In: Ardagna, C.A., Zhou, J. (eds.) WISTP 2011. LNCS, vol. 6633, pp. 224–233. Springer, Heidelberg (2011). https://doi.org/10.1007/978-3-642-21040-2_15

14. Zhang, F., et al.: Persistent fault analysis on block ciphers. IACR Trans. Cryptogr. Hardw. Embed. Syst. **2018**(3), 150–172 (2018)

15. Zhang, F., Xu, G., Yang, B., Liang, Z., Ren, K.: Theoretical analysis of persistent fault attack. Sci. China Inf. Sci. **63**(3), 1–3 (2020). https://doi.org/10.1007/s11432-018-9818-y

16. Zhang, F., et al.: Persistent fault attack in practice. IACR Trans. Cryptogr. Hardw. Embed. Syst. **2020**(2), 172–195 (2020)

17. Zhao, X., Guo, S., Zhang, F., Wang, T., Shi, Z., Ji, K.: Algebraic differential fault attacks on LED using a single fault injection. IACR Cryptol. ePrint Arch. **2012**, 347 (2012)

On Configurable SCA Countermeasures Against Single Trace Attacks for the NTT

A Performance Evaluation Study over Kyber and Dilithium on the ARM Cortex-M4

Prasanna Ravi[1,2]([✉]), Romain Poussier[1], Shivam Bhasin[1], and Anupam Chattopadhyay[1,2]

[1] Temasek Laboratories, Nanyang Technological University, Singapore, Singapore
{rpoussier,sbhasin}@ntu.edu.sg
[2] School of Computer Science and Engineering, Nanyang Technological University, Singapore, Singapore
{prasanna.ravi,anupam}@ntu.edu.sg

Abstract. The Number Theoretic Transform (NTT) is a critical sub-block used in several structured lattice-based schemes, including Kyber and Dilithium, which are finalist candidates in the NIST's standardization process for post-quantum cryptography. The NTT was shown to be susceptible to single trace side-channel attacks by Primas et al. in CHES 2017 and Pessl et al. in Latincrypt 2019 who demonstrated full key recovery from single traces on the ARM Cortex-M4 microcontroller. However, the cost of deploying suitable countermeasures to protect the NTT from these attacks on the same target platform has not yet been studied. In this work, we propose novel shuffling and masking countermeasures to protect the NTT from such single trace attacks. Firstly, we exploit arithmetic properties of *twiddle constants* used within the NTT computation to propose efficient and generic masking strategies for the NTT with configurable SCA resistance. Secondly, we also propose new variants of the shuffling countermeasure with varying granularity for the NTT. We perform a detailed comparative evaluation of the runtime performances for our proposed countermeasures within open source implementations of Kyber and Dilithium from the *pqm4* library on the ARM Cortex-M4 microcontroller. Our proposed countermeasures yield a reasonable runtime overhead in the range of **7%–78%** across all procedures of Kyber, while the runtime overheads are much more pronounced for Dilithium, ranging from **12%–197%** for the key generation procedure and **32%–490%** for the signing procedure.

1 Introduction

The NIST standardization process for post-quantum cryptography is currently in its third and final round with seven finalist candidates and eight alternate candidates [2] for Public Key Encryption (PKE), Key Establishment Mechanisms (KEM) and Digital Signature (DS) schemes. While criteria such as theoretical

© Springer Nature Switzerland AG 2020
L. Batina et al. (Eds.): SPACE 2020, LNCS 12586, pp. 123–146, 2020.
https://doi.org/10.1007/978-3-030-66626-2_7

post-quantum (PQ) security guarantees, implementation cost and performance were key selection criterion for the first two rounds, resistance against implementation attacks such as side-channel attacks is also being increasingly considered as an important criteria for the final round. In fact, NIST also explicitly states that it "hopes to collect more information about the costs of implementing these algorithms in a way that provides resistance to such attacks" [2].

Five out of the seven finalist candidates derive their hardness from hard problems over structured lattices. Side-channel Analysis (SCA) and Fault Injection Analysis (FIA) of structured lattice-based schemes has received considerable attention with several works on practical attacks [25,27,28] as well as protected implementations [23,31,33]. While most reported works on protected implementations focus on Differential Power Analysis (DPA) style attacks [23,31] that operate over multiple traces, they offer very little or no protection against the more powerful single trace attacks [25,27]. Of particular interest is the attack of Primas *et al.* [27] in CHES 2017, which is the first single trace attack on lattice-based schemes targeting the Number Theoretic Transform (NTT), a critical sub-block used for polyomial multiplication in several lattice-based schemes including finalist candidates such as Kyber KEM [3] and Dilithium DS [8]. This attack required about 1 million templates, but Pessl *et al.* [25] reduced the requirement to just 213 templates for full key recovery using a single trace on the ARM Cortex-M4 microcontroller. They propose *shuffling the order of operations* as the only concrete countermeasure against this attack. However, the runtime overhead due to the shuffling countermeasure on the ARM Cortex-M4 is not known while the possibility of employing randomization-based countermeasures has not yet been studied.

We in this work, propose novel shuffling and masking countermeasures to protect the NTT against the aforementioned single trace attacks and evaluate their runtime performance on the ARM Cortex-M4 microcontroller. As a *first contribution*, we utilize the efficient arithmetic properties of the special *twiddle constants* used within the NTT to mask the atomic operations of the NTT and subsequently build upon the same to construct a generic masked NTT with configurable SCA resistance. As a *second contribution*, we also propose several novel variants of the shuffling countermeasure with varying granularity for the NTT. As a *third contribution*, we practically evaluate the runtime performance of our shuffling and masking countermeasures when integrated within open source implementations of Kyber and Dilithium scheme available in the public *pqm4* library on the ARM Cortex-M4 microcontroller [15]. While our countermeasures yield a reasonable overhead in the range of **7%–78%** across all procedures of Kyber, the performance impact is much more pronounced for Dilithium with overheads in the range of **12%–197%** over its key generation procedure and **32%–490%** over the signing procedure.

Availability of Software. All softwares utilized for this work is placed into public domain. They are available at https://github.com/PRASANNA-RAVI/Configurable_SCA_Countermeasures_for_NTT.

2   Preliminaries

Notation: For a prime number q, we denote by $\mathbb{Z}_q$ the field of integers modulo q. The polynomial ring $\mathbb{Z}_q[x]/\phi(x)$ is denoted as R_q where $\phi(x) = x^n + 1$ is a cyclotomic polynomial with n being a power of 2. Multiplication of two polynomials $\mathbf{a}, \mathbf{b} \in R_q$ is denoted as $\mathbf{a} \cdot \mathbf{b} \in R_q$. Matrices and vectors of polynomials in R_q are referred to as *modules* and are denoted using bold letters viz. $\mathbf{a} \in R_q^{k \times l}, \mathbf{b} \in R_q^l$. Point-wise multiplication of two polynomials $\mathbf{a}$ and $\mathbf{b} \in R_q$ is denoted as $\mathbf{c} = \mathbf{a} \circ \mathbf{b}$ while scalar multiplication of two integers a and $b \in \mathbb{Z}_q$ is denoted as $c = a \cdot b$.

Lattice-Based Cryptography: Most of the efficient lattice-based cryptographic schemes derive their hardness from two average-case hard problems, known as the Ring Learning With Errors problem (RLWE) and the Ring Short Integer Solutions problem (RSIS) [20]. Both the problems reduce to provably worst-case hard problems over structured ideal lattices. Given a public key $(\mathbf{a}, \mathbf{t}) \in (R_q, R_q)$, an RLWE attacker is asked to find two small polynomials $\mathbf{s}_1, \mathbf{s}_2 \in R_q$ with $\mathbf{s}_1, \mathbf{s}_2 \in S_\eta$ such that $\mathbf{t} = \mathbf{a} \cdot \mathbf{s}_1 + \mathbf{s}_2$. Given m uniformly random elements $\mathbf{a}_i \in R_q$, an RSIS attacker is asked to find out a non-zero vector $\mathbf{z}$ with a small norm $\mathbf{z} \in S_\eta^m$ such that $\sum_i^m \mathbf{a}_i \cdot \mathbf{z}_i = 0 \in R_q$. The more generalized versions of these problems known as Module-LWE (MLWE) and Module-SIS (MSIS) respectively deal with computations over the space $R_q^{k \times \ell} = \mathbb{Z}_q^{k \times \ell}[X]/(X^n + 1)$ for $k, l > 1$ (as opposed to R_q for their ring variants) and also provide better security guarantees compared to their corresponding ring variants [17]. Any change in the security of a scheme (based on either MLWE or MSIS) can be obtained by simply changing the module dimensions (k, ℓ) without any change to the underlying implementation, thus warranting very minimal changes from a implementer's perspective.

2.1   Number Theoretic Transform:

The polynomial multiplication operation in the ring R_q is considered to be one of the most computationally expensive operations in structured lattice-based schemes. Hence, there have been several reported works devoted to increasing the efficiency and performance of polynomial multiplication in structured lattice-based schemes [5,26]. Among the many known techniques for polynomial multiplication such as the schoolbook multiplier, Toom-Cook [6] and Karatsuba [16], the Number Theoretic Transform (NTT) based polynomial multiplication is one of the most widely adopted techniques in several lattice-based schemes [7], owing to its quasilinear run-time complexity ($\mathcal{O}(nlog(n))$ time) in the degree of the polynomial and a compact design. The NTT is nothing but a bijective mapping from one polynomial to another in the same operating ring. Considering an $(n - 1)$ degree polynomial $\mathbf{p}$ in R_q, the polynomial $\mathbf{p}$ in the *normal* domain is mapped to its alternate representation $\hat{\mathbf{p}}$ in the *NTT domain* through the NTT as follows:

$$\hat{\mathbf{p}}_j = \sum_{i=0}^{n-1} \mathbf{p}_i \cdot \omega^{i \cdot j}$$

where $j \in [0, n-1]$ and ω is the nth root of unity in the operating ring $\mathbb{Z}_q$. There is also a corresponding inverse operation named Inverse NTT (denoted as INTT) that maps $\hat{\mathbf{p}}$ in the NTT domain back to $\mathbf{p}$ in the normal domain. The use of NTT requires to choose an NTT-friendly polynomial ring R_q such that the integer ring $\mathbb{Z}_q$ consists of either the $2n^{\text{th}}$ or n^{th} root of unity which we denote as ω and ψ respectively with $\psi^2 = \omega$. Schemes such as Kyber, Dilithium and NewHope operate in the NTT friendly anti-cyclic polynomial ring $R_q = \mathbb{Z}_q[x]/(x^n + 1)$. Powers of ψ and ω (i.e) $t = \psi^i$ for $i \in [0, 2n-1]$ or $t = \omega^i$ for $i \in [0, n-1]$ denoted as *twiddle constants* are used in the NTT computation. The multiplication of $\mathbf{z} = \mathbf{x} \times \mathbf{y} \in R_q$ can be efficiently done using the NTT as:

$$\mathbf{z} = \text{INTT}(\text{NTT}(\mathbf{x}) \circ \text{NTT}(\mathbf{y})).$$

The NTT of an $n-1$ degree polynomial with n coefficients can be recursively broken down into p smaller NTTs, which can be further broken down into atomic operations called *butterfly* operations which themselves are NTTs of size r with $r = 2$ being the most common choice.

$$c = a + b \cdot w \qquad\qquad\qquad c = a + b$$
$$d = a - b \cdot w, \qquad (1) \qquad\qquad d = (a - b) \cdot w, \qquad (2)$$

Each butterfly operation takes two inputs $(a, b) \in \mathbb{Z}_q^2$ and a known twiddle constant w (either a power of ψ or ω) and produces two outputs $(c, d) \in \mathbb{Z}_q^2$. There are two types of butterfly operations: (1) Cooley-Tukey (CT) butterfly [7] (Eq. 1) and (2) Gentleman-Sande (GS) butterfly [10] (Eq.2). Both the butterfly structures can be interchangeably used to perform both the NTT and INTT operation. The NTT/INTT of size n is typically computed in stages $\log(n)$ stages with each stage consisting of $n/2$ butterfly operations. Refer Fig.1(a)–(b) for the data-flow graphs of two widely used NTT configurations for an input sequence with length $n = 8$. The $(n/2)$ butterflies in each stage can be divided into non overlapping *butterfly groups* and every butterfly in a given group uses the same twiddle constant w. For example, the data flow graph of the NTT in Fig.1(b) consists of a single butterfly group in stage 1 with the number of groups increasing in power of two with every stage. Based on the progression of the number of groups with every stage - we classify the NTT configurations into two types: (1) Shrinking NTT (Fig.1(a)) and (2) Expanding NTT (Fig.1(b)) named based on the appearances of the respective data flow graphs. We refer the reader to [26] for more details on optimized embedded software implementations of the NTT.

2.2   CRYSTALS Package

The "Cryptographic Suite for Algebraic Lattices" (CRYSTALS) consists of two schemes - Kyber [3] and Dilithium [19] both of which are finalist candidates in the NIST's standardization process.

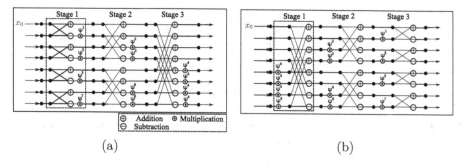

Fig. 1. Data flow graphs of two most commonly used configurations of the NTT (a) Expanding NTT (b) Shrinking NTT

Kyber: Kyber is a chosen-ciphertext secure (CCA-secure) KEM based on the MLWE problem and is considered to be a promising candidate for standardization owing to its strong theoretical security guarantees and implementation performance [2]. Computations are performed over modules in dimension $(k \times k)$ (i.e) $R_q^{k \times k}$ and Kyber provides three security levels with Kyber-512 (NIST Security Level 1), Kyber-768 (Level 3) and Kyber-1024 (Level 5) with $k = 2, 3$ and 4 respectively. Kyber operates over the anti-cyclic ring R_q with an NTT-friendly prime modulus $q = 3329$ and degree $n = 256$ such that the base ring $\mathbb{Z}_q$ contains ω but not ψ. The CCA-secure Kyber contains in its core, a CPA-secure Kyber encryption scheme called Kyber.CPA which is converted to a CCA-secure KEM using the Fujisaki-Okamoto transformation [9]. Please refer to Algorithm 1 in appendix for the description of its key-generation, encryption and decryption procedures.

Dilithium: Dilithium is also one of the leading candidates among digital signature schemes for standardization owing to its balanced security and efficiency guarantees. Dilithium is built upon the well known *Fiat-Shamir with Aborts* framework [18] and its security is based on the combination of the MLWE and MSIS problems. Dilithium involves computations over modules $R_q^{k \times \ell}$ with $k, \ell > 1$ and provides three different security levels with Dilithium2 (Level 1) : $(k, \ell) = (4, 3)$, Dilithium3 (Level 3) : $(k, \ell) = (5, 4)$ and Dilithium4 (Level 5) : $(k, \ell) = (6, 5)$. Dilithium also operates in a similarly structured base polynomial ring as Kyber with the same $n = 256$ albeit with a different modulus $q = 2^{23} - 2^{13} - 1$, such that the base ring $\mathbb{Z}_q$ contains both ψ and ω. Please refer to Algorithm 2 in appendix for the key-generation and signing procedures of the Dilithium signature scheme.

2.3 Related Works

Side-channel attacks can be broadly classified into two categories: (1) Multi trace attacks and (2) Single trace attacks. Most reported works on protected implementations of lattice-based schemes have focussed on protection against

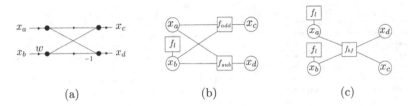

Fig. 2. Factor Graphs of the CT butterfly shown in (a) used by the attacks of (b) Primas et al. [27] and (b) Pessl et al. [25]

Differential Power Analysis (DPA) style attacks that work over multiple traces. There exists a large body of work on masking countermeasures for lattice-based schemes [23,29] (i.e) a secret polynomial $\mathbf{s} \in R_q$ is split into two shares $\mathbf{r}$ and $\mathbf{s} - \mathbf{r}$ and each share is computed upon in an independent manner. This type of additive sharing is convenient as most operations within lattice-based schemes are linear. There have also been proposals for alternate countermeasures against multi trace attacks such as blinding and shifting [31]. Blinding involves multiplying a secret polynomial $\mathbf{s} \in R_q$ with a scalar $a \in \mathbb{Z}_q$ (i.e) $a \cdot \mathbf{s} \in R_q$ while shifting involves multiplying the secret polynomial $\mathbf{s}$ with x^i for $i \in [0, n-1]$ which rotates the coefficient vector of $\mathbf{s}$ by i positions to the left. All the aforementioned countermeasures ensure randomization of computations across multiple executions. On the other hand, single trace attacks such as horizontal DPA [4] and algebraic attacks [27] work by collating information from SCA leakage of different operations within a single execution. Thus, defeating such single trace attacks requires to randomize computations within a single execution. In that respect, shuffling or randomizing the order of operations is a concrete countermeasure against single trace attacks, including the attack on the NTT [25,27] which remains the focus of our work. While Ziljstra *et al.* [33] investigated the cost of the shuffling countermeasure for the NTT on the Artix-7 FPGA, there exists no prior work on investigation or evaluation of countermeasures to protect the NTT on an embedded software platform, given that prior attacks were conducted on software implementations on the ARM Cortex-M4 microcontroller. In this work, we propose several novel shuffling and masking countermeasures for the NTT and conduct a detailed performance assessment of the proposed countermeasures when implemented within Kyber and Dilithium on the ARM Cortex-M4 microcontroller.

2.4   Side-Channel Attacks on NTT

Primas *et al.* [27] proposed the first SCA of NTT through a single trace template style attack using Soft-Analytical Side-Channel Attack (SASCA) based techniques [32]. They targeted the INTT instance used within the decryption procedure to recover the long term secret key (line 4 in CPA.Decrypt procedure of Algorithm 1). Their attack works in two steps. Firstly, a side-channel template attack is performed on certain targeted intermediates within the NTT computation to yield the corresponding probabilities conditioned upon the observed side-channel leakage. Secondly, the obtained probabilities are incorporated into a bipartite *factor graph* modelled based on the NTT/INTT and the Belief Propagation (BP) algorithm [24] is executed over the factor graph. The BP algorithm effectively combines the information from the various conditional probabilities to retrieve the marginal probabilities for the targeted inputs and intermediates within the NTT/INTT.

A factor graph consists of two types of nodes - variable nodes and factor nodes. The variable nodes x_i for $i = \{0, \ldots, N-1\}$ represent the targeted intermediates, which are the inputs and outputs of every stage of the NTT/INTT. The factor nodes f_i for $i = \{0, \ldots, M-1\}$ model the relationship between the different variable nodes. Refer Fig. 2(b) for a simple factor graph of a single CT butterfly operation (Fig. 2(a)) utilized by the attack of Primas *et al.* [27]. It has four variable nodes for inputs (x_a, x_b) and outputs (x_c, x_d) depicted using circles and three factor nodes f_{ADD}, f_{SUB} and f_ℓ depicted using squares. Factor nodes can be of two types - (1) probabalistic or (2) deterministic based on the relation between the connected variable node/s. Here, f_ℓ is a probabilistic factor node which models the leakage from multiplication $b \cdot w$ (i.e) $f_\ell(i) = Pr(b = i/l)$, while f_{ADD} and f_{SUB} are deterministic nodes with f_{ADD} given as follows (similarly for f_{SUB}):

$$f_{ADD}(x_a, x_b, x_c) = \begin{cases} 1 & \text{if } x_a + x_b \cdot \omega = x_c \bmod q \\ 0 & \text{otherwise} \end{cases}$$

Any relation between the variable nodes can be modelled and integrated as additional factor nodes into the factor graph thus making this approach very flexible. Primas *et al.* [27] also utilized the timing information from variable time modular reduction used in their targeted implementation. Templating the multiplication required roughly 1 million $(q \cdot n/2)$ templates using 100 million traces (100 traces for each template) and they subsequently demonstrated full key recovery using a single trace on the ARM Cortex-M4 microcontroller [27]. Subsequently, Pessl *et al.* [25] used a number of optimization techniques to mainly improve trace complexity of the profiling phase. Firstly, they switched to using hamming weight templates and targeted the loads and stores of the inputs and outputs of the butterfly instead of templating the multiplication operation resulting in a factor graph shown in Fig. 2(c). The factor nodes f_A and f_B model the leakage from loading of the inputs, while f_{BF} is the deterministic node modelled as follows:

$$f_{BF}(x_a, x_b, x_c, x_d) = \begin{cases} 1 & \text{if } x_a + x_b \cdot \omega = x_c \bmod q \text{ and } x_a - x_b \cdot \omega = x_d \bmod q \\ 0 & \text{otherwise} \end{cases}$$

Furthermore, they targeted the NTT over the ephemeral secret in the encryption procedure (Line 5 in CPA.Encrypt procedure in Alg.1) to exploit the very narrow support of its inputs (i.e) ($[-2, 2]$), to successfully recover the key in just a single trace for Kyber on the ARM Cortex-M4 only using 213 templates. This to date, is the most efficient single trace attack on the NTT, also potentially applicable to

NTT instances used in Dilithium for key recovery. This attack was also shown to be applicable to masking countermeasures, albeit in the presence of a high SNR. Thus, the aforementioned single trace attacks against NTT heavily motivate the need for evaluation of concrete countermeasures to protect the NTT/INTT operation against SCA on the ARM Cortex-M4 microcontroller.

3   Masking Countermeasures for the NTT

Several previous works on practical SASCA over block ciphers such as AES [11, 12] have shown significant degradation of the attack success rate in an unknown plaintext scenario compared to a known plaintext scenario (Figure 2 of [11] and Figure 9–10 of [12]). That is, the leakage from $SBOX(p \oplus k)$ provides significantly more information with known p compared to unknown p. In case of the NTT, the twiddle constants (powers of ω or ψ) are the only known values used within the NTT computation with both the inputs and outputs unknown. This knowledge about the twiddle constants is incorporated into construction of the factor graph thus potentially aiding the attack. This motivates us to investigate randomizing the twiddle constants as a potential mitigation technique against SASCA style attacks on the NTT.

Though the SASCA on AES involves different computations than the one in NTT/INTT, we expect a similar decrease in terms of extracted information. An attacker can indeed construct an alternative factor graph with twiddle constants as variable nodes, however we believe that the degradation in information will significantly affect the performance of the BP algorithm. In this section, we propose an efficient multiplicative masking strategy using *twiddle constants as masks* to randomize the twiddle constants used in the NTT. We adopt a bottom-up approach to propose generic masking strategies for the atomic butterfly operation and subsequently use the same to construct a generic masked NTT. For generality, we use n to denote the length of the input to the NTT and N for the number of stages within the NTT.

3.1   Generic Masked Butterfly Construction:

Let us consider the CT butterfly as in Eq. 1 computed with inputs (a, b) and the twiddle constant $w_x = \psi^x$ for $x \in [0, n-1]$ to output (c, d). We introduce a random twiddle constant mask $w_y = \psi^y$ and compute a modified butterfly as shown in Eq. 3. The resulting butterfly utilizes randomized twiddle constants w_y and $w_{(x+y)}$ with its outputs multiplicatively masked with the twiddle constant w_y. This masked butterfly only requires one additional multiplication $(a \cdot w_y)$ compared to an unmasked butterfly.

$$c' = c \cdot w_y$$
$$= (a + b \cdot w_x) \cdot w_y$$
$$= a \cdot w_y + b \cdot w_x \cdot w_y$$

$$= a \cdot w_y + b \cdot w_{(x+y)} \ (\because w_{(x+y)} = \psi^x \cdot \psi^y = \psi^{(x+y)})$$
$$d' = d \cdot w_y$$
$$= (a - b \cdot w_x) \cdot w_y$$
$$= a \cdot w_y - b \cdot w_{(x+y)} \ (\because w_{(x+y)} = \psi^x \cdot \psi^y = \psi^{(x+y)}) \tag{3}$$

An unmasked butterfly with a known twiddle constant w_x is a bijection from (a, b) to (c, d) in $\mathbb{Z}_q^2$. Thus, the inputs and outputs share a strong link potentially aiding the performance of the BP algorithm. However, the modified butterfly as in Eq. 3 is a many-to-one function with inputs $(a, b, w_y) \in \mathbb{Z}_q^3$ mapping to outputs $(c', d') \in \mathbb{Z}_q^2$ where the input space size is $(q^2 \cdot 2n)$ and the output space size is (q^2). Thus, breaking the inherent bijection in the butterfly weakens the link between the inputs and outputs similar to breaking the bijection between the input and output of the SBOX [12], which hinders the performance of the loopy BP algorithm. We only provide intuition for SCA resistance of our masking approach, while the main focus of our work is on its runtime performance. We thus leave concrete security analysis of our masking approach (e.g.) using LRPM [12] for future work. Our choice of using twiddle constants as masks instead of random integers in $\mathbb{Z}_q$ comes several advantages. Firstly, sampling a twiddle constant only requires to sample the position y of the twiddle constant w_y within the twiddle constant array (8–9 bits for typical parameters), as opposed to using costly approaches such as rejection sampling to sample in $\mathbb{Z}_q$. Secondly, multiplication of two twiddle constants can be done by simply summing their indices since the product of two twiddle constants is another twiddle constant (i.e) $w_x \cdot w_y = w_{(x+y)}$, saving one multiplication operation per butterfly. We extend this approach to two cases where the inputs are masked with (1) same mask w_i (i.e) $(a', b') = (a \cdot w_i, b \cdot w_i)$ and (2) different masks (w_i, w_j) (i.e) $(a', b') = (a \cdot w_i, b \cdot w_j)$. For inputs with same masks, the masked butterfly is computed as (computation of d' follows similarly as c'):

$$c' = (a' + b' \cdot w_x) \cdot w_y$$
$$= a \cdot w_i \cdot w_y + b \cdot w_i \cdot w_x \cdot w_y$$
$$= a \cdot w_{(i+y)} + b \cdot w_{(i+x+y)}$$
$$= c \cdot w_{(i+y)}$$
$$d' = a \cdot w_{(i+y)} - b \cdot w_{(i+x+y)} \tag{4}$$

The random twiddle constants used are $w_{(i+y)}$ and $w_{(i+x+y)}$ and the outputs are masked with $w_{(i+y)}$. We denote this butterfly as MSISO_BF where SISO denotes same masks for input (SI) and same masks for output (SO). We see that the masked outputs are computed without explicitly un-masking the inputs. However, when the inputs have different masks, the same approach cannot be used. Here, we exploit another property of the twiddle constants (i.e) $\psi^{2n} = 1$, to efficiently bypass the unmasking process and integrate the same into the butterfly operation. For example, an integer $a' = a \cdot w_i$ can be re-masked with a different twiddle constant w_k using a single multiplication as follows:

$$a'' = a' \cdot w_{(2n-i+k)}$$
$$= a \cdot w_i \cdot w_{(2n-i+k)}$$
$$= a \cdot w_k \tag{5}$$

We thus utilize the same strategy to compute the masked butterfly as shown in Eq. 6. We denote this masked butterfly as MDISO_BF where DISO denotes different masks for input (DI) and same masks for output (SO).

$$c' = (a' \cdot w_{(2n-i)} + b' \cdot w_{(2n-j)} \cdot w_x) \cdot w_y$$
$$= a' \cdot w_{(2n-i+y)} + b' \cdot w_{(2n-j+y+x)}$$
$$= a \cdot w_i \cdot w_{(2n-i+y)} + b \cdot w_j \cdot w_{(2n-j+y+x)}$$
$$= c \cdot w_y$$
$$d' = a' \cdot w_{(2n-i+y)} - b' \cdot w_{(2n-j+y+x)} \tag{6}$$

While both MSISO_BF and MDISO_BF butterflies mask the outputs with the same twiddle constant, we can use similar techniques to generate different output masks. We consider the most generic case where both inputs and outputs masked with different masks (i.e) inputs $(a', b') = (a \cdot w_i, b \cdot w_j)$ and outputs $(c', d') = (c \cdot w_k, d \cdot w_\ell)$ and such a masked butterfly can be computed as follows:

$$c' = a' \cdot w_{(2n-i+k)} + b' \cdot w_x \cdot w_{(2n-j+k)}$$
$$= a \cdot w_i \cdot w_{(2n-i+k)} + b \cdot w_j \cdot w_{(2n-j+k+x)}$$
$$= a \cdot w_k + b \cdot w_{(k+x)}$$
$$= c \cdot w_k$$
$$d' = a' \cdot w_{(2n-i+\ell)} - b' \cdot w_x \cdot w_{(2n-j+\ell)}$$
$$= a \cdot w_\ell - b \cdot w_{(\ell+x)}$$
$$= d \cdot w_\ell \tag{7}$$

We denote this masked butterfly as MDIDO_BF since both inputs and outputs are masked with different twiddle constants. The MSIDO_BF (same input masks, different output masks) can also be computed in a very similar manner. Both MDIDO_BF and MSIDO_BF are inherently costlier than MSISO_BF and MDISO_BF as they require 4 multiplication operations, as opposed to only 2 multiplication operations in the case of the MSISO_BF and MDISO_BF butterflies. All the aforementioned masking strategies can also be applied similarly to the GS butterfly as well as using powers of ω if ψ is not present in the ring (using $\omega^n = 1$). The presence of $\psi \in \mathbb{Z}_q$ ensures $2n$ possibilities, while its absence only ensures n possibilities for the twiddle constant masks. While Dilithium contains ψ in its operating ring, Kyber only contains ω in its operating ring. In the following discussion, we propose a generic and configurable masked NTT/INTT implemented using a combination of the aforementioned masked butterfly operations.

3.2   Configurable Masked NTT Construction

Usage of the aforementioned masked butterflies ensures that all intermediates within the NTT remain masked with random twiddle constants. The number of random masks and their allotment within each stage decides the type of masked butterflies used within the NTT.

3.2.1   Coarse-Masked NTT

We consider the simplest case of using a single mask for every stage and the resulting NTT can be computed only using MSISO_BF butterflies in the following manner. Let $W = \{w_{x_i}\}$ for $i \in \{0, N-1\}$ be a twiddle mask set with random masks for every stage of the NTT. Upon employing the MSISO_BF butterfly, the intermediate output at the end of stage ℓ is multiplicatively masked with the twiddle factor $\prod_{i=0}^{i=\ell-1} w_{x_i}$. Thus, final masked NTT output would typically require a post-scaling step. However, we bypass the post-scaling by exploiting the property that $w_{k \cdot 2n} = \psi^{k \cdot 2n} = 1$ for $k \geq 0$. If the sum of randomly chosen indices of the twiddle constants is a multiple of $2n$ (i.e) $\sum_{i=0}^{N-1} (x_i) = k \cdot 2n$, then the output is automatically unmasked. The mask space for the Coarse-Masked NTT is $(2n)^{(N-1)}$ (when using ψ) and $(n)^{(N-1)}$ (when using ω). For Kyber, this amounts to about $2^{(8 \times 6)} = 2^{48}$ (256 masks in each stage and independent masks in 6 out of the 7 stages) and 2^{63} for Dilithium. An adversary with a huge computational power could potentially brute-force SASCA over the complete mask space to perform key recovery. Secondly, reuse of same twiddle masks across different butterflies in a stage also creates additional links which could potentially be used as additional factor nodes in the factor graph.

3.2.2   Fine-Masked NTT

To alleviate the issues of Coarse-Masked NTT, one can employ more masks in every stage. We consider the other extreme case of using n twiddle masks for every stage (one mask each for every point), which we denote as the Fine-Masked NTT. This masked NTT can be constructed only using MDIDO_BF butterflies by choosing a set of n masks $W_t = \{w_i\}$ for $i \in \{0, n-1\}$ for every stage t such that the outputs of stage t are masked with W_t. The mask space for the Fine-Masked NTT is $2n^{(n \times N)}$ (when using ψ) and $n^{(n \times N)}$ (when using ω). For Kyber, this amounts to 2^{2048} just for a single stage (2^{4196} for Dilithium). Morover, every butterfly utilizes independent masks and thus additional links cannot be created between the masks used in different butterflies, thus intuitively providing improved SCA resistance compared to the Coarse-Masked NTT.

3.2.3   Generic-Masked NTT

One can also straddle between the two extremes of Coarse-Masked and Fine-Masked NTT, by choosing a random "u" number of masks per stage with $1 < u < n$. We illustrate the idea with $u = 2$ (2 masks per stage) using an 8-point NTT. We consider two cases here: (1) Shrinking NTT (Fig. 3(a)) and (2) Expanding NTT (Fig. 3(b)). In case of the Shrinking NTT, MSISO_BF butterflies are used in all but the last stage and MDISO_BF butterflies are used in the last stage since the inputs have different masks ($w_{(13)}, w_{(14)}$). In the case of

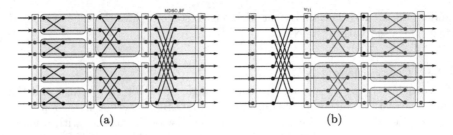

Fig. 3. Illustration of the masked NTT with $u = 2$ twiddle constant masks in each stage (a) Shrinking NTT (b) Expanding NTT

the Expanding NTT, the first stage utilizes the MSIDO_BF butterfly since the outputs need to be masked with different twiddle constants $(w_{(11)}, w_{(12)})$ while all the other stages can utilize the MSISO_BF butterfly. The number of masks per stage (u) can actually be randomly chosen at run-time for each masked NTT instance. In this work, we design a generic masked NTT denoted as Generic-u-Masked NTT (u: number of masks per stage) which uses a randomly generated u at run-time for each NTT instance. We limit our choices for u to powers of 2 (i.e) $u = 2^i$ for $i \in [0, \log(n)]$ since n being a power of 2 ensures even distribution of masks to all the coefficients in each stage which simplifies the control logic. This results in $\log(n)$ possible configurations for the masked NTT (8 for typical parameters of Kyber and Dilithium). However, we note that it is possible to design for any value of u between 1 and n at the cost of a more convoluted control logic. While the Generic-u-Masked NTT maintains same number of masks u for every stage of a given NTT instance (Fig. 3(a)–(b)), one can also increase the granularity by choosing a different u for each NTT stage. A generic control logic can be designed that tracks the input and output masks for each butterfly and uses the appropriate masked butterfly for computation. If u is limited to powers of 2, this in itself brings about about $\log(n)^N$ possible configurations for the NTT. For parameters of Kyber and Dilithium, it amounts to 2^{56} and 2^{64} possibilities respectively. The resulting NTT runs in variable time (secret independent) and has sufficient entropy to randomize the sequence of computations within the NTT. It has been shown that single trace template style attacks require precise knowledge of the underlying computations within the NTT [25,27]. Thus, randomizing the computations makes it significantly harder from a practical side-channel perspective, though not impossible to identify the underlying targeted operations within the NTT and utilize the leakage from the same for attack.

4   Shuffling Countermeasures for the NTT

Shuffling the order of operations is a well known countermeasure against SASCA [32] and is also the only known concrete countermeasure against similar attacks on the NTT [25,27]. Shuffling ensures that leakages cannot be trivially assigned to the corresponding nodes in the factor graph, provided there is sufficient entropy which is beyond realistic brute-force. Ziljstra *et al.* [33] utilized LFSR based on irreducible polynomials and a novel permutation network to implement the shuffling countermeasure for the NTT on Artix-7 FPGAs, but there exists no prior work of the same for an embedded software implementation, which was the target of reported attacks [25,27]. We propose three novel variants of the shuffling countermeasure with varying granularity for the NTT. They are (1) Coarse-Full-Shuffle, (2) Coarse-In-Group-Shuffle and (3) Fine-Shuffle.

4.1 Coarse-Full-Shuffled NTT

It is known that all butterflies within any stage of the NTT can be computed independent of one another. This allows us to randomly shuffle the order of execution of the $(n/2)$ butterfly operations within any stage of the NTT. While there are several algorithms to generate a random permutation, we in this work utilize the well known *Knuth-Yates* shuffling algorithm [30], which has also been used by several previous works for SCA protection of cryptographic schemes [13, 30]. Generating a full shuffling order for $n/2$ butterflies using the Knuth-Yates shuffle requires about $(n/2 - 1) \cdot \log(n)$ random bits and provides an entropy of $(n/2)!$, which is beyond realistic brute-force for typical parameter sets. One can also use LFSRs based on irreducible polynomials for generating permutations as done by Ziljstra *et al.* [33], but they offer a much limited permutation space (i.e) For $n = 256$, it amounts to about 2^{55} which can be considered to within the realm of brute-force for large organizations with very high computational power.

4.2 Coarse-In-Group-Shuffled NTT

Instead of performing a full $n/2$ length shuffle for every stage, one can limit to generating a unique shuffle within each *butterfly group*. In that stage of the NTT where every butterfly forms a unique group, we propose to do a full $n/2$ length shuffle. This shuffle provides an entropy of $((n/2m)!)^m$ for any stage with m butterfly groups and $n/2m$ butterflies in every group for $m < n/2$. This is much less than the $(n/2)!$ offered by the full length $n/2$ shuffle, but still beyond reach by realistic brute-force for any combination of (n, m) used in Kyber and Dilithium. While both Coarse-In-Group-Shuffle and Coarse-Full-Shuffle incur the same cost to generate the shuffle. However, all butterflies within a single group utilize the same twiddle factor and hence a single twiddle factor load per group will suffice, whereas a full $n/2$ length shuffle requires to twiddle factor load from memory for every butterfly. However, as shown in Sect. 5, the performance advantage compared to the Coarse-Full-Shuffle countermeasure is only minimal.

4.3 Fine-Shuffled NTT

The attack of Pessl *et al.* [25] targeted SCA leakage from the loading of inputs of every butterfly. So, a direct way to counter their attack is to simply randomize

```
1    m = -1*rand();      // rand() = 0 or 1 and m = 0x0000 or 0xFFFF
2
3    op1 = p[j+ r*len];
4    op2 = p[j+ (1-r)*len];
5
6    temp = (op1 ^ op2);
7    temp = temp & m;
8    op1 = op1 ^ temp;
9    op2 = op2 ^ temp;
```

Fig. 4. C code snippet for randomized loading using arithmetic cswap operation

the order of the input loads and output stores of each butterfly. Since we only shuffle the loads and stores, the modular multiplication can still be targeted similar to the first attack of Primas *et al.* [27]. But, constructing $(q \cdot n/2)$ templates for the multiplication operation and assuming 100 traces per template (similar to [27]) would amount to 42 million traces for Kyber and 214 billion for Dilithium which makes it highly difficult if not impossible to measure. Thus, this can be considered as a weaker mitigation technique compared to the Coarse-Shuffle countermeasures, nevertheless could be used to significantly increase the attacker's effort or could be used in conjunction with other countermeasures for the NTT.

We utilize an arithmetic conditional swap technique (arithmetic cswap) previously used in embedded implementations of elliptic curve cryptography [14] to shuffle the order of loads and stores. This technique neither uses lookups from secret addresses nor secret branch conditions and its code snippet randomizing the loading of p[j] and p[j+len] is shown in Fig. 4. Firstly, a random bit r is generated to create a mask m = -r (m = 0x0000 or 0xFFFF assuming operands are 16-bits long as in Kyber). The random bit decides the order of loading of p[j] and p[j+len] into op1 and op2. Subsequently, a conditional swap is executed using bitwise operations in lines 7–10 of Fig. 4. If m = 0x0000, op1 and op2 are swapped, while if m = 0xFFFF, op1 and op2 retain their values.

The arithmetic cswap operation has been the target of side-channel attacks in embedded ECC implementations [21,22] which work by building templates for the AND operation with the mask (line 8) and the leakage is mainly due to the difference in hamming weight of m = 0x0000 (0) and m = 0xFFFF (16). While the reported attacks used leakage from 16 such AND operations per mask, we only have a single AND operation and thus the leakage is significantly suppressed. Nevertheless, we propose a technique to further reduce the SNR by replacing the single 16-bit AND operation with 16 single bit iterative AND operations. Distinguishing between 0 and 1 is significantly harder than distinguishing between (0x0000 and 0xFFFF). Though we do not claim full protection against their attack, we significantly reduce the leakage. We refer to the original technique as Full-Fine-Shuffle and our modified approach as the Bitwise-Fine-Shuffle technique. In terms of the randomness requirement, every butterfly needs two bits (one each for load and store) thus amounting to about $n \cdot N$ bits for the complete NTT. Since there are $n/2$ butterflies in each stage, the total entropy is about $4^{(n/2)} = 2^n$ possibilities for a single stage which is well beyond practical brute-force for typical parameters (2^{256} for Kyber and Dilithium).

5   Experimental Results

We perform a practical performance evaluation of all the proposed countermeasures when integrated into open source implementations of Kyber and Dilithium available in the public *pqm4* library [15], a benchmarking framework for PQC schemes on the ARM Cortex-M4 microcontroller.

5.1   Target Platform and Implementation Details

All implementations were compiled with the arm-none-eabi-gcc-9.2.1 compiler using compiler flags -O3 -mthumb -mcpu=cortex-m4 -mfloat-abi=hard -mfpu=fpv4-sp-d16. Our target platform is the STM32F4DISCOVERY board (DUT) housing the STM32F407, ARM Cortex-M4 microcontroller and the clock frequency is 24 MHz. The unprotected NTT within Kyber and Dilithium is implemented in pure assembly, however we report results for countermeasures implemented over the C-based NTT/INTT implementations for Kyber and Dilithium. For randomness generation, we utilize the hardware TRNG running at 48 MHz that consumes about 215 cycles (including overheads) to generate 32 bits. We utilize true randomness from the TRNG for all our proposed countermeasures, however one could also use NIST approved PRNGs such as eXtendable Output Functions based on SHA3 or AES in counter mode, seeded with true randomness from the TRNG. This could speed up the sampling process especially on devices such as the STM32L4 MCUs with support for hardware accelerators for AES [1].

Both Kyber and Dilithium utilize the same configuration for their respective NTTs and INTTs [3,8]. The NTT is implemented using the CT butterfly with inputs in standard order and outputs in bit-reversed order. The INTT is implemented using the GS butterfly with inputs in bit-reversed order and outputs in standard order. Kyber operates in a ring with the modulus $q = 3329$ (12 bit) and only contains ω while Dilithium operates with a modulus $q = 2^{23} - 2^{17} - 1$ (23 bit) which contains both ψ and ω. The NTT/INTT used in Kyber is considerably faster than that in Dilithium, since Dilithium operates over larger integers (32-bit unsigned integers) compared to Kyber (16-bit signed integers). (Refer Table 1–2). Due to the presence of the ψ in Dilithium, Dilithium can use up to 512 twiddle constant masks as compared to 256 in the case of Kyber. Both schemes perform the NTT and INTT computations in the Montgomery domain.

5.2   Performance Evaluation of Protected NTT/INTTs

Please refer Table 1 and 2 for the performance impact of our proposed masking and shuffling countermeasures respectively, on the NTT/INTTs of Kyber and Dilithium. For the shuffled NTTs, the overheads come from the shuffling operation as well as sampling randomness required to generate the shuffling order. For the masked NTTs, the overheads come from the additional multiplications as well sampling randomness for mask generation. We also report cycle counts separately for shuffling (denoted as Shuffle) and randomness generation (Rand.)

Table 1. Performance evaluation of masking countermeasures for NTT and INTT in Kyber KEM and Dilithium DS on the ARM Cortex-M4 MCU. The cycle counts are reported in units of **thousand (10^3) clock cycles**.

Countermeasures	KCycles ($\times 10^3$)					
	NTT			INTT		
	Count	Overhead (%)	Rand.	Count	Overhead (%)	Rand.
Kyber						
Unprotected	31.0	-	-	50.6	-	-
Coarse-Masked	44.6	**43.7**	0.2 (**0.4%**)	63.9	**26.3**	0.2 (**0.3%**)
Generic-2-Masked	66.5	**114.5**	0.5 (**0.7%**)	83.7	**65.3**	0.5 (**0.6%**)
Generic-4-Masked	72.1	**132.7**	1.0 (**1.4%**)	87.2	**72.3**	1.0 (**1.3%**)
Fine-Masked	171.1	**451.7**	65.7 (**38.4%**)	177.6	**250.9**	65.7 (**36.9%**)
Dilithium						
Unprotected	55.2	-	-	66.2	-	-
Coarse-Masked	91.3	**65.4**	0.4 (**0.4%**)	103.2	**55.8**	0.2 (**0.2%**)
Generic-2-Masked	125.5	**127.3**	0.5 (**0.4%**)	142.6	**115.3**	0.5 (**0.4%**)
Generic-4-Masked	139.0	**151.7**	0.9 (**0.6%**)	154.9	**133.7**	1.1 (**0.7%**)
Fine-Masked	297.3	**438.2**	70.2 (**23.6%**)	303.7	**358.4**	70.3 (**23.1%**)

as well their contribution to the NTT/INTT runtime in % (Table 1-2). For the masked NTTs, we report numbers for the Coarse-Masked (1 mask per stage), Fine-Masked (256 masks), Generic-2-Masked (2 masks) and Generic-4-Masked (4 masks) NTTs.

When comparing the masking countermeasures (Table 1), we observe that the overhead increases with the number of masks used in each stage since more MSIDO and MDIDO butterflies are used within the NTT. We thus see a clear trade-off between security and performance for the masked NTTs. We also observe that the overheads due to randomness generation significantly increases with increasing number of masks. While less than 1% of the runtime is occupied by randomness generation in Coarse-Masked NTT/INTTs, it increases to about 36–38% for Kyber and to about 23% for Dilithium for the Fine-Masked NTT/INTTs.

Among the shuffling countermeasures (Table 2), the Basic-Fine-Shuffle countermeasure incurs the least performance overhead followed by the Coarse-In-Group-Shuffle, Coarse-Full-Shuffle and the Bitwise-Fine-Shuffle NTT. The Coarse-In-Group-Shuffled NTT only performs marginally better than the Coarse-Full-Shuffled NTT thus showing that the advantage due to reduced loading of twiddle factors is minimal. Notably, we also see that the Bitwise-Fine-Shuffled NTT has the largest runtime and the overhead mainly arises from multiple single bit AND operations. This is evident from the results which show that 70% and 88% of the NTTs' runtime in Kyber and Dilithium respectively is occupied by the arithmetic swap operation. We also observe that the Bitwise-Fine-Shuffled NTT in Dilithium incurs a much higher overhead than in Kyber due to the higher number of iterations (32) of the bitwise AND operations as compared to Kyber (16). When comparing the overheads separately due to shuffling operation and

Table 2. Performance evaluation of the shuffling countermeasures for the NTT and INTT of Kyber and Dilithium on the ARM Cortex-M4 MCU. The cycle counts are reported in units of **thousand** (10^3) **clock cycles.**

Countermeasures	Shuffle Algo.	KCycles ($\times 10^3$)			
		Count	Overhead (%)	Shuffle	Rand.
Kyber NTT					
Unprotected	NA	31.0	-	-	-
Coarse-Full-Shuffled	Knuth-Yates	87.2	181.1	16.6 (19%)	38.4 (**44.1%**)
Coarse-In-Group-Shuffle		84.4	**172.2**	17.1 (**20.3%**)	32.4 (**38.4%**)
Basic-Fine-Shuffled	Arith. cswap	76.7	147.4	35.1 (**45.7%**)	9.5 (**12.4%**)
Bitwise-Fine-Shuffle		142.6	**356**	100.1 (**70.2%**)	9.5 (**6.7%**)
Kyber INTT					
Unprotected	NA	50.6	-	-	-
Coarse-Full-Shuffled	Knuth-Yates	113.3	**123.8**	16.6 (**14.6%**)	38.4 (**33.9%**)
Coarse-In-Group-Shuffled		101.2	99.9	16 (**15.8%**)	33 (**32.6%**)
Basic-Fine-Shuffled	Arith. cswap	101.8	101.1	40.9 (**40.1%**)	9.5 (**9.4%**)
Bitwise-Fine-Shuffled		172.4	240.8	102.2 (**59.3%**)	9.6 (**5.5%**)
Dilithium NTT					
Unprotected	NA	55.2	-	-	-
Coarse-Full-Shuffled	Knuth-Yates	120.2	117.5	18.9 (**15.7%**)	43.9 (**36.6%**)
Coarse-In-Group-Shuffled		114.6	107.5	19 (**16.6%**)	37.8 (**33%**)
Basic-Fine-Shuffled	Arith. cswap	109.7	98.7	42.2 (**38.5%**)	10.9 (**10%**)
Bitwise-Fine-Shuffled		630.9	1042.1	554.7 (**87.9%**)	10.9 (**1.7%**)
Dilithium INTT					
Unprotected	NA	66.2	-	-	-
Coarse-Full-Shuffled	Knuth-Yates	130.4	96.9	18.9 (**14.5%**)	43.9 (**33.7%**)
Coarse-In-Group-Shuffled		125.3	89.1	18.4 (**14.7%**)	37.8 (**30.1%**)
Basic-Fine-Shuffled	Arith. cswap	117.6	77.7	41.2 (**35%**)	10.9 (**9.3%**)
Bitwise-Fine-Shuffled		640.9	867.5	560.5 (**87.4%**)	10.9 (**1.7%**)

sampling randomness, sampling randomness consumes a significant portion of run-time in the Coarse-Masking countermeasures (32-44% in Kyber and 30-36% in Dilithium) while the arithmetic swap operations form the main bottleneck in the Fine-Shuffled NTTs.

5.3   Performance Evaluation of Protected Kyber and Dilithium

We now discuss the runtime overheads due to our countermeasures on procedures in Kyber and Dilithium. We report numbers for key generation, encapsulation and decapsulation procedures for kyber, while we limit to the key generation and signing procedures for Dilithium as verification only operates upon public information. Moreover, we only incorporate countermeasures for those NTT instances that operate over sensitive intermediate variables.Please refer Algorithm 1–2 where the SCA protected NTT and INTT instances are highlighted in blue.

Table 3. Performance evaluation of all our proposed countermeasures across various procedures of Kyber768 on the ARM Cortex-M4 MCU. The results are reported in units of **million (10^6) clock cycles**.

Countermeasures	MCycles ($\times 10^6$)					
	KeyGen	Overhead (%)	Encaps	Overhead (%)	Decaps	Overhead (%)
No Protection						
Unprotected	1.178	-	1.301	-	1.358	-
Masking						
Coarse-Masked	1.259	**6.9**	1.395	**7.2**	1.466	**7.9**
Generic-2-Masked	1.383	**17.5**	1.54	**18.3**	1.63	**20**
Generic-4-Masked	1.411	**19.8**	1.571	**20.7**	1.665	**22.5**
Generic-Random-Masked	1.507	**27.9**	1.676	**28.8**	1.764	**29.8**
Fine-Masked	1.979	**68**	2.229	**71.3**	2.413	**77.6**
Shuffling						
Coarse-Full-Shuffled	1.534	**30.2**	1.72	**32.2**	1.841	**35.4**
Coarse-In-Group-Shuffled	1.49	**26.5**	1.664	**27.9**	1.772	**30.4**
Basic-Fine-Shuffled	1.468	**24.7**	1.643	**26.3**	1.752	**28.9**
Bitwise-Fine-Shuffled	1.878	**59.4**	2.123	**63.2**	2.303	**69.5**

Firstly, we observe that all our proposed countermeasures have no impact on the dynamic memory consumption in both Kyber and Dilithium (refer Table 5). Refer Table 3–4 for the performance impact of our countermeasures on individual procedures of Kyber and Dilithium. For brevity, we only report results for the recommended parameters (NIST security level 3) of Kyber (Kyber768) and Dilithium (Dilithium3) while similar trends are observed over all security levels. We report averaged cycle counts over 100 executions for Kyber, and 1000 executions for Dilithium since its signing procedure inherently runs in secret independent variable time. We observe much reduced overheads due to our countermeasures since the NTT/INTT only make up part of the computation within each of these procedures. We also notice that Dilithium's signing procedure incurs the highest overheads since a significant portion of its runtime is dominated by the NTT/INTTs, while the overheads for Kyber are much lesser since the majority of runtime (about 54–69%) is dominated by the PRNG using Keccak permutations [5].

Among the masking countermeasures, we observe that the performance overhead increases with increasing number of masks used per stage, starting from the Coarse-Masked NTTs with the best performance and the Fine-Masked NTTs incurring the largest overheads. The Generic-Random-Masked NTTs where u is chosen randomly at runtime with $u = 2^i$ for $i \in [1, \log(n)]$ incurs a reasonable overhead of about 27–29% in Kyber and 36% for Dilithium's key generation and 77% for Dilithium's signing procedure. Overall, the masking countermeasures incur a performance overhead in the range of 6–77% for Kyber, while the key generation and signing procedure have much more pronounced overheads

Table 4. Performance evaluation of all our proposed countermeasures across various procedures of Dilithium3 on the ARM Cortex-M4 MCU. The results are reported in units of **million** (10^6) **clock cycles.**

Countermeasures	MCycles ($\times 10^6$)			
	KeyGen	Overhead (%)	Sign	Overhead (%)
No Protection				
Unprotected	2.626	-	15.144	-
Masking				
Coarse-Masked	2.955	12.5	17.253	32.9
Generic-2-Masked	3.289	25.2	21.585	66.3
Generic-4-Masked	3.404	29.6	22.765	75.3
Generic-Random-Masked	3.594	36.8	23.082	77.8
Fine-Masked	4.781	82.1	39.752	206.2
Shuffling				
Coarse-Full-Shuffled	3.206	22.1	20.581	58.5
Coarse-In-Group-Shuffled	3.159	20.3	20.257	56
Basic-Fine-Shuffled	3.101	18.1	20.865	60.7
Bitwise-Fine-Shuffled	7.802	197.1	76.614	490.2

in the range of 12–82% and 32–206% respectively. The impact of all the shuffling countermeasures on Kyber is also reasonable with a 24–69% overhead over all procedures. Excepting the Bitwise-Fine-Shuffled NTTs, the other shuffling countermeasures incur an overhead in the range of 18–22% for Dilithium's Key-Gen and 58–60% for Dilithium's Sign procedure. However, the overheads due to the Bitwise-Fine-Shuffle countermeasure is more pronounced with 197% for Dilithium's KeyGen and 490.2% for Dilithium's Sign procedure respectively.

6 Conclusion

We thus propose novel shuffling and masking countermeasures for the NTT against single trace attacks. Our masking strategy centers around the utilization of twiddle constants as masks to construct a generic masked NTT. We also propose three variants of the shuffling countermeasure with varying granularity. Finally, we analyze the performance impact of our countermeasures within *pqm4* implementations of Kyber and Dilithium on the ARM Cortex-M4 microcontroller. While our countermeasures yield a reasonable overhead in the range of 7–78% across all procedures of Kyber, the overhead on Dilithium's key generation and signing procedure are on the higher side in the range of **12-197%** and **32–490%** respectively. We leave the practical side-channel security analysis of our proposed countermeasures for future work.

Acknowledgment. The authors acknowledge the support from the Singapore National Research Foundation ("SOCure" grant NRF2018NCR-NCR002-0001 – www.green-ic.org/secure).

A   Stack Memory Consumption of Protected and Unprotected Implementations of Kyber and Dilithium

Table 5. Stack memory Consumption of our protected and unprotected implementations of Kyber and Dilithium across all parameter sets.

Stack Usage (Bytes)			
Kyber	**KeyGen**	**Encaps**	**Decaps**
Kyber512	2432	2496	2520
Kyber768	3296	2992	3024
Kyber1024	3808	3504	3536
Dilithium	**KeyGen**	**Sign**	**Verify**
Dilithium2	32328	54184	31464
Dilithium3	45640	72616	43760
Dilithium4	61008	93096	58096

B   Algorithmic Description of Kyber Encryption scheme and Dilithium Signature Scheme

Algorithm 1: CPA-Kyber Encryption scheme Kyber.CPA (v2). The sensitive NTTs and INTTs within the individual procedures which are protected with countermeasures are highlighted in blue.

1 **Procedure** CPA.KeyGen()
2      $\rho, \sigma \leftarrow \{0,1\}^{256} \times \{0,1\}^{256}$
3      $\hat{\mathbf{a}} \in R_q^{k \times k} \leftarrow$ SampleUniform(ρ)
4      $\mathbf{s}, \mathbf{e} \in R_q^k \leftarrow$ SampleCBD(σ)
5      $\hat{\mathbf{s}} \leftarrow$ NTT$(\mathbf{s})$
6      $\mathbf{t} \leftarrow$ INTT$(\hat{\mathbf{a}} \cdot \hat{\mathbf{s}})$+$\mathbf{e}$
7      $\hat{\mathbf{t}} =$ NTT$(\mathbf{t})$ return $pk = (\rho, \hat{\mathbf{t}})), sk = \hat{\mathbf{s}}$

8 ───
1 **Procedure** CPA.Encrypt$(pk = (\rho, \hat{\mathbf{t}}), m \in \{0,1\}^{256}, \mu \in \{0,1\}^{256})$
2      $\hat{\mathbf{a}} \in R_q^{k \times k} \leftarrow$ SampleUniform(ρ)
3      $\mathbf{r}, \mathbf{e}_1 \in R_q^k \leftarrow$ SampleCBD(μ)
4      $\mathbf{e}_2 \in R_q \leftarrow$ SampleCBD(μ)
5      $\hat{\mathbf{r}} \leftarrow$ NTT$(\mathbf{r})$
6      $\mathbf{u} \leftarrow$ INTT$(\hat{\mathbf{a}}^T \circ \hat{\mathbf{r}})$+$\mathbf{e}_1$
7      $\mathbf{m} \in R_q =$ Encode(m)
8      $\mathbf{v} \leftarrow$ INTT$(\hat{\mathbf{t}}^T \circ \hat{\mathbf{r}})$+$\mathbf{e}_2$+$\mathbf{m}$
9   return $\mathbf{u}' =$ Compress$(\mathbf{u}), \mathbf{v}' =$ Compress$(\mathbf{v})$

10 ───
1 **Procedure** CPA.Decrypt$(sk, \mathbf{u}', \mathbf{v}')$
2      $\mathbf{u} =$ Decompress$(\mathbf{u}')$
3      $\mathbf{v} =$ Decompress$(\mathbf{v}')$
4      $\mathbf{m}' \leftarrow \mathbf{v}-$INTT$(\hat{\mathbf{s}}^T \circ$ NTT$(\mathbf{u}))$
5      $m \in \{0,1\}^{256} =$ Decode$(\mathbf{m}')$
6   return m

Algorithm 2: Dilithium Signature scheme. The sensitive NTTs and INTTs within the individual procedures which are protected with countermeasures are highlighted in blue.

```
 1  Procedure KeyGen()
 2  |   ρ, ρ' ← {0, 1}^256
 3  |   K ← {0, 1}^256
 4  |   N = 0
 5  |   for i from 0 to ℓ − 1 do
 6  |   |   s_1[i] = Sample(PRF(ρ', N))
 7  |   |   N := N + 1
 8  |   end
 9  |   for i from 0 to k − 1 do
10  |   |   s_2[i] = Sample(PRF(ρ', N))
11  |   |   N := N + 1
12  |   end
13  |   ŝ_1 = NTT(s_1)
14  |   â ∼ R_q^{k×ℓ} = ExpandA(ρ)
15  |   t = INTT(â ∘ ŝ_1) + s_2
16  |   t_1 = Power2Round_q(t, d)
17  |   tr ∈ {0, 1}^384 = CRH(ρ∥t_1)
18  |   return pk = (ρ, t_1), sk = (ρ, K, tr, s_1, s_2, t_0)
19
```

```
 1  Procedure Sign(sk = (ρ, K, tr, s_1, s_2, t_0), M ∈ {0, 1}∗)
 2  |   â ∈ R_q^{k×ℓ} := ExpandA(ρ)
 3  |   μ = CRH(tr∥M)
 4  |   κ = 0, (z, h) = ⊥
 5  |   ρ' ∈ {0, 1}^384 := CRH(K∥μ) (or ρ' ← {0, 1}^384 for randomized signing)
 6  |   ŝ_1 = NTT(s_1), ŝ_2 = NTT(s_2), t̂_0 = NTT(t_0)
 7  |   while (z, h) = ⊥ do
 8  |   |   y ∈ S_{γ_1−1}^ℓ := ExpandMask(ρ'∥κ)
 9  |   |   ŷ = NTT(y)
10  |   |   w = INTT(â ∘ ŷ)
11  |   |   (w_1, w_0) = D_q(w, 2γ_2)
12  |   |   c ∈ B_{60} = H(μ∥w_1)
13  |   |   ĉ = NTT(c)
14  |   |   z = y + INTT(ĉ ∘ ŝ_1)
15  |   |   r = INTT(ĉ ∘ ŝ_2)
16  |   |   (r_1, r_0) := D_q(w − r, 2γ_2)
17  |   |   if ∥z∥_∞ ≥ γ_1 − β or ∥r_0∥_∞ ≥ γ_2 − β or r_1 ≠ w_1 then
18  |   |   |   (z, h) = ⊥
19  |   |   else
20  |   |   |   g = INTT(ĉ ∘ t̂_0)
21  |   |   |   h = MH_q(−g, w − r + g, 2γ_2)
22  |   |   |   if ∥r∥_∞ ≥ γ_2 or wt(h) > ω then
23  |   |   |   |   (z, h) = ⊥
24  |   |   end
25  |   |   κ = κ + 1
26  |   end
27  |   return σ = (z, h, c)
```

References

1. Reference Manual for STM32L47xxx, STM32L48xxx, STM32L49xxx and STM32L4Axxx advanced Arm-based 32-bit MCUs (2020)
2. Alagic, G., et al.: Status report on the second round of the NIST PQC standardization process. NIST, Technical report, July (2020)
3. Avanzi, R., et al.: CRYSTALS-Kyber (version 2.0) - Algorithm Specifications And Supporting Documentation (April 1, 2019). Submission to the NIST post-quantum project (2019)
4. Aysu, A., Tobah, Y., Tiwari, M., Gerstlauer, A., Orshansky, M.: Horizontal side-channel vulnerabilities of post-quantum key exchange protocols. In: 2018 IEEE International Symposium on Hardware Oriented Security and Trust (HOST), pp. 81–88. IEEE (2018)
5. Botros, L., Kannwischer, M.J., Schwabe, P.: Memory-efficient high-speed implementation of kyber on cortex-M4. In: Buchmann, J., Nitaj, A., Rachidi, T. (eds.) AFRICACRYPT 2019. LNCS, vol. 11627, pp. 209–228. Springer, Cham (2019). https://doi.org/10.1007/978-3-030-23696-0_11
6. Cook, S.: On the minimum computation time for multiplication. Doctoral dissertation, Harvard U., Cambridge, Mass 1 (1966)
7. Cooley, J.W., Lewis, P.A., Welch, P.D.: Historical notes on the fast Fourier transform. Proc. IEEE **55**(10), 1675–1677 (1967)
8. Ducas, L., et al.: CRYSTALS-Dilithium: Algorithm Specifications and Supporting Documentation. Submission to the NIST post-quantum project (2020)
9. Fujisaki, E., Okamoto, T.: Secure integration of asymmetric and symmetric encryption schemes. In: Wiener, M. (ed.) CRYPTO 1999. LNCS, vol. 1666, pp. 537–554. Springer, Heidelberg (1999). https://doi.org/10.1007/3-540-48405-1_34
10. Gentleman, W.M., Sande, G.: Fast Fourier transforms: for fun and profit. In: Proceedings of the November 7–10, 1966, Fall Joint Computer Conference, pp. 563–578. ACM (1966)
11. Grosso, V., Standaert, F.-X.: ASCA, SASCA and DPA with enumeration: which one beats the other and when? In: Iwata, T., Cheon, J.H. (eds.) ASIACRYPT 2015. LNCS, vol. 9453, pp. 291–312. Springer, Heidelberg (2015). https://doi.org/10.1007/978-3-662-48800-3_12
12. Guo, Q., Grosso, V., Standaert, F.X., Bronchain, O.: Modeling soft analytical side-channel attacks from a coding theory viewpoint. IACR Trans. Cryptographic Hardw. Embedded Syst. (2020)
13. Howe, J., Khalid, A., Rafferty, C., Regazzoni, F., O'Neill, M.: On practical discrete Gaussian samplers for lattice-based cryptography. IEEE Trans. Comput. (2016)
14. Hutter, M., Schwabe, P.: NaCl on 8-Bit AVR microcontrollers. In: Youssef, A., Nitaj, A., Hassanien, A.E. (eds.) AFRICACRYPT 2013. LNCS, vol. 7918, pp. 156–172. Springer, Heidelberg (2013). https://doi.org/10.1007/978-3-642-38553-7_9
15. Kannwischer, M.J., Rijneveld, J., Schwabe, P., Stoffelen, K.: PQM4: Post-quantum crypto library for the ARM Cortex-M4. https://github.com/mupq/pqm4
16. Karatsuba, A.: Multiplication of multidigit numbers on automata. Soviet physics doklady **7**, 595–596 (1963)
17. Langlois, A., Stehlé, D.: Worst-case to average-case reductions for module lattices. Des. Codes Cryptogr. **75**(3), 565–599 (2014). https://doi.org/10.1007/s10623-014-9938-4

18. Lyubashevsky, V.: Fiat-Shamir with aborts: applications to lattice and factoring-based signatures. In: Matsui, M. (ed.) ASIACRYPT 2009. LNCS, vol. 5912, pp. 598–616. Springer, Heidelberg (2009). https://doi.org/10.1007/978-3-642-10366-7_35

19. Lyubashevsky, V., et al.: CRYSTALS-dilithium. Technical report, National Institute of Standards and Technology (2017). https://csrc.nist.gov/projects/post-quantum-cryptography/round-1-submissions

20. Lyubashevsky, V., Peikert, C., Regev, O.: On ideal lattices and learning with errors over rings. J. ACM **60**(6), 43 (2013)

21. Nascimento, E., Chmielewski, Ł.: Applying horizontal clustering side-channel attacks on embedded ECC implementations. In: Eisenbarth, T., Teglia, Y. (eds.) CARDIS 2017. LNCS, vol. 10728, pp. 213–231. Springer, Cham (2018). https://doi.org/10.1007/978-3-319-75208-2_13

22. Nascimento, E., Chmielewski, L., Oswald, D., Schwabe, P.: Attacking embedded ECC implementations through cmov side channels. In: Avanzi, R., Heys, H. (eds.) SAC 2016. LNCS, vol. 10532, pp. 99–119. Springer, Cham (2017). https://doi.org/10.1007/978-3-319-69453-5_6

23. Oder, T., Schneider, T., Pöppelmann, T., Güneysu, T.: Practical CCA2-secure and masked ring-LWE implementation. IACR Trans. Cryptographic Hardware Embedded Syst. **2018**(1), 142–174 (2018)

24. Pearl, J.: Fusion, propagation, and structuring in belief networks. Artif. Intell. **29**(3), 241–288 (1986)

25. Pessl, P., Primas, R.: More practical single-trace attacks on the number theoretic transform. In: Schwabe, P., Thériault, N. (eds.) LATINCRYPT 2019. LNCS, vol. 11774, pp. 130–149. Springer, Cham (2019). https://doi.org/10.1007/978-3-030-30530-7_7

26. Pöppelmann, T., Oder, T., Güneysu, T.: High-performance ideal lattice-based cryptography on 8-bit ATxmega microcontrollers. In: Lauter, K., Rodríguez-Henríquez, F. (eds.) LATINCRYPT 2015. LNCS, vol. 9230, pp. 346–365. Springer, Cham (2015). https://doi.org/10.1007/978-3-319-22174-8_19

27. Primas, R., Pessl, P., Mangard, S.: Single-trace side-channel attacks on masked lattice-based encryption. In: Fischer, W., Homma, N. (eds.) CHES 2017. LNCS, vol. 10529, pp. 513–533. Springer, Cham (2017). https://doi.org/10.1007/978-3-319-66787-4_25

28. Ravi, P., Roy, S.S., Chattopadhyay, A., Bhasin, S.: Generic side-channel attacks on CCA-secure lattice-based PKE and KEMs. IACR Trans. Cryptographic Hardware Embedded Syst. 307–335 (2020)

29. Reparaz, O., Sinha Roy, S., Vercauteren, F., Verbauwhede, I.: A masked ring-LWE implementation. In: Güneysu, T., Handschuh, H. (eds.) CHES 2015. LNCS, vol. 9293, pp. 683–702. Springer, Heidelberg (2015). https://doi.org/10.1007/978-3-662-48324-4_34

30. Roy, S.S., Reparaz, O., Vercauteren, F., Verbauwhede, I.: Compact and Side Channel Secure Discrete Gaussian Sampling. IACR ePrint Archive, p. 591 (2014)

31. Saarinen, M.J.O.: Arithmetic Coding and Blinding Countermeasures for Ring-LWE. IACR Cryptology ePrint Archive **2016**, 276 (2016)

32. Veyrat-Charvillon, N., Gérard, B., Standaert, F.-X.: Soft analytical side-channel attacks. In: Sarkar, P., Iwata, T. (eds.) ASIACRYPT 2014. LNCS, vol. 8873, pp. 282–296. Springer, Heidelberg (2014). https://doi.org/10.1007/978-3-662-45611-8_15

33. Zijlstra, T., Bigou, K., Tisserand, A.: FPGA implementation and comparison of protections against SCAs for RLWE. In: Hao, F., Ruj, S., Sen Gupta, S. (eds.) INDOCRYPT 2019. LNCS, vol. 11898, pp. 535–555. Springer, Cham (2019). https://doi.org/10.1007/978-3-030-35423-7_27

HEDrone: Privacy-Preserving Proof-of-Alibi for Drone Compliance Based on Homomorphic Encryption

Ganeshsai Garikipati$^{(\boxtimes)}$, Roshani, Anish Mathuria, and Priyanka Singh

Dhirubhai Ambani Institute of Information and Communication Technology,
Gandhinagar, Gujarat, India
ganeshsaigarikipati@gmail.com

Abstract. The proliferation of unmanned aerial Vehicles (UAVs) might be impeded because of rising concerns about citizen privacy in today's society. Though some protocols and standards like no-fly-zones (NFZs) have been proposed for drone compliance, they expose the operational logistics of the drone in terms of its flight data. AliDrone is a recent protocol that verifies NFZ violations by proof-of-alibi (PoA) via sharing of drone's trace with a trusted third party Auditor. The protocol leverages upon a trusted execution environment (TEE) to prevent malicious drone operators from forging geo-location information. In AliDrone, since the auditor learns the drone's flight trace, the privacy of the drone is compromised. HEDrone addresses this issue of drone privacy: it uses homomorphic encryption to enable PoA over encrypted traces.

Keywords: Drone/Drone operator · No fly zone · Homomorphic encryption · Alidrone · Trusted Execution Environment (TEE)

1 Introduction

Unmanned Aerial Vehicles (UAVs), also known as drones, are widely being put to use in diverse fields such as Aeronautics, Software Development, Cinematography, Retail markets, and many other areas. The adoption of drones among consumers and retailers has also been increasing rapidly. For instance, Amazon has announced its Prime Air service to deliver lightweight packets efficiently. Alphabet is in a partnership with FedEx for the delivery of health and wellness products. Walmart also has started its drone delivery services. With the inclusion of drones in these services, the expected delivery time can be reduced than the current state of delivering in person.

Though drone availability has opened up an entire gamut of possible applications, it has also posed unprecedented threats to society's privacy and security. Drones come with much technology on board that can be GPS, high-definition cameras, Lidars, etc. that can accumulate much sensitive information. The information collected by the drone, if leaked, may cause heavy losses that can be in the

© Springer Nature Switzerland AG 2020
L. Batina et al. (Eds.): SPACE 2020, LNCS 12586, pp. 147–166, 2020.
https://doi.org/10.1007/978-3-030-66626-2_8

form of commercial losses, location leakage of a sensitive military site, aircraft collisions [1], smuggling [2] or even assassination attempts [3]. Privacy-aware society has already shown its concern to this alarming issue and many measures like law enforcement on the drones [4–7], drone registration with trusted authorities [8], etc. are being put in effect to control the scenario.

The issue of drone compliance and the privacy threat posed by drones' usage has been widely discussed [9,10]. One such work involves regulating the entry of a drone into a host region/No-Fly-Zone (NFZ) [11]. An NFZ is an area owned by an entity or a person in which a drone cannot enter. This is done to safeguard the privacy of the NFZ owner. The drone would be required to take permission from the host region/NFZ owner to enter the region and also abide by the policies established by the NFZ owner. Once the drone has received the owner's policy, it enforces the policy on its trusted hardware and ensures the NFZ owner that it is in compliance.

Some of the works propose different restrictions applied to the drone that enters a particular NFZ [9]. Like the images captured during flight must be processed locally, i.e., the drone can not export any image from the system to any cloud. In this way, it ensures that none of the images/information inside the NFZ is leaked. For cases where images need to be uploaded to the cloud, the drone must ensure that it uploads blurred images, similar to that of the google maps that blurs the faces of persons captured in the street view. Another restriction that could be put on the drone is restricting its path.

One such framework named Privaros [12] has been designed to enforce privacy policies on commercial delivery drones. It employs access control mechanisms to make the delivery drones abide by these policies during their flight. The framework is built on top of the robot Operating system (ROS) and integrated with India's Digital Sky portal. A similar framework is proposed in the paper [13], where they describe an infrastructure to build a framework for privacy-aware Unmanned Aerial systems (UAS) for flying over restricted areas. The work discusses how the protocol can be used to enable a proactive approach where the consent of the private property owner is taken into consideration before flying over it, using geospatial data.

The Alidrone is a geo-location-based alibi protocol that enables drones to generate proof-of-non-entrance to an NFZ [8]. In this protocol, the drone reveals its trace to the auditor, who is a trusted third-party and checks for any violations. It tries to achieve this by holding the drone/flyer responsible for proving innocence against any violation reported by NFZ owners. This is done by submitting the GPS trace of the trip along with timestamps to an auditing party. An on-board trusted execution environment (TEE) is used to secure the GPS readings and provide data integrity.

The Alidrone protocol sacrifices the data privacy of the operator. The need to check for violations of NFZs is just as important as respecting the data privacy of a personal or business drone. In this paper, we propose a privacy-preserving protocol HEDrone that will help check for drone compliance while preserving the privacy of the drone. We develop a proof-of-alibi (PoA) based on the encrypted trace of the drone and it ensures that no information about the drone's trace is revealed to the auditor. We adopt HE1 family of somewhat homomorphic encryption (SHE) schemes for our protocol as it requires a fixed number of multiplications and additions during its execution [14]. All the computations on the drone's end occur inside the TEE, so the drone operator can not tamper with it. The key differences between Alidrone and our proposed HEDrone protocol are as follows:

- Unlike Alidrone, the GPS samples are stored encrypted in HEDrone protocol.
- Verification of airspace violation for Alidrone compromises drone's flight data, whereas in HEDrone protocol, only encrypted flight data is made available to the auditor.
- PoA aims to show that there is no possibility for any of GPS co-ordinates corresponding to the drone's trace, to lie inside any NFZ. In Alidrone, it is verified with plaintext co-ordinates whereas in HEDrone, this is done for the encrypted trace.

The rest of the paper is organized as follows: Sect. 2 gives a brief overview of the HE1 encryption schemes. Section 3 discusses about the Alidrone Trustworthy Protocol, and the associated PoA is briefed in Sect. 4. Section 5 presents the proposed HEDrone protocol and the corresponding PoA. In Sect. 6, we perform the security analysis and evaluation is presented in Sect. 7. Section 8 concludes the work and discusses some potential future applications of the same.

2   HE1 and HE1N Encryption Schemes

There are three types of homomorphic encryption (HE) [15,16] schemes: Partially HE, Somewhat HE, and Fully HE. The difference between these three types boils down to the operations that can be performed on the ciphertexts. For our protocol we require a small but fixed number of multiplications and additions to be done on the encrypted data and therefore we aim to use a Somewhat Homomorphic Encryption Scheme - HE1 [14].

HE1 is a somewhat homomorphic encryption scheme over integers that supports both addition and multiplication. We say HE1 is only somewhat homomorphic but not entirely because the arithmetic operations it supports are to be executed under the modulus of a semiprime. So if the result of any operation ends up greater than the seceret key used to encrypt it, the plaintext result is unobtainable, i.e. the homomorphic nature of HE1 has a limit. Assume we have integers inputs $m_1, m_2, \ldots, m_n \in [0, M)$ distributed with an entropy ρ.

We consider a large enough security parameter λ. Let p and q be two large prime numbers such that, $p \in [2^{\lambda-1}, 2^\lambda]$ and $p > (n+1)^d M^d$ and $q \in [2^{\eta-1}, 2^\eta]$ where, $\eta \approx \frac{\lambda^2}{\rho} - \lambda$ and d is number of multiplications needed for the use-case. The security parameter λ is chosen in way such the keys can not be found out by factorising pq. Once the two keys p and q are chosen, we encrypt a plaintext message m as,

$$c = Enc(m, p) = m + rp \pmod{pq} \tag{1}$$

where, $r \leftarrow [1, q)$ is a random noise. The ciphertext c is decrypted by,

$$Dec(c, p) = c \pmod{p} \tag{2}$$

We need to choose the entropy large enough so that brute force attacks do not happen. The probability of any correct guess in $2^{\rho/2}$ is $2^{-\rho/2}$ in the worst case scenario. Therefore, if ρ is large enough, a brute force attack is infeasible to be carried out.

Insufficient Entropy: HE1N. If the entropy ρ of the input is not large enough to negate a brute force attack against HE1 cipher, we increase the entropy of the plaintext by adding an additional noise to the ciphertext.

This noise that we add to the cipher-text is a multiple s of an integer κ, such that the new entropy would be $\rho' = \rho + \log \kappa$ which would be large enough to negate a brute force attack.

Let P be a polynomial we wish to evaluate over a given input of integer, and let P' be its homomorphic equivalent in ciphertext space, then we need to choose such the integer $\kappa > (n+1)^d M^d$ so that $P(m_1, m_2, ..., m_n) < \kappa$ where P is denoted as given in [14]. However, due to an extra linear term in the ciphertext we compute $P(m_1, m_2, ..., m_n, \kappa)$.

A plaintext m is encrypted in the following way,

$$Enc(m, s\kappa) = c = m + s\kappa + rp \pmod{pq} \tag{3}$$

where, $r \leftarrow [1, q)$ and $s \leftarrow [0, \kappa)$. The ciphertext is decrypted by,

$$Dec(c, s\kappa) = (c \bmod p) \mod \kappa \tag{4}$$

Let us consider two ciphertexts $c = m + s\kappa + rp$ and $c' = m' + s'\kappa + r'p$, then the addition of two cipher texts would be,

$$Add(c, c') = m + m' + (s + s')\kappa + (r + r')p \pmod{pq} \tag{5}$$

This decrypts to,

$$Dec(c + c', (s + s')\kappa) = m + m' \tag{6}$$

Similarly we can check for multiplication of two ciphertexts that decrypt to mm'. In our proposed protocol we use both HE1 and HE1N.

Key Generation. The parameters of the homomorphic encryption schemes are chosen after considering the various constraints under which they are to be operated, such as the number of multiplicative operations a HE1 encrypted ciphertext must support before overflowing the message beyond retrieval.

In our proposed protocol the maximum number of multiplicative operations supported throughout the protocol is 15. The range of the latitude and longitude is substituted in the constraints to obtain the range of the security keys.

- Maximum possible value of the input, $M = 180$ (in general for Latitude & Longitude)

- Number of elements in the trace, n
- Number of multiplications to be supported, $d = 15$ for our protocol
- $\lambda > 192$ bits (for security against brute-force attack)
- $\eta > 960$ bits (for security against brute-force attack)
- p is picked randomly from $(2^{\lambda-1}, 2^{\lambda})$
- q is picked randomly from $(2^{\eta-1}, 2^{\eta})$

For a better understanding of the key-generation, refer to [14].

3 Architecture of Alidrone

In this section we provide a high level overview of AliDrone. In the following section, we explain AliDrone's design of proof-of-alibi which makes it possible to determine if a drone has entered any NFZ during that flight.

3.1 System Model

The system consists of three entities:

- Zone Owner: Owns a No Fly Zone (NFZ).
- Drone Operator: Operates a drone and controls/plans its navigation through an area.
- Auditor: An authorized third party (e.g., local agent of the FAA) that keeps track of drones and NFZs and responsible for imposing fines on non-compliance of No-Fly Zone (NFZ) regulations.

For the protocol to be secure, we must ensure that the GPS samples are not tampered with or stored in some other place. An on-board TEE helps sample GPS readings and record them securely along with providing data integrity. In our privacy-preserving protocol we make use of the on-board TEE for secure communication with the drone.

All the NFZs are assumed to be circular in nature. Thus, each NFZ is represented using the notation,

$$z = (lat, lon, r)$$

where lat and lon are the coordinates (latitude and longitude) of the center of the NFZ and r is the radius of the NFZ. The Auditor has a list of all the NFZs which can be queried by the drone operator to plan its route.

The trace of the drone is a series of samples recorded at a frequency (generally the maximum GPS sample frequency). Each sample of the trace is denoted by,

$$S = (lat, lon, t)$$

where, lat, lon stands for the latitude, longitude of the position at which the drone is present and t is the timestamp at which the location was recorded. A series of GPS samples would be represented as $(S_0, S_1, S_2, ..., S_n)$.

3.2   Cryptographic Keys and Proof of Alibi

The various cryptographic keys involved in the system are given below:

- The TEE (Secure OS/World) has a pair of asymmetric keys (T^-, T^+), where T^- is the private key accessible only to the TEE. The verification key T^+ is known to the drone operator at the time of purchase of the drone.
- The drone also has of a pair of asymmetric keys $D = (D^+, D^-)$. The private key D^- is used to sign a random nonce when the drone queries for NFZ information in order to calculate the path it would take.

GPS Data Signed by TEE. The GPS data is signed by the TEE sign key T^- before it leaves the secure world. We define the Proof-of-Alibi (PoA) as a series of GPS samples along with the TEE signatures, with the help of which the drone can provide alibi against the claims of violating a no-fly-zone i.e.,

$$PoA := (S_0, Sig(S_0, T^-)), (S_1, Sig(S_1, T^-)), ...$$

Sig denotes the signature scheme and sign key T^- is only available to TEE such that a drone operator in the untrusted environment cannot forge the signatures. The verification key T^+ is known to the auditor at registration stage, and thus the auditor is able to detect if the GPS data is modified. The signature scheme used here can be any scheme of our choice.

3.3   Registration and Operating Model

The different stages of the registration process are shown in Fig. 1 part A.

Drone Registration. Whenever a new drone is registered, a unique drone id: id_{drone} is issued to the drone that helps to identify the drone. This identifier is similar to a vehicle license plate, which must be carried on the drone when it operates. The public keys D^+, T^+ are provided to the Auditor. Therefore, an entry of registered drone can be expressed as (id_{drone}, D^+, T^+). The private key D^- will be used when the drone queries for the NFZs from the Auditor.

Zone Registration. Each new zone would be given an id id_{zone}. When a Zone owner wants to register his/her NFZ, the entry is done in the form of (id_{zone}, z), where z is the representation of that particular NFZ.

The different stages of operation after registration are shown in Fig. 1 part B.

Drone's Query for NFZ Information. Every registered drone, before its flight, queries the local auditor for NFZ information in a specified area, ideally the area in which the flight happens. The drone specifies the start and end coordinates of the area whose NFZ information is required. Along with the query it must add its signature to it so that the auditor can verify the authenticity of

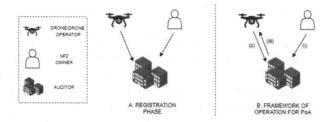

Fig. 1. Figure showing the interaction between the entities during A. Registration Phase and B. Alidrone Framework of Operation. In part B the stages are (i) NFZ owner registers a compliant against a drone (ii) Drone sends the trace for PoA to the Auditor (iii) Auditor responds whether the drone has violated the compliance laws or not

the query. The query comprises of the drone id, the start and end co-ordinates of the navigation area, and a random nonce signed by the drone sign key D^-:

$$(id_{drone}, (x_1, y_1), (x_2, y_2), nonce, Sig(nonce, D^-))$$

Auditor's Response to the Drone. After verifying the authenticity of the query received, the auditor responds with the information on all the NFZs in the specified area so that the drone can either plan the route or move dynamically according to the information.

Auditor Complaint Reception. Meanwhile the auditor stays dormant until there is a privacy violation on any NFZ areas. The NFZ area is responsible for detection and reporting it to the local auditor. All these complaints are persisted in memory and are dealt with in the next stage.

Verification. The drone's trace will be checked for violation only if a complaint is raised by a NFZ owner. Once the complaint is raised the drone operator then submits the trace to the auditor for verification.

4 Proof of Alibi for Alidrone

A proof-of-alibi aims to show that none of the samples lie inside any NFZ nor is it possible to enter any NFZ in the interval between any two consecutive GPS samples i.e. in the time when GPS information is not available.

Consider two GPS samples $S_1 = (x_1, y_1, t_1)$ and $S_2 = (x_2, y_2, t_2)$. Denote the location of the drone at any arbitrary time $t \in [t_1, t_2]$ as (x, y), then the possible traveling range/locus of position can be described as an ellipse with (x_1, y_1) and (x_2, y_2) as its foci:

$$(S_1, S_2) = \{(x, y) | d_1 + d_2 \leq v_{max}(t_2 - t_1)\}$$

where $d_i = \sqrt{(x - x_i)^2 + (y - y_i)^2}$ and v_{max} is the maximum velocity the drone can achieve.

Suppose the drone operates near an NFZ $z = (x_0, y_0, r_0)$ as shown in Fig. 2. The alibi can be proved if the ellipse formed by the two consecutive samples does not intersect with the circle representing zone z. The drone's alibi is accepted if and only if no sample lies in a NFZ and every pair of consecutive GPS samples prove impossibility of travelling into any NFZ, i.e.,

$$(S_i, S_{i+1}) \cap (\cup z) = \phi, \forall i < n$$

The equation of the NFZ is given by,

$$(x - lat)^2 + (y - lon)^2 \leq r^2 \tag{7}$$

where (x, y) represent the point anywhere inside or on the NFZ. (lat, lon) are the co-ordinates of the center of the NFZ and r is the radius of the NFZ. Any parametric point on the rotated ellipse can be represented as

$$x = a \cos \alpha \cos A - b \sin \alpha \sin A$$
$$y = a \cos \alpha \sin A + b \sin \alpha \cos A \tag{8}$$

where α is the angle of made by the point with the major axis of the ellipse.

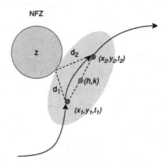

Fig. 2. Possible traveling range and a single NFZ. The possible traveling range should not intersect with the NFZ to produce sufficient alibi

As shown in the Fig. 3, (h, k) is the center of ellipse formed with S_1, S_2 as focii. A is the angle made by ellipse's major axis with the X-axis and B is the angle made by the line joining the centers of circle and ellipse with X-axis.

Substituting (8) in (7) we get,

$$c^4 \cos^4 \alpha + 4asc^2 \sin(A + B) \cos^3 \alpha + [4b^2 s^2 \cos^2(A + B) + 2c^2(s^2 + b^2)$$
$$+ 4a^2 s^2 \sin^2(A + B) - 2r^2 c^2] \cos^2 \alpha + [4as(s^2 + b^2 - r^2) \sin(A + B)] \cos \alpha \tag{9}$$
$$+ [s^2 + b^2 + r^4 - 4b^2 s^2 \cos^2(A + B)] = 0$$

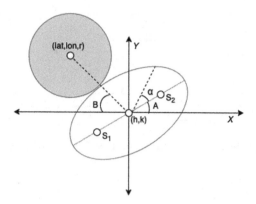

Fig. 3. Geometry of the NFZ and ellipse formed by two consecutive GPS samples

In Eq. 9, if we consider $i = 1$, then $s^2 = (h - lat)^2 + (k - lon)^2$. (a, b, c) are the ellipse parameters and (lat, lon, r) are latitude, longitude, and radius of the NFZ respectively. The ellipse parameters (a, b, c) can be obtained by solving Eqs. 10.

$$d_1 + d_2 = 2a \implies 2a \leq v_{max}(t_2 - t_1)$$
$$c = \sqrt{(x_1 - h)^2 + (y_1 - k)^2} \qquad (10)$$
$$b = \sqrt{a^2 - c^2}$$

Equation 9 is obtained by solving for the intersection between the NFZ and the ellipse formed by the two GPS samples S_1, S_2 as focii. Depending on the solutions of the equation we can verify drone/flyer's alibi as given below:

- *No real roots*: It means no intersection, there is no violation
- *No real root in [−1,1]*: In this case as well there is no intersection so no violation
- *At least one real root in [−1,1]*: There is intersection, possible violation, alibi not accepted and will be fined.

5 Proof of Alibi for Proposed HEDrone

In our proposed HEDrone protocol, we check the range in which the roots lie. However, as the auditor has access only to the encrypted roots, it can not determine whether the drone entered the NFZ. To serve this purpose, we need the auditor to communicate with the drone operator to fetch decrypted roots in a format that does not hinder the privacy of the drone operator. The verification stage of our proposed protocol has been shown in Fig. 4.

As stated above, the Quadratic Polynomial 9 obtained has to be solved for every pair of consecutive samples in order to verify the drone's alibi. If the roots of the equation lie in $[-1, 1]$ i.e. the range of cosine function, then the non-compliance of the drone will be proved.

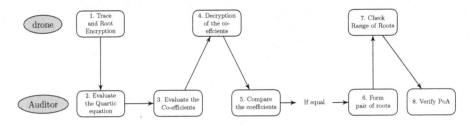

Fig. 4. Verification stage of proposed HEDrone protocol

5.1 Threat Model

Different from AliDrone, in our proposed protocol we assume that the auditor is a semi-honest party. The auditor will follow the protocol but may try to break the privacy of the drone by attempting to learn the plaintext values of GPS samples from the encrypted trace.

5.2 Setup

Encryption of Trace. The trace of the drone is encrypted using HE1N key p which is known only to the drone.

Let a trace be represented by S. We represent the samples as $S_i, i = 1, 2, ..., n$. The encrypted samples are of the form:

$$c_{i_{latitude}} = S_{i_{latitude}} + p \times r_i$$
$$c_{i_{longitude}} = S_{i_{longitude}} + p \times r_i \tag{11}$$

where r_i is a random number from $[0, q)$.

Encryption of Roots. Each root of the polynomial is represented as tuple of $(real, imaginary)$, consisting of the real and imaginary parts. The roots are encrypted using the same key p. As there would be lesser entropy in the roots we add noise$(s\kappa)$, the minimal number of bits with which the root can be represented is considered as the measure of entropy here.

$$c'_{i_{real}} = real + s\kappa + p \times r'_{real}$$
$$c'_{i_{imag}} = imaginary + s\kappa + p \times r'_{imag} \tag{12}$$

where r'_{real} and r'_{imag} are random numbers from $[0, q)$ After encrypting the trace and the roots they are sent to the auditor in the form of an ordered pair $(c'_{i_{real}}, c'_{i_{imag}})$ for each root.

5.3 HEDrone Protocol Flow

The high-level idea of the protocol is that the drone operator convinces the auditor that the encrypted trace sent is consistent with the encrypted roots.

Using the encrypted roots, it tries to prove that the plaintext roots lie in a particular range, without revealing the roots. As the encrypted trace can not be tampered by the drone operator, the range proofs of the encrypted roots serve as the PoA of the drone. The detailed steps involved in the protocol are as follows:

Step 1. The drone sends encrypted trace $S = (c_{i_{latitude}}, c_{i_{longitude}})$ and encrypted roots $roots = (c'_{i_{real}}, c'_{i_{imag}})$ as shown in 11 and 12, to the auditor. The auditor then performs computational actions on the encrypted trace for the PoA.

Using the encrypted trace the auditor computes a modified form of Eq. 9 for every consecutive pair of samples of the encrypted trace.

$$c^4 cos^4\alpha + 4asc^2 sin(A+B)cos^3\alpha + [4b^2s^2cos^2(A+B) + 2c^2(s^2+b^2)$$
$$+ 4a^2s^2 sin^2(A+B) - 2r^2c^2]cos^2\alpha + [4as(s^2+b^2-r^2)sin(A+B)]cos\alpha \quad (13)$$
$$+ [s^2 + b^2 + r^4 - 4b^2s^2cos^2(A+B)] + X = 0$$

where X is obtained due to the parameters of encryption of trace. The equation computed by the auditor will consist of coefficients that are encrypted. This ensures that the auditor can not find the actual roots of the equation, which would otherwise compromise the privacy of the drone operator.

Using the encrypted roots the auditor calculates the coefficients of 13, by substituting the values of the roots in Eqs. 14, 15, 16 and 17.

$$c_1 = -(\alpha + \beta + \gamma + \delta) \quad (14)$$

$$c_2 = \prod_{x \neq y} xy, \ \forall \ x, y \in \{\alpha, \beta, \gamma, \delta\} \quad (15)$$

$$c_3 = -(\prod_{x \neq y \neq z} xyz) \ \forall \ x, y, z \in \{\alpha, \beta, \gamma, \delta\} \quad (16)$$

$$c_4 = \alpha\beta\gamma\delta \quad (17)$$

where $\alpha, \beta, \gamma, \delta$ are the encrypted roots. The equation formed using these coefficients would be

$$x^4 + c_1 x^3 + c_2 x^2 + c_3 x + c_4 = 0 \quad (18)$$

The roots passed by the drone are non-integral values, thus the integral part and non-integral parts are isolated and are operated on as shown below,

Let m, n be two roots whose product is to be evaluated

$$m = (m_i, m_{!i}), \quad n = (n_i, n_{!i}) \quad (19)$$

$$m \times n = m_i \times n_i + m_i \times n_{!i} + n_i \times m_{!i} + m_{!i} \times n_{!i} \quad (20)$$

Operations on the roots are broken down as shown in Eq. 20. This way we work on the roots without merging integral and non-integral parts into one single value.

The coefficients of Eqs. 13 and 18 are obfuscated and passed to drone as pairs in the form of (P_{i1}, P_{i2}) where,

$$P_{i1} = (c_{i1}a_i + R_i)$$
$$P_{i2} = (c_{i2}a_i + R_i)$$
(21)

where c_{i2} are the coefficients of Eq. 18 multiplied by c_0 (coefficient of the first term), c_{i1} are the coefficients of Eq. 13. The auditor then sends these values to the drone for decryption.

Step 2. The values sent by the auditor are obfuscated and thus the drone can not map any passed value to its message. For every pair of values sent by the auditor, the first value is decrypted by key p, second value is first decrypted by key p (and then by κ if noise was added to the roots before encrypting).

$$d_{i1} = P_{i1} \mod p, \quad d_{i2} = P_{i2} \mod p$$
(22)

if noise was added to the roots before encrypting, then:

$$d_{i2} = (P_{i2} \mod p) \mod \kappa$$

Not using the corresponding key for decryption is undesirable for the drone since it might jeopardise its alibi. The drone then multiplies both decrypted values of every pair with a random number for obfuscation and sends them back to the auditor. The obfuscation is to prevent the auditor from compromising the privacy of the drone.

$$D_{i1} = R_i d_{i1}, \quad D_{i2} = R_i d_{i2}$$
(23)

NOTE: Above specified multiplication is done by splitting the decrypted values into integral and non-integral counterparts.

Step 3. On receiving the values the auditor checks if $D_{i1} \approx D_{i2}$ holds. If the equality does not hold the verification process will be terminated and the drone operator would be fined for passing wrong values of the encrypted roots. If the equality holds the protocol continues.

Step 4. After verification of the roots, we check for the range in which the roots lie. The auditor creates n random obfuscations for each of the four roots, refer to Step 2 for obfuscation. The four sets each consisting of $n + 1$ elements (the n obfuscations along with the root) are then sent to the drone for decryption.

$$(root_i, o_{i_1}, o_{i_2}, ..., o_{i_n})$$
(24)

where $root_i$ is an encrypted root and o_{i_j} are its the obfuscations. For roots that are complex in nature no sets are formed as they do not lie in the cosine range.

Step 5. Once these sets are received by the drone it decrypts all the elements present in the sets and sends back the interval in which the values are present. The intervals are of the form $(x, x+1], x \in Z^+$, where Z^+ is the set of all positive integers and for $x = 0$ the range is $[0,1]$. Each value will lie in only one interval marked by bounds that are consecutive integers, therefore only a single interval will be mapped for each value in a set.

For verification the intervals sent by the drone the auditor removes the obfuscations from the roots and checks if they lie in the intervals provided by the drone.

$$x < root_i \leq (x+1) => (ax+R) < obf \leq (ax+a+R), i.e. 0 < (obf - ax - R) \leq a$$

where m is the root and obf are the obfuscations applied by the auditor, refer to Step 2 for obfuscation. Once this is verified for all the roots, the auditor can then fine the drone if any of the roots lie in the range of cosine function.

6 Security and Privacy Analysis

This section we dwell into explaining how secure our methods are in each interaction (stated above) and why they can not be broken. We also discuss the various security constraints and parameters taken into consideration at each step.

6.1 Security of the Encrypted Trace

The first concern in this protocol would be the security of the encrypted trace sent by the drone to the auditor. It is to be ensured that the auditor can not find out the real trace of the drone.

We can say that the encrypted trace is as secure as our encryption scheme (HE1 and HE1N) is against brute-force attack. A brute-force attack against HE1 would be successful in polynomial time if and only if one can factorise the semiprime modulus used, in polynomial time. We consider a variant of brute force attack which is known as *collision attack*. Let us suppose that we have a pair of equal plaintexts $m_1 = m_2$. This would result in difference of the ciphertexts to be an encryption of 0, and the scheme is subject to Known-plaintext attack (KPA). However, this attack is not possible if the entropy is high. The complexity of this problem is similar to that in RSA cryptosystem, which currently remains impractical to be attacked against.

The probability that any two plaintext messages are equal will be $P(m_1 = m_2) \leq 2^{-\rho}$, where ρ is the entropy with which the messages are distributed. Therefore, if we have n messages then the probability of a collision attack to take place is at most $\binom{n}{2} 2^{-\rho}$. If $n < 2^{-\rho/3}$, then the probability will be lesser than $2^{-\rho/3}$, which is smaller than the inverse polynomial in λ. Therefore, if λ is large enough collision attack is impractical. The similar case would be for HE1N.

6.2 Security of Auditor's Obfuscation Function

The main essence of using a obfuscation function is to mask the original value from the recipient. This obfuscation needs to work while the drone already has knowledge of the original values being obfuscated by the auditor, i.e. the drone already knows which values' obfuscations it is looking at but must be unable to map them with their original values.

For the privacy preserving protocol we build the obfuscation function as

$$C = c + R \qquad (25)$$

where R is a random number, c is any message and C is its obfuscated value. In order to actually/practically provide any obfuscation at all the lower bound of R needs to be atleast as large as the values being obfuscated.

Consider a scenario where there is a large difference between some of the c's being obfuscated and the choice of the Rs doesn't help reduce the difference between them, in such a scenario the auditor has an easy way of predicting atleast two among all the values being obfuscated.

Now if we add a new term in the function,

$$C = ac + R \qquad (26)$$

In order to address our earlier concern of possibility of there being too great differences between the values being obfuscated, we introduce the parameter a, using which we bring all our values into a range where the mutual difference isn't too great.

The possibility of the drone predicting the original values is further reduced greatly. The drone will have a hard time trying to map obfuscations to their original values as there can be multiple values of (a, R) with which one original value can generate more than one obfuscation from the list on hand.

6.3 Security of Drone's Obfuscation Function

This obfuscation doesn't have the constraint the auditor's obfuscation function faces, i.e. the auditor doesn't have the knowledge of the original values being obfuscated by the drone. Though the auditor doesn't know original values, the decrypted values still retain the form of the obfuscation used by the auditor, making it easy to retrieve the underlying value of root.

After decrypting the obfuscated values sent by the auditor, the drone multiplies all the values by a random number. This is done so that the auditor can not figure out the actual roots of the equation.

It is observed that the auditor has knowledge of $C = ac + R$, the value returned to the auditor by drone after obfuscation is

$$M = (am + R') \times T \qquad (27)$$

where $c = m + rp$, $R' = R \bmod p$ and T is drone's obfuscation factor. The auditor can not figure out the real roots from the values sent by the drone just by the knowledge of a as R' is unknown to the auditor.

Note: The comparison between two quartic coefficients is possible only if the obfuscations terms a, R, T remain same for both quartic coefficients in every pair formed to test for equality.

6.4   Security of the Range-Check

The information regarding which encrypted root/s lie in the cosine range can not be revealed to the auditor, as we have considered a semi-honest model. The set of obfuscations generated by the auditor for each encrypted root must use the same terms a, R, T so that when the drone returns the ranges of the roots and their obfuscations, the auditor is unable to figure out which set of ranges maps to which root's set.

7   Evaluation

Due to the availability of limited storage we are required to limit the sampling rate at which the GPS samples are recorded. In this section we discuss the maximum sampling rate and also the storage requirements that would be required for the functioning of the proposed protocol.

7.1   Practical Sampling Rate

In the proposed protocol, the *latitude/longitude* of the locations are scaled by the drone, to convert them into integers before encrypting them using the encrypting protocol (HE1 or HE1N). For encrypting we require a certain entropy of the input. In order to achieve that we need to scale the *latitude/longitude* up to 10 decimal places. Thus, any decimal place beyond that will be ignored/truncated. Therefore, we can limit the maximum sampling rate of the GPS hardware to detect changes in the co-ordinates only up to 10th decimal place, since any additional sensitivity will cause no change in the values considered by the drone in the protocol. Considering the above changes the maximum sampling frequency is 2.81 MHz of the GPS hardware.

The memory that can be stored on the drone is limited and hence we need to restrict the number of GPS samples that are stored. To tackle this problem we use the Adaptive Sampling [8] (as discussed in Alidrone) method, which ensures that the sampling frequency is adjusted depending upon the proximity of the drone with the NFZ.

On applying the Adaptive Sampling to the GPS hardware the following results are obtained. The red circles represent the NFZs, and the yellow dots indicate the co-ordinates at which the GPS samples are recorded using Adaptive Sampling. The trace of the drone is indicated using the blue line (Figs. 5, 6 and 7).

The Table 1 below shows us the number of GPS samples recorded in the above three cases,

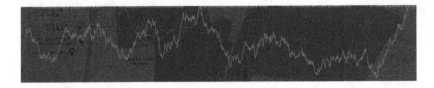

Fig. 5. Samples recorded when there are no NFZs in the proximity of the drone (Color figure online)

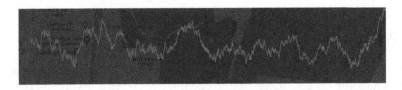

Fig. 6. Samples recorded when there are a few NFZs in the proximity of the drone (Color figure online)

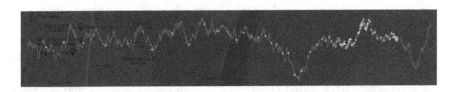

Fig. 7. Samples recorded when there are NFZs in proximity of the drone's path (Color figure online)

Table 1. Table showing number of samples recorded for three different cases where (1) When there is no NFZ in the proximity of the drone's trace, (2) & (3) When there are a few NFZs in the proximity of the drone's Trace.

Case	No. of samples	
	Highest freq	Adaptive sampling
1	1000	26
2	1000	58
3	1000	99

Case 1 shows us that the number of samples recorded are lesser in number when there are no NFZs on the drone's path. On the other hand we see that in Case 2 and Case 3 the sampling frequency increases as the drone flies near a NFZ, thus we see that the samples collected near a NFZ increases. The sampling rate completely depends upon the density of the NFZs present in the navigation area of the drone.

7.2 Data Storage

In this section we try and compare the amount of storage required by AliDrone and our proposed protocol.

- Maximum flight time of drone: 20 mins
- Maximum GPS sampling frequency: 2.81 Mhz
- No. of samples recorded in worst case scenario: 336×10^7 (when samples are recorded at maximum frequency)
- The average conversion rate for adaptive sampling algorithm is 65 samples out of 10,000.
- The key space considered is the minimum possible with respect to [14]

Table 2. Comparison of the size of trace in plaintext and encrypted domain Since AliDrone operates in plaintext domain and HEDrone operates in encrypted domain, this actually is a comparison between storage requirements of AliDrone and HEDrone

	Co-ordinates	Timestamp	Size of Trace	Size of trace (after Adaptive sampling)
Alidrone (Plaintext Domain)	64 bits	20 bits	75.6 TB	2.3 GB
HEDrone (Encrypted Domain)	2302 bits	20 bits	10.38 PB	2.5 TB

In case of encrypted domain on considering the size of trace after taking adaptive sampling into account, the value comes down to 2.5 TB out of which only 0.5 TB needs to be persisted on the drone, that is nearly 219 $times$ the storage space needed in plaintext domain per a trip of 20 min (Table 2).

It can be clearly seen that all the storage and communication is constrained by the size of trace/roots, hence if the trip is planned, it would rather be a lot easier on the system to take a longer but less dense path rather than a very dense path of no-fly-zones. This would help reducing the size of the trace and making it practical to fly.

8   Limitations

Other than the limitations inherited from AliDrone, this section focuses on this paper's limitations and suggests some possible solutions/workarounds.

8.1   Storage Space

Considering the various drone models available, no model can offer the amount of storage space required by HEDrone. In case of drones being used for logistics, the use of route planning software to come up with a predefined path can greatly reduce the amount of storage required. While in the case of free flyers, areas densely populated with NFZs are not areas where free-flying is possible without violating the guidelines, so compelling flyers to choose locations with less densely packed NFZs and suitable speeds for drone operation will enable us to greatly reduce the storage demands of the proposed protocol.

8.2   Computational Requirements

The encryption schemes used demand quite some computational power from the hardware to be able to perform the operations involved in HEDrone in real-time. The computations can be broadly classified into two categories: i) computations involved in encrypted trace generation during flight, ii) computations involved in the verification stage of the proposed protocol.

Case I: Computations Involved in Encrypted Trace Generation (PoA). These computations are to be performed on-the-fly since only the encrypted trace is allowed to be persisted in the storage. As discussed in the above subsection, if we are able to reduce the number of locations to be persisted, then the time between the processing of two consecutive samples also increases, allowing us to relax the computational requirements to some extent. Despite everything, it all comes down to the hardware being used and any decent piece of hardware today is capable of handling encryption and concurrency. So case i should not be a problem.

Case II: Computations Involved in Verification Stage of HEDrone. The real problem with computations being run on the drone will present themselves in this case, where the operations involve numbers with more than 1000 bits. Unlike encrypted trace generation, HEDrone doesn't require the verification stage be performed in real-time, the drone can be enabled to process each trip's data and when complete save the data in a secure cloud so that it's own memory can be freed except the metadata for each trip which help the drone decrypt the data in the cloud.

9   Conclusion

With the increasing use of drones for commercial purposes many works have been done in the direction to ensure the privacy of the NFZ owners, by making sure that the drone complies to the policy of the NFZ owner before entering the property. Through our proposed policy we build upon the Alidrone protocol by ensuring compliance of the drone with the NFZ along with protecting the privacy of the drone operator. Our proposed protocol would help in protecting the Trace of the drone from being revealed as well as checking for violations, thereby protecting the privacy of both the entities.

References

1. Young, A.: Passenger jet carrying 240 people nearly hits a drone at 15,000ft, The Daily Mail, UK, 15 September 2018
2. British broadcasting corporation. Big rise in drone jail smuggling incidents, February 2016. http://www.bbc.com/news/uk-35641453
3. Javaid, A.Y., Sun, W., Devabhaktuni, V.K., Alam, M.: Cyber security threat analysis and modeling of an unmanned aerial vehicle system. In: 2012 IEEE Conference on Technologies for Homeland Security (HST), pp. 585–590. IEEE (2012)
4. Birnbach, S., Baker, R., Martinovic, I.: Wi-fly?: detecting privacy invasion attacks by consumer drones (2017)
5. Busset, J., et al.: Detection and tracking of drones using advanced acoustic cameras. In: Unmanned/Unattended Sensors and Sensor Networks XI; and Advanced Free-Space Optical Communication Techniques and Applications, vol. 9647, p. 96470F, International Society for Optics and Photonics (2015)
6. Nguyen, P., Truong, H., Ravindranathan, M., Nguyen, A., Han, R., Vu, T.: Matthan: drone presence detection by identifying physical signatures in the drone's RF communication. In: Proceedings of the 15th Annual International Conference on Mobile Systems, Applications, and Services, pp. 211–224 (2017)
7. Rozantsev, A., Lepetit, V., Fua, P.: Flying objects detection from a single moving camera. In: Proceedings of the IEEE Conference on Computer Vision and Pattern Recognition, pp. 4128–4136 (2015)
8. Liu, T., Hojjati, A., Bates, A., Nahrstedt, K.: AliDrone: enabling trustworthy proof-of-alibi for commercial drone compliance. In: 2018 IEEE 38th International Conference on Distributed Computing Systems (ICDCS), pp. 841–852 (2018)
9. Brasser, F., Kim, D., Liebchen, C., Ganapathy, V., Iftode, L., Sadeghi, A.-R.: Regulating arm trustzone devices in restricted spaces. In: Proceedings of the 14th Annual International Conference on Mobile Systems, Applications, and Services, MobiSys 2016, pp. 413–425, Association for Computing Machinery, New York (2016)
10. Javaid, A.Y., Sun, W., Devabhaktuni, V.K., Alam, M.: Cyber security threat analysis and modeling of an unmanned aerial vehicle system. In: 2012 IEEE Conference on Technologies for Homeland Security (HST), pp. 585–590 (2012)
11. Vijeev, A., Ganapathy, V., Bhattacharyya, C.: Regulating drones in restricted spaces. In: Proceedings of the 20th International Workshop on Mobile Computing Systems and Applications, HotMobile 2019, pp. 27–32, Association for Computing Machinery, New York (2019)
12. Beck, R.R., Vijeev, A., Ganapathy, V.: Privaros: a framework for privacy-compliant drones, arXiv preprint arXiv:2002.06512 (2020)
13. Blank, P., Kirrane, S., Spiekermann, S.: Privacy-aware restricted areas for unmanned aerial systems. IEEE Secur. Priv. 16(2), 70–79 (2018)
14. Dyer, J., Dyer, M., Xu, J.: Practical homomorphic encryption over the integers, arXiv preprint arXiv:1702.07588 (2017)

15. Peng, Y., Li, H., Cui, J., Zhang, J., Ma, J., Peng, C.: hope: improved order preserving encryption with the power to homomorphic operations of ciphertexts. Sci. China Inf. Sci. **60**(062101), 2017 (2017)
16. Cheon, J.H., Kim, A., Kim, M., Song, Y.: Homomorphic encryption for arithmetic of approximate numbers. In: Takagi, T., Peyrin, T. (eds.) ASIACRYPT 2017. LNCS, vol. 10624, pp. 409–437. Springer, Cham (2017). https://doi.org/10.1007/978-3-319-70694-8_15

Fiat-Shamir with Aborts: From Identification Schemes to Linkable Ring Signatures

Dipayan Das$^{(\boxtimes)}$

National Institute of Technology, Durgapur, Durgapur, India
dasdipayan.crypto@gmail.com

Abstract. Fiat-Shamir with aborts is a technique to transform a lattice-based identification scheme to a signature scheme introduced by Lyubashevsky (in Asiacrypt 2009). The scheme is also provably secure based on some standard lattice problems. In this paper, we show how to generically transform a signature scheme, obtained by Fiat-Shamir transformation from the ring learning with errors problem (RLWE), to a ring signature. The ring signature obtained with this transformation possesses standard security notions like unforgeability and anonymity. We also show how to achieve a linkable ring signature from the ring signature using a collision-resistant hash function. Linkable ring signatures are an important cryptographic tool as it protects signer anonymity and link signatures from the same signer. The linkable ring signature obtained from this transformation performs at par with the other lattice-based solutions for linkable ring signature, which does not require high-end zero-knowledge proofs.

1 Introduction

An identification scheme [1] is a three-round authentication protocol that is used by a prover to convince a verifier that he holds a secret information (his identity). The prover, who holds a secret key sk, first sends a commitment $\mathbf{w}$ to the verifier using an efficient probabilistic algorithm P_1, verifier in return replies with a random challenge $\mathbf{c}$ from the challenge space C, the prover again replies with a response $\mathbf{z}$ (which depends on the verifier's challenge and prover's commitment) using an efficient algorithm P_2. The verifier accepts if the transcript $(\mathbf{w}, \mathbf{c}, \mathbf{z})$ is valid, which is done using a deterministic verification algorithm V. This is shown in Fig. 1.

Fiat-Shamir transformation converts an identification scheme into a signature scheme with an additional hash function H. This is done by simply replacing verifier's random challenge $\mathbf{c}$ by a hash output of the prover's (signer in case of signature scheme) commitment along with the message denoted by $H(\mathbf{w}, M)$. The signature of the message M is $(\mathbf{c}, \mathbf{z})$, which is a valid signature if $(\mathbf{w}, \mathbf{c} = H(\mathbf{w}, M), \mathbf{z})$ is a valid transcript of the identification scheme. The Fiat-Shamir transformation from an identification scheme to a signature scheme is given in Fig. 2.

L. Batina et al. (Eds.): SPACE 2020, LNCS 12586, pp. 167–187, 2020.
https://doi.org/10.1007/978-3-030-66626-2_9

Prover(sk)   Verifier(pk)
$\mathbf{w} \leftarrow P_1(sk)$ $\xrightarrow{\quad \mathbf{w} \quad}$

                                  $\xleftarrow{\quad \mathbf{c} \quad}$ $\mathbf{c} \leftarrow C$
$\mathbf{z} \leftarrow P_2(sk, \mathbf{w}, \mathbf{c})$ $\xrightarrow{\quad \mathbf{z} \quad}$ $V(pk, \mathbf{w}, \mathbf{c}, \mathbf{z}) \in \{0, 1\}$

Fig. 1. Identification scheme

The above framework works well in a factoring-based scheme, but in lattice-based scheme, there is some known attack which exploits the valid transcript to get information about the signer's secret key [23,42]. Authors in [23,42] have shown how to recover the signer's secret key using valid transcripts in the preliminary lattice signatures, like GGHsign [28] and NTRUsign [30]. To mitigate the transcript attack, Lyubashevsky proposed Fiat-Shamir with abort technique [38], which provably (information-theoretically) withstand the transcript attack (see Fig. 3). In this technique, a prover (or a signer) sends a response $\mathbf{z}$ only if $\mathbf{z}$ follows some extra condition. The technique of transcript secure signature scheme has been studied further in [39], which has been the foundation of some recent advances of lattice signatures [7,11,21]. The transcript secure NTRUsign has been studied in [19] using a variant of Fiat Shamir with aborts technique.

Signer(sk, M)   Verifier(pk)
$\mathbf{w} \leftarrow P_1(sk)$
$\mathbf{c} = H(\mathbf{w}, M)$
$\mathbf{z} \leftarrow P_2(sk, \mathbf{w}, \mathbf{c})$ $\xrightarrow{\quad (\mathbf{c}, \mathbf{z}, M) \quad}$ $V(pk, \mathbf{c}, \mathbf{z}, M) \in \{0, 1\}$

Fig. 2. Fiat-Shamir transformation

In some applications, including e-voting system and cryptocurrency, it is also crucial to have an additional signer anonymity property (to hide signer's identity) in a signature scheme. In order to impose the additional property of hiding signer's identity on a signature scheme, the idea of *ring signature* was first proposed in [49]. A Ring signature is a unique type of signature where a signer can sign on behalf of an ad-hoc group (which is called a ring), while keeping himself anonymous. In addition, in a ring signature, there is generally no trusted third party who can reveal the identity of the signer and manage group membership. This makes a ring signature superior to a group signature, where a third party manages new signer's identity.

Signer(sk, M)   Verifier(pk)
$\mathbf{w} \leftarrow P_1(sk)$
$\mathbf{c} = H(\mathbf{w}, M)$
$\mathbf{z} \leftarrow P_2(sk, \mathbf{w}, \mathbf{c})$
If $\mathbf{z} \in G$ $\xrightarrow{\quad (\mathbf{c}, \mathbf{z}, M) \quad}$ $V(pk, \mathbf{c}, \mathbf{z}, M) \in \{0, 1\}$

Fig. 3. Fiat-Shamir transformation with aborts

Let us give a hypothetical example where the ring signature can be useful. A member of a company wants to inform all the company members about her boss's misdeeds, yet at the same time wants to remain anonymous, so that the company does not fire her when she tells the world about the misdeeds. The ring signature can be valuable in this regard. Since she is a member of the company (which is the ring here), she can sign on a message on behalf of the company. Every other member of the company can verify that a valid member of the company has signed, and with the anonymity property of a ring signature, the member remains anonymous.

Later, ring signature with linkable property is introduced in [36], which is known as the *linkable ring signature*. The linkable property allows linking a signer when he signs two messages (same or different), keeping the anonymity property of a ring signature intact. The linkable ring signature is useful in cryptocurrencies to prevent double-spending while preserving the anonymity of a spender [46]. Also, it has applications for other real-life scenarios, like big data privacy [34], e-voting [55], etc.

1.1 Related Work

There has been a sequence of work that proposes (linkable) ring signatures based on the traditional number theoretical problems [10, 35, 36, 53, 55]. Number theoretic cryptographic problems are known to be vulnerable against quantum adversary [51], which may lead to weakness in long-term anonymity. Lattice-based problems are known to be quantum-resistant, which may help to withstand quantum threats. Further, lattice problems enjoy worst-case security guarantees [3, 48], which makes it one of the promising alternatives of the number-theoretic cryptography. This fact is demonstrated by the NIST competition for post-quantum security [43], where lattice-based solutions contributed to the majority.

Recently, there have been some lattice-based solutions for the (linkable) ring signatures. In [13], a linkable ring signature scheme is proposed from the module SIS problem [32], which can be seen as the generalization of a variant of Dilithium (Dilithium-G) lattice-based digital signature [21]. Dilithium [21] is one of the candidates for the third round NIST post-quantum cryptography competition [45]. In [54], a linkable ring signature is proposed from the ring SIS problem, which can be seen as the generalization of the BLISS lattice-based digital signature [20]. Both [13, 54] uses Gaussian based rejection sampling, which requires sampling from discrete Gaussian distribution. Currently, sampling from discrete Gaussian distribution is a major obstacle for the community, with some known vulnerabilities studied in [15, 47].

To avoid sampling from discrete Gaussian distribution, [18] proposed a linkable ring signature that uses uniform rejection sampling method as used in previous lattice-based digital signatures [21, 29, 38]. Additionally, the authors instantiated the scheme using a variant of learning with errors problem, known as the middle-product learning with errors (MPLWE) problem [11, 50]. MPLWE problem is known to be hard by a reduction from RLWE problem, over many polynomials that define the RLWE problem. But such reductions increase the parameter choice for the MPLWE problem, making a cryptographic construction less efficient. In order to get better efficiency, [18] uses aggressive parameters that do not support the reduction from [11].

In Raptor [37], a linkable ring signature is proposed, which is a generalization of Falcon digital signature [25] using Chameleon Hash Plus function. Falcon is also a candidate for the NIST third round post-quantum competition [45]. The core idea behind Raptor is a trapdoor generation for lattices from [27], which is still a complex operation after many years of investigation [16,22,41]. Also, it is to be noted that the optimized version of Raptor uses NTRU problem [30,31] as the underlying hardness assumptions, which is only heuristically secure, unlike the SIS/LWE variants which enjoy worst-case security guarantees.

In addition, there have been some lattice-based solutions for ring signatures using zero-knowledge arguments [24,33], but the inefficiency of the underlying zero-knowledge arguments does not make the schemes too practical.

1.2 Our Contribution

The main contribution of this paper is to introduce a method to transform an identification scheme into a linkable ring signature. The transformation is quite simple and efficient. The direction of the transformation achieved in this paper is given below.

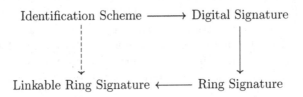

We instantiated the transformation using RLWE problem as the underlying lattice problem over the ring $\mathbb{Z}[x]/(x^{2^k}+1)$, for some integer k. Such polynomials are useful for cryptographic applications as it supports the search to decision reduction for the RLWE problem [40]. The transformation is generic and can be instantiated using any variants of LWE. The choice of the RLWE problem in this paper is due to the fact that the underlying polynomial multiplications can be done effectively using NTT than module LWE [32] or middle-product LWE [11,50].

We achieve the security notion of unforgeability, anonymity, linkability of a linkable ring signature in the random oracle model. The unforgeability result is attained using "lossy" key technique as introduced in [18] in the context of ring signatures. The anonymity result is achieved by a technique of game swapping, as done in [54]. The linkability result is achieved by a reduction from finding a collision in a cryptographic hash function to unlinking two messages by the same signer.

Table 1. Comparison with different lattice-based linkable ring signatures

	This paper	[37]	[18]	[54]
Secret key size (in Kb)	2	9.1	4.3	0.59
Public key size (in Kb)	1.4	0.9	2.5	1.15
Signature size (in Kb) (ring size1)	5	3	19.5	51
Signature size (in Kb) (ring size5)	21	7.8	19.8	89
Signature size (in Kb) (ring size10)	41	14.2	20.1	136

Though lattice problems enjoy worst-case security reductions, to get better parameter estimates, it is generally the attacks that are considered before choosing concrete parameters for a lattice-based construction. Considering the general approach, the parameters of the (linkable) ring signature are chosen such that it withstands all known attacks. We give a brief comparison for the linkable ring signature with the other lattice-based solutions in Table 1.

2 Preliminaries

2.1 Notations

We will use R to represent the polynomial ring $\mathbb{Z}[x]/(x^n + 1)$, where n is a power of two. For such a choice of ring, multiplication in the ring can be done faster (in time $\tilde{O}(n)$) using Fast Fourier Transformation. The result obtained in the paper can be easily achieved for some other polynomial f, where there is a meaningful worst-case reduction. We will denote R_q, where q is a large prime, to represent polynomials in R with coefficients in $\left[\frac{-(q-1)}{2}, \frac{(q-1)}{2}\right]$. We will also use $R_k \subset R_q$ to represent polynomials with coefficients in $[-k, k]$. In this paper, we will treat a polynomial in R (or R_q) and a vector in $\mathbb{Z}^n$ (or $\mathbb{Z}_q^n$) as a similar data type. We will use $[n]$ to denote natural numbers between 1 to n.

For a vector $\mathbf{a}$, $\|\mathbf{a}\|_\infty := \max_i |a_i|$, $\|\mathbf{a}\|_1 := \sum_i |a_i|$, $\|\mathbf{a}\|_2 := \sqrt{\sum_i a_i^2}$. We will use low norm vector to mean vector whose norm is $<<q$. We will denote $\langle , \rangle$ to represent the inner product of two vectors. For a set S, we will use $\mathbf{a} \xleftarrow{\$} S$ to sample uniformly at random from the set S. For a distribution, Ψ, we will use $\mathbf{a} \xleftarrow{\$} \Psi$ to sample according to the distribution Ψ. All operations done in this paper will end up with a mod q operation unless stated otherwise. All log used in this paper will have base 2.

Ring Learning with Errors Problem (RLWE) [1]

Definition 1 ((search) Ring Learning with errors problem). *Let Ψ_1, Ψ_2 be two distributions over $\mathbb{Z}_q[x]/(f)$. For a fix $s \xleftarrow{s} \Psi_1$, given samples of the form $(a_i, b_i = a_i s + e_i) \in \mathbb{Z}_q[x]/(f) \times \mathbb{Z}_q[x]/(f)$, where $a_i \xleftarrow{s} \mathbb{Z}_q[x]/(f)$, $e_i \xleftarrow{s} \Psi_2$, find s.*

The samples (a_i, b_i) obtained as above, is said to follow RLWE distribution over $\mathbb{Z}[x]/(f)$. The search version of the RLWE problem was first introduced in [52] to speed up LWE based cryptosystem, which could be shown as hard as the (worst-case) approximate shortest vector problem in any ideal lattices of $\mathbb{Z}_q[x]/(f)$. The reduction works when f is monic, irreducible, and have bounded expansion factor. In many applications, including public key encryptions, it is difficult to achieve security reductions with a mere search problem. In such cases, it is crucial to have a decisional analog of a search problem that was introduced in [40].

Definition 2 ((decisional) Ring Learning with errors problem). *Given samples of the form $(a_i, b_i) \in R_q \times R_q$, decide (with non-negligible probability) if it comes from RLWE distribution or uniform distribution.*

[40] provides a decision to search reduction for cyclotomic polynomials. In general, the power of two cyclotomics plays an important role in cryptographic applications as multiplication in the ring can be done efficiently. In this paper, we will consider the following version of the RLWE problem.

Definition 3. *Let k is any integer less than q. The (decisional) RLWE problem is said to have a distinguishing advantage ϵ, if for any polynomial-time adversary $\mathcal{A}$, the distinguishing advantage of RLWE distribution when $(s, e) \xleftarrow{s} R_k \times R_k$ is less than or equal to ϵ. That is*

$$|\Pr[\mathcal{A}(a, b = as + e \in R_q \times R_q) = 1] - \Pr[\mathcal{A}(a, b \xleftarrow{s} R_q \times R_q) = 1]| \leq \epsilon$$

The RLWE assumption says that the distinguishing advantage ϵ is negligible for all polynomial time adversary $\mathcal{A}$.

2.2   Fiat Shamir with Aborts from RLWE Problem

Fiat-Shamir with abort technique was initially introduced in [38] to prevent the transcript attack in the initial lattice signatures, like GGHsign, NTRUsign. The transcript secure lattice signatures are achieved using a technique called *rejection sampling*. In rejection sampling, the response z of the prover (signer in case of the signature scheme) is sent to the verifier only if it lies within a specific range, aborting otherwise. This enables the distribution of z independent of the secret key of the signer. In Fig. 4, we have shown how RLWE based

---

[1] The ring in Ring LWE refer to the mathematical ring structure which is different from the ring in the ring signatures. The ring in the ring signatures signifies an ad-hoc group.

$H : \{0,1\}^* \rightarrow C = \{\mathbf{c} : \mathbf{c} \in R_2 \wedge \|\mathbf{c}\|_1 \leq \kappa\}$
$\mathbf{a} \xleftarrow{\$} R_q; (\mathbf{s}, \mathbf{e}) \xleftarrow{\$} R_{k_1} \times R_{k_1}$
$\mathbf{b} = \mathbf{as} + \mathbf{e} \in R_q$

Signer$(\mathbf{s}, \mathbf{e}, M)$	Verifier$(\mathbf{a}, \mathbf{b})$
$(\mathbf{y}_1, \mathbf{y}_2) \xleftarrow{\$} R_{k_2} \times R_{k_2}; \mathbf{w} = \mathbf{ay}_1 + \mathbf{y}_2$	Accept if
$\mathbf{c} = H(\mathbf{w}, M)$	
$\mathbf{z}_1 = \mathbf{sc} + \mathbf{y}_1$	
$\mathbf{z}_2 = \mathbf{ec} + \mathbf{y}_2$	$\mathbf{z}_1, \mathbf{z}_2 \in R_{k_2 - \kappa k_1}$
If $\mathbf{z}_1, \mathbf{z}_2 \in R_{k_2 - \kappa k_1}$ $\xrightarrow{\quad (\mathbf{c}, \mathbf{z}_1, \mathbf{z}_2, M) \quad}$	$\mathbf{c} = H(\mathbf{az}_1 + \mathbf{z}_2 - \mathbf{bc}, M)$
Else Repeat	

Fig. 4. Fiat-Shamir signatures from RLWE problem

Fiat-Shamir signatures work using the rejection sampling procedure. In [38], the author considered (ring) SIS problem for constructing the signature scheme. In the full version of [39], a signature scheme on the (ring) LWE was proposed, which can be shown more efficient than the (ring) SIS ones. The Fiat-Shamir signature scheme on the (ring) LWE problem was further studied in [12,29] to optimizing the basic signature scheme. Dilithium [21] and qTESLA [7] are two lattice-based signature schemes from Fiat-Shamir with aborts technique, which is in the second round of the NIST competion [44].

In this setting, the public key $(\mathbf{a}, \mathbf{b})$ is a RLWE sample, secret key $(\mathbf{s}, \mathbf{e})$ is the RLWE secrets. The commitment $\mathbf{w}$ is a polynomial in R_q, the challenge space $C = \{\mathbf{c} : \mathbf{c} \in R_2 \wedge \|\mathbf{c}\|_1 \leq \kappa\}$, response $\mathbf{z} = (\mathbf{z}_1, \mathbf{z}_2)$ is pair polynomials in R_q with the low norm. Since $\mathbf{z}_1, \mathbf{z}_2$ depends on the secrets $(\mathbf{s}, \mathbf{e})$, and they are far away from being uniform in R_q; thus there is a direct dependency on the secrets when a response $\mathbf{z}$ is outputted as a signature. This observation is exploited in the transcript attacks from [23,42]. Thus to mitigate the threat, a response $\mathbf{z}$ is sent along with the commitment as a potential signature only when the coefficients of $\mathbf{z}$ is within a certain interval, where there is no dependency on the secrets.

3 Ring Signatures

A ring signature consists of four efficient algorithms:

- **Parameter Generation Algorithm** (λ): It takes the security parameter λ as input, and outputs public parameter $\mathcal{P}$.
- **Key Generation Algorithm** $(\mathcal{P})$: It takes the public parameter $\mathcal{P}$ as input, and output a pair of keys (pk^i, sk^i), where pk^i is called the public key (or verification key), and sk^i is called the secret key (or signing key) of a user.
- **Signature Generation Algorithm** $((M, sk^i), L)$: It takes the message M to be signed, secret key sk^i, and the list L of public keys (which is called the ring) as input such that $pk^i \in L$, and output a signature $\sigma_L(M)$.

- **Signature Verification Algorithm** $(M, \sigma_L(M), L)$: It takes the message M, signature $\sigma_L(M)$, and the list L of public keys in the ring as input, and output Accept or Reject.

Correctness: The signature verification algorithm should output Accept when a signature is constructed by a member of the list L.

Security of Ring Signatures

- **Unforgeability:** It is computationally infeasible for an adversary, who does not possess a secret key to any public keys in the list L, to create a signature $\sigma_L(M)$ for any chosen message M that will output Accept by the signature verification algorithm.
- **Anonymity:** It is computationally infeasible for an adversary to guess the identity of a signature $\sigma_L(M)$ for a given message M of the adversary's choice.

3.1 Linkable Ring Signatures

In a linkable ring signature, we have an additional linking algorithm that will help to link a signer of two messages.

The Framework. A linkable ring signature consists of five efficient algorithms:

- **Parameter Generation Algorithm** (λ): It takes the security parameter λ as input, and outputs public parameter $\mathcal{P}$.
- **Key Generation Algorithm** $(\mathcal{P})$: It takes the public parameter $\mathcal{P}$ as input, and output a pair of keys (pk^i, sk^i), where pk^i is called the public key (or verification key), and sk^i is called the secret key (or signing key).
- **Signature Generation Algorithm** $((M, sk^i), L)$: It takes the message M to be signed, secret key sk^i, and the list L of public keys in the ring as input such that $pk^i \in L$, and output a signature $\sigma_L(M)$.
- **Signature Verification Algorithm** $(M, \sigma_L(M), L)$: It takes the message M, signature $\sigma_L(M)$, and the list L of public keys in the ring as input, and output Accept or Reject.
- **Signature Linking Algorithm** $(\sigma_L(M), \sigma_{L'}(M'))$: It takes two signatures $\sigma_L(M), \sigma_{L'}(M')$ as input and output Linked or Unlinked.

Correctness. The correctness of a linkable ring signature is two-fold.

- **Correctness in Signature Verification Algorithm:** The algorithm should output Accept when a signature is constructed by a member of the ring L.
- **Correctness in Signature Linking Algorithm:** The algorithm should output Linked if the two signatures are from the same signer, regardless of the ring L.

Security of Linkable Ring Signatures.

- **Unforgeability:** It is computationally infeasible for an adversary who does not possess a secret key to any public keys in the ring L to create a signature $\sigma_L(M)$ for any chosen message M of his choice that will output Accept by the signature verification algorithm.
- **Anonymity:** It is computationally infeasible for an adversary to guess the identity of a signature $\sigma_L(M)$ in the ring L for any given message M, (nonnegligibly) better than a random guess.
- **Linkability:** It is computationally infeasible for a signer in the ring L to create two signatures that will output Unlinked by the signature linking algorithm.

3.2 Security Model of a (Linkable) Ring Signature

In this subsection, we present the security model of three different types of adversaries used in unforgeability, anonymity, and linkability game. We will also assume that the adversaries will have access to the following oracles:

1. **Joining Oracle($\mathcal{JO}$):** The adversary can request the oracle to add a new user to the scheme. The oracle outputs the corresponding public key to the adversary.
2. **Corruption Oracle($\mathcal{CO}$):** The adversary can request the oracle to supply the secret key of any public key, which is an output of the Joining oracle. The oracle outputs the corresponding secret keys.
3. **Signing Oracle($\mathcal{SO}$):** The adversary can request the oracle to provide signatures of messages of his choice on inputting the ring and a public key from the ring, which are the output of the joining oracle. The oracle returns a signature corresponding to the ring, which is verified in the verification algorithm.

Unforgeability. In this game, the adversary has access to the $\mathcal{JO}$, $\mathcal{SO}$ oracle, which is maintained by a simulator. The adversary can query these oracle in any adaptive strategy. The adversary wins the unforgeable game if he can output a signature $\sigma_L(M)$ corresponding to a ring L on a message M of his choice such that

1. L is the output of $\mathcal{JO}$.
2. The signature $\sigma_L(M)$ is verified in the verification algorithm.
3. The adversary hasn't queried $\mathcal{CO}$ on any public key corresponding to the ring L.
4. $\sigma_L(M)$ is not an output of $\mathcal{SO}$.

A (linkable) ring signature is said to have unforgeability security notion if the probability of success of any polynomial-time adversary is negligible.

Anonymity. In this game, the adversary has access to the $\mathcal{JO}$ oracle, which is maintained by a simulator. The adversary can query these oracle in any adaptive strategy. The adversary chooses a ring L, which is the output of the $\mathcal{JO}$ oracle, and a message M of his choice and sends it to the simulator. The simulator chooses a public key pk^i uniformly from the ring L and run the $\mathcal{SO}$ oracle on (pk^i, L, M) to get a signature $\sigma_L(M)$. The simulator sends $\sigma_L(M)$ to the adversary. The adversary makes a guess i' and wins the game if $i = i'$. A (linkable) ring signature is said to have anonymity security notion if the probability of success of any polynomial-time adversary is negligibly better than a random guess.

Linkability. In this game, the adversary has access to the $\mathcal{JO}, \mathcal{CO}$ oracle, which is maintained by a simulator. The $\mathcal{JO}$ oracle is allowed for multiple calls, but $\mathcal{CO}$ is allowed for a single call. The adversary wins the linkability game if he can output two signatures $\sigma_L(M)$ and $\sigma_{L'}(M')$ corresponding to two (similar or different) rings L and L' on two messages of his choice and

1. L and L' are the output of $\mathcal{JO}$.
2. The two signatures $\sigma_L(M)$, $\sigma_{L'}(M')$ are verified in the verification algorithm.
3. The two signatures $\sigma_L(M)$, $\sigma_{L'}(M')$ get Unlinked in the signature linking algorithm.

A linkable ring signature is said to have a linkability security notion if the probability of success of any polynomial-time adversary is negligible.

4   Ring Signatures Using Fiat-Shamir with Aborts Paradigm

In this section, we give the framework on how to achieve a ring signature using Fiat-Shamir framework. The framework using RLWE problem is given in Fig. 5. In this setting, the public key of each user in the ring of size w is $(\mathbf{a}, \mathbf{b}_\pi)$, which is a RLWE sample, with secrets $(\mathbf{s}_\pi, \mathbf{e}_\pi)$. Note that the public key of each user in the ring corresponds to different RLWE samples because in each key the secret $\mathbf{s}_\pi$ is different. The commitment $\mathbf{w}$ is a polynomial in R_q, the challenge space $C = \{\mathbf{c} : \mathbf{c} \in R_2 \wedge \|\mathbf{c}\|_1 \leq \kappa\}$, response $\mathbf{z}^{(\pi)} = (\mathbf{z}_\pi, \mathbf{z}'_\pi)$ is a pair polynomial in R_q with the low norm. As discussed previously, we apply a rejection sampling step on the response so that there is no dependency on the secrets. Now in order to get the anonymity property, we need to hide the index π, which is done by randomly selecting $w - 1$ other responses $\mathbf{z}^{(i)}_{i \in [w] \wedge i \neq \pi}$ as part of the signature output. Now it is hard for one to know information about the index π from w similar responses. We give the details in the next subsection.

Parameter Generation Algorithm. On inputting the security parameter, the Parameter Generation Algorithm outputs

$H : \{0,1\}^* \to C = \{\mathbf{c} : \mathbf{c} \in R_2 \wedge \|\mathbf{c}\|_1 \leq \kappa\}$

$\mathbf{a} \xleftarrow{\$} R_q$

$(\mathbf{s}_\pi, \mathbf{e}_\pi) \xleftarrow{\$} R_{k_1} \times R_{k_1}$

$\mathbf{b}_\pi = \mathbf{a}\mathbf{s}_\pi + \mathbf{e}_\pi \in R_q$

$L = \{\mathbf{b}_i\}_{i \in [w]}; \ \pi \in [w]$

Signer$(\mathbf{s}_\pi, \mathbf{e}_\pi, M, L)$

$(\mathbf{y}_1, \mathbf{y}_2) \xleftarrow{\$} R_{k_2} \times R_{k_2}; \ \mathbf{w} = \mathbf{a}\mathbf{y}_1 + \mathbf{y}_2$

$\mathbf{c}_{\pi+1} = H(\mathbf{w}, M, L)$

For $i \in [w] \wedge i \neq \pi$

$(\mathbf{z}_i, \mathbf{z}_i') \xleftarrow{\$} R_{k_2 - \kappa k_1} \times R_{k_2 - \kappa k_1}$

$\mathbf{c}_{i+1} = H(\mathbf{a}\mathbf{z}_i + \mathbf{z}_i' - \mathbf{b}_i\mathbf{c}_i, M, L)$

$\mathbf{z}_\pi = \mathbf{s}_\pi \mathbf{c}_\pi + \mathbf{y}_1$

$\mathbf{z}_\pi' = \mathbf{e}_\pi \mathbf{c}_\pi + \mathbf{y}_2$

If $(\mathbf{z}_\pi, \mathbf{z}_\pi') \in R_{k_2 - \kappa k_1} \times R_{k_2 - \kappa k_1}$

Else Restart

Verifier(L)

For $i \in [w]$

$\mathbf{c}_{i+1} = H(\mathbf{a}\mathbf{z}_i + \mathbf{z}_i' - \mathbf{b}_i\mathbf{c}_i, M, L)$

Accept If

$\{\mathbf{z}_i, \mathbf{z}_i'\}_{i \in [w]} \in R_{k_2 - \kappa k_1}$

$\mathbf{c}_1 = H(\mathbf{a}\mathbf{z}_w + \mathbf{z}_w' - \mathbf{b}_w\mathbf{c}_w, M, L)$

$$\xrightarrow{\left(\mathbf{c}_1, \{\mathbf{z}_i, \mathbf{z}_i'\}_{i \in [w]}, M\right)}$$

Fig. 5. Fiat-Shamir ring signatures from RLWE problem

1. q: a large modulus.
2. n: defining ring.
3. κ: defining norm of the Hash function H.
4. k_1: defining distribution of secret and error, respectively, which is small.
5. k_2: Rejection sampling parameter.

The Parameter Generation Algorithm also chooses a cryptographic Hash function $H : \{0,1\}^* \to C = \{\mathbf{c} : \mathbf{c} \in R_2 \wedge \|\mathbf{c}\|_1 \leq \kappa\}$. We will use the hash function as the random oracle in the proof. The Parameter Generation Algorithm also generates $\mathbf{a} \xleftarrow{\$} R_q$, which can be shared among all users. In practice, this can be done using a hash function exploiting a common seed.

Key Generation Algorithm. The π-th user of the ring L chooses $\mathbf{s}_\pi \xleftarrow{\$} R_{k_1}$, $\mathbf{e}_\pi \xleftarrow{\$} R_{k_1}$, and construct $\mathbf{b}_\pi = \mathbf{a}\mathbf{s}_\pi + \mathbf{e}_\pi$. Note that $\mathbf{b}_\pi$ is a RLWE instance. The public key is $(\mathbf{a}, \mathbf{b}_\pi) \in R_q \times R_q$, and the secret key is $(\mathbf{s}_\pi, \mathbf{e}_\pi)$.

Signature Generation Algorithm. To sign a message M, the signer $\pi \in [w]$ does the following: The signer chooses $(\mathbf{y}_1, \mathbf{y}_2) \xleftarrow{\$} R_{k_2} \times R_{k_2}$ and computes $\mathbf{w} = \mathbf{a}\mathbf{y}_1 + \mathbf{y}_2$. Then he assigns $\mathbf{c}_{\pi+1} = H(\mathbf{w}, M, L)$. Now, for $i \in [w]$ and $i \neq \pi$, he chooses $(\mathbf{z}_i, \mathbf{z}_i') \xleftarrow{\$} R_{k_2 - \kappa k_1} \times R_{k_2 - \kappa k_1}$, then assigns $\mathbf{c}_{i+1} = H(\mathbf{a}\mathbf{z}_i + \mathbf{z}_i' - \mathbf{c}_i\mathbf{b}_i, M, L)$. Finally, the signer computes $\mathbf{z}_\pi = \mathbf{c}_\pi\mathbf{s}_\pi + \mathbf{y}_1$ and $\mathbf{z}_\pi' = \mathbf{c}_\pi\mathbf{e}_\pi + \mathbf{y}_2$, continues if $\|\mathbf{z}_\pi\|_\infty, \|\mathbf{z}_\pi'\|_\infty \leq k_2 - \kappa k_1$. The probability of getting both $\|\mathbf{z}_\pi\|_\infty, \|\mathbf{z}_\pi'\|_\infty, \leq k_2 - \kappa k_1$ is $\left(\frac{2(k_2 - \kappa k_1) + 1}{2k_2 + 1}\right)^{2n}$. The parameters can be chosen carefully such that the success of the above step is maximized. The signer Outputs $\left(\mathbf{c}_1, \{\mathbf{z}_i, \mathbf{z}_i'\}_{i \in [w]}\right)$ as the signature of the message M.

Signature Verification Algorithm. In the Verification algorithm, the verifier first computes $c_{i+1} = H(az_i + z'_i - c_i b_i, M, L)$ for $i \in [w]$. The verifier accepts the signature if

1. for $i \in [w]$, $\|z_i\|_\infty, \|z'_i\|_\infty \leq k_2 - \kappa k_1$,

2. $c_1 = H(az_w + z'_w - c_w b_w, M, L)$.

4.1   Linkable Ring Signature from Ring Signature

In this subsection, we provide the general framework on how to achieve linkability property in a ring signature. The framework is given in Fig. 6. In this case, we need to tweak the key generation slightly to include the tag of a signer, which will be used in the signature linking algorithm. For this, we need an additional collision-resistant hash function $\mathcal{H}$, which will be chosen in the parameter generation algorithm, that map elements from R_q to R_q. In the key generation algorithm, instead of a RLWE sample b_π as the signer's public key, we now randomize it by adding $\mathcal{H}$ output of the signer's tag h_π, which is a new RLWE sample. During the signing algorithm, the signer eliminates the additional randomization step to go back to the RLWE sample b_π for his share of public key in the ring L. The signature generation algorithm is almost similar, except an additional tag, which is the output along with the signature. In the verification step, the verifier first eliminates the additional randomization step using the signer's tag to go back to the RLWE sample for the signer's public key π (without verifier's knowledge on π). The rest of the procedure is identical.

$H : \{0,1\}^* \to C = \{c : c \in R_2 \wedge \|c\|_1 \leq \kappa\}$
$\mathcal{H} : R_q \to R_q$
$(a, h) \xleftarrow{\$} R_q \times R_q$
$(s_\pi, e_\pi, e'_\pi) \xleftarrow{\$} R_{k_1} \times R_{k_1} \times R_{k_1}$
$b_\pi = as_\pi + e_\pi \in R_q$, $h_\pi = hs_\pi + e'_\pi \in R_q$
$b'_\pi = b_\pi + \mathcal{H}(h_\pi)$
$L = \{b'_i\}_{i \in [w]}; \pi \in [w]$

Signer$(s_\pi, e_\pi, e'_\pi, h_\pi, M, L)$
For $i \in [w]$ $b''_i = b'_i - \mathcal{H}(h_\pi)$
$(y_1, y_2, y_3) \xleftarrow{\$} R_{k_2} \times R_{k_2} \times R_{k_2}$
$w = ay_1 + y_2$, $v = hy_1 + y_3$
$c_{\pi+1} = H(w, v, h_\pi, M, L)$
For $i \in [w] \wedge i \neq \pi$
$(z_i, z'_i, z''_i) \xleftarrow{\$} R_{k_2 - \kappa k_1} \times R_{k_2 - \kappa k_1} \times R_{k_2 - \kappa k_1}$
$c_{i+1} = H(az_i + z'_i - b''_i c_i, hz_i + z''_i - h_\pi c_i, h_\pi, M, L)$
$z_\pi = s_\pi c_\pi + y_1$
$z'_\pi = e_\pi c_\pi + y_2$
$z''_\pi = e'_\pi c_\pi + y_3$
If $(z_\pi, z'_\pi, z''_\pi) \in R_{k_2 - \kappa k_1} \times R_{k_2 - \kappa k_1} \times R_{k_2 - \kappa k_1}$
Else Restart

Verifier(L)
For $i \in [w]$

$b''_i = b'_i - \mathcal{H}(h_\pi)$
$c_{i+1} = H(az_i + z'_i - b''_i c_i, hz_i + z''_i - h_\pi c_i, h_\pi, M, L)$
Accept If

$\{z_i, z'_i, z''_i\}_{i \in [w]} \in R_{k_2 - \kappa k_1}$
$c_1 = H(az_w + z'_w - b''_w c_w, hz_w + z''_w - h_\pi c_w, M, L)$

$\xrightarrow{\left(c_1, \{z_i, z'_i, z''_i\}_{i \in [w]}, h_\pi, M\right)}$

Fig. 6. Fiat-Shamir Linkable ring signatures from RLWE problem

Signature Linking Algorithm. In the signature linking algorithm, the algorithm takes two signatures $\sigma_L(M), \sigma_{L'}(M')$. It outputs Linked if generated by the same signer. This can be done by simply checking if the tag $\mathbf{h}_\pi$, outputted along with the signatures in the signature generation algorithm, of the two signatures are the same.

4.2 Correctness of Signature Generation Algorithm

The Signature generation algorithm is correct if $\mathbf{c}_{\pi+1}$ in the signature generation algorithm is equal to $\mathbf{c}_{\pi+1}$ in the signature verification algorithm. That is we have to show (no need for the second step in case of ring signatures)

1. $\mathbf{ay}_1 + \mathbf{y}_2 = \mathbf{az}_\pi + \mathbf{z}'_\pi - \mathbf{b}_\pi \mathbf{c}_\pi$,

2. $\mathbf{hy}_1 + \mathbf{y}_3 = \mathbf{hz}_\pi + \mathbf{z}''_\pi - \mathbf{h}_\pi \mathbf{c}_\pi$.

Note that

$$\mathbf{az}_\pi + \mathbf{z}'_\pi - \mathbf{b}_\pi \mathbf{c}_\pi = \mathbf{a}\left(\mathbf{s}_\pi \mathbf{c}_\pi + \mathbf{y}_1\right) + \left(\mathbf{e}_\pi \mathbf{c}_\pi + \mathbf{y}_2\right) - \mathbf{c}_\pi \left(\mathbf{as}_\pi + \mathbf{e}_\pi\right)$$
$$= \mathbf{ay}_1 + \mathbf{y}_2$$

And

$$\mathbf{hz}_\pi + \mathbf{z}''_\pi - \mathbf{h}_\pi \mathbf{c}_\pi = \mathbf{h}\left(\mathbf{s}_\pi \mathbf{c}_\pi + \mathbf{y}_1\right) + \left(\mathbf{e}'_\pi \mathbf{c}_\pi + \mathbf{y}_3\right) - \mathbf{c}_\pi \left(\mathbf{hs}_\pi + \mathbf{e}'_\pi\right)$$
$$= \mathbf{hy}_1 + \mathbf{y}_3$$

4.3 Correctness of Signature Linking Algorithm

The Linking algorithm is correct if the tag generated by the same signer always gets Linked. Note that the tag generated in the key generation algorithm is deterministic and the signer with secrets $(\mathbf{s}_\pi, \mathbf{e}_\pi, \mathbf{e}'_\pi)$ always generates the same tag $\mathbf{h}_\pi = \mathbf{hs}_\pi + \mathbf{e}'_\pi$.

5 Security Analysis of the (Linkable) Ring Signature

5.1 Unforgeability

Theorem 1. *If RLWE distribution has the advantage ϵ of distinguishing from a uniform distribution, then any probabilistic polynomial-time adversary querying w public keys, sign queries, and random oracle queries, the advantage of winning the unforgeability game is $w\epsilon + \epsilon_1$, where ϵ_1 is a negligible function in the security parameter.*

The proof uses the technique of the "lossy" keys (introduced in [2,18]), we give the sketch of the proof here due to space constraint. In the proof, we change the original game by a sequence of games, such that each game has the only negligible advantage of distinguishing from the previous. In the final game, the probability of winning the unforgeability game for any probabilistic polynomial time adversary is negligible.

We change the original game with the following modification at a time.

1. **Random oracle simulation** During any random oracle queries, the simulator chooses c and output to the adversary. He has to be consistent if the same response appears twice. The change in this game is indistinguishable from adversary's point of view based on enough entropy of the hash function H.
2. **Signature simulation** During any signature queries corresponding to a signer $\pi \in [w]$, the simulator chooses $(\mathbf{z}_\pi, \mathbf{z}'_\pi, \mathbf{z}''_\pi)$ at random with probability $\left(\frac{2(k_2 - \kappa k_1) + 1}{2k_2 + 1} \right)^{3n} 2$ from the correct domain and programs the random oracle such that it appears as the true signature for π. The change in this game is indistinguishable from adversary's point of view based on enough entropy of the hash function H and identical distribution of the simulated and original signature.
3. **Lossy key generation** During each public key queries of user $\pi \in [w]$, the simulator chooses $\mathbf{b}_\pi \xleftarrow{\$} R_q$ and sets $\mathbf{b}'_\pi = \mathbf{b}_\pi + \mathcal{H}(\mathbf{h}_\pi)$ as the public of π. Note that in case of ring signature, we do not need to compute $\mathbf{b}'_\pi$. The change in this game is indistinguishable from adversary's point of view based on the decisional RLWE assumption.

In the final game, if possible, the adversary produces a signature

$$\left(c_1, \{ \mathbf{z}_i, \mathbf{z}'_i, \mathbf{z}''_i \}_{i \in [w]} \right)$$

on a message M that is verified in the verification algorithm. It has to be that the adversary must have queried the random oracle on

$$\mathbf{a} \mathbf{z}_i + \mathbf{z}'_i - \mathbf{b}''_i \mathbf{c}_i \tag{1}$$

for some $i \in [w]$, otherwise, the right output of the adversary is a random guess from C (which is of negligible probability). Since each $\mathbf{b}_i$ is chosen uniformly at random, the probability that there exists a corresponding RLWE secret is with negligible probability. Thus, the probability that there exists $(\mathbf{z}_i, \mathbf{z}'_i, \mathbf{z}''_i)$ on the signature domain satisfying $\mathbf{p} = \mathbf{a} \mathbf{z}_i + \mathbf{z}'_i - \mathbf{b}''_i \mathbf{c}_i$ for some $\mathbf{p} \in R_q$ is also negligible.

5.2   Anonymity

Theorem 2. *If RLWE distribution has the advantage ϵ of distinguishing from a uniform distribution, then any probabilistic polynomial-time adversary querying w public keys, and oracle queries, the advantage of winning the anonymity game is $1/w + 2\epsilon + \epsilon_2$, where ϵ_2 is a negligible function in the security parameter.*

The proof is similar to the proof of anonymity provided in [18,54]. The idea is that in the anonymity game, the adversary is given a signature of a signer π at random from a list of w users (of adversary's choice), the adversary wins the

---

2 $\left(\frac{2(k_2 - \kappa k_1) + 1}{2k_2 + 1} \right)^{2n}$ in case of ring signature.

game if he outputs the right guess, which is π. We replace the original game by a sequence of games, which is indistinguishable to each other, such that in the final game, there is no dependency on the signer's index π. Thus adversary's winning chance in the modified game is always equivalent to a random guess.

5.3 Linkability

Theorem 3. *If there exists any probabilistic polynomial-time adversary who can break the linkability game with non-negligible probability, then there exists a probabilistic algorithm with same time complexity which can find a collision in the cryptographic hash function $\mathcal{H}$.*

Proof. During the linkability game, the adversary expects public keys from the simulator. The simulator runs the key generation algorithm and provides public keys $\mathbf{b}_i'$ of adversary's choice. The adversary also gets a corresponding secret key $(\mathbf{s}_\pi, \mathbf{e}_\pi, \mathbf{e}_\pi', \mathbf{h}_\pi)$ of some index, say π. $\mathbf{h}_\pi$ is the tag of the adversary, which is a part of the secret key. The adversary wins the game if he can output a tag different from $\mathbf{h}_\pi$. If possible, let the adversary outputs a new tag $\mathbf{h}_\pi^*$. Then with the new tag, the simulator can compute $\mathbf{b}_\pi''' = \mathbf{b}_\pi' - \mathcal{H}(\mathbf{h}_\pi^*)$. Also, with the original tag, the simulator computes $\mathbf{b}_\pi'' = \mathbf{b}_\pi' - \mathcal{H}(\mathbf{h}_\pi)$. Since $\mathbf{b}_\pi'' = \mathbf{b}_\pi'''$ (otherwise, the verification step will fail for $\mathbf{b}_\pi'''$), so we get a collision on the cryptographic hash function $\mathcal{H}$.

6 Parameter Selection

The security of the (linkable) ring signature depends on the public keys. We chose the parameters such that it bypasses the known attacks which we discuss next.

6.1 Known Attacks on the Public Keys

Lattice reduction technique is known to be the most fruitful way to attack (R)LWE based constructions. In literature, there are mainly two attacks on the (R)LWE problem, as discussed in [6].

1. **Primal attack.** The attacker solves the decoding problem to obtain the secret of the (R)LWE problem.
2. **Dual attack.** The attacker finds a short vector in the (scaled) dual lattice to distinguish the (R)LWE distribution with a uniform.

Primal Attack. Given a RLWE sample $\mathbf{b} = \mathbf{a}\mathbf{s} + \mathbf{e}$ with $\|\mathbf{s}\|_\infty, \|\mathbf{e}\|_\infty \leq k_1$, the attacker can build a lattice spanned by the rows of the matrix

$$\begin{bmatrix} qI_n & \mathbf{0} & \mathbf{0} \\ \mathrm{Rot}_f^T(\mathbf{a}) & I_n & \mathbf{0} \\ \mathbf{b} & \mathbf{0} & 1 \end{bmatrix}$$

where $\mathrm{Rot}_f(\mathbf{a})$ represents the matrix of order $n \times n$ whose i-th row represents the coefficients of $x^{i-1}\mathbf{a} \bmod f$ and I_n represents the identity matrix. The lattice has dimension $\dim = 2n + 1$ and determinant value $\det = q^n$. The attacker is able to solve the RLWE instance if he can find a vector $\mathbf{v} = (\mathbf{e}, -\mathbf{s}, 1)$ in the lattice sufficiently shorter than the Gaussian heuristics. The attacker needs to find a vector $\mathbf{v}$ such that $\|\mathbf{v}\|_2 \leq \sqrt{2nk_1^2 + 1}$. We know from the result of [26], the hardness of finding a short vector in a lattice depends on a factor $\gamma^{\frac{1}{\dim}}$ (which is called root Hermite factor), where

$$\gamma = \sqrt{\frac{\dim}{2\pi e} \det^{\frac{1}{\dim}} \frac{1}{\|\mathbf{v}\|_2}} = \sqrt{\frac{2n+1}{2\pi e} \frac{q^{\frac{n}{2n+1}}}{\sqrt{2nk_1^2 + 1}}}$$

To achieve a bit security of 128 against BKZ attacks [17] under quantum-Core-sieve model [8], we will aim $\gamma^{\frac{1}{\dim}} \leq 1.0045$. In the concrete parameter, we achieve $\gamma^{\frac{1}{\dim}} = 1.002$.

Dual Attack. The dual attack does not play a role in the security estimates for a single RLWE sample $(\mathbf{a}, \mathbf{b})$. In the dual attack, the adversary tries to find a short vector $\mathbf{x}$ in the dual lattice generated by the Rot matrix, that is in $\Lambda_q^{\perp}(\mathbf{a}) = \{\mathbf{y} \in \mathbb{Z}^n : \mathrm{Rot}_f(\mathbf{a}) \cdot \mathbf{y} = 0 \bmod q\}$. Then the sample $\mathbf{b}$ can be distinguished by simply checking $\langle \mathbf{b}, \mathbf{x} \rangle$, which is always small for a RLWE sample. But in case of the lattice $\Lambda_q^{\perp}(\mathbf{a})$, there exists no small lattice vector (except $\mathbf{0}$) with very high probability.

Other Attacks. There are also some non-lattice attacks, known as the *combinatorial attack*, to solve the (R)LWE problem. For instance, BKW algorithm [14] and it's variants [4,5] requires many (R)LWE sample to be applicable in our case. Similarly, the algorithm of Arora et al. [9] also requires many samples of the (R)LWE instance to be applicable here. In general, it is known that asymptotically the combinatorial attacks perform better than the lattice attacks; the main disadvantage is the requirement of too many samples to be applicable in practice.

6.2 Estimating Size for Ring Signatures

1. **Secret key size.** The secret of the ring signatures are two polynomials of degree less than n and coefficients bounded by k_1. Thus the secret key size is $2n \log(2k_1 + 1)$ bits.
2. **Public key size.** The public key is a polynomial of degree less than n and coefficients bounded by $\frac{q}{2}$. Thus the public key size is $n \log(q)$ bits.
3. **Signature size.** The signature size of the ring signature of ring size w will mainly depend on the size of $(\{\mathbf{z}_i, \mathbf{z}_i'\}_{i=1}^w)$, where each $\mathbf{z}_i, \mathbf{z}_i'$ is a polynomial of degree less than n and coefficients bounded by $k_2 - \kappa k_1$. The signature size is calculated by the individual sum of the bit lengths of $\mathbf{z}_i$ and $\mathbf{z}_i'$, which gives the total signature size of $2nw \log(2(k_2 - \kappa k_1) + 1)$ bits (Table 2).

Table 2. Parameters for the Ring signature (I) and Linkable Ring signature (II)

Parameters	I	II
$\log(q)$	23	23
n	512	512
k_1	50	50
k_2	2^{20}	2^{20}
κ	17	17
Expected number of restart	2	3
Secret key size per user	0.8 Kb	2 Kb
Public key size per user	1.4 Kb	1.4 Kb
Signature size ($w = 1$)	2 Kb	5 Kb
Signature size ($w = 5$)	13 kb	21 Kb
Signature size ($w = 10$)	26 kb	41 Kb

6.3 Estimating Size for Linkable Ring Signatures

1. **Secret key size.** The secret of the linkable ring signatures are three polynomials of degree less than n and coefficients bounded by k_1, plus a polynomial of degree less than n and coefficients bounded by $\frac{q}{2}$. Thus the secret key size is $3n \log(2k_1 + 1) + n \log(q)$ bits.
2. **Public key size.** The public key is a polynomial of degree less than n and coefficients bounded by $\frac{q}{2}$. Thus the public key size is $n \log(q)$ bits.
3. **Signature size.** The signature size of the ring signature of ring size w will mainly depend on the size of $\left(\{ \mathbf{z}_i, \mathbf{z}'_i, \mathbf{z}''_i \}_{i=1}^{w}, \mathbf{h}_\pi \right)$, where each $\mathbf{z}_i, \mathbf{z}'_i, \mathbf{z}''_i$ is a polynomial of degree less than n and coefficients bounded by $k_2 - \kappa k_1$, $\mathbf{h}_\pi$ is a polynomial of degree less than n and coefficients bounded by $\frac{q}{2}$. Thus the total signature size is given by $3nw \log(2(k_2 - \kappa k_1) + 1) + n \log q$ bits.

7 Open Problems

One advantage of using (R)LWE instance over (R)SIS instance is to achieve low key and signature size, as shown in [39]. But instantiating with RLWE instance, we could only prove computational anonymity property in the (linkable) ring signature. The unconditional property in [54] is achieved by applying the Leftover Hash Lemma (LHL), which states that for a particular choice of parameters, (R)SIS distribution is statistically close to a uniform distribution. But how to achieve unconditional anonymity result using (R)LWE instances are not clear to us at this moment. Thus proposing a (linkable) ring signature using (R)LWE instance, which will achieve unconditional anonymity property, is a nice open problem.

Optimizing the (linkable) ring signature proposed in this paper to achieve better parameter estimates is another open problem. One way to do this is by applying the compression technique for lattice-based digital signatures introduced in [12] and studied further in [21]. We leave the investigation of this potential optimization to future work.

References

1. Abdalla, M., An, J.H., Bellare, M., Namprempre, C.: Minimizing assumptions for security and forward-security: from identification to signatures via the Fiat-Shamir transform. In: Proceedings of the EUROCRYPT 2002, pp. 418–433 (2002)
2. Abdalla, M., Fouque, P.-A., Lyubashevsky, V., Tibouchi, M.: Tightly secure signatures from lossy identification schemes. J. Cryptol. **29**(3), 597–631 (2016)
3. Ajtai, M.: Generating hard instances of lattice problems. Electron. Colloq. Comput. Compl. (ECCC), **3**(7) (1996)
4. Albrecht, M.R., Cid, C., Faugère, J.-C., Fitzpatrick, R., Perret, L.: On the complexity of the BKW algorithm on LWE. Des. Codes Cryptogr. **74**(2), 325–354 (2015)
5. Albrecht, M.R., Faugère, J.-C., Fitzpatrick, R., Perret, L.: Lazy modulus switching for the BKW algorithm on LWE. In: Krawczyk, H. (ed.) PKC 2014. LNCS, vol. 8383, pp. 429–445. Springer, Heidelberg (2014). https://doi.org/10.1007/978-3-642-54631-0_25
6. Albrecht, M.R., Player, R., Scott, S.: On the concrete hardness of learning with errors. J. Math. Cryptol. **9**(3), 169–203 (2015)
7. Alkim, E., Bindel, N., Buchmann, J.A., Dagdelen, Ö.: TESLA: tightly-secure efficient signatures from standard lattices. IACR Cryptology ePrint Archive 2015:755 (2015)
8. Alkim, E., Ducas, L., Pöppelmann, T., Schwabe, P.: Post-quantum key exchange - a new hope. In: Proceedings of USENIX 2016, pp. 327–343 (2016)
9. Arora, S., Ge, R.: New algorithms for learning in presence of errors. In: Aceto, L., Henzinger, M., Sgall, J. (eds.) ICALP 2011. LNCS, vol. 6755, pp. 403–415. Springer, Heidelberg (2011). https://doi.org/10.1007/978-3-642-22006-7_34
10. Au, M.H., Chow, S.S.M., Susilo, W., Tsang, P.P.: Short linkable ring signatures revisited. In: Atzeni, A.S., Lioy, A. (eds.) EuroPKI 2006. LNCS, vol. 4043, pp. 101–115. Springer, Heidelberg (2006). https://doi.org/10.1007/11774716_9
11. Bai, S., et al.: MPSign: a signature from small-secret middle-product learning with errors. In: Kiayias, A., Kohlweiss, M., Wallden, P., Zikas, V. (eds.) PKC 2020. LNCS, vol. 12111, pp. 66–93. Springer, Cham (2020). https://doi.org/10.1007/978-3-030-45388-6_3
12. Bai, S., Galbraith, S.D.: An improved compression technique for signatures based on learning with errors. In: Benaloh, J. (ed.) CT-RSA 2014. LNCS, vol. 8366, pp. 28–47. Springer, Cham (2014). https://doi.org/10.1007/978-3-319-04852-9_2
13. Baum, C., Lin, H., Oechsner, S.: Towards practical lattice-based one-time linkable ring signatures. In: Naccache, D., Xu, S., Qing, S., Samarati, P., Blanc, G., Lu, R., Zhang, Z., Meddahi, A. (eds.) ICICS 2018. LNCS, vol. 11149, pp. 303–322. Springer, Cham (2018). https://doi.org/10.1007/978-3-030-01950-1_18
14. Blum, A., Kalai, A., Wasserman, H.: Noise-tolerant learning, the parity problem, and the statistical query model. J. ACM **50**(4), 506–519 (2003)
15. Groot Bruinderink, L., Hülsing, A., Lange, T., Yarom, Y.: Flush, gauss, and reload - a cache attack on the BLISS lattice-based signature scheme. In: Gierlichs, B., Poschmann, A.Y. (eds.) CHES 2016. LNCS, vol. 9813, pp. 323–345. Springer, Heidelberg (2016). https://doi.org/10.1007/978-3-662-53140-2_16

16. Chen, Y., Genise, N., Mukherjee, P.: Approximate trapdoors for lattices and smaller hash-and-sign signatures. IACR Cryptology ePrint Archive 2019:1029 (2019)

17. Chen, Y., Nguyen, P.Q.: BKZ 2.0: better lattice security estimates. In: Lee, D.H., Wang, X. (eds.) ASIACRYPT 2011. LNCS, vol. 7073, pp. 1–20. Springer, Heidelberg (2011). https://doi.org/10.1007/978-3-642-25385-0_1

18. Das, D., Au, M.H., Zhang, Z.: Ring signatures based on middle-product learning with errors problems. In: Buchmann, J., Nitaj, A., Rachidi, T. (eds.) AFRICACRYPT 2019. LNCS, vol. 11627, pp. 139–156. Springer, Cham (2019). https://doi.org/10.1007/978-3-030-23696-0_8

19. Das, D., Hoffstein, J., Pipher, J., Whyte, W., Zhang, Z.: Modular lattice signatures, revisited. Des. Codes Cryptogr. 88(3), 505–532 (2020)

20. Ducas, L., Durmus, A., Lepoint, T., Lyubashevsky, V.: Lattice signatures and bimodal Gaussians. In: Canetti, R., Garay, J.A. (eds.) CRYPTO 2013. LNCS, vol. 8042, pp. 40–56. Springer, Heidelberg (2013). https://doi.org/10.1007/978-3-642-40041-4_3

21. Ducas, L., et al.: Crystals-Dilithium: a lattice-based digital signature scheme. IACR Trans. Cryptogr. Hardw. Embed. Syst. 2018(1), 238–268 (2018)

22. Ducas, L., Lyubashevsky, V., Prest, T.: Efficient identity-based encryption over NTRU lattices. In: Sarkar, P., Iwata, T. (eds.) ASIACRYPT 2014. LNCS, vol. 8874, pp. 22–41. Springer, Heidelberg (2014). https://doi.org/10.1007/978-3-662-45608-8_2

23. Ducas, L., Nguyen, P.Q.: Learning a zonotope and more: cryptanalysis of NTRUSign countermeasures. In: Wang, X., Sako, K. (eds.) ASIACRYPT 2012. LNCS, vol. 7658, pp. 433–450. Springer, Heidelberg (2012). https://doi.org/10.1007/978-3-642-34961-4_27

24. Esgin, M.F., Steinfeld, R., Sakzad, A., Liu, J.K., Liu, D.: Short lattice-based one-out-of-many proofs and applications to ring signatures. In: Deng, R.H., Gauthier-Umaña, V., Ochoa, M., Yung, M. (eds.) ACNS 2019. LNCS, vol. 11464, pp. 67–88. Springer, Cham (2019). https://doi.org/10.1007/978-3-030-21568-2_4

25. Fouque, P.-A., et al.: Fast-fourier lattice-based compact signatures over NTRU, Falcon (2018)

26. Gama, N., Nguyen, P.Q.: Predicting lattice reduction. In: Smart, N. (ed.) EUROCRYPT 2008. LNCS, vol. 4965, pp. 31–51. Springer, Heidelberg (2008). https://doi.org/10.1007/978-3-540-78967-3_3

27. Gentry, C., Peikert, C., Vaikuntanathan, V.: Trapdoors for hard lattices and new cryptographic constructions. In: ACM Symposium on Theory of Computing 2008, pp. 197–206 (2008)

28. Goldreich, O., Goldwasser, S., Halevi, S.: Public-key cryptosystems from lattice reduction problems. In: Kaliski, B.S. (ed.) CRYPTO 1997. LNCS, vol. 1294, pp. 112–131. Springer, Heidelberg (1997). https://doi.org/10.1007/BFb0052231

29. Güneysu, T., Lyubashevsky, V., Pöppelmann, T.: Practical lattice-based cryptography: a signature scheme for embedded systems. In: Prouff, E., Schaumont, P. (eds.) CHES 2012. LNCS, vol. 7428, pp. 530–547. Springer, Heidelberg (2012). https://doi.org/10.1007/978-3-642-33027-8_31

30. Hoffstein, J., Howgrave-Graham, N., Pipher, J., Silverman, J.H., Whyte, W.: NTRUSign: digital signatures using the NTRU lattice. In: Joye, M. (ed.) CT-RSA 2003. LNCS, vol. 2612, pp. 122–140. Springer, Heidelberg (2003). https://doi.org/10.1007/3-540-36563-X_9

186   D. Das

31. Hoffstein, J., Pipher, J., Silverman, J.H.: NTRU: a ring-based public key cryptosystem. In: Buhler, J.P. (ed.) ANTS 1998. LNCS, vol. 1423, pp. 267–288. Springer, Heidelberg (1998). https://doi.org/10.1007/BFb0054868
32. Langlois, A., Stehlé, D.: Worst-case to average-case reductions for module lattices. Des. Codes Cryptogr. 75(3), 565–599 (2015)
33. Libert, B., Ling, S., Nguyen, K., Wang, H.: Zero-knowledge arguments for lattice-based accumulators: logarithmic-size ring signatures and group signatures without trapdoors. In: Fischlin, M., Coron, J.-S. (eds.) EUROCRYPT 2016. LNCS, vol. 9666, pp. 1–31. Springer, Heidelberg (2016). https://doi.org/10.1007/978-3-662-49896-5_1
34. Liu, J.K., Au, M.H., Huang, X., Susilo, W., Zhou, J., Yu, Y.: New insight to preserve online survey accuracy and privacy in big data era. In: Kutyłowski, M., Vaidya, J. (eds.) ESORICS 2014. LNCS, vol. 8713, pp. 182–199. Springer, Cham (2014). https://doi.org/10.1007/978-3-319-11212-1_11
35. Liu, J.K., Au, M.H., Susilo, W., Zhou, J.: Linkable ring signature with unconditional anonymity. IEEE Trans. Knowl. Data Eng. 26(1), 157–165 (2014)
36. Liu, J.K., Wei, V.K., Wong, D.S.: Linkable spontaneous anonymous group signature for ad hoc groups. In: Wang, H., Pieprzyk, J., Varadharajan, V. (eds.) ACISP 2004. LNCS, vol. 3108, pp. 325–335. Springer, Heidelberg (2004). https://doi.org/10.1007/978-3-540-27800-9_28
37. Lu, X., Au, M.H., Zhang, Z.: Raptor: a practical lattice-based (linkable) ring signature. In: Deng, R.H., Gauthier-Umaña, V., Ochoa, M., Yung, M. (eds.) ACNS 2019. LNCS, vol. 11464, pp. 110–130. Springer, Cham (2019). https://doi.org/10.1007/978-3-030-21568-2_6
38. Lyubashevsky, V.: Fiat-Shamir with aborts: applications to lattice and factoring-based signatures. In: Matsui, M. (ed.) ASIACRYPT 2009. LNCS, vol. 5912, pp. 598–616. Springer, Heidelberg (2009). https://doi.org/10.1007/978-3-642-10366-7_35
39. Lyubashevsky, V.: Lattice signatures without trapdoors. In: Pointcheval, D., Johansson, T. (eds.) EUROCRYPT 2012. LNCS, vol. 7237, pp. 738–755. Springer, Heidelberg (2012). https://doi.org/10.1007/978-3-642-29011-4_43
40. Lyubashevsky, V., Peikert, C., Regev, O.: On ideal lattices and learning with errors over rings. J. ACM 60(6), 43:1–43:35 (2013)
41. Micciancio, D., Peikert, C.: Trapdoors for lattices: simpler, tighter, faster, smaller. In: Pointcheval, D., Johansson, T. (eds.) EUROCRYPT 2012. LNCS, vol. 7237, pp. 700–718. Springer, Heidelberg (2012). https://doi.org/10.1007/978-3-642-29011-4_41
42. Nguyen, P.Q., Regev, O.: Learning a parallelepiped: cryptanalysis of GGH and NTRU signatures. J. Cryptol. 22(2), 139–160 (2009)
43. NIST. Post-Quantum Cryptography - Round 1 Submissions. https://csrc.nist.gov/Projects/Post-Quantum-Cryptography/Round-1-Submissions
44. NIST. Post-Quantum Cryptography - Round 2 Submissions. https://csrc.nist.gov/projects/post-quantum-cryptography/round-2-submissions
45. NIST. Post-Quantum Cryptography - Round 3 Candidate Announcement. https://csrc.nist.gov/News/2020/pqc-third-round-candidate-announcement
46. Noether, S., Mackenzie, A.: Ring confidential transactions. Ledger 1, 1–18 (2016)
47. Pessl, P.: Analyzing the shuffling side-channel countermeasure for lattice-based signatures. In: Dunkelman, O., Sanadhya, S.K. (eds.) INDOCRYPT 2016. LNCS, vol. 10095, pp. 153–170. Springer, Cham (2016). https://doi.org/10.1007/978-3-319-49890-4_9

48. Regev, O.: On lattices, learning with errors, random linear codes, and cryptography. In: Symposium on Theory of Computing 2005, pp. 84–93 (2005)
49. Rivest, R.L., Shamir, A., Tauman, Y.: How to leak a secret. In: Boyd, C. (ed.) ASIACRYPT 2001. LNCS, vol. 2248, pp. 552–565. Springer, Heidelberg (2001). https://doi.org/10.1007/3-540-45682-1_32
50. Roşca, M., Sakzad, A., Stehlé, D., Steinfeld, R.: Middle-product learning with errors. In: Katz, J., Shacham, H. (eds.) CRYPTO 2017. LNCS, vol. 10403, pp. 283–297. Springer, Cham (2017). https://doi.org/10.1007/978-3-319-63697-9_10
51. Shor, P.W.: Polynomial time algorithms for discrete logarithms and factoring on a quantum computer. In: Adleman, L.M., Huang, M.-D. (eds.) ANTS 1994. LNCS, vol. 877, pp. 289–289. Springer, Heidelberg (1994). https://doi.org/10.1007/3-540-58691-1_68
52. Stehlé, D., Steinfeld, R., Tanaka, K., Xagawa, K.: Efficient public key encryption based on ideal lattices. In: Matsui, M. (ed.) ASIACRYPT 2009. LNCS, vol. 5912, pp. 617–635. Springer, Heidelberg (2009). https://doi.org/10.1007/978-3-642-10366-7_36
53. Sun, S.-F., Au, M.H., Liu, J.K., Yuen, T.H.: RingCT 2.0: a compact accumulator-based (linkable ring signature) protocol for blockchain cryptocurrency Monero. In: Foley, S.N., Gollmann, D., Snekkenes, E. (eds.) ESORICS 2017. LNCS, vol. 10493, pp. 456–474. Springer, Cham (2017). https://doi.org/10.1007/978-3-319-66399-9_25
54. Alberto Torres, W.A., et al.: Post-quantum one-time linkable ring signature and application to ring confidential transactions in blockchain (lattice RingCT v1.0). In: Susilo, W., Yang, G. (eds.) ACISP 2018. LNCS, vol. 10946, pp. 558–576. Springer, Cham (2018). https://doi.org/10.1007/978-3-319-93638-3_32
55. Tsang, P.P., Wei, V.K.: Short linkable ring signatures for E-voting, E-cash and attestation. In: Deng, R.H., Bao, F., Pang, H.H., Zhou, J. (eds.) ISPEC 2005. LNCS, vol. 3439, pp. 48–60. Springer, Heidelberg (2005). https://doi.org/10.1007/978-3-540-31979-5_5

An Insecurity Study of Ethereum Smart Contracts

Bishwas C. Gupta, Nitesh Kumar, Anand Handa$^{(\boxtimes)}$, and Sandeep K. Shukla

C3i Center, Department of CSE, Indian Institute of Technology, Kanpur,
Kanpur, India
{bishwas,niteshkr,ahanda,sandeeps}@cse.iitk.ac.in

Abstract. Ethereum is the second most valuable cryptocurrency, right
after Bitcoin. The most distinguishing feature of Ethereum was the introduction of smart contracts which are essentially small computer programs
that sit on top of the blockchain. They are written in programming languages like Solidity and are executed by the Ethereum Virtual Machine
(EVM). Since these contracts are present on the blockchain itself, they
become immutable as long as the blockchains integrity is not compromised. This makes it a nightmare for security researchers as the vulnerabilities found cannot be patched. Also, since Ethereum is a public
blockchain, all the contract bytecodes are available publicly. The DAO
and the Parity attack are two prominent attacks that have caused great
monetary losses. There are many tools that have been developed to cope
with these challenges. However, the lack of a benchmark to compare these
tools, non-standard vulnerability naming conventions, etc. make the job
of a security analyst very difficult.

This paper provides the first ever comprehensive comparison of smart
contract vulnerability discovery tools which are available in the public domain based on a comprehensive benchmark developed here. The
benchmark development is based on a novel taxonomy of smart contract
vulnerabilities which has been created after a thorough study of security
vulnerabilities present in smart contracts.

Keywords: Ethereum blockchain · Smart contracts · Security
vulnerability discovery tools

1 Introduction

1.1 Ethereum

Ethereum is also a cryptocurrency backed blockchain like Bitcoin. It uses similar
techniques like proof of work (it will eventually move to a proof of stake based
consensus algorithm called Casper), hash pointers (Ethereum uses KECCAK-
256), etc. However, the main difference between Ethereum and Bitcoin is that

Partially Supported by Office of National Cyber Security Coordinator (NCSC),
Government of India.

© Springer Nature Switzerland AG 2020
L. Batina et al. (Eds.): SPACE 2020, LNCS 12586, pp. 188–207, 2020.
https://doi.org/10.1007/978-3-030-66626-2_10

unlike Bitcoin which is just a distributed ledger of transactions, Ethereum can also run small computer programs which allow developers to develop decentralized applications (or dApps). Also, unlike Bitcoin whose founder(s) are unknown, Ethereum is the vision of Vitalik Buterin, who wrote the white paper [9]. It is maintained by the Ethereum Foundation.

Unlike Bitcoin, Ethereum has two kinds of addresses [12] - **Externally Owned Accounts (EOAs)** which are owned through public-private key pairs and **Contract Accounts** these are special accounts which are controlled by the smart contract deployed on them. They can be triggered only by an EOA. Like Bitcoin, the users have to pay a small transaction fees for each transaction they want to be included in the blockchain. This is paid in Ethereum's native currency called Ether.

1.2 Smart Contracts

Smart Contracts are essentially small programs that exist on the blockchain and are executed by the Ethereum Virtual Machine (EVM). They do not need any centralised trusted authority like banks since all the functionality required is implemented in the smart contract logic, and since the code itself resides on the blockchain, we can be sure that it has not been tampered with. This property of being immutable is crucial in financial applications like escrow and other payments. Also, it allows developers to develop other smart applications by utilizing the power of blockchain technology. However, the concept of smart contracts is not new. It was introduced by Nick Szabo [46] in 1997.

1. **EVM:** EVM stands for Ethereum Virtual Machine which serves a similar purpose that Java Virtual Machine (JVM) does for Java by providing a layer of abstraction between the code and the machine. This also makes the code portable across machines. It also gives the developers an option to code in their smart contract language of choice, as finally all the programs written in different languages are translated by their respective compilers to EVM byte-code. The Ethereum Yellow Paper [51] explains the intricate workings of the Ethereum Virtual Machine in great detail.

2. **Smart Contract Programming:** The most popular programming language for Ethereum Smart Contracts is Solidity. It is a language similar to Javascript and C++, making it easy for existing software developers to write solidity code. Other languages, though not as popular are Vyper and Bamboo. Before Solidity was released, languages like Serpent and Mutan were used which have since been deprecated [29]. The compiler (solidity's compiler is called `solc`) converts the source code to EVM bytecode. This code is called the contract creation code. This is like a constructor to put the contract bytecode on the blockchain and can be executed by the EVM only once to put the run-time bytecode on the chain. The run-time bytecode is the code that is executed by the EVM on every call of the contract. The run-time bytecode also contains a swarm hash of the metadata file. This file can contain information like functions, compiler version, etc. However, this is still an experimental feature and not many have uploaded the metadata to the Swarm network [29].

3. **Ether and Gas:** Ether is the native cryptocurrency of the Ethereum network. Gas is another feature of Ethereum that separates it from Bitcoin. Since different smart contracts require varying amounts of computational power and time, it would be unfair to the miners to base the transaction fees just on the length of the transaction or have a constant transaction fees. Gas is a unit introduced by Ethereum that measures the computational work done. Each operation has an associated gas cost. However, gas is different from Ether as the value of the latter is market dependent but that does not change the 'computational power' required to execute the contract. Therefore, every transaction mentions a gas price which is the price a person is willing to pay in ether per unit of gas. The combination of these two give the transaction fees in ether.

1.3   Smart Contract Security

The biggest advantage of smart contracts - their immutability also poses the biggest threat from a security standpoint. This is because any bug found in the smart contract after deployment cannot be patched. Recent attacks like the DAO attack and the Parity attack have caused massive monetary losses. In such a scenario it becomes imperative to develop and interact with smart contracts that are secure. To achieve this goal, various tools have been developed by security researchers. However, the lack of organized information around smart contract security issues, a proper vulnerability naming convention and classification, and a benchmark to compare existing tools make the job of a security researcher very difficult.

The remainder of the paper is organized as follows - Sect. 2 introduces the various smart contract vulnerabilities. Section 3 describes the need for a new taxonomy and our novel taxonomy for smart contract vulnerabilities. In Sect. 4, we demonstrate our Vulnerability Benchmark for analyzing the security tools. Section 5 introduces the different security tools and highlights the results of the tools on the benchmark. Finally, we have past related works in Sect. 6 and concluding remarks in Sect. 7.

2   Smart Contract Security Vulnerabilities

We divide the security vulnerabilities in Ethereum into two broad categories - Blockchain 1.0 and Blockchain 2.0 vulnerabilities. Blockchain 1.0 vulnerabilities include security vulnerabilities that are present in most blockchain based systems and that Ethereum shares with its predecessors like Bitcoin. Blockchain 2.0 vulnerabilities include vulnerabilities introduced in the system because of the presence of smart contracts. Our work is concerned with the Blockchain 2.0 (Smart Contract) vulnerabilities. However, the Blockchain 1.0 vulnerabilities are introduced for completeness.

2.1 Blockchain 1.0 Vulnerabilities

1. **51% attack:** In proof of work, the miners try finding the nonce value to solve the given cryptographic puzzle. However, if miner(s) get control of more than 51% of the compute power in the network then they essentially control what goes into the blockchain - compromising its integrity [35].

2. **Double Spending:** Double spending [32] occurs when the attacker uses the same cryptocurrency more than once. This is done by leveraging race conditions, forks in the chain, or 51% attacks.

3. **Selfish Mining:** In selfish mining [23,41], a malicious miner does not publish the block immediately after solving the proof of work puzzle. Instead, reveals it only to its pool members which then work on the next block, while the other network continues working for essentially nothing [31].

4. **Eclipse Attack:** In eclipse attacks [28], the victim's incoming and outgoing connections are taken over by attacker (using a botnet or otherwise). This gives a filtered view of the blockchain to the victim.

5. **BGP Hijacking Attack:** The border gateway protocol (BGP) is used for handling routing information over the internet. BGP hijacking is a common attack. However in the context of public blockchains, it can be used to create unwanted delays in the network [34].

6. **Private key security:** Private keys are used to control the addresses in Ethereum. It is a security problem in itself to store these keys securely. As blockchain is a decentralised system, there is no way to report a stolen private key and prevent its misuse.

2.2 Blockchain 2.0 Vulnerabilities

1. **Re-entrancy:** A re-entrancy condition is when a malicious party can call a vulnerable function of the contract again before the previous call is completed: once or multiple times. This type of function is especially problematic in case of payable functions, as a vulnerable contract might be emptied by calling the payable function repeatedly. The `call()` function is especially vulnerable as it triggers code execution without setting a gas limit. To avoid re-entrancy bugs, it is recommended to use `transfer()` and `send()` as they limit the code execution to 2300 gas [40]. Also, it is advised to always do the required work (i.e. change the balances, etc.) before the external call. The DAO Attack is the most famous re-entrancy attack which lead to a loss of US$50 Million [13] and resulted in the chain being forked into two - Ethereum and Ethereum Classic.

2. **Authorization through `tx.origin`:** This can be interpreted as a type of a phishing attack. In solidity, `tx.origin` and `msg.sender` are separate. The account calling a contract is defined by `msg.sender`. `tx.origin` is the original sender of the transaction, which might lead to a string of other calls. However, if `tx.origin` is used for authorization, and the actual owner is conned to call a malicious contract which in turn calls the victim contract, then the authorization fails.

3. **Unprotected Ether Withdrawal:** Due to missing or inadequate access control mechanisms, it might be the case that anyone is able to withdraw Ether from the contract which is highly undesirable.

4. **Unprotected Selfdestruct:** `selfdestruct` kills a contract on the blockchain and send the contract balance to the specified address. Opcode `SELFDESTRUCT` is one of the few operations that costs negative gas as it frees up space on the blockchain. This construct is important because contracts may need to be killed if they are no longer required or if some bug is discovered. However, if this construct is put without proper protection mechanisms in place then anyone can kill the contract.

5. **Unexpected Ether:** Usually, when you send ether to a contract, its fallback function is executed. However, if the transfer of ether happens as a result of a `selfdestruct()` call, then the fallback function is not called. Therefore, a contract's balance should never be used in an if condition as it can be manipulated by a malicious user.

6. **Function and Variable Visibility:** Solidity has four visibility specifiers for functions and variables. However, being declared `public` is the most tricky from a security standpoint. If an important function like a payable function or a constructor with a wrong name is declared as public, then it can cause great monetary losses. This was observed in the Rubixi Contract which was the copy of the DynamicPyramid contract. However, the constructor name was not changed, making the original constructor a public function which anyone could call. This constructor decided the owner of the contract. Since anyone could now become the owner of the contract, it was compromised. Variable visibility does not have such drastic consequences as public variables get a public getter function. The Parity wallet attack also consisted of a function visibility bug.

7. **Integer Overflow and Underflow:** Solidity can handle up to 256 bit numbers, and therefore increasing (or decreasing) a number over (or below) the maximum (or minimum) value can result in overflows (or underflows). It is recommended to use OpenZeppelin's `SafeMath` library to mitigate such attacks.

8. **Variable Shadowing:** Variable shadowing occurs when a variable with the same name can be declared again. This can happen in case of a single contract (at the contract and function level) and also with multiple contracts. For example, a contract A inherits B, but both contracts have declared a variable x.

9. **Exception Handling:** Like in any object oriented programming language, exceptions may arise due to many reasons. These must be properly handled at the programmer level. Also, lower level calls do not throw an exception. They simple return a false value which needs to be checked and the exception should be handled manually.

10. **Denial of Service:** A denial of service attack from a smart contract's perspective happens when a smart contract becomes inaccessible to its users. Common reasons include failure of external calls or gas costly programming patterns.

11. **Call to the Unknown:** Ethereum Smart Contracts can make calls to other smart contracts. If the addresses of these smart contracts may be user provided then a malicious actor can utilize improper authentication to call a malicious contract. If the address is hard-coded, then it does not give the flexibility to update the contract to be called over time. Another issue is a special method called `delegatecall`. This makes the dynamically loaded code run in the caller's context. Therefore, if a `delegatecall` is made to a malicious contract, they can change storage values and potentially drain all funds from the contract.

12. **Bad Randomness:** Online games and lotteries are common dApp use cases. For these applications, a common choice for the seed of the random number generator is the hash or timestamp of some block that appears in the future. This is considered secure as the future is unpredictable. However, a malicious attacker can bias the seed in his favour.

13. **Untrustworthy Data Feeds:** In context of blockchains, a data feeds (also referred to as oracle) is an agent that verifies the integrity of the information before putting it on the blockchain. Once the data is published on the chain, its integrity can be guaranteed. However, the problem of making sure that the data feeds themselves are trustworthy is an active research problem.

14. **Transaction Order Dependence:** The order in which the transactions are picked up by miners might not be the same as the order in which they arrive. This creates a problem for contracts that rely on the state of the storage variables. Gas sent is usually important as it plays an important role in determining which transactions are picked first. A malicious transaction might be picked first, causing the original transaction to fail. This kind of race-condition vulnerability is referred to as transaction order dependence.

15. **Timestamp Dependence:** A lot of applications have a requirement to implement a notion of time in their applications. The most common method of implementing this is using the `block.timestamp` either directly or indirectly. However, a malicious miner with a significant computational power can manipulate the timestamp to get an output in his/her favour.

3 New Taxonomy for Ethereum Smart Contract Vulnerabilities

3.1 Existing Taxonomies and the Need for a New Taxonomy

The first taxonomy for smart contract vulnerabilities was given by Atzei et al. [5]. They divided the vulnerabilities into three broad categories based on their source. This included Solidity, EVM and blockchain. The vulnerabilities discussed did not give a holistic picture as it did not even contain common vulnerabilities like access control, function visibility, and transaction order dependence. These vulnerabilities have been proven to be quite disastrous as shown in the infamous Parity bug. Also, it was felt that only one level of hierarchy was less for proper analysis. Dika [21] in his Master's Thesis addressed many of the shortcomings of the Atzei taxonomy. More vulnerability categories were added and an associated severity level was also given for each vulnerability. However, the single level hierarchy was carried forward from the previous work. Also, we noticed that some vulnerability classes do not pose an immediate security risk. For example, use of `tx.origin` was labelled as a vulnerability. However, just using `tx.origin` does not cause a security breach. The problem occurs when it is used for authorization. Similarly, `blockhash` may cause a security vulnerability if used as a source of randomness. However just using it in the code does not make a contract vulnerable. Because of these issues in the existing work, we felt that there was a need for an improved taxonomy that was more hierarchical - for better analysis and understanding. Also, issues of improper vulnerability naming and incomplete vulnerability listing also needed refinement.

3.2   A New Taxonomy of Ethereum Smart Contract Vulnerabilities

Based on our research and study of Ethereum smart contract vulnerabilities as discussed in Sect. 1, we have come up with a new and unified vulnerability taxonomy as shown in Table 1. With this new taxonomy, we try to overcome the problems in the existing literature. We try to cover almost all the security vulnerabilities that have been reported. Since, these are usually reported under different names, a security analyst would find that he/she is able to put any *existing* vulnerability he/she encounters under one of the many categories we have created. Also, unlike previous works, we have tried to eliminate any redundancies and/or incorrect categorizations. The taxonomy is hierarchical and therefore analysis using this taxonomy would give the security researcher better insights into the root security issues in smart contracts.

Based on the existing literature [21] and the OWASP Risk Rating Methodology [50], the severity levels are color-coded. The authors in this work categorized various severity levels according to their criticality level - high, medium, and low. In our work, the severity level is color-coded with red being high, orange being medium, and green being low.

4   Vulnerability Benchmark

4.1   Need for a Benchmark

It is observed that many security tools have come up for Ethereum smart contracts over the years. However, it is also observed that these tools are usually tested on different test-instances and in some cases even the ground truth is unknown. Therefore, as a smart contract developer or a user, it becomes difficult to actually compare the performance of different tools without a proper benchmark.

Dika [21] tried to solve this issue. However, he tested only three tools on just 23 vulnerable and 21 audited-safe contracts. A contract was called vulnerable if it had *any* vulnerability. However, it was not checked that a tool properly detected the vulnerability claimed and the results were presented as is.

Table 1. A new taxonomy of ethereum smart contract vulnerabilities

Solidity	Re-entrancy	
	Access Control	Protection Issues
		Authorization through `tx.origin`
		Unprotected Ether Withdrawal
		Unprotected `selfdestruct`
		Unexpected Ether
		Visibility Issues
		Function Visibility
		Variable Visibility
	Arithmetic Issues	Integer Overflow & Underflow
		Floating Point & Precision
	Solidity Programming Issues	Uninitialized Storage Pointers
		Variable Shadowing
		Keeping Secrets
		Type Casts
		Lack of Proper Signature Verification
		Write to Arbitrary Storage Location
		Incorrect Inheritance Order
		Typographical Errors
		Use of Assembly
		Use of Deprecated Functions/Constructions
		Floating or No Pragma
		Outdated Compiler Version
	Exception Handling	Unchecked Call
		Gasless Send
		Call Stack Limit
		Assert Violation
		Requirement Violation
	Call to the Unknown	Dangerous Delegate Call
		External Contract Referencing
	Denial of Service	DoS with block gas limit
		DoS with failed call
EVM	Short Address Attack	
	Immutable bugs	
	Stack size limit	
Blockchain	Bad Randomness	
	Untrustworthy Data Feeds	
	Transaction Order Dependence	
	Timestamp Dependence	
	Unpredictable state (Dynamic Libraries)	

4.2   Benchmark Creation Methodology

To create the benchmark, we collected contracts known to be vulnerable from various sources. This included:

- Smart Contract Weakness Classification (SWC) Registry [16]
- (Not So) Smart Contracts [17]
- EVM Analyzer Benchmark Suite [14]
- Research papers, theses and books [3–6,21]
- Various blog posts, articles, etc. [8,11,24,26,33,37,42,43,47,52]

After collecting all the instances, we manually removed the duplicate contracts - this was important as we found that there was notable overlap between contracts gathered from different sources. After this, we manually checked the contracts and classified them as per the new taxonomy. Finally we compiled the smart contracts into run-time bytecode. However, as each contract required a different version of solidity, and solc-select [20] did not support such a large range of compiler versions, we leveraged Remix IDE [25] to manually generate the run-time byte-codes for each contract and stored it separately. This was not done for the on-chain contracts and the run-time byte-codes for these were directly taken from the blockchain. A summary of the benchmark creation methodology is depicted in Fig. 1.

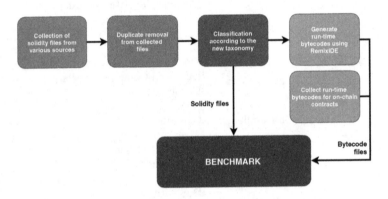

Fig. 1. Vulnerability benchmark creation

4.3   Benchmark Statistics

Unlike the previous work by Dika where only 23 vulnerable contracts were used, we have identified 162 unique vulnerable contracts. We have collected 34 on-chain vulnerable contracts. A few of them are - SmartBillions, Lottery, EthStick, UGToken, etc. including infamous contracts like the DAO, Parity Wallet, Rubixi and King of the Ether Throne.

It has been observed that Ethereum smart contracts have been used for creating ponzi-schemes to scam innocent people into loosing money by promising extraordinarily high returns [6]. Even though a ponzi contract might not be a direct security vulnerability, we have included them in our study because of the high monetary impact of such contracts. Apart from ponzi schemes like Govern-Mental, FirePonzi and Rubixi which have already been included, we added ponzi schemes corresponding to the vulnerabilities - Does not Refund, Allow Owner to withdraw funds from contracts namely - DynamicPyramid, GreedPit, NanoPyramid, Tomeka, ProtectTheCastle, and EthVentures that exhibited one or more of the following properties - contracts that do not refund and contracts that allow the owner to withdraw funds. These properties are typical in ponzi schemes, however they cannot be classified as security vulnerabilities directly without knowing the context.

The final benchmark consists of 180 contracts spread over all the categories. Out of these we have 162 unique contracts. This includes 40 on-chain contracts (including six additional ponzi schemes). This is very high in comparison to the 23 vulnerable smart contracts identified by [21].

5 Study of Security Tools

5.1 Tools Available for Ethereum Smart Contracts

There are many different tools available for Ethereum Smart Contracts. These tools have been gathered from research publications and through Internet searches. In this section, we classify the various tools available into different categories, so that the end users can easily find which tool to use for their particular application. Even though our work is primarily concerned with Security Tools, the other tools are included for the reader's convenience.

1. **Security Tools:** These are tools which take as input either the source code or the bytecode of a contract and give outputs on the security issues present. These are the tools that we are primarily concerned in with our work. Examples of security tools include Mythril [15], and Securify [49].
2. **Visualization Tools:** Visualization tools help give graphical outputs like control flow graphs, dependency graphs, etc. of the given contract to help in analysis. Tools like solgraph [44] and rattle [18] fall under this category.
3. **Disassemblers and Decompilers:** A dis-assembler converts the binary code back into the high level language code while a decompiler converts the binary code to a low level language for better understanding. evm-dis [30] is a popular dis-assembler for smart contracts.
4. **Linters:** Linters are static analysis tools primarily focused on detecting poor coding practices, programming errors, etc. Ethlint [22] is a common linting tool of Ethereum smart contracts.
5. **Miscellaneous Tools:** This includes tools like SolMet [27] which help give common code metrics like number of lines of code, number of functions per contract, etc. for solidity source files.

5.2 Methods Employed by the Security Tools

1. **Static Analysis:** Static Analysis essentially means evaluating the program code without actually running it. It looks at the code structure, the decompiled outputs, and control flow graphs to identify common security issues.

SmartCheck [48], Slither [19] and Remix IDE [25] are static analysis security tools for Ethereum smart contracts.

2. **Symbolic Execution:** Symbolic execution is considered to be in the middle of static and dynamic analysis. It explores possible execution paths for a program without any concrete input values. Instead of values, it uses symbols and keeps track of the symbolic state. It leverages constraint solvers to make sure that all the properties are satisfied. Mythril [15] and Oyente [36] are the popular Symbolic Execution tools for smart contract security.

3. **Formal Verification:** Formal Verification incorporates mathematical models to make sure that the code is free of errors. Bhargavan et al. [7] conducted a study of smart contracts using F*. However, the work is not available as open source to the best of our knowledge.

5.3   Experimental Setup

For the purpose of the study, we select the security tools that are actively maintained, open-sourced, ready for use and cover a fairly large section of the vulnerabilities. Keeping the above constraints in mind, the following tools were selected -

1. **Remix IDE:** Remix IDE [25] is primarily an integrated development environment (IDE) for developing Solidity smart contracts. It can connect to the Ethereum network using Metamask and developers can directly deploy smart contracts from Remix. It is developed and maintained by the Ethereum Foundation. The IDE has a security module to help developers with common security issues like re-entrancy, etc. It requires the solidity file of the contract to work. As a web interface was available, the testing using the benchmark instances was carried out manually.

2. **SmartCheck:** SmartCheck [48] is a static analysis tool for Solidity and Vyper smart contracts. It is developed by SmartDec and the University of Luxembourg. Like other static analysis tools, it does not work on byte-codes and requires the source codes to be present for analysis. It works by transforming the source codes into an intermediate representation which is XML-based. This representation is then checked against XPath patterns to highlight potential vulnerabilities in the code. The tool is open sourced and also has a web interface hosted at [45].

3. **Slither:** Slither [19] is a static analysis tool for solidity source files written in Python 3. It is open sourced and is developed by Trail of Bits. It works on contracts written in solidity >= 0.4 and requires the solidity files for analysis. It leverages an intermediate representation call SlithIR for code analysis. However, it requires the correct solidity version to be installed in the system. For this, we utilize another tool by Trail of Bits called `solc-select` [20] to switch to the right compiler version which is predetermined manually.

4. **Oyente:** Oyente [36] is one of the earliest security tools for Solidity smart contracts. It was developed by security researchers at the National University of Singapore and is now being maintained by Melonport. Oyente leverages

symbolic execution to find potential vulnerabilites in the smart contracts. It works with both byte-codes and solidity files. Being one of the first tools in this area, Oyente has been extended by many researchers over the years. For example, the control flow graphs generated by Oyente are also used by EthIR [1], which is a high level analysis tool for Solidity. A web interface for the tool is also available [38].

5. **Securify:** Securify [49] has been created by researchers at ETH Zurich in collaboration with ChainSecurity for security testing of Ethereum smart contracts. It works on both solidity source files and byte-codes. It has also received funding from the Ethereum Foundation to help mitigate the security issues in smart contracts. It analyzes the contract symbolically to get semantic information and then checks against patterns to see if a particular property holds or not. A web interface is also available at [10].

6. **Mythril:** Mythril [15] is a security tool developed by ConsenSys. It uses as a combination of symbolic execution and taint analysis to identify common security issues. Recently, a new initiative called MythX was launched with a similar core as Mythril for smart contract developers to provide security as a service. However, it is still in beta testing and is not available as open source. Therefore, we use Mythril Classic for our testing purposes.

Table 2 summarizes the tools selected for the study along with versions of the tools used. Table 3 shows the vulnerability coverage as claimed by the tools. According to the claims, we observe that the vulnerability coverage across all the tools is fairly good with most vulnerabilities being covered by one tool or another. All the experiments were carried out on a machine running Ubuntu 18.04.2 LTS on an Intel® Core™ i7-4770 CPU with 16 GB DDR3 RAM. Also, the tools that worked on both solidity and bytecode files were tested on bytecode files only. The results output by each tool were then converted to the new taxonomy as shown in Table 3 to allow us to compare the tools uniformly.

Table 2. Summary of tools used in the study

	Remix IDE	Smart-Check	Slither	Oyente	Securify	Mythril
Version/ Date Used	4-Mar-2019	2.0.1	0.4.0	0.2.7	17-Apr-19	0.20.4
Technique	Static Analysis	Static Analysis	Static Analysis	Symbolic Execution	Symbolic Execution	Symbolic Execution
WUI/ CLI	WUI	WUI + CLI	CLI	WUI + CLI	WUI + CLI	WUI + CLI
Works on src-file/ bytecode	src-file	src-file	src-file	src-file + bytecode	src-file + bytecode	src-file + bytecode
Developed by	Ethereum Foundation	SmartDec	Trail of Bits	NUS + Melonport	ETH Zurich	ConsenSys

Table 3. Vulnerability mapping to the new taxonomy

Reported by the Tool	Mapping to the new Taxonomy
Remix IDE	
Transaction origin	Authorization through tx.origin
Check-effects	Re-entrancy
Block timestamp usage	Timestamp Dependence
block.blockhash usage	Bad randomness
inline assembly	Use of Assembly
Use of selfdestruct	Unprotected selfdestruct
Low level calls/use of send	Unchecked Call
SmartCheck	
Deprecated Constructions	Use of Deprecated Functions/Constructions
Gas limit in loops	DoS with block gas limit
Upgrade to 0.5.0	Outdated Compiler Version
Pragmas version	Floating or No Pragma
Send, Unchecked call, Call without data	Unchecked Call
Using inline assembly	Use of Assembly
Incorrect Blockhash	Bad Randomness
Transfer in loop	DoS with failed call
Exact time	Timestamp dependence
Div mul	Floating Point and Precision
Visibility	Function Default Visibility
Locked money	Ponzi Scheme – Do Not Refund
Redundant fallback reject, Balance equality	Unexpected Ether
Array length manipulation	Write to Arbitrary Storage Location
Slither	
Reentrancy-eth,reentrancy-no-eth,reentrancy-benign	Re-entrancy
tx-origin	Authorization through tx.origin
timestamp	Timestamp dependence
Uninitialized-state, uninitialized-local, uninitialized-storage	Uninitialized storage pointers
suicidal	Unprotected selfdestruct
assembly	Use of Assembly
deprecated-standards	Use of Deprecated Functions or Constructions
solc-version	Outdated Compiler Version
calls-loop	Denial of Service with failed call
arbitrary-send	Unprotected Ether Withdrawal
incorrect-equality	Unexpected Ether
Unused-return, low-level-calls	Unchecked External Call
Shadowing-builtin, shadowing-local, shadowing-state	Shadowing State Variables
controlled-delegatecall	Dangerous Delegate Call
locked-ether	Ponzi scheme – Does not Return
OYENTE	
Call stack	Stack size limit
Re-entrancy	Re-entrancy
Time Dependency	Timestamp Dependence
Integer Overflow, Integer Underflow	Integer Overflow & Underflow
Money Concurrency	Transaction Order Dependence
Mythril Classic	
Integer Underflow, Integer Overflow	Integer Overflow & Underflow
Unchecked Call Return Value	Unchecked Call
Unprotected Selfdestruct	Unprotected selfdestruct
Unprotected Ether Withdrawal	Unprotected Ether Withdrawal
Use of tx.origin	Authorization through tx.origin
Exception State	Exception Handling
External Call To Fixed/User-Supplied Address	Dangerous Delegate Call
Use of callcode	Use of Deprecated Functions/Constructs
Dependence on predictable variable/environment variable	Bad Randomness
Multiple Calls in a Single Transaction	Denial of Service
Securify	
DAO, DAOConstantGas	Re-entrancy
LockedEther	Ponzi Scheme – Do not Refund
MissingInputValidation	Type Casts
RepeatedCall	Dangerous Delegate Call
TODAmount, TODReceiver	Transaction Ordering Dependence
UnhandledException	Unchecked Call
UnrestrictedEtherFlow	Unprotected Ether Withdrawal
UnrestrictedWrite	Write to arbitrary storage location

6 Results

For each tool, we run it against the benchmark. Then, we identify the relevant entries using the Table 4 to identify the vulnerabilities which the tool claims to identify. We then, map the results using the mapping in Table 3 and present the results in a tabular format in Table 5 and Table 6. The table for each tool depicts the vulnerable contracts it detected successfully and correctly, the contracts it could not detect correctly, and the contracts on which the tool could not finish it's evaluation because of some error or exception being raised. Securify is the only tool in our study that marks a contract as 'safe' from a vulnerability. If a vulnerable contract was wrongly labelled as 'safe', we call it a false negative.

Table 4. Tool-vulnerability matrix as claimed by the tools

		Remix	Slither	SmartCheck	Oyente	Mythril	Securify	SUM
	Re-entrancy	Y	Y		Y		Y	4
	Authorization through tx.origin	Y	Y			Y		3
	Unprotected Ether Withdrawal		Y			Y	Y	3
	Unprotected selfdestruct	Y	Y			Y		3
	Unexpected Ether		Y	Y				2
	Function Visibility			Y				1
	Variable Visibility							0
	Integer Overflow & Underflow				Y	Y		2
	Floating Point & Precision			Y				1
	Uninitialized Storage Pointers		Y					1
	Variable Shadowing		Y					1
	Keeping Secrets			Y				1
SOLIDITY	Type Casts						Y	1
	Lack of Proper Signature Verification							0
	Write to Arbitrary Storage Location			Y			Y	2
	Incorrect Inheritance Order							0
	Typographical Errors							0
	Use of Assembly	Y	Y	Y				3
	Use of Deprecated Functions		Y	Y		Y		3
	Floating or No Pragma			Y				1
	Outdated Compiler Version		Y	Y				2
	Unchecked Call	Y	Y	Y			Y	4
	Gasless Send						Y	1
	Call Stack Limit						Y	1
	Assert Violation						Y	1
	Requirement Violation						Y	1
	Dangerous Delegate Call		Y			Y	Y	3
	External Contract Referencing							0
	DoS with block gas limit			Y			Y	2
	DoS with failed call		Y	Y			Y	3
	Short Address Attack							0
EVM	Immutable bugs							0
	Stack size limit				Y			1
	Bad Randomness	Y		Y		Y		3
	Untrustworthy Data Feeds							0
B/CHAIN	Transaction Order Dependence				Y		Y	2
	Timestamp Dependence	Y	Y	Y	Y			4
	Unpredictable state							0
PS	Does not Return		Y	Y			Y	3
	Allows Owner to Withdraw Funds							0
	TOTAL	7	15	15	5	7	14	

1. **Remix IDE:** The performance of Remix IDE is surprisingly good. As seen in Table 6, it detects vulnerabilities like tx.origin authorization, use of assembly, unchecked call and timestamp dependence with 100% accuracy. However,

we find that these vulnerabilities are caught by mere presence of certain constructs without checking whether they actually result in a vulnerability or not. For example, Timestamp Dependence flag is raised if `timestamp` is used anywhere in the code. Similarly, `tx.origin` flag is raised if `tx.origin` is used anywhere within the code without checking if any it causes any security issue or not. The `selfdestruct` module works similarly. However it could not detect the Parity Bug because it uses the older `suicide` construct. It was also observed that for solidity versions 0.3.1 and prior, the check-effects and the selfdestruct modules gave an error. This resulted in the famous DAO contract not being analysed by the tool.

2. **SmartCheck:** The performance of SmartCheck is given in Table 6. It has a good performance in only a few of the many categories that it can detect. They include security issues like use of deprecated functions, unchecked call, use of assembly, etc. However, the performance on other instances is not very good.

3. **Slither:** Slither has a very good performance across most of the categories as shown in Table 6. There was no category that it could not detect even one instance from. The biggest drawback of slither is that does not work with older solidity versions (prior to 0.4) and requires the correct version of solidity to be present on the system. Because of this, a lot of contracts in the benchmark gave errors with slither. However, it is a very good tool for smart contract developers who are developing in newer versions of solidity.

4. **Oyente:** Being one of the earliest tools, Oyente is now showing it's age. It covers a very low number of vulnerabilities. The results are shown in Table 6. Average EVM code coverage for the entire benchmark set was found to be 75.98%. Also, there was not a single report of integer overflow or underflow across the complete benchmark. We believe this is some bug in the tool causing this behaviour.

5. **Securify:** Securify is the only tool that reports a contract as 'safe' from a particular vulnerability. If the contract contains a vulnerability, and Securify reports it as 'safe', we call it false negative. From Table 5 we can see that Securify reports a lot of false negatives. However, it has a decent performance on re-entrancy bug detection.

Table 5. Results of securify on the vulnerability benchmark

Vulnerability	Total	Detected	Not Detected	Error	False Negative
Re-entrancy	10	6	0	2	2
Transaction Ordering Dependence	9	2	2	0	5
Dangerous Delegate Call	6	0	0	0	6
Unchecked Call	3	0	0	0	3
Type Casts	6	1	4	0	1
Ponzi – Do not Refund	4	0	0	0	4
Unprotected Ether Withdrawal	7	0	3	0	4
Write to arbitrary storage	2	0	2	0	0

Table 6. Results of various tools on the Vulnerability Benchmark

Results of Remix IDE on the Vulnerability Benchmark

Vulnerability	Total	Detected	Not Detected	Error
Auth through tx.origin	2	2	0	0
Use of Assembly	1	1	0	0
Timestamp Dependence	6	6	0	0
Unchecked Call	3	3	0	0
Unprotected selfdestruct	3	2	1	0
Re-entrancy	10	5	3	2
Bad Randomness	11	4	7	0

Results of Oyente on the Vulnerability Benchmark

Vulnerability	Total	Detected	Not Detected	Error
Stack Size Limit	1	1	0	0
Re-entrancy	10	5	5	0
Timestamp Dependence	6	2	4	0
Transaction Order Dependence	9	5	4	0

Results of Slither on the Vulnerability Benchmark

Vulnerability	Total	Detected	Not Detected	Error
Auth through tx.origin	2	2	0	0
Unprotected selfdestruct	3	2	0	1
Use of Assembly	1	1	0	0
Use of Deprecated Functions	1	1	0	0
Outdated Compiler Version	1	1	0	0
Unexpected Ether	2	2	0	0
Unchecked Call	3	1	0	2
Variable Shadowing	3	3	0	0
Uninitialized storage pointers	5	4	1	0
Dangerous Delegate Call	6	2	1	3
Re-entrancy	10	4	3	3
DoS with failed call	3	1	1	1
Timestamp dependence	6	1	2	3
Unprotected Ether Withdrawal	7	2	4	1
Ponzi – Does not Return	4	0	0	4

Results of SmartCheck on the Vulnerability Benchmark

Vulnerability	Total	Detected	Not Detected	Error
Outdated Compiler Version	1	0	0	1
Use of Deprecated	1	1	0	0
Unchecked Call	3	3	0	0
Use of Assembly	1	1	0	0
Function Visibility	12	9	3	0
Unexpected Ether	2	1	1	0
DoS with block gas limit	5	1	4	0
Time stamp dependence	6	1	5	0
Floating or No Pragma	2	0	1	1
Bad Randomness	11	0	10	1
DoS with failed call	3	0	3	0
Floating Point and Precision	2	0	2	0
Ponzi – Do Not Refund	4	0	4	0
Write to Arbitrary Storage	2	0	2	0

Results of Mythril on the Vulnerability Benchmark

Vulnerability	Total	Detected	Not Detected	Error
Unchecked Call	3	1	0	2
Auth through tx.origin	2	1	0	1
Use of Deprecated Functions	1	1	0	0
Unprotected selfdestruct	3	2	1	0
Unprotected Ether Withdrawal	7	4	3	0
Integer Overflow & Underflow	31	11	10	10
Dangerous Delegate Call	6	2	2	2
Exception Handling	29	12	14	3
Bad Randomness	11	1	4	6
Denial of Service	4	0	4	0

6. **Mythril:** The performance of Mythril on the benchmark is shown in Table 6. It is able to detect the attacks with a fair accuracy, however it encounters a lot of errors. This makes its performance inferior to some static analysis tools like Slither.

The effectiveness of the tools in detecting the vulnerabilities in the benchmark is shown in Table 7. The cells highlighted in green indicate that all the instances of that vulnerability present in the benchmark are successfully detected, while grey highlights the maximum vulnerabilities (though not all) accurately detected across all the tools. We observe that many vulnerabilities are not being detected by the tools. We also observe that even though the tools cover a wide spectrum of vulnerabilities, they are not very accurate in detecting them. The best tool from our study is Slither. It covers a wide range of vulnerabilities and is the only tool that detected at-least one from each category it could successfully evaluate. The only drawback is that it works on solidity versions greater than 0.4.0. Nevertheless, it is still a good tool for new smart contract developers.

7 Related Work

Atzei et al. [5] conducted the first survey of attacks on Ethereum smart contracts and also gave the first taxonomy of Ethereum smart contract vulnerabilities. They also look at some of the popular vulnerable contracts like the DAO, Rubixi, GovernMental and King of the Ether throne.

Table 7. Tool effectiveness for different vulnerabilities

		RemixIDE	Slither	SmartCheck	Oyente	Mythril	Securify
SOLIDITY	Re-entrancy	5	4		5		6
	Authorization through tx.origin	2	2			1	
	Unprotected Ether Withdrawal		2			4	0
	Unprotected selfdestruct	2	2			2	
	Unexpected Ether		2	1			
	Function Visibility			9			
	Variable Visibility						
	Integer Overflow & Underflow				-	11	
	Floating Point & Precision			0			
	Uninitialized Storage Pointers		4				
	Variable Shadowing		3				
	Keeping Secrets						
	Type Casts						1
	Lack of Proper Signature Verification						
	Write to Arbitrary Storage Location			0			0
	Incorrect Inheritance Order						
	Typographical Errors						
	Use of Assembly	1	1	1			
	Use of Deprecated Functions/Constructions		1	1		1	
	Floating or No Pragma			0			
	Outdated Compiler Version		1	0			
	Unchecked Call	3	1	3		1	0
	Gasless Send					0	
	Call Stack Limit					0	
	Assert Violation					12	
	Requirement Violation					0	
	Dangerous Delegate Call		2			2	0
	External Contract Referencing						
	DoS with block gas limit			1			0
	DoS with failed call		1	0			
EVM	Immutable bugs						
	Stack size limit				1		
B/CHAIN	Bad Randomness	4		0		1	
	Transaction Order Dependence				5		2
	Timestamp Dependence	6	1	1	2		
	Unpredictable state (Dynamic Libraries)						
PS	Does not Return		0	0			0
	Allows Owner to Withdraw Funds						

Dika [21] in his master's thesis, extended the taxonomy given by Atzei et al. [5]. He also tested the effectiveness of three security tools on a data-set of 23 vulnerable and 21 safe contracts. It is observed that the data-set and the number of tools used for the study is quite less. Also, the taxonomy needs hierarchy for better analysis. Mense et al. [39] look at the security analysis tools available for Ethereum smart contracts and cross reference them to the extended taxonomy given by Dika [21] to identify the vulnerabilities captured by each tool. However, the tool's effectiveness in catching those vulnerabilities is not studied. Buterin [8] in his post outlines the various vulnerable smart contracts with an elementary categorization. He also emphasises the need to experiment with various tools and standardization wherever possible to mitigate bugs in smart contracts. Angelo et al. [2] surveyed the various tools available to Ethereum smart contract developers. They do a very broad categorization of tools - those which are publicly available and those which are not publicly available. Antonopoulos et al. [3] in their book on Ethereum have dedicated a chapter on smart contract security. They cover the various vulnerabilities encountered by smart contract developers and give real world examples and preventative techniques. It is a good reference for smart contract developers.

8   Conclusion

Security researchers and smart contract developers face three problems when dealing with smart contracts - lack of an updated and organized study of the possible vulnerabilities and their causes, lack of a standard taxonomy and naming convention of these vulnerabilities and lack of a benchmark to compare and evaluate the performance of the different tools available for smart contract security, so that they can make an informed decision about which tool to use. In this work, we conduct an organized study of smart contract vulnerabilities and develop a novel taxonomy that is hierarchical and uses nomenclature used popularly by security researchers. We also develop a comprehensive vulnerability benchmark containing 180 vulnerable contracts across different vulnerability categories. This benchmark is based on the novel taxonomy explained in this work. Finally, we compare and analyze the performance of different security tools using the benchmark. We observe that the static analysis tools perform better than the symbolic execution tools. As this is an active research area, updation of the benchmark and the taxonomy is needed from time to time. Also, to detect false positives, we may develop a non-vulnerable benchmark that contains instances that might seem vulnerable at the first glance but do not pose a security risk. It would be interesting to see the performance of the tools on such instances.

References

1. Albert, E., Gordillo, P., Livshits, B., Rubio, A., Sergey, I.: ETHIR: a framework for high-level analysis of ethereum bytecode. In: Lahiri, S.K., Wang, C. (eds.) ATVA 2018. LNCS, vol. 11138, pp. 513–520. Springer, Cham (2018). https://doi.org/10.1007/978-3-030-01090-4_30
2. Di Angelo, M., Antipolis, S.: A survey of tools for analyzing ethereum smart contracts (2019)
3. Antonopoulos, A.M., Wood, G.: Mastering Ethereum: Building Smart Contracts and Dapps. O'Reilly Media, Sebastopol (2018)
4. Atzei, N., Bartoletti, M., Cimoli, T.: Attacks - A Survey of Attacks on Ethereum Smart Contracts. http://blockchain.unica.it/projects/ethereum-survey/attacks.html. Accessed 2 May 2019
5. Atzei, N., Bartoletti, M., Cimoli, T.: A survey of attacks on ethereum smart contracts (SoK). In: Maffei, M., Ryan, M. (eds.) POST 2017. LNCS, vol. 10204, pp. 164–186. Springer, Heidelberg (2017). https://doi.org/10.1007/978-3-662-54455-6_8
6. Bartoletti, M., Carta, S., Cimoli, T., Saia, R.: Dissecting ponzi schemes on ethereum: identification, analysis, and impact. arXiv preprint arXiv:1703.03779 (2017)
7. Bhargavan, K., et al.: Formal verification of smart contracts: short paper. In: Proceedings of the 2016 ACM Workshop on Programming Languages and Analysis for Security, pp. 91–96. ACM (2016)
8. Buterin, V.: Thinking About Smart Contract Security. https://blog.ethereum.org/2016/06/19/thinking-smart-contract-security/. Accessed 2 May 2019
9. Buterin, V., et al.: A next-generation smart contract and decentralized application platform. White paper (2014)

10. ChainSecurity. Securify Scanner for Ethereum Smart Contracts. https://securify. chainsecurity.com. Accessed 16 May 2019
11. CityMayor. How Someone Tried to Exploit a Flaw in Our Smart Contract and Steal All of Its Ether. https://blog.citymayor.co/posts/how-someone-tried-to-exploit-a-flaw-in-our-smart-contract-and-steal-all-of-its-ether/. Accessed 2 May 2019
12. Ethereum Community. Ethereum Homestead Documentation. http://ethdocs.org/en/latest/index.html. Accessed 10 May 2019
13. ConsenSys. Ethereum Smart Contract Best Practices - Known Attacks. https://consensys.github.io/smart-contract-best-practices/known_attacks/. Accessed 24 April 2019
14. Consensys. EVM Analyzer Benchmark Suite. https://github.com/ConsenSys/evm-analyzer-benchmark-suite. Accessed 2 May 2019
15. ConsenSys. Mythril Classic. https://github.com/ConsenSys/mythril-classic. Accessed 16 May 2019
16. Consensys. Smart Contract Weakness Classification and Test Cases. https://smartcontractsecurity.github.io/SWC-registry/. Accessed 2 May 2019
17. Crytic. (Not So) Smart Contracts. https://github.com/crytic/not-so-smart-contracts Accessed 2 May 2019
18. Crytic. rattle. https://github.com/crytic/rattle. Accessed 16 May 2019
19. Crytic. Slither, the Solidity source analyzer. https://github.com/crytic/slither. Accessed 2 May 2019
20. Crytic. solc-select. https://github.com/crytic/solc-select. Accessed 2 May 2019
21. Dika, A.: Ethereum smart contracts: Security vulnerabilities and security tools. Master's thesis, NTNU (2017)
22. Dua, R.: EthLint. https://github.com/duaraghav8/Ethlint. Accessed 16 May 2019
23. Eyal, I., Sirer, E.G.: Majority is not enough: bitcoin mining is vulnerable. Commun. ACM 61(7), 95–102 (2018)
24. Falkon, S.: The Story of the DAO - Its History and Consequences. https://medium. com/swlh/the-story-of-the-dao-its-history-and-consequences-71e6a8a551ee. Accessed 2 May 2019
25. Ethereum Foundation. Remix - Solidity IDE. https://remix.ethereum.org/. Accessed 2 May 2019
26. NCC Group. DASP - TOP 10. https://dasp.co/index.html. Accessed 2 May 2019
27. Hegedus, P.: Towards analyzing the complexity landscape of solidity based ethereum smart contracts. Technologies 7(1), 6 (2019)
28. Heilman, E., Kendler, A., Zohar, A., Goldberg, S.: Eclipse attacks on bitcoin's peer-to-peer network. In: 24th USENIX Security Symposium (USENIX Security 15), pp. 129–144 (2015)
29. Hollander, L.: The Ethereum Virtual Machine - How does it work? https://medium. com/mycrypto/the-ethereum-virtual-machine-how-does-it-work-9abac2b7c9e. Accessed 10 May 2019
30. Johnson, N.: evmdis. https://github.com/arachnid/evmdis. Accessed 16 May 2019
31. Karame, G.O., Androulaki, E.: Bitcoin and Blockchain Security. Artech House (2016)
32. Karame, G.O., Androulaki, E., Capkun, S.: Double-spending fast payments in bitcoin. In: Proceedings of the 2012 ACM Conference on Computer and Communications Security, pp. 906–917. ACM (2012)
33. KingoftheEther. Post-Mortem Investigation, February 2016. https://www.kingoftheether.com/postmortem.html. Accessed 2 May 2019
34. Li, X., Jiang, P., Chen, T., Luo, X., Wen, Q.: A survey on the security of blockchain systems. Future Gen. Comput. Syst. 107, 841–853 (2020). ISSN: 0167-739X

35. Lin, I.-C., Liao, T.-C.: A survey of blockchain security issues and challenges. IJ Netw. Secur. **19**(5), 653–659 (2017)
36. Luu, L., Chu, D.-H., Olickel, H., Saxena, P., Hobor, A.: Making smart contracts smarter. In: Proceedings of the 2016 ACM SIGSAC Conference on Computer and Communications Security, pp. 254–269. ACM (2016)
37. Manning, A.: Solidity Security: Comprehensive list of known attack vectors and common anti-patterns. https://blog.sigmaprime.io/solidity-security.html. Accessed 2 May 2019
38. Melonport. Oyente. https://oyente.melonport.com. Accessed 2 May 2019
39. Mense, A., Flatscher, M.: Security vulnerabilities in ethereum smart contracts. In: Proceedings of the 20th International Conference on Information Integration and Web-based Applications & Services, iiWAS 2018, pp. 375–380. ACM, New York (2018)
40. nick256. Smart Contract Security: Part 1 Reentrancy Attacks. https://hackernoon.com/smart-contract-security-part-1-reentrancy-attacks-ddb3b2429302. Accessed 24 Apr 2019
41. Niu, J., Feng, C.: Selfish Mining in Ethereum. arXiv e-prints, January 2019
42. PeckShield. New proxyOverflow Bug in Multiple ERC20 Smart Contracts. https://blog.peckshield.com/2018/04/25/proxyOverflow/. Accessed 2 May 2019
43. Reutov, A.: Predicting Random Numbers in Ethereum Smart Contracts. https://blog.positive.com/predicting-random-numbers-in-ethereum-smart-contracts-e5358c6b8620. Accessed 2 May 2019
44. Raine Revere. solgraph. https://github.com/raineorshine/solgraph. Accessed 16 May 2019
45. SmartDec. SmartCheck. https://tool.smartdec.net/. Accessed 2 May 2019
46. Szabo, N.: The idea of smart contracts. Nick Szabo's Papers and Concise Tutorials, 6 (1997)
47. Parity Technologies. Parity: Security Alert. https://www.parity.io/security-alert-2/. Accessed 2 May 2019
48. Tikhomirov, S., et al.: Smartcheck: static analysis of ethereum smart contracts. In: 2018 IEEE/ACM 1st International Workshop on Emerging Trends in Software Engineering for Blockchain (WETSEB), pp. 9–16. IEEE (2018)
49. Tsankov, P., Dan, A., Drachsler-Cohen, D., Gervais, A., Buenzli, F., Vechev, M.: Securify: practical security analysis of smart contracts. In: Proceedings of the 2018 ACM SIGSAC Conference on Computer and Communications Security, pp. 67–82. ACM (2018)
50. UcedaVelez, T.: OWASP Risk Rating Methodology. https://www.owasp.org/index.php?title=OWASP_Risk_Rating_Methodology&oldid=247702. Accessed 25 Apr 2019
51. Wood, G., et al.: Ethereum: A secure decentralised generalised transaction ledger. Ethereum Project Yellow Paper (2014)
52. Yuan, M.: Building a safer crypto token. https://medium.com/cybermiles/building-a-safer-crypto-token-27c96a7e78fd. Accessed 2 May 2019

Cryptographically Secure Multi-tenant Provisioning of FPGAs

Arnab Bag[1](✉), Sikhar Patranabis[1], Debapriya Basu Roy[2],
and Debdeep Mukhopadhyay[1]

[1] Indian Institute of Technology, Kharagpur, Kharagpur, India
amiarnabbolchi@gmail.com
[2] Technische Universität München, Munich, Germany

Abstract. Field-programmable gate arrays (FPGAs) have gained massive popularity today as accelerators for a variety of workloads, including big data analytics, and parallel and distributed computing. This has fueled the study of mechanisms to provision FPGAs among multiple tenants as general purpose computing resources on the cloud. Such mechanisms offer new challenges, such as ensuring IP protection and bitstream confidentiality for mutually distrusting clients sharing the same FPGA. A direct adoption of existing IP protection techniques from the single tenancy setting do not completely address these challenges, and are also not scalable enough for practical deployment.

In this paper, we propose a dedicated and scalable framework for secure multi-tenant FPGA provisioning that can be easily integrated into existing cloud-based infrastructures such as OpenStack. Our technique has *constant resource/memory overhead* irrespective of the number of tenants sharing a given FPGA, and is provably secure under well-studied cryptographic assumptions. A prototype implementation of our proposition on Xilinx Virtex-7 FPGAs is presented to validate its overheads and scalability when supporting multiple tenants and workloads. To the best of our knowledge, this is the first FPGA provisioning framework to be prototyped that achieves a desirable balance between security and scalability in the multi-tenancy setting.

Keywords: FPGAs · Security · Provisioning · Multi-tenant · Cloud computing

1 Introduction

The modern era of cloud computing has actualized the idea of ubiquitous provisioning of computational resources and services via a network. Cloud-based solutions are now marketed by all leading enterprise IT vendors such as IBM (PureApplication), Oracle (ExaData), Cisco (UCS) and Microsoft (Azure), as well as Web companies such as Amazon (AWS) and Google (Compute Engine). In the midst of this paradigm shift from traditional IT infrastructures

© Springer Nature Switzerland AG 2020
L. Batina et al. (Eds.): SPACE 2020, LNCS 12586, pp. 208–225, 2020.
https://doi.org/10.1007/978-3-030-66626-2_11

to the cloud, field-programmable gate arrays (FPGAs) have risen as attractive computational avenues for accelerating heavy workloads.

Modern FPGAs offer a number of advantages including reconfigurability, high throughput, predictable latency and low power consumption. They also offer *dynamic partial reconfiguration* (DPR) capabilities [21], that allow non-invasive run-time modification of existing circuitry for on-the-fly functionality enhancement. The recent trend of deploying FPGAs as computing resources on the cloud is visible in upcoming commercial applications such as Microsoft's Project Catapult [28], that integrates FPGAs with cloud-based data centers in a distributed architecture and enables using up to thousands of FPGAs to accelerate a single service.

In this paper, we examine the following question:

Can FPGAs be viewed and realized in the cloud as general purpose programmable resources that can be re-configured as on-demand devices?

There is a growing interest today into whether FPGA resources may be shared among multiple tenants and their applications, as opposed to the "all-or-nothing" philosophy where a single tenant has complete control over the FPGA [6]. It is interesting to note that the benefits of such sharing, which includes maximal resource utilization, are already being realized in the GPU domain. While GPUs were traditionally limited to only one user/tenant per host, a paradigm shift is occurring with Nvidia providing hardware support for multi-tenancy in its latest Kepler architecture GPU [1].

Very recently, Amazon has announced the addition of Xilinx FPGAs to their cloud services [8], signaling that major commercial institutions are seeing market demand in realizing FPGAs as general purpose shared computing resources in the cloud. In this work, we focus on the security challenges that arise when an FPGA accelerates multiple workloads from mutually distrusting tenants, and possible techniques to mitigate such challenges.

Security Challenges. Provisioning shared FPGAs on the cloud offers a number of challenges such as resource abstraction, ecosystem compatibility (libraries and SDKs) and, most importantly, *security*. While some of these challenges have been addressed comprehensively in the existing literature [6], security issues emerging from such a model are largely under-studied. One such security issue is *IP protection*. Multiple mutually distrusting tenants sharing a common pool of FPGA resources are likely to demand guarantees for bitstream confidentiality. Since FPGAs are inherently designed for single party access, FPGA vendors today focus on ensuring the privacy of bitstreams originating from *single users*, especially when deployed into hostile industrial/military environments.

Mitigation techniques typically used include bitstream encryption and authentication, combined with fault-tolerance. However, a direct adoption of such techniques in the multi-tenancy setting potentially blows up resource requirements, imposes significant key-management overheads, and leads to an overall lack of scalability.

In particular, a simpler solution based on traditional public key encryption would incur significant storage overheads since the secret key corresponding to each partition would have to be stored separately and securely. This motivates the need for dedicated and scalable security solutions tuned to the multi-tenancy setting where the storage required *does not grow* linearly with the number of partitions.

Existing Solutions. While a number of recent works [18,27,34] have helped develop general acceptance for FPGAs as general-purpose computing elements in portable ecosystems, security concerns regarding large-scale FPGA deployment have been discussed only in the context of specific applications. For example, the authors of [2] have looked into the security of specific applications such as building databases, where FPGAs are used as accelerators. Their security discussions are more at the application-level rather than the system-level.

Other works [6] focus on the threats originating from malicious tenants either crashing the system or attempting illegal memory accesses. Their proposed mitigations are mostly based on virtualization, in the sense that they use dedicated hypervisors and DMA units to regulate the memory access made by each tenant's bitstream file on the host FPGA node. However, they do not consider the threats posed by *co-resident VM attacks* [11,31], where data resident on a target VM can be stolen by a second malicious VM, so long as they co-exist on the same physical node. This poses a massive threat to IP security in the shared tenancy setting, and underlines the need for cryptographic security guarantees in addition to architectural barricading.

While a number of cryptographic solutions have been proposed for IP protection in the single tenancy scenario [10,16], there exist no equivalent solutions tuned to the shared tenancy setting to the best of our knowledge.

1.1   Our Contributions

In this paper, we propose a dedicated and scalable framework for secure multi-tenant FPGA provisioning on the cloud. Our framework also has following desirable features:

- Our framework guarantees bitstream confiden tiality in exchange for a constant amount of resource/memory overhead, *irrespective of the number of tenants sharing a given FPGA*. We achieve this using a novel technique known as *key-aggregation* that is provably secure under well-studied cryptographic assumptions.

- The only trusted agent in our framework is the FPGA vendor. Note that even in IP protection solutions in the single tenancy setting, the FPGA vendor is typically a trusted entity. Hence, this is a reasonable assumption. More importantly, the cloud service provider need not be trusted, which is desirable from a tenant's point of view.

Virtual Machine for Tenant

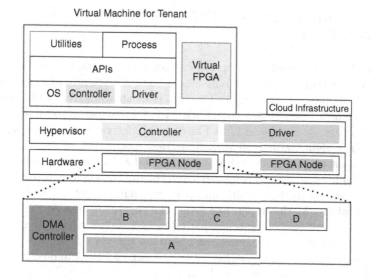

Fig. 1. FPGA provisioning on a cloud [6]

- Our framework can be easily integrated into existing cloud-based infrastructures such as OpenStack, and does not interfere with other desirable properties of an FPGA provisioning mechanism, such as resource virtualization/isolation and platform compatibility.

Prototype Implementation. We illustrate the scalability of our proposed approach via a prototype implementation on Xilinx Virtex-7 FPGAs. Our results indicate that the proposed approach has a fixed overhead of around $5-8\%$ of the available FPGA resources. This overhead remains unaltered for any number of tenants/workloads using the FPGA resources at any given point of time. Note the choice of the Virtex-7 FPGA family for our prototype is only for benchmarking, and may be extended to other FPGA vendors/families.

Applications in the Automotive Setting. FPGAs are being increasingly used as accelerators in automotive applications. In particular, the high parallel processing capabilities of FPGAs provide great advantages in applications such as ADAS, Smart Park Assist systems, and power control systems in modern vehicles. Most FPGAs also come with integrated peripheral cores that implement commonly-used functions like communication over controller area network (CAN) [12]. In an automotive setting, a single FPGA may be required to accelerate applications from multiple stakeholders, that are mutually distrusting and wish to protect their individual IPs. The core techniques underlying our proposed framework in this paper can be equivalently applied to build efficient and scalable IP protection units for such applications.

2   Secure Multi-tenant FPGA Provisioning: Our Proposition

In this section, we present our proposal for secure provisioning of FPGAs among multiple tenants on the cloud. We assume a basic FPGA provisioning setup on a cloud [6], as illustrated in Fig. 1. The idea is to abstract the FPGA resources to the client as an *accelerator pool*. Each FPGA is divided into multiple accelerator slots (e.g. A, B, C and D in Fig. 1), with one or more slots assigned to a tenant. The dynamic partial reconfiguration mechanism of modern FPGAs allows a tenant to view each such slot as a *virtual FPGA*, with specific resource types, available capacity and compatible interfaces. The DMA controller module is meant primarily for bandwidth and priority management across the various FPGA partitions. At the hypervisor layer, the controller module chooses available FPGA nodes based on their compatibility with a tenant's requirements, and helps configure them with the desired bitstream file via the service layer. The tenant essentially sees a VM, embedded with a virtual FPGA and containing the necessary APIs and controller modules to configure the FPGA. The allocation of resources to various tenants and the creation of corresponding VMs is handled by a separate controller module. More details of this basic setup can be found in [6]. Our aim is to propose an efficient and secure mechanism that ensures IP protection in this setup, without compromising on the other well-established features such as virtualization, inter-VM isolation and platform compatibility.

2.1   Bring Your Own Keys (BYOK)

The fundamental idea underlying our security proposal is as follows: each tenant encrypts her bitstream using a secret-key *of her own choice* before configuring the virtual FPGA with the same. Since bitstreams would potentially be encrypted in bulk, a symmetric-key encryption algorithm such as AES-128 is the ideal choice in this regard. Note that this approach immediately assures bitstream confidentiality. In particular, since neither the service provider nor any malicious agent can correctly guess the key chosen by a tenant (except with negligible probability), they can no longer gain access to her bitstream.

Notwithstanding its apparent benefits, the aforementioned BYOK-based bitstream encryption technique poses two major challenges in the shared FPGA setting - synchronizing bitstream encryption and decryption for different tenants, and efficient key-management. The main novelty of our proposal is in the application of *key-aggregation* [29] - a provably secure cryptographic technique - to efficiently solve both these challenges. We begin by providing a brief overview of a key-aggregate cryptosystem (KAC), along with a concrete construction for the same. We then demonstrate how KAC solves the key-management and synchronization challenges posed by the BYOK-based approach.

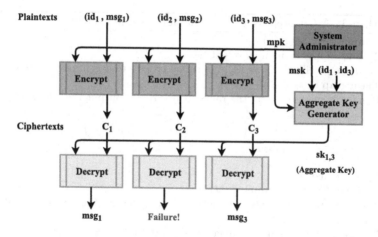

Fig. 2. An illustration of KAC over three entities

2.2   Key-Aggregate Cryptosystems (KAC)

KAC is a public-key mechanism to encapsulate multiple decryption-keys corresponding to an arbitrarily large number of independently encrypted entities into a single constant-sized entity. In a KAC, each plaintext message/entity is associated with a unique identity id, and is encrypted using a common master public-key mpk, generated by the system administrator. The system administrator also generates a master secret-key msk, which in turn is used to generate decryption keys for various entities. The main advantage of KAC is its ability to generate constant-size *aggregate decryption keys*, that combine the power of several individual decryption keys. In other words, given ciphertexts $C_1, C_2 \cdots, C_n$ corresponding to identities $id_1, id_2, \cdots, id_n$, it is possible to generate a constant-size aggregate decryption key sk_S for any arbitrary subset of identities $S \subseteq \{id_1, \cdots, id_n\}$. In addition, the aggregate key sk_S *cannot* be used to decrypt any ciphertext C_j corresponding to an identity $id_j \notin S$. Figure 2 illustrates the concept of a KAC scheme with a simple toy example. Observe that the individual secret-keys sk_1 and sk_3 for the identities id_1 and id_3 are compressed into a single aggregate-key $sk_{1,3}$, that can be used to decrypt both the ciphertexts C_1 and C_3, *but not* C_2. Additionally, $sk_{1,3}$ has the same size as either of sk_1 and sk_3, individually.

2.3   A Concrete KAC Construction on Elliptic Curves

Algorithm 1 briefly describes a provably secure construction for KAC to illustrate its key-aggregation property. The main mathematical structure used by the construction is a prime order sub-group of elliptic curve points $\mathbb{G}$, generated by a point P, and a bilinear map e that maps pairs of elements in $\mathbb{G}$ to a unique element in another group $\mathbb{G}_T$. The construction supports a maximum of

---

Algorithm 1. A Concrete KAC construction on Elliptic Curves

1: **procedure** KAC.Setup(n)
2:     Take as input the number of entities n
3:     Let P be an elliptic curve point of prime order q that generates a group $\mathbb{G}$ with a bilinear map $e : \mathbb{G} \times \mathbb{G} \longrightarrow \mathbb{G}_T$.
4:     Randomly choose α, γ in the range $[0, q-1]$ and output the following:

$$\mathsf{mpk} = \left(\{ \left[\alpha^j \right] P \}_{j \in [0,n] \cup [n+2, 2n]}, [\gamma] P \right)$$
$$\mathsf{msk} = \gamma$$

5: **end procedure**
6: **procedure** KAC.Encrypt(mpk, i, M)
7:     Take as input the master public key mpk, an entity identity $i \in [1, n]$ and a plaintext bitstream M.
8:     Randomly choose r in the range $[0,q-1]$ and set:

$$c_0 = [r] P$$
$$c_1 = [r] \left([\gamma] P + \left[\alpha^i \right] P \right)$$
$$c_2 = M \oplus H \left(e \left([\alpha^1] P, [\alpha^n] P \right)^r \right)$$

where H is a collision-resistant hash function and $\oplus$ denotes the bit-wise XOR operation
9:     Output the ciphertext $C = (c_0, c_1, c_2)$
10: **end procedure**
11: **procedure** KAC.AggregateKey(msk, mpk, $\mathcal{S}$)
12:     Take as input the master secret key $\mathsf{msk} = \gamma$, the master public key mpk and a subset of entities $\mathcal{S} \subseteq [1, n]$.
13:     Compute $a_\mathcal{S} = \sum_{j \in \mathcal{S}} \left[\alpha^{n+1-j} \right] P$
14:     Output the aggregate key $\mathsf{sk}_\mathcal{S} = [\gamma] a_\mathcal{S}$
15:     Also output $a_\mathcal{S}$ and $b_{i,\mathcal{S}} = \sum_{j \in \mathcal{S} \setminus \{i\}} \left[\alpha^{n+1-j+i} \right] P$ for each $i \in \mathcal{S}$
16: **end procedure**
17: **procedure** KAC.Decrypt($\mathsf{sk}_\mathcal{S}$, $a_\mathcal{S}$, $b_{i,\mathcal{S}}$, C)
18:     Take as input a ciphertext $C = (c_0, c_1, c_2)$ corresponding to an entity with identity i, an aggregate key $\mathsf{sk}_\mathcal{S}$ such that $i \in \mathcal{S}$, along with $a_\mathcal{S}$ and $b_{i,\mathcal{S}}$ as defined above.
19:     Output the decrypted message M as:

$$M = c_2 \oplus H \left(e \left(a_\mathcal{S}, c_1 \right) \cdot e \left(\mathsf{sk}_\mathcal{S} + b_{i,\mathcal{S}}, c_0 \right)^{-1} \right) \tag{1}$$

where H is the same collision-resistant hash function as used in KAC.Encrypt
20: **end procedure**

---

n entities, and is provably secure against chosen-plaintext-attacks under a variant of the bilinear Diffie-Hellman assumption [13]. We refer the reader to [29] for more details on the correctness and security of the construction. Note that the notations $P_1 + P_2$ and $[a]P$ denote point addition and scalar multiplication operations, respectively, over all elliptic curve points P, P_1, P_2 and all scalars a.

Observe that the aggregate key sk_S is a *single elliptic-curve point* (with a fixed representation size), irrespective of the size of the subset S.

2.4   Combining BYOK with KAC

The crux of our proposal lies in combining BYOK with KAC for efficient key-management and synchronization of bitstream encryption-decryption. We achieve this via the following three-step proposal:

Step-1: Setup. In this step, the FPGA vendor sets up a KAC system by generating a master public key and a master secret key. Without loss of generality, we assume that each manufactured FPGA can be divided into a maximum of n accelerator partitions, where each partition is associated with a unique partition identity id, and represents an independent virtual FPGA from the tenant point of view. A dedicated mapping between the virtual FPGA id and the corresponding partition id may be suitably defined; we avoid details of the same for simplicity. Each FPGA contains a KAC decryption engine, that is pre-programmed to use a single aggregate decryption key sk_S corresponding to the subset S of partition ids it hosts. As already mentioned, the KAC aggregate key is a constant-sized entity (typically 256-320 bits), and can be securely stored in either a dedicated non-volatile RAM, or in the eFUSE[1] of certain advanced FPGA families such as Xilinx Virtex-7.

Step-2: Bitstream Encryption. In keeping with the idea behind BYOK, each tenant encrypts her bitstream using her own custom AES-128 key. This may be done using commercially available software tools such as Xilinx Vivado. In our proposal, this functionality is augmented to additionally encrypt the AES-128 key using the master public key of the KAC. The second encryption is performed under the identity id of the partition assigned to the tenant.

Step-3: Bitstream Decryption. Bitstream encryption occurs on-chip in two steps. Each FPGA is provided with a single KAC decryption core, while each individual partition is provided with its own AES-128 decryption core. The KAC decryption engine is first used to recover the AES-128 key chosen by the tenant. Since a single tenant is expected to use the same AES-128 key in a given session, the KAC decryption core needs to be invoked only once per tenant. The recovered key is subsequently used to decrypt any number of encrypted bitstreams and program the FPGA partition with the same.

---

[1] https://www.xilinx.com/support/documentation/application_notes/xapp1239-fpga -bitstream-encryption.pdf.

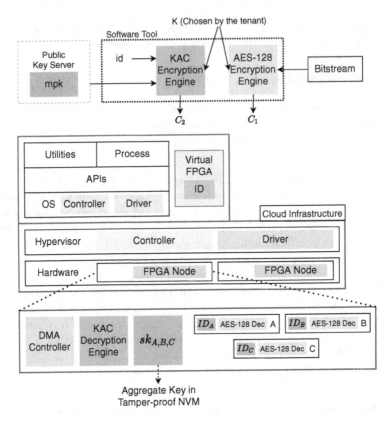

Fig. 3. Secure FPGA provisioning scheme: combining KAC with BYOK

3   Analysis of Our Proposal

3.1   Threat Models and Security

Our threat model considers the following potential IP stealing scenarios:

- **Malicious External Agents:** In this threat model, malicious external agents attempt to gain unauthorized access to a tenant's bitstream.
- **Malicious Co-tenants:** In this threat model, malicious co-tenants collude to try and expose the bitstream of an honest tenant sharing the same FPGA.
- **Malicious Service Provider:** In this threat model, the service provider itself attempts to steal the IP of a tenant (Fig. 3).

Note that in our proposal, bitstream decryption happens entirely on-chip. Hence, IP stealing is possible only if a malicious adversary gains access to the AES-128 key chosen by the tenant to encrypt her bitstream. This key is not known apriori to any third party, including the service provider. The AES-128 key is in turn encrypted using KAC, which is provably CPA secure [29], implying

Algorithm 2. Secure Multi-Tenant FPGA Provisioning

1: **procedure** INITIAL SETUP (FPGA VENDOR)
2:     $(\mathsf{mpk}, \mathsf{msk}) \leftarrow \mathsf{KAC}.\mathsf{Setup}$
3:     Publish the master public key mpk for the KAC scheme
4:     **for** each FPGA **do**
5:         Partition the FPGA into accelerator slots (the maximum number of such slots may be pre-defined depending on the FPGA family)
6:         **for** each FPGA partition **do**
7:             Assign a unique random identity id to the partition
8:         **end for**
9:         Let S denote the set of all id-s corresponding to partitions on the same FPGA
10:        $(\mathsf{sk}_S, a_S, \{b_{\mathsf{id},S}\}_{\mathsf{id}\in S}) \leftarrow \mathsf{KAC}.\mathsf{AggregateKey}\,(\mathsf{msk}, S)$
11:        Embed sk_S in a tamper-proof non-volatile memory segment on the FPGA
12:        Embed a_S in a non-volatile memory segment on the FPGA (*need not be secure/tamper-proof*).
13:        Embed each $b_{\mathsf{id},S}$ in a non-volatile memory segment of the partition with identity id (*again need not be secure/tamper proof*)
14:    **end for**
15:    Each FPGA is provisioned with a single KAC decryption engine, while each FPGA partition is provisioned with its own AES-128 decryption engine.
16: **end procedure**
17: **procedure** BITSTREAM ENCRYPTION(Bitstream)
18:    Suppose a tenant is assigned an FPGA partition with identity id.
19:    $K \leftarrow \mathsf{AES}.\mathsf{KeyGen}$
20:    $C_1 \leftarrow \mathsf{AES}.\mathsf{Encrypt}\,(K, \mathsf{Bitstream})$
21:    $C_2 \leftarrow \mathsf{KAC}.\mathsf{Encrypt}\,(\mathsf{mpk}, \mathsf{id}, K)$
22:    Submit (C_1, C_2) to the framework for configuring the FPGA partition.
23: **end procedure**
24: **procedure** BITSTREAM DECRYPTION(C_1, C_2)
25:    $K \leftarrow \mathsf{KAC}.\mathsf{Decrypt}\,(\mathsf{sk}_S, C_2)$
26:    Bitstream $\leftarrow \mathsf{AES}.\mathsf{Decrypt}\,(K, C_1)$
27: **end procedure**

that the encrypted key cannot be accessed without the appropriate aggregate decryption key for the KAC scheme. Since this key is constant-overhead and is stored in dedicated secure storage, an external adversary cannot gain access to the aggregate decryption key. Hence, our proposal ensures that neither an external adversary nor the service provider can steal the IP of a tenant in the shared FPGA setting.

As mentioned, we also consider threats from malicious co-tenants, who could collude to try and expose the IP of an honest tenant sharing the same FPGA. Note that the malicious tenants have access to the aggregate key(s) corresponding to their own accelerator partitions, and not the aggregate key corresponding to the partitions being used by the honest tenant. However, the KAC scheme is provably collusion resistant against an unbounded number of malicious parties [29], implying that, irrespective of the number of malicious tenants colluding, the aggregate decryption key of an honest tenant cannot be exposed. Thus, our proposal guarantees IP security in the malicious co-tenant setting.

Note that, some recent works on side-channel attacks [20,30] target multi-tenant FPGA systems. Currently, our proposal provides a secure solution for multi-tenant FPGA use on the cloud which focuses on the performance and storage (resource) efficiency, but not security against implementation-level attacks. We shall consider the possible applicability of these attacks against the proposed scheme and necessary countermeasures (if needed) in our future works. .

3.2   Performance and Efficiency

Our proposal has the following desirable features from the point of view of efficiency as well as security.

Constant Secure Storage Overhead per FPGA: Each FPGA stores a single aggregate decryption key that suffices for all its partitions. As already mentioned, KAC generates constant-overhead aggregate-keys irrespective of the number of entities they correspond to. Hence, the memory requirement per FPGA for secure key storage remains the same irrespective of the maximum number of partitions n. In other words, the framework scales to any arbitrarily large n without incurring any additional overhead for secure key storage.

Constant Encryption and Decryption Latency: The encryption and decryption latencies for both KAC and AES-128 are constant, and independent of the maximum number of partitions n supported by an FPGA. In particular, the encryption and decryption sub-routines in the KAC scheme of [29] involve a constant number of elliptic curve operations, and hence require a constant amount of time.

No Leakage to the Cloud Service Provider: The new scheme achieves synchronization between the encryption and decryption engines via a public-key mechanism that is set up by the FPGA vendor. Since the entire bitstream decryption happens on-chip, the confidentiality of the bitstream as well as that of the AES-128 key from the cloud service provider (as well as any external malicious agents) are guaranteed by the security of AES-128 and the CPA security of the KAC scheme, respectively.

4   Prototype Implementation

In this section, we present a prototype implementation of our proposed protocol on the Xilinx Virtex-7 family of FPGAs. In particular, we focus on the overhead and performance results for the security-related components, namely KAC and AES-128. The results are presented in two parts. The first part focuses on the on-chip decryption engines, while the second part focuses on the software tool for generating the encrypted bitstreams and encrypted AES-128 keys.

Table 1. Implementation Details: Elliptic Curve Operations, Optimal-Ate Pairing and AES-128

Elliptic Curve Operations	Module/ Algorithm	#Clock Cycles	Operating Frequency (in MHz)	Latency (in ms)
	Point Addition	705		3.905×10^{-3}
	Point Doubling	528	180.505	2.925×10^{-3}
	Scalar Multiplication	279552		1.548
Opt-Ate Pairing Operations	Module/ Algorithm	#Clock Cycles	Operating Frequency (MHz)	Latency (ms)
	Miller's Loop	1669941	180.505	9.252
	Final Exponentiation	882403		4.888
AES-128 Operations	Module/ Algorithm	#Clock Cycles	Operating Frequency (MHz)	Latency (ms)
	Encryption/ Decryption	10	180.505	5.54×10^{-5}

4.1   On-Chip Decryption Engines

The two main components of our prototype implementation are the AES-128 and KAC decryption engines. To implement the AES-128 decryption core, we adopt a distributed look-up table (LUT)-based approach [23] for efficient and low-latency implementations. While other benchmark implementations for AES-128 using composite field based approaches (such as polynomial, normal, redundant and mixed bases) are well-known [32,35], distributed LUT-based approach is especially tuned to FPGA-based implementations, and is hence chosen.

The KAC Decryption Engine. The KAC decryption engine, adopted from Algorithm 1 [29], requires the implementation of an elliptic curve core that also supports bilinear pairing operations, such as Tate and Optimal-Ate pairing [7,9,36]. Since pairing-friendly elliptic curves with small characteristics [7,17,26] have recently been analyzed as vulnerable to DLP attacks [14,15], we choose an elliptic curve with a 256-bit characteristic prime from the family of pairing-friendly Barreto-Naehrig (BN) curves [4]. All elliptic-curve operations, including point addition, and scalar multiplication are implemented using a Montgomery ladder [5] for constant-time operations. Other constant-time approaches such as window-non-adjacent form (w-NAF) [22] may also be used. We used Miller's algorithm [24] for Optimal-Ate pairing computation with combined point operations and line function evaluation to reduce computation time.

Table 2. Overhead Comparison for Comparable Throughput: BYOK + Authenticated Key Exchange v/s BYOK + KAC for 10 partitions

Bitstream Decryption Methodology	Resource Consumption					Secure Storage Requirement(in Kb) (10 partitions)
	#Slices (%)	#LUTs (%)	#Registers (%)	#DSPs (%)	#BRAMs (%)	
BYOK+Auth. DHKE (Naive Approach)	32880 (30.30)	70380 (16.24)	85848 (9.90)	400 (11.11)	200 (13.60)	3.84
BYOK+KAC (Our Proposal)	5330 (4.91)	12747 (2.94)	11839 (1.36)	40 (1.11)	20 (1.36)	0.256

We would like to point out that the choice of curve for our prototype implementation is only for demonstration; our proposal may be easily adopted and implemented efficiently using standard curve choices, including Hessian, Edwards, NIST and Koblitz curves [3,19,33], subject to the restriction that the characteristics of these chosen curves is large.

Use of DSP Blocks. A novel feature of our implementation is the use of DSP blocks to design efficient prime-field multipliers, which in turn are used in the elliptic curve-based operational modules. Modern FPGAs such as the Xilinx Virtex-7 are inherently equipped with numerous DSP blocks, which can be used to design low-latency circuits for arithmetic operations. We exploited this fact to design a high-speed prime field multiplier, that optimally uses these DSP blocks based on an efficient high-radix Montgomery algorithm [25] for modular multiplication. The post-route timing reports for the elliptic curve operations and the AES-128 operations are summarized in Table 1. Although we have chosen the Xilinx Virtex-7 FPGA (xc7vx690tffg1761) family for the prototype implementation, our implementation may be readily ported to other FPGA families with minimal effort.

Comparison with Naïve Approach. In Table 2, we compare the resource overhead of our approach with an alternative naïve approach where each tenant chooses her own key and exchanges the same via a secure and authenticated Diffie-Hellman key exchange (DHKE) protocol. The second approach requires elliptic curve scalar multiplication operations, that required dedicated scalar multiplication units per FPGA partition. For the purpose of comparison, we assume a total of 10 partitions on a given FPGA. Quite evidently, for a comparable throughput, the area requirement of our proposed approach (BYOK+KAC) is significantly more resource-thrifty, which may be attributed to the constant-size aggregate key generation feature of the KAC scheme.

4.2 Software Encryption Engine

The software encryption engine in our prototype implementation allows a tenant to encrypt her bitstream using an AES-128 key of her own choice, and subsequently, encrypt this key under the KAC scheme. As mentioned previously,

Table 3. Implementation Details: KAC Encryption Engine

Operation	Point addition	Point doubling	Pairing	KAC encryption
Latency (ms)	1.351×10^{-2}	1.098×10^{-2}	82.025	104.333

BYOK-based bitstream encryption can be readily availed using commercial design tools such as Xilinx Vivado.

We implemented the KAC encryption engine in software using the open-source Pairing-Based Cryptography (PBC) library[2], that provides APIs to compute pairings over the BN family of elliptic curves. The only pre-requisite for using the PBC library is the open-source GNU Multiple Precision Arithmetic Library[3] (GMP). The PBC library works on a variety of operating systems, including Linux, Mac OS, and Windows (32 and 64 bits).

It is important to note that similar to the decryption operation, the latency for KAC encryption is also independent of the number of partitions a given FPGA can support.

We present implementation results for the KAC encryption engine using the PBC library in Table 3. The target platform is a standard desktop computer, with an Intel Core i5-4570 CPU, 3.8 GB RAM, and an operating frequency of 3.20GHz. Use of PBC is primarily for demonstrating the utility of the framework. Modern libraries like RELIC[4] or MIRACL[5] may be used for better performance.

5 Scalability of Our Framework

In order to elucidate the scalability of our proposed framework, we demonstrate how the following parameters of our prototype implementation scale with the maximum number of tenants/partitions per FPGA:

Secure Storage on FPGA. In Fig. 4, we compare the amount of secure key storage required per FPGA in our proposed framework (combining KAC with BYOK) against a framework that simply uses BYOK with authenticated Diffie-Hellman key exchange. The latter scheme would require to store the AES-128 key for every tenant on the corresponding FPGA partition allocated to her. Naturally, the storage requirement grows with the number of partitions that a given FPGA can support. In our proposition, the aggregation capability of KAC ensures that the tamper-resistant non-volatile storage requirement is independent of number of partitions that a given FPGA can support. In other words, our FPGA provisioning scheme has a far superior scalability in terms of secure key storage, as compared to a simple BYOK-based provisioning scheme.

---

[2] https://crypto.stanford.edu/pbc/.
https://crysp.uwaterloo.ca/software/PBCWrapper/.
[3] https://gmplib.org/.
[4] https://github.com/relic-toolkit/relic.
[5] https://github.com/miracl/MIRACL.

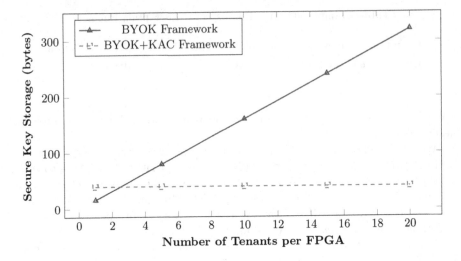

Fig. 4. On-chip secure-storage requirements

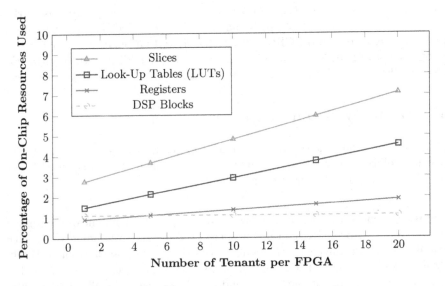

Fig. 5. On-chip resource requirements for BYOK + KAC

On-Chip Resource Overhead. Since our framework requires only a single KAC decryption engine per FPGA, the on-chip resource overhead remains almost constant with respect to the number of partitions that a given FPGA can support. This is illustrated in Fig. 5. The only slight increase is due to the presence of an AES-decryption engine in every FPGA partition. The overall on-chip resource overhead for up to 20 partitions on a single FPGA device is less than 5% for LUTs and is less than 7% for Slices, which highlights the scalability of our proposal.

Bitstream Encryption/Decryption Performance. Finally, as already mentioned, the bitstream encryption/decryption latency (both KAC and AES-128) of our framework is independent of the number of partitions that a given FPGA can support.

In summary, the incorporation of KAC plays a crucial role in ensuring that our framework retains the same levels of performance and efficiency for arbitrarily large number of tenants sharing a single FPGA node. To the best of our knowledge, this is the first FPGA provisioning framework to be prototyped that achieves a desirable balance between security and scalability in the multi-tenancy setting.

6 Conclusion

In this paper, we proposed a dedicated and scalable framework for secure multi-tenant FPGA provisioning on the cloud. Our framework guarantees bitstream confidentiality with constant amount of resource/memory overhead, *irrespective of the number of tenants sharing a given FPGA*. We achieved this using a novel technique known as *key-aggregation* that is provably secure under well-studied cryptographic assumptions. Our framework can be easily integrated into existing cloud-based infrastructures such as OpenStack, and does not interfere with other desirable properties of an FPGA provisioning mechanism, such as resource virtualization/isolation and platform compatibility. We illustrated the scalability of our proposed approach via a prototype implementation on Xilinx Virtex-7 FPGAs. Our results indicate that the proposed approach has a fixed overhead of less than 5% of the available FPGA resources (LUT). This overhead remains unaltered for any number of tenants/workloads using the FPGA resources at any given point of time.

References

1. Nvidia Inc. GRID GPUs
2. Arasu, A., Eguro, K., Kaushik, R., Kossmann, D., Ramamurthy, R., Venkatesan, R.: A secure coprocessor for database applications. In: 2013 23rd International Conference on Field Programmable Logic and Applications (FPL), pp. 1–8. IEEE (2013)
3. Azarderakhsh, R., Reyhani-Masoleh, A.: Efficient FPGA implementations of point multiplication on binary Edwards and generalized Hessian curves using Gaussian normal basis. IEEE Trans. Very Large Scale Integr. (VLSI) Syst. **20**(8), 1453–1466 (2012)
4. Barreto, P.S.L.M., Naehrig, M.: Pairing-friendly elliptic curves of prime order. In: Preneel, B., Tavares, S. (eds.) SAC 2005. LNCS, vol. 3897, pp. 319–331. Springer, Heidelberg (2006). https://doi.org/10.1007/11693383_22
5. Bernstein, D.J., Lange, T., Schwabe, P.: The security impact of a new cryptographic library. In: Hevia, A., Neven, G. (eds.) LATINCRYPT 2012. LNCS, vol. 7533, pp. 159–176. Springer, Heidelberg (2012). https://doi.org/10.1007/978-3-642-33481-8_9

6. Chen, F., Shan, Y., Zhang, Y., Wang, Y., Franke, H., Chang, X., Wang, K.: Enabling FPGAs in the cloud. In: Proceedings of the 11th ACM Conference on Computing Frontiers, p. 3. ACMD (2014)

7. Duursma, I., Lee, H.S.: Tate pairing implementation for hyperelliptic curves $\hat{y}\,2= \hat{x}\,p\text{-}x+$ d. In: ASIACRYPT, vol. 2894, pp. 111–123. Springer (2003). https://doi.org/10.1007/978-3-540-40061-5_7

8. Freund, K.: Amazon's Xilinx FPGA Cloud: Why This May Be A Significant Milestone (2016)

9. Frey, G., Muller, M., Ruck, H.G.: The Tate pairing and the discrete logarithm applied to elliptic curve cryptosystems. IEEE Trans. Inf. Theory **45**(5), 1717–1719 (1999)

10. Guajardo, J., Kumar, S.S., Schrijen, G.-J., Tuyls, P.: FPGA intrinsic PUFs and their use for IP protection. In: Paillier, P., Verbauwhede, I. (eds.) CHES 2007. LNCS, vol. 4727, pp. 63–80. Springer, Heidelberg (2007). https://doi.org/10.1007/978-3-540-74735-2_5

11. Irazoqui, G., Inci, M.S., Eisenbarth, T., Sunar, B.: Wait a minute! a fast, cross-VM attack on AES. In: Stavrou, A., Bos, H., Portokalidis, G. (eds.) RAID 2014. LNCS, vol. 8688, pp. 299–319. Springer, Cham (2014). https://doi.org/10.1007/978-3-319-11379-1_15

12. Johansson, K.H., Törngren, M., Nielsen, L.: Vehicle applications of controller area network. In: Hristu-Varsakelis, D., Levine, W.S. (eds.) Handbook of Networked and Embedded Control Systems, pp. 741–765 (2005). https://doi.org/10.1007/0-8176-4404-0_32

13. Joux, A.: A one round protocol for tripartite Diffie-Hellman. J. Cryptol. **17**(4), 263–276 (2004). https://doi.org/10.1007/s00145-004-0312-y

14. Joux, A., Pierrot, C.: Technical history of discrete logarithms in small characteristic finite fields - the road from subexponential to quasi-polynomial complexity. Des. Codes Cryptograph. **78**(1), 73–85 (2016). https://doi.org/10.1007/s10623-015-0147-6

15. Joux, A., Vitse, V.: Elliptic curve discrete logarithm problem over small degree extension fields. Application to the static Diffie-Hellman problem on E(Fq5) (2010)

16. Kean, T.: Cryptographic rights management of FPGA intellectual property cores. In: Proceedings of the 2002 ACM/SIGDA Tenth International Symposium on FIeld-programmable Gate Arrays, pp. 113–118. ACM (2002)

17. Kerins, T., Marnane, W.P., Popovici, E.M., Barreto, P.S.L.M.: Efficient hardware for the tate pairing calculation in characteristic three. In: Rao, J.R., Sunar, B. (eds.) CHES 2005. LNCS, vol. 3659, pp. 412–426. Springer, Heidelberg (2005). https://doi.org/10.1007/11545262_30

18. Kirchgessner, R., Stitt, G., George, A., Lam, H.: VirtualRC: a virtual FPGA platform for applications and tools portability. In: Proceedings of the ACM/SIGDA International Symposium on Field Programmable Gate Arrays, pp. 205–208. ACM (2012)

19. Koblitz, N.: Elliptic curve cryptosystems. Math. Comput. **48**(177), 203–209 (1987)

20. Krautter, J., Gnad, D.R., Schellenberg, F., Moradi, A., Tahoori, M.B.: Active fences against voltage-based side channels in multi-tenant FPGAS. IACR Cryptol. ePrint Arch 2019:1152 (2019)

21. Lie, W., Feng-Yan, W.: Dynamic partial reconfiguration in FPGAs. In: 2009 Third International Symposium on Intelligent Information Technology Application, IITA 2009, vol. 2, pp. 445–448. IEEE (2009)

22. Longa, P., Miri, A.: New Multibase Non-Adjacent Form Scalar Multiplication and its Application to Elliptic Curve Cryptosystems (extended version). IACR Cryptology ePrint Archive 2008:52 (2008)
23. McLoone, M., McCanny, J.V.: Rijndael FPGA implementations utilizing look-up tables. J. VLSI Signal Process. Syst. Signal Image Video Technol. **34**(3), 261–275 (2003)
24. Miller, V.S.: The Weil pairing, and its efficient calculation. J. Cryptol. **17**(4), 235–261 (2004)
25. Mukhopadhyay, D., Roy, D.B.: Revisiting FPGA implementation of montgomery multiplier in redundant number system for efficient ECC application in GF (p). In: 2018 28th International Conference on Field Programmable Logic and Applications (FPL), pp. 323–3233. IEEE (2018)
26. Oliveira, L.B., Aranha, D.F., Morais, E., Daguano, F., López, J., Dahab, R.: Tinytate: computing the Tate pairing in resource-constrained sensor nodes. In: Sixth IEEE International Symposium on Network Computing and Applications, 2007. NCA 2007, pp. 318–323, IEEE (2007)
27. Opitz, F., Sahak, E., Schwarz, B.: Accelerating distributed computing with FPGAs. Xcell J. **3**, 20–27 (2012)
28. Ovtcharov, K., Ruwase, O., Kim, J.Y., Fowers, J., Strauss, K., Chung, E.S.: Accelerating deep convolutional neural networks using specialized hardware. Microsoft Res. Whitepaper **2**(11), 1–4 (2015)
29. Patranabis, S., Shrivastava, Y., Mukhopadhyay, D.: Provably secure key-aggregate cryptosystems with broadcast aggregate keys for online data sharing on the cloud. IEEE Trans. Comput. **66**(5), 891–904 (2017)
30. Provelengios, G., Holcomb, D., Tessier, R.: Characterizing power distribution attacks in multi-user FPGA environments. In: 2019 29th International Conference on Field Programmable Logic and Applications (FPL), pp. 194–201. IEEE (2019)
31. Ristenpart, T., Tromer, E., Shacham, H., Savage, S.: Hey, you, get off of my cloud: exploring information leakage in third-party compute clouds. In: Proceedings of the 16th ACM Conference on Computer and Communications Security, pp. 199–212. ACM (2009)
32. Rudra, A., Dubey, P.K., Jutla, C.S., Kumar, V., Rao, J.R., Rohatgi, P.: Efficient Rijndael encryption implementation with composite field arithmetic. In: Koç, Ç.K., Naccache, D., Paar, C. (eds.) CHES 2001. LNCS, vol. 2162, pp. 171–184. Springer, Heidelberg (2001). https://doi.org/10.1007/3-540-44709-1_16
33. Shu, C., Gaj, K., El-Ghazawi, T.: Low latency elliptic curve cryptography accelerators for NIST curves over binary fields. In: Proceedings of the 2005 IEEE International Conference on. Field-Programmable Technology, 2005, pp. 309–310. IEEE (2005)
34. So, H.K.H., Brodersen, R.: A unified hardware/software runtime environment for FPGA-based reconfigurable computers using BORPH. ACM Trans. Embed. Comput. Syst. (TECS) **7**(2), 14 (2008)
35. Ueno, R., Homma, N., Sugawara, Y., Nogami, Y., Aoki, T.: Highly efficient GF (2^8) g f $(2\ 8)$ inversion circuit based on redundant GF arithmetic and its application to AES design. In: International Workshop on Cryptographic Hardware and Embedded Systems, pp. 63–80. Springer (2015). https://doi.org/10.1007/978-3-662-48324-4_4
36. Vercauteren, F.: Optimal pairings. IEEE Trans. Inf. Theory **56**(1), 455–461 (2009)

Experimental Results on Higher-Order Differential Spectra of 6 and 8-bit Invertible S-Boxes

Subhamoy Maitra[1], Bimal Mandal[2(✉)], Manmatha Roy[1], and Deng Tang[3]

[1] Indian Statistical Institute, Kolkata 700108, India
subho@isical.ac.in, reach.manmatha@gmail.com
[2] Department of Mathematics, Indian Institute of Technology Madras,
Chennai 600036, India
bimalmandal90@gmail.com
[3] School of Electronic Information and Electrical Engineering,
Shanghai Jiao Tong University, Shanghai 200240, China
dtang@foxmail.com

Abstract. Designing S-box with good cryptographic properties still remains as one of the most important areas of research in symmetric key cryptography. For quite sometime, inverse function ($x \mapsto x^{-1}$, i.e., x^{2^n-2}) over $\mathbb{F}_{2^n}$ has been the most popular choice for S-boxes due to good resistance against differential and linear cryptanalysis. Very recently Tang et. al. (2020) proved that inverse function admits a bias (error) of $\frac{1}{2^{n-2}}$ when considered in its second-order differential spectrum. In this paper we present experimental results related to higher-order differential spectrum of multiplicative inverse functions for $n = 6$ and 8 and compare the result with APN permutation for $n = 6$. In particular, we observe that APN permutation over $\mathbb{F}_{2^6}$ has larger bias in its second-order differential spectrum with probability $\frac{1}{8}$ ($> \frac{1}{2^{n-2}}$). This fact admits the possibility of higher-order differential attacks against block ciphers which employ APN permutations as a nonlinear layer.

Keywords: Symmetric key cryptography · S-box · Higher-order differential attack · Inverse function · Almost perfectly nonlinear (APN) permutation

1 Introduction

S-boxes are used as the basic building block to design a secure symmetric cipher, especially block cipher. Cryptanalysis on such ciphers are broadly considered in two directions. One is differential cryptanalysis [3], and the other one is linear cryptanalysis [11]. The basic idea of differential cryptanalysis of a cipher E is to measure the probability of occurrence of input messages P satisfying $E(P) + E(P + \Delta P) = \Delta C$, where ΔP and ΔC are inputs and corresponding outputs differences, respectively. The idea of higher-order differential cryptanalysis was first proposed by Lai [10] which is mainly generalization of first-order

© Springer Nature Switzerland AG 2020
L. Batina et al. (Eds.): SPACE 2020, LNCS 12586, pp. 226–237, 2020.
https://doi.org/10.1007/978-3-030-66626-2_12

differential cryptanalysis. It is required to compute a good higher-order differential of a block cipher of $(r-1)$th round outputs for recovering the last round key. There are many works done on (higher-order) differential attacks. Knudsen [9] used the partial and higher-order differential cryptanalysis to the DES. Tsunoo et al. [17] analyzed the higher-order differential cryptanalysis on the reduced round MISTY1. For more details on (higher-order) differential attacks, we refer to [1,4,7,8,16].

We want to emphasize on the fact that core part of S-box design process involves choosing a suitable Boolean function with good cryptographic properties (e.g. balanced, high nonlinearity, high algebraic degree, strong avalanche criteria etc). It is difficult to construct a bijective S-box with good cryptographic properties, and most of the methods published in the literature to design them are based on algebraic constructions [5]. Recent other efforts mostly involve computer-aided (meta) heuristic search including but not limited to genetic algorithm [6], evolutionary computation [15] and cellular automata [13]. As the dimension grows, search space (2^{2^n}) explodes limiting the scope of computer-aided search. Currently there are two well known candidates for invertible S-boxes, one is called multiplicative inverse function and another is APN permutation. The multiplicative inverse functions are constructed for any n-bit and it provides optimal resistance to linear approximation, optimal algebraic degree and good differential properties. It is in use for last three decades and survived many of the state-of-the-art attack formulated in these years. On the other hand APN permutations are new candidates, mostly famous for their provably optimal resistance against provided the optimal resistance for first-order differential attack, but $n = 6$ is the only even value of n where an APN permutation defined over $\mathbb{F}_{2^n}$ is known up to now. Very recently Tang et al. [18] proved that inverse function admits a bias (error) of $\frac{1}{2^{n-2}}$ when considered in its second-order differential spectrum. In this paper we derive experimental results related to higher-order differential spectrum of inverse functions for $n = 6$ and 8 and APN permutation for $n = 6$. Higher-order differential cryptanalysis, a natural generalization of first-order differential cryptanalysis, is study of biases in its higher-order differential spectrum. In particular we could analyze higher-order differential characteristics of both of APN permutation and inverse functions to list suitable candidates which admit more bias. In general our experimentation shows that despite its optimality with respect to first-order differential characteristics, APN permutation performs worse than inverse function when we consider the higher-order differential characteristics. To the best of our knowledge it is first such work, especially for APN permutations. One of the objectives of this paper is review candidacy of APN permutations in comparison with inverse functions as S-box primitive in context of higher-order differential attacks. Various techniques of higher-order differential techniques are known since many years. Results from this paper can be motivation for researchers to revisit higher-order differential attacks for block ciphers employing APN permutations in nonlinear layer to review its candidacy as a substitute for inverse functions.

1.1   Contribution and Organization

We mainly focus on the experimental results on higher-order differential spectrum of two well known S-boxes, multiplicative inverse functions in 6 and 8-bit and APN permutation in 6-bit. In particular, we first experimentally calculate their second and third-order differential spectrum and compare their spectrum values. The experimental results of this paper are given below.

- We identify the $\alpha, \beta \in \mathbb{F}_{2^n}^*$ with $\alpha \neq \beta$ and $y \in \mathbb{F}_{2^n}$ such that $\mathcal{N}_I(\alpha, \beta, y) = 8$ for multiplicative inverse functions I for $n = 6$ and 8, also $\mathcal{N}_F(\alpha, \beta, y) = 12$ for APN permutation F for $n = 6$, where

$$\mathcal{N}_I(\alpha, \beta, y) = \#\{x \in \mathbb{F}_{2^n} : I(x) + I(x + \alpha) + I(x + \beta) + I(x + \alpha + \beta) = y\}$$

  is second-order differential characteristics of multiplicative inverse function I and similarly $N_F(\alpha, \beta, y)$ is second-order differential characteristics of APN permutation F.
- Thus, we get a non negligible bias in second-order spectrum of APN permutation in 6-bit with probability $\frac{1}{8}$ ($> \frac{1}{2^{n-2}}$), and it is required 4 ($p = \frac{1}{16}$ and $q = 2$ since $\frac{3}{16} = \frac{1}{16}(1+2)$, so $\frac{1}{pq^2} = 4$) many inputs to identify this error with a success probability significantly higher that half. This might be a weakness of a block cipher if we used an APN permutation as a primitive.
- We also inspect third-order differentials of both of the functions which confirms again the superiority of multiplicative inverse function over APN permutation. We observe that inverse functions admit bias of $\frac{1}{32}$ and $\frac{1}{8}$ for $n = 8$ and 6, respectively, in its third-order differential spectrum, and APN permutation over $\mathbb{F}_{2^6}$ have a bias $\frac{7}{8}$, which is much higher than the inverse function for $n = 6$.
- We observe that the second derivatives of inverse functions for $n = 4$ and 5 take the possible value with uniform probability $\frac{1}{4}$ and $\frac{1}{8}$, respectively, which are optimal for any S-box.

The rest of this paper is organized as follows. In Sect. 2 we present some basic definitions and notations of S-boxes. We also derive some basic results on APN permutations in Sect. 3. The experimental observations on higher-order differential spectrum of different S-boxes are given in Sect. 4, and in Sect. 5 we compare the experimental results in context of cryptographic implications. Section 6 concludes the paper.

2   Preliminaries

For any positive integer n, we denote by $\mathbb{F}_2^n$ the vector space of n-tuples over the finite field $\mathbb{F}_2 = \{0, 1\}$, and by $\mathbb{F}_{2^n}$ the finite field of order 2^n. For simplicity, we denote by $\mathbb{F}_2^{n*}$ the set $\mathbb{F}_2^n \setminus \{(0, 0, \ldots, 0)\}$, and $\mathbb{F}_{2^n}^*$ denotes the set $\mathbb{F}_{2^n} \setminus \{0\}$. It is known that the vector space $\mathbb{F}_2^n$ is isomorphic to the finite field $\mathbb{F}_{2^n}$ through the choice of some basis of $\mathbb{F}_{2^n}$ over $\mathbb{F}_2$. Indeed, if $\{\lambda_1, \lambda_2, \ldots, \lambda_n\}$ is a basis of $\mathbb{F}_{2^n}$ over $\mathbb{F}_2$, then every vector $\mathbf{x} = (x_1, x_2, \ldots, x_n)$ of $\mathbb{F}_2^n$ can be identified with the element $x_1\lambda_1 + x_2\lambda_2 + \cdots + x_n\lambda_n \in \mathbb{F}_{2^n}$. The finite field $\mathbb{F}_{2^n}$ can then be viewed as an n-dimensional vector space over $\mathbb{F}_2$. The Hamming weight of an element $\mathbf{x} \in \mathbb{F}_2^n$, denoted by $wt(\mathbf{x})$, is defined by $wt(\mathbf{x}) = \sum_{i=1}^{n} x_i$, the sum is over integer. The inner product of $\mathbf{x}, \mathbf{y} \in \mathbb{F}_2^n$ is defined by $\mathbf{x} \cdot \mathbf{y} = x_1 y_1 + x_2 y_2 + \cdots + x_n y_n$. Given two Boolean functions f and g in n variables, the Hamming distance between f and g is defined as $d_H(f, g) = \#\{\mathbf{x} \in \mathbb{F}_2^n : f(\mathbf{x}) \neq g(\mathbf{x})\}$. Any Boolean function f in n variables can also be expressed in terms of a polynomial in $\mathbb{F}_2[x_1, \ldots, x_n]/(x_1^2 + x_1, \ldots, x_n^2 + x_n)$:

$$f(x_1, \ldots, x_m) = \sum_{\mathbf{u} \in \mathbb{F}_2^m} a_{\mathbf{u}} \left(\prod_{j=1}^{n} x_j^{u_j} \right) = \sum_{\mathbf{u} \in \mathbb{F}_2^m} a_{\mathbf{u}} \mathbf{x}^{\mathbf{u}},$$

where $a_{\mathbf{u}} \in \mathbb{F}_2$. This representation is called the algebraic normal form (ANF) of f. The algebraic degree, denoted by $\deg(f)$, is the maximal value of $wt(\mathbf{u})$ such that $a_{\mathbf{u}} \neq 0$. A Boolean function is called affine if its algebraic degree is at most one. Any affine function can be written by $l_{\mathbf{a}, \varepsilon}(\mathbf{x}) = \mathbf{a} \cdot \mathbf{x} + \varepsilon$ for all $\mathbf{x} \in \mathbb{F}_2^n$, where $\mathbf{a} \in \mathbb{F}_2^n$ and $\varepsilon \in \mathbb{F}_2$. If $\varepsilon = 0$, then $l_{\mathbf{a}, 0}$ is called a linear function.

2.1   S-Boxes over Vector Space $\mathbb{F}_2^n$ and Finite Field $\mathbb{F}_{2^n}$

Any function $F : \mathbb{F}_2^n \to \mathbb{F}_2^m$ is called an $n \times m$ S-box, which is often called an (n, m)-function or a vectorial Boolean function if the values n and m are omitted. An $n \times m$ S-box can be considered as the parallelization of m Boolean functions $f_i : \mathbb{F}_2^n \to \mathbb{F}_2$, where $1 \leq i \leq m$, such that $F(\mathbf{x}) = (f_1(\mathbf{x}), f_2(\mathbf{x}), \ldots, f_m(\mathbf{x}))$ for all $\mathbf{x} \in \mathbb{F}_2^n$. We represent the set of all n-variable Boolean functions by $\mathcal{B}_n$. In addition, the Boolean functions f_i's are called the coordinate functions of F. Further, the Boolean functions, which are the linear combinations with non all-zero coefficients of the coordinate functions of F, are called component functions of F. The component functions of F can be expressed as $\mathbf{v} \cdot F$, denoted by $F_{\mathbf{v}}$, where $\mathbf{v} \in \mathbb{F}_2^{m*}$. If we identify every element of $\mathbb{F}_2^m$ with an element of finite field $\mathbb{F}_{2^m}$, then the nonzero component functions F_v of F can be expressed as $\mathrm{Tr}_1^m(vF)$, where $v \in \mathbb{F}_{2^m}^*$ and $\mathrm{Tr}_1^m(x) = \sum_{i=0}^{m-1} x^{2^i}$.

2.2   Cryptographic Properties of S-Boxes

We now briefly review the basic definitions regarding to the cryptographic properties of Boolean functions and then extend those definitions to S-boxes by using component functions. For further details we refer to [5]. We say that a Boolean function $f \in \mathcal{B}_n$ is balanced if its truth table contains an equal number of ones and zeros, that is, if its Hamming weight equals 2^{n-1}, where the Hamming weight of f is defined as the size of the support of f in which the support of f is defined as $\mathrm{supp}(f) = \{\mathbf{x} \in \mathbb{F}_2^n : f(\mathbf{x}) \neq 0\}$. The nonlinearity of f, denoted by $nl(f)$, is the minimum Hamming distance between f and all the functions with algebraic degree at most 1. The Walsh–Hadamard transform of $f \in \mathcal{B}_n$ at point $\mathbf{a}$ is defined by $\widehat{f}(\mathbf{a}) = \sum_{\mathbf{x} \in \mathbb{F}_2^n} (-1)^{f(\mathbf{x}) + \mathbf{a} \cdot \mathbf{x}}$. The multiset constituting of the values of the Walsh–Hadamard transform is called the Walsh–Hadamard spectrum of f. It can be easily seen that, for any Boolean function $f \in \mathcal{B}_n$, its nonlinearity can be computed as $\mathrm{nl}(f) = 2^{n-1} - \frac{1}{2} \max_{\mathbf{a} \in \mathbb{F}_2^n} |\widehat{f}(\mathbf{a})|$. The cryptographic properties of any S-box mainly depends on its component functions. The algebraic degree of an S-box is the maximum algebraic degree of its component functions. The nonlinearity of an (n, m)-function F is dependent on its component functions, and is defined by the minimum nonlineartiy of its all component functions, that is,

$$\mathrm{nl}(F) = \min_{\mathbf{v} \in \mathbb{F}_2^{m*}} \{\mathbf{v} \cdot F\} = 2^{n-1} - \frac{1}{2} \max_{\mathbf{a} \in \mathbb{F}_2^n, \mathbf{v} \in \mathbb{F}_2^{m*}} |\widehat{\mathbf{v} \cdot F}(\mathbf{a})|.$$

The nonlinearity $\mathrm{nl}(F)$ is upper bounded by $2^{n-1} - 2^{\frac{n-1}{2}}$ when $m = n$. This upper bound is tight for odd $n = m$. For even $m = n$, the best known value of the nonlinearity of (n, n)-functions is $2^{n-1} - 2^{\frac{n}{2}}$ and achieved by multiplicative inverse functions for even n. The rth order nonlinearity of an (n, m)-function F is the minimum rth order nonlineartiy of its all component functions.

The derivative of $f \in \mathcal{B}_n$ with respect to $\mathbf{a} \in \mathbb{F}_2^n$, denoted by $D_{\mathbf{a}}f$, is defined by $D_{\mathbf{a}}f(\mathbf{x}) = f(\mathbf{x} + \mathbf{a}) + f(\mathbf{x})$. By successively taking derivatives with respect to any k linearly independent vectors in $\mathbb{F}_2^n$ we obtain the kth-derivative of $f \in \mathcal{B}_n$. Suppose $\mathbf{u}_1, \ldots, \mathbf{u}_k$ are linearly independent vectors of $\mathbb{F}_2^n$ generating the subspace V of $\mathbb{F}_2^n$. The kth-derivative of $f \in \mathcal{B}_n$ with respect to $\mathbf{u}_1, \ldots, \mathbf{u}_k$, or alternatively with respect to the subspace V, is defined as

$$D_V f(\mathbf{x}) = D_{\mathbf{u}_1, \ldots, \mathbf{u}_k} f(\mathbf{x}) = \sum_{\mathbf{a} \in \mathbb{F}_2^k} f(\mathbf{x} + a_1 \mathbf{u}_1 + \cdots + a_k \mathbf{u}_k) = \sum_{\mathbf{v} \in V} f(\mathbf{x} + \mathbf{v}).$$

It can be easily seen that $D_V f$ is independent of the choice of basis for V. If any one vector $\mathbf{u}_i$ is linearly dependent on other vectors $\mathbf{u}_j$, $j \neq i$, then $D_{\mathbf{u}_1, \ldots, \mathbf{u}_k} f(\mathbf{x}) = 0$ for all $\mathbf{x} \in \mathbb{F}_2^n$ and $f \in \mathcal{B}_n$. We call it by trivial kth order differential. Let $V_k \subseteq \mathbb{F}_2^n$ be a vector space with dimension k and F be an arbitrary (n, m)-function. The kth-derivative of F with respect to V_k is defined as $D_{V_k} F(\mathbf{x}) = \sum_{\mathbf{v} \in V_k} F(\mathbf{x} + \mathbf{v})$. Let V be an k dimensional subspace of $\mathbb{F}_2^n$. The kth order differential of a S-box F [9, Definition 4.2] is the number of inputs $\mathbf{x} \in \mathbb{F}_2^n$ such that

$$\sum_{\mathbf{v} \in V} F(\mathbf{x} + \mathbf{v}) = \beta, \quad \beta \in \mathbb{F}_2^n. \tag{1}$$

Definition 1 [9, Definition 4.2]. *An $n \times m$ S-box F is called the kth-order differentially δ_k-uniform if the equation $\sum_{\mathbf{v} \in V_k} F(\mathbf{x} + \mathbf{v}) = \beta$ has at most δ_k solutions for all k-dimensional vector space V_k and $\beta \in \mathbb{F}_2^m$. Accordingly, δ_k is called the kth-order differential uniformity of F.*

It is clear that if $\mathbf{x} \in \mathbb{F}_2^n$ satisfy (1), then $\mathbf{x} + \mathbf{v}$, $v \in V$ are also satisfied. Thus, the cardinality of the solution spaces of (1) for any k-dimensional subspace of $\mathbb{F}_2^n$ and $\beta \in \mathbb{F}_2^n$ is divisible by 2^k. It is clear that $\delta_k \equiv 0 \pmod{2^k}$. The first-order differential uniformity δ_1, simply denoted by δ, of F is well-known as differential uniformity which was introduced by Nyberg in [14] for considering the quality of F to resist the differential attack [3]. The smaller value of δ provides good resistance against differential attack. It is clear that the values of δ are always even since if $\mathbf{x}$ is a solution of equation $F(\mathbf{x}) + F(\mathbf{x} + \mathbf{a}) = \alpha$ then $\mathbf{x} + \mathbf{a}$ is also a solution. This implies that the smallest possible value of δ of (n, m)-functions is 2 and the functions achieving this value are called *almost perfect nonlinear* (APN) functions. Till now only known APN permutation was proposed by Browning et al. [2] for $n = 6$. Algebraic degree of this APN permutation is 4.

A cryptographically desirable S-box is required to have low differential uniformity ($\delta = 2$ is optimal, $\delta = 4$ is good), which makes the probability of occurrence of a particular pair of input and output differences $(\mathbf{a}, \alpha)$ low, and hence provides resistance against differential cryptanalysis. For every k-dimensional vector space V_k and every $\beta \in \mathbb{F}_2^m$, we denote by $\delta_k(V_k, \beta)$ the size of the set $\{\mathbf{x} \in \mathbb{F}_2^n : \sum_{\mathbf{v} \in V_k} F(\mathbf{x} + \mathbf{v}) = \beta\}$ and therefore δ_k equals the maximum value of $\delta_k(V_k, \beta)$. The multi-set $[\delta_k(V_k, \beta) : V_k \subseteq \mathbb{F}_2^k, \beta \in \mathbb{F}_2^m]$ is called the *kth-order differential spectrum* of F. For $k = 1$, this spectrum is represented as a well known table, called difference distribution table (DDT), and the maximum value of DDT is called differential uniformity of F.

For any finite field $\mathbb{F}_{2^n}$, the multiplicative inverse function of $\mathbb{F}_{2^n}$, denoted by I, is defined as $I(x) = x^{2^n-2}$. In the sequel, we will use x^{-1} or $\frac{1}{x}$ to denote x^{2^n-2} with the convention that $x^{-1} = \frac{1}{x} = 0$ when $x = 0$. We can see that, for any $v \neq 0$, $I_v(x) = \mathrm{Tr}_1^n(vx^{-1})$ is a component function of I. The Walsh–Hadamard transform of I_1 at any point α is well known as a Kloosterman sum over $\mathbb{F}_{2^n}$ at α, which is usually denoted by $\mathcal{K}(\alpha)$, i.e., $\mathcal{K}(\alpha) = \widehat{I_1}(\alpha) = \sum_{x \in \mathbb{F}_{2^n}} (-1)^{\mathrm{Tr}_1^n(x^{-1}+\alpha x)}$. The algebraic degree of I is $n - 1$, i.e., optimal, and provided best known nonlinearly among S-boxes in even dimension n.

3   Results on APN Permutation

Let $F : \mathbb{F}_2^n \longrightarrow \mathbb{F}_2^n$ be an APN permutation. Then the equation $F(\mathbf{x}) + F(\mathbf{x} + \mathbf{a}) = \mathbf{b}$ has at most two solutions for any nonzero $\mathbf{a}, \mathbf{b} \in \mathbb{F}_2^n$. Suppose $F(\mathbf{x}) = (f_1(\mathbf{x}), f_2(\mathbf{x}), \dots, f_n(\mathbf{x}))$, where $f_i \in \mathcal{B}_n$ is a coordinate function of F, $i = 1, 2, \dots, n$, and define

$$\mathcal{A}_F(\mathbf{a}, i, \varepsilon_i) = \{\mathbf{x} \in \mathbb{F}_2^n : f_i(\mathbf{x}) + f_i(\mathbf{x} + \mathbf{a}) = \varepsilon_i\}, \tag{2}$$

for all $1 \leq i \leq n$. It is clear that $\mathcal{A}_F(\mathbf{a}, i, 1) = supp(D_{\mathbf{a}} f_i)$, for all $i = 1, 2, \dots, n$ and nonzero $\mathbf{a} \in \mathbb{F}_2^n$, and $\delta_F(\mathbf{a}, \mathbf{b}) = \cap_{i=1}^n \mathcal{A}_F(\mathbf{a}, i, b_i)$.

Remark 1. Let f_i be a coordinate function of $F : \mathbb{F}_2^n \longrightarrow \mathbb{F}_2^n$ such that $supp(D_{\mathbf{a}} f_i) = \emptyset$ for some $\mathbf{a} \in \mathbb{F}_2^n$. Then the cardinality of $\delta_F(\mathbf{a}, \mathbf{b})$ is 0 for all $\mathbf{b} \in \mathbb{F}_2^n$ such that $b_i = 1$ and when $b_i = 0$, $\delta_F(\mathbf{a}, \mathbf{b}) = \cap_{i=1:i \neq j}^n \mathcal{A}_F(\mathbf{a}, i, b_i)$

Proof. If $supp(D_{\mathbf{a}} f_i) = \emptyset$, then $\mathcal{A}_F(\mathbf{a}, i, 1) = \{x \in \mathbb{F}_2^n : f_i(\mathbf{x}) + f_i(\mathbf{x} + \mathbf{a}) = 1\} = \emptyset$, and we get the results.

From the above remark, we get directly the next results for APN permutations.

Theorem 1. *Let* $F : \mathbb{F}_2^n \longrightarrow \mathbb{F}_2^n$ *be an APN permutation and* $\mathcal{A}_F(\mathbf{a}, i, \varepsilon_i)$ *is defined as in* (2). *Then we have the following results.*

1. *The cardinality of* $\cap_{i=1}^n \mathcal{A}_F(\mathbf{a}, i, \varepsilon_i)$ *is either* 0 *or* 2, *for all nonzero* $\mathbf{a} \in \mathbb{F}_2^n$ *and* ε_i, *not all zero.*
2. *For any* $\mathbf{x}, \mathbf{a} \in \mathbb{F}_2^n$ *with* $\mathbf{a} \neq \mathbf{0}$ *such that* $f_i(\mathbf{x}) \neq f_i(\mathbf{x} + \mathbf{a})$, *i.e.,* $\mathbf{a} \neq \mathbf{0}$, $\mathbf{x}, \mathbf{x} + \mathbf{a} \in supp(D_{\mathbf{a}} f_i)$ *for at least one* $i = 1, 2, \ldots, n$.

4   Experimental Results

In this section we experimentally derive higher-order differential spectrums of multiplicative inverse function for $n = 6$ and 8 and APN permutation for $n = 6$. Let F be an $n \times m$ S-box.

$$\mathcal{N}_F(\mathbf{a}, \mathbf{b}, \mathbf{y}) = \#\{\mathbf{x} \in \mathbb{F}_2^n : F(\mathbf{x}) + F(\mathbf{x}+\mathbf{a}) + F(\mathbf{x}+\mathbf{b}) + F(\mathbf{x}+\mathbf{a}+\mathbf{b}) = \mathbf{y}\}, \quad (3)$$

where $\mathbf{a}, \mathbf{b} \in \mathbb{F}_2^n$ and $\mathbf{y} \in \mathbb{F}_2^m$. Then the derivations of all possible values of $\mathcal{N}_I(a, b, y)$ for inverse functions are given in next theorem.

Theorem 2 [18, Theorem 3]. *Let* $n \geq 3$ *be a positive integer. When* (a, b, y) *ranges over* $\mathbb{F}_{2^n}^3$ *such that* $a, b \in \mathbb{F}_{2^n}^*$ *and* $a \neq b$, *we have*

$$\mathcal{N}_I(a, b, y) = \begin{cases} 0, \ 3 \cdot 2^{3n-2} - 2^{2n+1} - \left(10(-1)^{\mathrm{Tr}_1^n(1)} - 3(-1)^{\mathrm{Tr}_1^n(1)} \widehat{I}_1(1) + 1\right) \cdot 2^{n-2} \\ \quad - \frac{3}{4}(-1)^{\mathrm{Tr}_1^n(1)} \widehat{I}_1(1) + \frac{5}{2}(-1)^{\mathrm{Tr}_1^n(1)} + \frac{3}{2} \ [\text{times}] \\ 4, \ 2^{3n-2} - 5 \cdot 2^{2n-2} + \left(10(-1)^{\mathrm{Tr}_1^n(1)} - 3(-1)^{\mathrm{Tr}_1^n(1)} \widehat{I}_1(1) + 8\right) \cdot 2^{n-1} \\ \quad + \frac{3}{2}(-1)^{\mathrm{Tr}_1^n(1)} \widehat{I}_1(1) - 5(-1)^{\mathrm{Tr}_1^n(1)} - 3 \ [\text{times}] \\ 8, \ 2^{2n-2} + \left(3(-1)^{\mathrm{Tr}_1^n(1)} \widehat{I}_1(1) - 10(-1)^{\mathrm{Tr}_1^n(1)} - 7\right) \cdot 2^{n-2} \\ \quad - \frac{3}{4}(-1)^{\mathrm{Tr}_1^n(1)} \widehat{I}_1(1) + \frac{5}{2}(-1)^{\mathrm{Tr}_1^n(1)} + \frac{3}{2} \ [\text{times}] \end{cases},$$

where $\widehat{I}_1(1) = \mathcal{K}(1)$.

Tang et al. [18] computationally checked that there is no such tuple $(a, b, y) \in \mathbb{F}_{2^n} \times \mathbb{F}_{2^n} \times \mathbb{F}_{2^n}$ such that $\mathcal{N}_I(a, b, y) = 8$ for multiplicative inverse function I when $n = 4$ and 5. We know that if n is odd, then multiplicative inverse functions is APN permutations. Thus, from Theorem 2 we have the maximum second-order differential spectrum value of a inverse function for odd n which is also a APN permutations is 8.

4.1   First-Order Differential Characteristics

We recap some known results of multiplicative inverse functions and APN permutation. For first-order differential of a S-box F, we try to find the pairs of the form (a, y), where $y = D_a F(x) = F(x) + F(x + a)$ with $a \neq 0$, which admits larger than trivial number of x as solution to the aforesaid equation. Clearly more the number of feasible such x, larger the differential uniformity.

Multiplicative Inverse Function: Nyberg [14] proved that if n is odd, then the inverse function over $\mathbb{F}_{2^n}$ is APN, and if n is even, then each row of its DDT has exactly one 4 and $2^{n-1} - 2$ occurrences of the number 2.

Case(i): Suppose n is odd. There exist exactly $2^{n-1}(2^n - 1)$ pairs of (a, y) such that $y = D_a F(x)$ has no solution, and $2^{n-1}(2^n - 1)$ many pairs of (a, y) such that $y = D_a F(x)$ has 2 solutions, where $a, y \in \mathbb{F}_{2^n}$ with $a \neq 0$.
Case (ii): Suppose n is even. There exist exactly $(2^{n-1} + 1)(2^n - 1)$, $(2^{n-1} - 2)(2^n - 1)$ and $2^n - 1$ pairs of (a, y) such that $y = D_a F(x)$ has no solution, 2 solutions and 4 solutions, respectively, where $a, y \in \mathbb{F}_{2^n}$ with $a \neq 0$.

APN Permutation over $\mathbb{F}_{2^6}$: By the definition of APN function, we have 2016 many pairs of (a, y) such that $y = D_a F(x)$ has no solution, and also 2016 many pairs has 2 solutions, where $a, y \in \mathbb{F}_{2^6}$ with $a \neq 0$.

4.2 Second-Order Differential Characteristics

The second derivative of a S-box F at $(a, b) \in \mathbb{F}_{2^n} \times \mathbb{F}_{2^n}$ is defined by

$$D_{a,b}F(x) = F(x) + F(x + a) + F(x + b) + F(x + a + b),$$

where $x \in \mathbb{F}_2^n$. We try to find tuples of the form (a, b, y), where $y = D_{a,b}F(x)$ with $a \neq 0$, $b \neq 0$ and $a \neq b$, admitting larger than trivial number of x as solution to the aforesaid equation. Clearly more the number of feasible such x, larger the second-order differential uniformity.

Multiplicative Inverse Function: We calculate the second-order differential spectrum of multiplicative inverse functions.

Case (i): We observe that for $n = 4$ and $a, b \in \mathbb{F}_{2^4}^*$ with $a \neq b$, there exist exactly 2520 triplets of (a, b, y) none of them admits any solution, and 840 many triplets such that $y = D_{a,b}F(x)$ has 4 solutions.
Case (ii): We observe that for $n = 5$ and $a, b \in \mathbb{F}_{2^5}^*$ with $a \neq b$, there exist exactly 22320 triplets of (a, b, y) none of them admits any solution, and 7440 many triplets such that $y = D_{a,b}F(x)$ has 4 solutions.
Case (iii): We observe that for $n = 6$ and $a, b \in \mathbb{F}_{2^6}^*$ with $a \neq b$, there exist exactly 187866 triplets of (a, b, y) none of them admits any solution, and 61740 many triplets such that $y = D_{a,b}F(x)$ has 4 solutions. Also there exist 378 many such triplets (a, b, y) which admits 8 solutions.
Case (iv): We observe that for $n = 7$ and $a, b \in \mathbb{F}_{2^7}^*$ with $a \neq b$, there exist exactly 1541526 triplets of (a, b, y) none of them admits any solution, and 501396 many triplets such that $y = D_{a,b}F(x)$ has 4 solutions. Also there exist 5334 many such triplets (a, b, y) which admits 8 solutions.
Case (v): We observe that for $n = 8$ and $a, b \in \mathbb{F}_{2^8}^*$ with $a \neq b$, there exist exactly 12457260 triplets of (a, b, y) none of them admits any solution, and 4102440 many triplets such that $y = D_{a,b}F(x)$ has 4 solutions. Also there exist 21420 many such triplets (a, b, y) which admits 8 solutions.

APN Permutation over $\mathbb{F}_{2^6}$: We observe that there exist exactly 194880 triplets of (a, b, y) none of them admits any solution, and 48048 many triplets such that $y = D_{a,b}F(x)$ has 4 solutions, where $a, b \in \mathbb{F}_{2^6}^*$ with $a \neq b$. Also there exist 6720 and 336 many such triplets (a, b, y) which admits 8 and 12 solutions, respectively.

4.3   Third-Order Differential Characteristics

The third derivative of a S-box F at $(a, b, c) \in \mathbb{F}_{2^n} \times \mathbb{F}_{2^n} \times \mathbb{F}_{2^n}$ is defined as

$$D_{a,b,c}F(x) = F(x) + F(x + a) + F(x + b) + F(x + a + b) + F(x + c)$$
$$+ F(x + a + c) + F(x + b + c) + F(x + a + b + c),$$

where $x \in \mathbb{F}_2^n$. We try to find quadruple of the form (a, b, c, y) where $y = D_{a,b,c}F(x)$ with a, b and c are linearly independent, which admits larger than trivial number of x as solution to the aforesaid equation. Clearly more the no of feasible such x, larger the third-order differential uniformity.

Multiplicative Inverse Function: We calculate the third-order differential spectrum of multiplicative inverse functions.

Case (i): We observe that for $n = 4$ and $a, b, c \in \mathbb{F}_{2^4}^*$, third derivatives of inverse functions becomes constant functions and there exist exactly 37800 quadruples of (a, b, c, y) admits no solution, and also 2520 many quadruples such that $y = D_{a,b,c}F(x)$ has 16 solutions.

Case (ii): We observe that for $n = 5$ and $a, b, c \in \mathbb{F}_{2^5}^*$, there exist exactly 729120 quadruples of (a, b, c, y) none of them admits any solution, also 104160 many quadruples such that $y = D_{a,b,c}F(x)$ has 8 solutions.

Case (iii): We observe that for $n = 6$ and $a, b, c \in \mathbb{F}_{2^6}^*$, there exist exactly 13177080 quadruples of (a, b, c, y) none of them admits any solution, and 1769040 many quadruples such that $y = D_{a,b,c}F(x)$ has 8 solutions. Also there exist 52920 many quadruples (a, b, c, y) which admits 16 solutions.

Case (iv): We observe that for $n = 7$ and $\mathbf{a}, \mathbf{b}, \mathbf{c} \in \mathbb{F}_{2^7}^*$, there exist exactly 222555816 quadruples of (a, b, c, y) none of them admits any solution, and 31107888 many quadruples such that $y = D_{a,b,c}F(x)$ has 8 solutions. Also there exist 32040 many quadruples (a, b, c, y) which admits 16 solutions.

Case (v): We observe that for $n = 8$ and nonzero $a, b, c \in \mathbb{F}_{2^8}^*$, there exist exactly 3658321800 quadruples of (a, b, c, y) none of them admits any solution, and 517935600 many quadruples such that $y = D_{a,b,c}F(x)$ has 8 solutions. Also there exist 2184840 many quadruples (a, b, c, y) which admits 16 solutions.

APN Permutation over $\mathbb{F}_{2^6}$: We observe that there exist exactly 14030856 quadruples of (a, b, c, y) each of them admits no solution, and 688128 many quadruples such that $y = D_{a,b,c}F(x)$ has 8 solutions, where $a, b, c \in \mathbb{F}_{2^6}^*$. Also there exist 263424 and 16632 many quadruples (a, b, c, y) which admits 32 and 64 solutions, respectively. Therefore, there are many three dimensional subspaces V of $\mathbb{F}_{2^6}$ such that the derivative of the APN permutation over $\mathbb{F}_{2^6}$ with respect to V are constant.

5 Comparison and Cryptographic Significance

Lai [10] first proposed the concept of higher-order differential cryptanalysis of block ciphers which is mainly generalization of first order differential cryptanalysis, and claim that if a nontrivial ith derivative of $r-1$ round function of block cipher takes a value with high probability, then it is possible to derive the key from last round from known 2^i inputs and anticipated derivative value. We know that one can use mixed-integer linear programming techniques [12,19] for finding differential trails in multiple rounds of a block ciphers. In this paper we observe that both inverse functions and APN permutation have non negligible biases in its second and higher-order differential spectrum. In fact, APN permutation admits more bias in its second and third-order differential spectrum in comparison with the inverse functions. The following tables provides their first, second and third-order spectrum values with multiplicity. Let h_i be the total number of inputs of some fixed ith derivatives of a S-box such that output value also fixed, where $i = 1, 2, 3$. Thus, for any non-trivial values a, b, c and y,

$$h_1 = \#\{x \in \mathbb{F}_{2^n} : y = D_a F(x)\},$$
$$h_2 = \#\{x \in \mathbb{F}_{2^n} : y = D_{a,b} F(x)\},$$
$$\text{and } h_3 = \#\{x \in \mathbb{F}_{2^n} : y = D_{a,b,c} F(x)\}.$$

Using above mentioned notation, we summarize our experimental results in Tables 1, 2 and 3.

Table 1. First-order differential spectrum

Function	n	$h_1 = 0$	$h_1 = 2$	$h_1 = 4$
Inverse functions	4	135	90	15
	5	496	496	0
	6	2079	1890	63
	7	8128	8128	0
	8	32895	32130	255
APN permutation	6	2016	2016	0

Table 2. Second-order differential spectrum

Function	n	$h_2 = 0$	$h_2 = 4$	$h_2 = 8$	$h_2 = 12$
Inverse functions	4	2520	840	0	0
	5	22320	7440	0	0
	6	187866	61740	378	0
	7	1541526	501396	5334	0
	8	12457260	4102440	21420	0
APN permutation	6	184880	48048	6720	336

Table 3. Third-order differential spectrum

Function	n	$h_3 = 0$	$h_3 = 8$	$h_3 = 16$	$h_3 = 32$	$h_3 = 64$
Inverse functions	4	37800	2520	0	0	0
	5	729120	104160	0	0	0
	6	13177080	1769040	52920	0	0
	7	222555816	31107888	320040	0	0
	8	3658321800	517935600	2184840	0	0
APN permutation	6	14030856	688128	0	263424	16632

Above mentioned results might be helpful in devising a higher-order distinguisher of a block cipher where these functions are used as a primitive for S-box design. As of now, we suggest MILP based tools to find higher order differential trails as a starting point in this line of research.

6   Conclusion

In this paper we experimentally derive the higher-order differential spectra for two well known S-boxes for inverse functions in 6 and 8-bit and APN permutation for 6-bit. We observe that APN permutation over $\mathbb{F}_{2^6}$ have bias in its second and third-order differential spectrum with probability $\frac{1}{8}$ and $\frac{7}{8}$ which is higher than inverse functions and that occurs for several values of inputs. On the other hand known APN functions are of low algebraic degree. The above two facts together indicates possible weakness of APN based S-boxes in context of differential attacks. Our research advocates against APN function as an alternative of inverse function in S-box design.

Acknowledgments. The authors would like to thank the anonymous reviewers for the detailed comments that improved the technical as well as editorial quality of this paper significantly. The work of Bimal Mandal was supported by the Science and Engineering Research Board, India (Project number: MA1920334SERB008668).

References

1. Biryukov, A., Lamberger, M., Mendel, F., Nikolić, I.: Second-order differential collisions for reduced SHA-256. In: Lee, D.H., Wang, X. (eds.) ASIACRYPT 2011. LNCS, vol. 7073, pp. 270–287. Springer, Heidelberg (2011). https://doi.org/10.1007/978-3-642-25385-0_15
2. Browning, K.A., Dillon, J.F., McQuistan, M.T., Wolfe, A.J.: An APN permutation in dimension six. Contemp. Math. **518**, 3–42 (2010)
3. Biham, E., Shamir, A.: Differential cryptanalysis of DES-like cryptosystems. J. Cryptol. **4**(1), 3–72 (1991)
4. Biham, E., Shamir, A.: Differential cryptanalysis of the full 16-round DES. In: Brickell, E.F. (ed.) CRYPTO 1992. LNCS, vol. 740, pp. 487–496. Springer, Heidelberg (1993). https://doi.org/10.1007/3-540-48071-4_34

5. Carlet, C.: Vectorial Boolean functions for cryptography. In: Crama, Y., Hammer, P.L. (eds.) Boolean Models and Methods in Mathematics, Computer Science, and Engineering, pp. 398–469. Cambridge University Press (2010)
6. Ivanov, G., Nikolov, N., Nikova, S.: Reversed genetic algorithms for generation of bijective S-boxes with good cryptographic properties. Commun. Crypt. 8(2), 247–276 (2016)
7. Knudsen, L., Wagner, D.: Integral cryptanalysis. In: Daemen, J., Rijmen, V. (eds.) FSE 2002. LNCS, vol. 2365, pp. 112–127. Springer, Heidelberg (2002). https://doi.org/10.1007/3-540-45661-9_9
8. Knudsen, Lars R.: Truncated and higher order differentials. In: Preneel, Bart (ed.) FSE 1994. LNCS, vol. 1008, pp. 196–211. Springer, Heidelberg (1995). https://doi.org/10.1007/3-540-60590-8_16
9. Knudsen, L.R.: Partial and higher order differentials and applications to the DES. BRICS Report Series, RS-95-9 (1995)
10. Lai, X.: Higher order derivatives and differential cryptanalysis. Commun. Crypt. 276, 227–233 (1994)
11. Matsui, M.: Linear cryptanalysis method for DES cipher. In: Helleseth, T. (ed.) EUROCRYPT 1993. LNCS, vol. 765, pp. 386–397. Springer, Heidelberg (1994). https://doi.org/10.1007/3-540-48285-7_33
12. Mouha, N., Wang, Q., Gu, D., Preneel, B.: Differential and linear cryptanalysis using mixed-integer linear programming. In: Wu, C.-K., Yung, M., Lin, D. (eds.) Inscrypt 2011. LNCS, vol. 7537, pp. 57–76. Springer, Heidelberg (2012). https://doi.org/10.1007/978-3-642-34704-7_5
13. Mariot, L., Picek, S., Leporati, A., Jakobovic, D.: Cellular automata based S-boxes. Commun. Cryptogr. 11(1), 41–62 (2019)
14. Nyberg, K.: Differentially uniform mappings for cryptography. In: Helleseth, T. (ed.) EUROCRYPT 1993. LNCS, vol. 765, pp. 55–64. Springer, Heidelberg (1994). https://doi.org/10.1007/3-540-48285-7_6
15. Picek, S., Cupic, M., Rotim, L.: A New Cost Function for Evolution of S-Boxes. Evol. Comput. 24(4), 695–718 (2016)
16. Shamir, A.: Impossible differential attacks. Crypto 1998 rump session
17. Tsunoo, Y., Saito, T., Shigeri, M., Kawabata, T.: Higher order differential attacks on reduced-round MISTY1. In: Lee, P.J., Cheon, J.H. (eds.) ICISC 2008. LNCS, vol. 5461, pp. 415–431. Springer, Heidelberg (2009). https://doi.org/10.1007/978-3-642-00730-9_26
18. Tang, D., Mandal, B., Maitra, S.: Further Cryptographic Properties of the Multiplicative Inverse Function. IACR Cryptol. ePrint Arch, vol. 920 (2020)
19. Wu, S., Wang, M.: Security Evaluation Against Differential Cryptanalysis for Block Cipher Structures. IACR Cryptol. ePrint Arch, vol. 511 (2011)

Quantum Resource Estimates of Grover's Key Search on ARIA

Amit Kumar Chauhan$^{(\boxtimes)}$ and Somitra Kumar Sanadhya

Indian Institute of Technology Ropar, Rupnagar, India
amit.iitropar@gmail.com, somitra@iitrpr.ac.in

Abstract. Grover's algorithm provides a quantum attack against block ciphers by searching for a k-bit key using $O(\sqrt{2^k})$ calls to the cipher, when given a small number of plaintext-ciphertext pairs. Recent works by Grassl et al. in PQCrypto'16 and Almazrooie et al. in QIP'18 have estimated the cost of this attack against AES by analyzing the quantum circuits of the cipher.

We present a quantum reversible circuit of ARIA, a Korean standardized block cipher that is widely deployed in government-to-public services. Firstly, we design quantum circuits for the main components of ARIA, and then combine them to construct the complete circuit of ARIA. We implement Grover's algorithm-based exhaustive key-search attack on ARIA. For all three variants of ARIA-{128, 192, 256}, we establish precise bounds for the number of qubits and the number of Clifford+T gates that are required to implement Grover's algorithm.

We also estimate the G-cost as the total number of gates, and DW-cost as the product of circuit depth and width. To find the circuit depth of various circuits such as squaring, multiplier, and permutation layer, we implement them in an open-source quantum computing platform QISKIT developed by IBM.

Keywords: Quantum cryptanalysis · Quantum circuit · Grover's search algorithm · Block cipher · ARIA

1 Introduction

Recent advancements in quantum computing technologies have enhanced the viability of a large-scale quantum computer. Consequently, much of the traditional public-key cryptosystems such as RSA, ECDSA, ECDH will be completely broken due to Shor's algorithm [22]. However, it is widely believed that symmetric cryptosystems like block ciphers and hash functions are quantum-immune. The only known principle is the square-root speed-up over classical key search or pre-image search attacks with Grover's algorithm [11].

The national institute of standards and technology (NIST) has also initiated a process to standardize the cryptographic primitives that are designed to remain secure in the presence of quantum computers. NIST [19] defined various security categories defined based on the concrete cost of an exhaustive key search on the

© Springer Nature Switzerland AG 2020
L. Batina et al. (Eds.): SPACE 2020, LNCS 12586, pp. 238–258, 2020.
https://doi.org/10.1007/978-3-030-66626-2_13

block cipher AES and collision search for the hash function SHA-3 as a reference point. The relevant cost metrics include the number of qubits, the number of Clifford+T gates, and the T-depth and overall circuit-depth. The NIST proposal derives security categories on gate cost estimates from the gate-level descriptions of the AES oracle by Grassl et al. [10].

Related Work. Grassl et al. [10] studied the quantum circuits of AES and estimated the cost of quantum resources needed to apply Grover's algorithm to the AES oracle for key search. Almazrooie et al. [1] improved the quantum circuit of AES-128. The work by Grassl et al. [10] focused on minimizing the number of qubits. In contrast, Almazrooie et al. [1] focused on reducing the total number of Toffoli gates by saving one multiplication in a binary field inversion circuit. Amy et al. [3] estimated the cost of generic quantum pre-image attacks on SHA-2 and SHA-3. Later, Kim et al. [15] discussed the time-space trade-off cost of quantum resources on block ciphers in general and used AES as an example.

Recently, Langenberg et al. [17] developed the quantum circuits for AES that demonstrate the significant improvements over the works by Grassl et al. [10] and Almazrooie et al. [1]. Their work was based on the different S-box design derived by Boyar and Peralta [6], which significantly reduces the number of Toffoli gates in the S-box and its Toffoli-depth. Jaques et al. [13] further studied the quantum key-search attacks under a depth restriction. As a working example, they implemented the AES Grover oracle in Q# quantum programming language. They provided lower-cost estimates by considering different time-space trade-offs based on the NIST security categories for maximum depth.

Bonnetain et al. [5] also studied the post-quantum security of AES within a new framework for classical and quantum structured search. They used the work by Grassl et al. [10] for deducing concrete gate counts for reduced-round attacks.

Our Contribution. In this work, we present a reversible quantum circuit of the block cipher ARIA-k [16], where $k = 128, 192, 256$ are the different key sizes. To implement the full quantum circuit of ARIA, we separately present the quantum circuits for squaring, multiplier, S-box, and the diffusion layer. For the invertible linear map, we adopt an in-place PLU decomposition algorithm as implemented in SageMath[1] [24]. For each circuit used in ARIA, we establish the cost of quantum resources for the number of qubits and the number of Pauli-X gates, controlled-NOT gates, and Toffoli gates. We also compute their circuit depth by implementing them in an open-source quantum computing platform Qiskit[2] [9]. The source code of Qiskit and Sagemath implementations of squaring, multiplier, S-boxes, and diffusion matrix for ARIA is publicly available[3] under a free license to allow independent verification of our results. For all three variants of ARIA-{128, 192, 256}, we first provide the entire cost of these oracles for the number

---

[1] https://www.sagemath.org.

[2] https://qiskit.org.

[3] https://github.com/amitcrypto/ARIA-Blocks-Qiskit.git.

of qubits, Pauli-X gates, controlled-NOT gates, Toffoli gates, and Toffoli-depth and overall circuit depth. Later, when we apply Grover's search algorithm [11] to all three ARIA oracles, we consider the decomposition of reversible circuits into a universal fault-tolerant gate set that can be implemented as the Clifford+T gate set.

The Clifford group consists of Hadamard gate, Phase gate, and controlled-NOT gate. An important non-Clifford gate is a Toffoli gate, which is universal and composed of a few T gates and Clifford gates. For implementing the Toffoli gate, we use Amy et al. [2]'s Toffoli decomposition that requires 7 T-gates and 8 Clifford gates with T-depth of 4 and a total depth of 8. However, Selinger [21] offers a Toffoli decomposition with 7 T-gates and 18 Clifford gates, with T-depth 1 and 4 ancillae. To realize an ℓ-fold controlled-NOT gate in terms of T-gates, we use the result by Wiebe and Roetteler [23] and the estimated cost as $(32 \cdot \ell - 84)$.

We then provide the precise cost estimate of quantum resources for Grover's based key search attack in the Clifford+T model. We also compute the G-cost as the total number of gates and DW-cost as the product of circuit depth and width (the number of qubits) as defined by Jaques and Schanck [14]. We provide the results in Table 6. We believe that like the work by Grassl et al. [10], our work will further help to assess the security of ARIA against more advanced quantum reduced-round attacks.

Organization. First, we briefly discuss quantum computation and Grover's algorithm in Sect. 2. Next, we recall the structure of block cipher ARIA in Sect. 3. We rewrite the SubBytes function to get an advantage over the reversible implementation of ARIA. We then separately evaluate the cost of each operation for one round of ARIA, and the cost of round subkeys generation. In Sect. 4, we present the full quantum reversible circuit of ARIA-128, and give overall cost estimates of resources used in the quantum reversible circuit of ARIA-{128, 192, 256}. In Sect. 5, we provide the total resource estimates of an exhaustive key search with Grover's algorithm for ARIA-{128, 192, 256}. In Sect. 6, we compare the quantum resource estimates of ARIA and AES [10,14]. In Sect. 7, we conclude our work.

2   Preliminaries

2.1   Quantum Computation

A quantum computer acts on quantum states by applying quantum gates to its quantum bits (qubits). A qubit ($|0\rangle$ or $|1\rangle$) is a quantum system defined over a finite set $B = \{0, 1\}$. The state of a 2-qubit quantum system $|\psi\rangle$ is the superposition defined as $|\psi\rangle = \alpha |0\rangle + \beta |1\rangle$, where $\alpha, \beta \in \mathbb{C}$ and $|\alpha|^2 + |\beta|^2 = 1$. In general, the states of an n-qubit quantum system can be described as unit vectors in $\mathbb{C}^{2^n}$ under the orthonormal basis $\{|0\ldots00\rangle, |0\ldots01\rangle, \ldots |1\ldots11\rangle\}$, alternatively written as $\{|i\rangle : 0 \le i < 2^n\}$. Any quantum algorithm is described by a sequence of gates in the form of a quantum circuit, and all quantum computations are reversible. For circuit design, we use the standard quantum circuit model [18] and adopt the basic gate set {Pauli-X, H, CNOT, T, Toffoli}. We briefly define the basic gates in Table 1. To estimate the cost of resources, we consider the decomposition of reversible circuits over the Clifford+T gate set.

Table 1. Commonly used 1-, 2-, 3-qubit quantum gates, along with their corresponding unitary matrices, circuit symbols, and a description of their actions.

Gate type	Qubits	Circuit symbol	Unitary matrix	Description
Pauli-X	1	$\oplus$	$\begin{bmatrix} 0 & 1 \\ 1 & 0 \end{bmatrix}$	Analogous to classical NOT gate, switches $|0\rangle$ to $|1\rangle$ and vice-versa.
H	1	$\boxed{H}$	$\frac{1}{\sqrt{2}}\begin{bmatrix} 1 & 1 \\ 1 & -1 \end{bmatrix}$	Transforms a basis state into an even superposition of the two basis states.
T	1	$\boxed{T}$	$\begin{bmatrix} 1 & 0 \\ 0 & e^{i\pi/4} \end{bmatrix}$	Adds a relative phase shift of $\pi/4$ between contributing basis states.
CNOT	2		$\begin{bmatrix} 1 & 0 & 0 & 0 \\ 0 & 1 & 0 & 0 \\ 0 & 0 & 0 & 1 \\ 0 & 0 & 1 & 0 \end{bmatrix}$	Controlled-not, a reversible analog to classical XOR gate. The input connected to solid dot is a controlled input to make the operation reversible.
Toffoli	3		$\begin{bmatrix} 1 & 0 & 0 & 0 & 0 & 0 & 0 & 0 \\ 0 & 1 & 0 & 0 & 0 & 0 & 0 & 0 \\ 0 & 0 & 1 & 0 & 0 & 0 & 0 & 0 \\ 0 & 0 & 0 & 1 & 0 & 0 & 0 & 0 \\ 0 & 0 & 0 & 0 & 1 & 0 & 0 & 0 \\ 0 & 0 & 0 & 0 & 0 & 1 & 0 & 0 \\ 0 & 0 & 0 & 0 & 0 & 0 & 0 & 1 \\ 0 & 0 & 0 & 0 & 0 & 0 & 1 & 0 \end{bmatrix}$	Controlled-controlled-not, a 3-qubit gate that switches the 3rd bit for states where the first two bits are 1 (that is, switches $|110\rangle$ to $|111\rangle$ and vice-versa).

2.2 Grover's Search Algorithm

We briefly recall the interface that we need to provide for realizing a key search, namely Grover's algorithm [11]. The Grover searching procedure takes as an input a quantum circuit implementing a Boolean function $f : \{0,1\}^k \to \{0,1\}$ in the usual way, i.e., via a quantum circuit U_f that implements $|x\rangle |y\rangle \mapsto |x\rangle |y \oplus f(x)\rangle$, where $x \in \{0,1\}^k$ and $y \in \{0,1\}$. The basic Grover's algorithm finds an element x_0 such that $f(x_0) = 1$. The Grover's algorithm consists of repeatedly applying the operation G to the initial state $|\psi\rangle \otimes |\phi\rangle$, where $|\psi\rangle = \frac{1}{\sqrt{2^k}} \sum_{x \in \{0,1\}^k} |x\rangle$ and $|\phi\rangle = \frac{1}{\sqrt{2}}(|0\rangle - |1\rangle)$. The Grover operator G is defined as

$$G = U_f \left(\left(H^{\otimes k} \left(2 |0\rangle \langle 0| - 1_{2^k} \right) H^{\otimes k} \right) \otimes 1_2 \right)$$

where $|0\rangle$ denotes the all zero basis state of the appropriate size. In order to find a solution x_0 such that $f(x_0) = 1$, G has to be applied $\mathcal{O}(\sqrt{N})$ times to the cipher, where $N = 2^k$ is the total number of possible solutions, and provided that there is only one solution. This means that we can find a solution by applying $H^{\otimes k+1}$ to the initial state $|0\rangle^{\otimes k} \otimes |1\rangle$ and then applying G^ℓ, where $\ell = \lfloor \frac{\pi}{4} \sqrt{2^k} \rfloor$, followed by a measurement of the entire quantum register which will yield a solution x_0 with high probability [7].

In finding the unique solution using Grover's algorithm, we study the number of gates and space requirements needed to apply Grover's algorithm to the block cipher ARIA.

3   Quantum Circuits to Implement ARIA

ARIA [16] is a 128-bit block cipher standardized as a Korean standard block cipher. Its design is based on a substitution-permutation network such as AES. ARIA supports three different key sizes – 128, 192 and 256 bits with different number of rounds – 12, 14, 16 respectively. The 128-bit internal state and key state are treated as a bytes matrix of 4×4 size, where the bytes are numbered from 0 to 15 column-wise.

0	4	8	12
1	5	9	13
2	6	10	14
3	7	11	15

We will devote 128 qubits to hold the current internal state.

The ARIA cipher consists of two parts:

1. **Round transformation** – Each round of the ARIA cipher consists of the following three basic operations, except the last round.
   - **Substitution layer (SL):** a non-linear byte-wise substitution applied to every byte of the state matrix in parallel, where two different substitution layers exist for odd and even rounds.
   - **Diffusion layer (DL):** a linear matrix multiplication of the state matrix with a 16×16 involution matrix.
   - **Add round key (ARK):** simply XORing of the state and a 128-bit round key, which is derived from the master key.
   Before the first round, an initial ARK operation is applied, and the DL operation is omitted in the last round.

2. **Key scheduling algorithm** – It generates the round keys for different rounds from a master key K of 128, 192, or 256 bits. It works in two phases:
   - **Initialization phase:** Four 128-bit values W_0, W_1, W_2, W_3 are generated from the master key MK, by using a 3-round Feistel cipher.
   - **Round key generation phase:** By combining four values W_0, W_1, W_2, W_3, the round subkeys for encryption are generated. The number of round keys for ARIA-{128, 192, 256} are 13, 15, 17 respectively.

Next, we separately describe each operation of ARIA and measure the quantum resource estimates for its reversible implementation.

3.1 Add Round Key (ARK)

In the implementation of the key expansion, we ensure that the current round key is available on 128 dedicated wires. Then we simply XOR the 128-bit round key with the current state.

Quantum Resource Estimates for ARK. Implementing the bit-wise XOR of the round key needs 128 CNOT gates, which can be executed in parallel, and therefore the circuit depth is 1.

3.2 Substitution Layer (SL)

ARIA has two different substitution layers for even and odd rounds. In each odd round, the substitution layer consist of four 8-bit S-boxes in the following order $(S_1, S_2, S_1^{-1}, S_2^{-1})$, and in each even round the substitution layer consists of the following 4 S-boxes $(S_1^{-1}, S_2^{-1}, S_1, S_2)$ operating on one column. Each S-box replaces one byte of the current state with a new value. We treat a state byte as an element $\alpha \in \mathbb{F}_2[x]/(x^8 + x^4 + x^3 + x + 1)$.

1. The first S-box $S_1 : GF(2^8) \rightarrow GF(2^8)$ is defined as

$$S_1(\alpha) := \mathbf{A}.\alpha^{-1} + \mathbf{a} \tag{1}$$

where $\mathbf{A} = \begin{bmatrix} 1 & 0 & 0 & 0 & 1 & 1 & 1 & 1 \\ 1 & 1 & 0 & 0 & 0 & 1 & 1 & 1 \\ 1 & 1 & 1 & 0 & 0 & 0 & 1 & 1 \\ 1 & 1 & 1 & 1 & 0 & 0 & 0 & 1 \\ 1 & 1 & 1 & 1 & 1 & 0 & 0 & 0 \\ 0 & 1 & 1 & 1 & 1 & 1 & 0 & 0 \\ 0 & 0 & 1 & 1 & 1 & 1 & 1 & 0 \\ 0 & 0 & 0 & 1 & 1 & 1 & 1 & 1 \end{bmatrix}$ and $\mathbf{a} = \begin{bmatrix} 1 \\ 1 \\ 0 \\ 0 \\ 0 \\ 1 \\ 1 \\ 0 \end{bmatrix}$.

The inverse of S-box S_1 can be defined as

$$S_1^{-1}(\alpha) := (\mathbf{A}^{-1}.(\alpha + \mathbf{a}))^{-1} \tag{2}$$

where $\mathbf{A}^{-1} = \begin{bmatrix} 0 & 0 & 1 & 0 & 0 & 1 & 0 & 1 \\ 1 & 0 & 0 & 1 & 0 & 0 & 1 & 0 \\ 0 & 1 & 0 & 0 & 1 & 0 & 0 & 1 \\ 1 & 0 & 1 & 0 & 0 & 1 & 0 & 0 \\ 0 & 1 & 0 & 1 & 0 & 0 & 1 & 0 \\ 0 & 0 & 1 & 0 & 1 & 0 & 0 & 1 \\ 1 & 0 & 0 & 1 & 0 & 1 & 0 & 0 \\ 0 & 1 & 0 & 0 & 1 & 0 & 1 & 0 \end{bmatrix}$ and $\mathbf{a} = \begin{bmatrix} 1 \\ 1 \\ 0 \\ 0 \\ 0 \\ 1 \\ 1 \\ 0 \end{bmatrix}$.

2. The second S-box $S_2 : GF(2^8) \rightarrow GF(2^8)$ is defined as

$$S_2(\alpha) := \mathbf{B}.\alpha^{247} + \mathbf{b} \tag{3}$$

$$
\text{where } \mathbf{B} = \begin{bmatrix} 0 & 1 & 0 & 1 & 1 & 1 & 1 & 0 \\ 0 & 0 & 1 & 0 & 1 & 1 & 1 & 1 \\ 1 & 0 & 0 & 1 & 0 & 1 & 1 & 1 \\ 1 & 1 & 0 & 0 & 1 & 0 & 1 & 1 \\ 1 & 1 & 1 & 1 & 0 & 0 & 1 & 0 \\ 0 & 1 & 1 & 1 & 1 & 0 & 0 & 1 \\ 1 & 0 & 1 & 1 & 1 & 1 & 0 & 0 \\ 0 & 1 & 0 & 1 & 1 & 1 & 1 & 0 \end{bmatrix} \text{ and } \mathbf{b} = \begin{bmatrix} 0 \\ 1 \\ 0 \\ 0 \\ 0 \\ 1 \\ 1 \\ 1 \end{bmatrix}.
$$

We rewrite the Eq. (3) as

$$
S_2(\alpha) := \mathbf{B}.(\alpha^{-1})^8 + \mathbf{b} = \mathbf{B}.\mathbf{C}.\alpha^{-1} + \mathbf{b}
$$
$$
= \mathbf{D}.\alpha^{-1} + \mathbf{b} \tag{4}
$$

$$
\text{where } \mathbf{D} = \begin{bmatrix} 0 & 1 & 0 & 1 & 0 & 1 & 1 & 1 \\ 0 & 0 & 1 & 1 & 1 & 1 & 1 & 1 \\ 1 & 1 & 1 & 0 & 1 & 1 & 0 & 1 \\ 1 & 1 & 0 & 0 & 0 & 0 & 1 & 1 \\ 0 & 1 & 0 & 0 & 0 & 0 & 1 & 1 \\ 1 & 1 & 0 & 0 & 1 & 1 & 1 & 0 \\ 0 & 1 & 1 & 0 & 0 & 0 & 1 & 1 \\ 1 & 1 & 1 & 1 & 0 & 1 & 1 & 0 \end{bmatrix} \text{ and } \mathbf{b} = \begin{bmatrix} 0 \\ 1 \\ 0 \\ 0 \\ 0 \\ 1 \\ 1 \\ 1 \end{bmatrix}.
$$

The inverse of S-box S_2 can be defined as

$$
S_2^{-1}(\alpha) = (\mathbf{D}^{-1}.(\alpha + \mathbf{b}))^{-1} \tag{5}
$$

$$
\text{where } \mathbf{D}^{-1} = \begin{bmatrix} 0 & 0 & 0 & 1 & 1 & 0 & 0 & 0 \\ 0 & 0 & 1 & 0 & 0 & 1 & 1 & 0 \\ 0 & 0 & 0 & 0 & 1 & 0 & 1 & 0 \\ 1 & 1 & 1 & 0 & 0 & 0 & 1 & 1 \\ 1 & 1 & 1 & 0 & 1 & 1 & 0 & 0 \\ 0 & 1 & 1 & 0 & 1 & 0 & 1 & 1 \\ 1 & 0 & 1 & 1 & 1 & 1 & 0 & 1 \\ 1 & 0 & 0 & 1 & 0 & 0 & 1 & 1 \end{bmatrix} \text{ and } \mathbf{b} = \begin{bmatrix} 0 \\ 1 \\ 0 \\ 0 \\ 0 \\ 1 \\ 1 \\ 1 \end{bmatrix}.
$$

Quantum Resource Estimates for Substitution Layer (SL). In the implementation of substitution layer, we first compute α^{-1} used in SubBytes functions S_1, S_1^{-1} and S_2, S_2^{-1} given in Eqs. (1), (2), (3), (5) and then we apply the corresponding affine transformations.

To compute α^{-1}, we use Itoh-Tsujii multiplier [12] that is a series of multiplication and squaring operations in $GF(2^n)$. ARIA's operations work in $GF(2^8)$ with irreducible polynomial $P(x) = x^8 + x^4 + x^3 + x + 1$. Specifically, we can write α^{-1} as

$$
\alpha^{-1} = \alpha^{254} = ((\alpha.\alpha^2).(\alpha.\alpha^2)^4.(\alpha.\alpha^2)^{16}.\alpha^{64})^2. \tag{6}
$$

The squaring in $GF(2^8)$ can be implemented with only 12 CNOT gates, and the circuit depth is 7. The resulting circuit is shown in Fig. 1.

The multiplication in $GF(2^8)$ can be realized by using a classical Mastrovito multiplier, which is adopted by Maslov et al. [8]. For the inputs $\mathbf{a} = [a_0, \ldots, a_7]^{\mathsf{T}}$ and $\mathbf{b} = [b_0, \ldots, b_7]^{\mathsf{T}}$ in $GF(2^8)$, let the product of $\mathbf{a}$ and $\mathbf{b}$ is denoted by $\mathbf{c} = [c_0, \ldots, c_7]^{\mathsf{T}}$. The multiplier circuit for computing $\mathbf{c}$ can be implemented with 64 Toffoli gates and 21 CNOT gates, and the circuit depth is 37 and Toffoli-depth is 28. The resulting circuit is shown in Fig. 2.

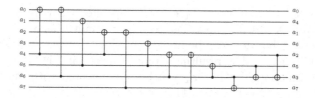

Fig. 1. Circuit for squaring in $\mathbb{F}_2[x]/(x^8 + x^4 + x^3 + x + 1)$.

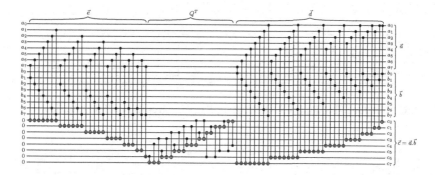

Fig. 2. Circuit for multiplier in $\mathbb{F}_2[x]/(x^8 + x^4 + x^3 + x + 1)$.

The SubBytes functions S_1 and S_2 given in Eqs. (1) and (3) can be implemented with 33 squarings and 7 multiplications and the required number of qubits are only 40. The resulting circuit is shown in Fig. 3. The same circuit with 40 qubits was also given by Kim et al. [15].

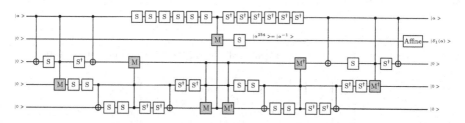

Fig. 3. Circuit for SubBytes functions S_1 and S_2. The gates labelled with S represent the squaring circuit shown in Fig. 1, and the gates labelled with M represent the multiplier circuit shown in Fig. 2. The gates labelled with $S^\dagger$ and $M^\dagger$ represent the inverse squaring and inverse multiplication respectively. Different affine transformations are used for computing S_1 and S_2 (see Fig. 4 and Fig. 6). The first wire represents the input, the second wire represents the S-box output by computing the multiplicative inverse α^{-1} which is equivalent to α^{254} in Galois field $\mathsf{GF}[2^8]$, and other three wires are used as workspace (ancillary qubits).

The affine function of S-box S_1 can be implemented with only 26 CNOT gates and 4 Pauli-X (NOT) gates. The resulting circuit is shown in Fig. 4. The affine function of S-box S_1^{-1} can be implemented with only 18 CNOT gates and 4 Pauli-X (NOT) gates. The resulting circuit is shown in Fig. 5.

The affine function of S-box S_2 can be implemented with only 35 CNOT gates and 4 Pauli-X (NOT) gates. The resulting circuit is shown in Fig. 6. The affine function of S-box S_2^{-1} can be implemented with only 27 CNOT gates and 4 Pauli-X (NOT) gates. The resulting circuit is shown in Fig. 7.

Fig. 4. Circuit for affine function of S_1.

Fig. 5. Circuit for affine function of S_1^{-1}.

Fig. 6. Circuit for affine function of S_2.   **Fig. 7.** Circuit for affine function of S_2^{-1}.

3.3 Diffusion Layer (DL)

The diffusion layer is defined by an invertible map $D : GF(2^8)^{16} \to GF(2^8)^{16}$ which is given by

$$(x_0, x_1, \ldots, x_{15}) \mapsto (y_0, y_1, \ldots, y_{15}), \tag{7}$$

where $(y_0, y_1, \ldots, y_{15})$ can be computed by a matrix multiplication as follows.

$$
\begin{bmatrix} y_0 \\ y_1 \\ y_2 \\ y_3 \\ y_4 \\ y_5 \\ y_6 \\ y_7 \\ y_8 \\ y_9 \\ y_{10} \\ y_{11} \\ y_{12} \\ y_{13} \\ y_{14} \\ y_{15} \end{bmatrix}
=
\begin{bmatrix}
0&0&0&1&1&0&1&0&1&1&0&0&0&1&1&0 \\
0&0&1&0&0&1&0&1&1&1&0&0&1&0&0&1 \\
0&1&0&0&1&0&1&0&0&0&1&1&1&0&0&1 \\
1&0&0&0&0&1&0&1&0&0&1&1&0&1&1&0 \\
1&0&1&0&0&1&0&0&1&0&0&1&0&0&1&1 \\
0&1&0&1&1&0&0&0&0&1&1&0&0&0&1&1 \\
1&0&1&0&0&0&0&1&0&1&1&0&1&1&0&0 \\
0&1&0&1&0&0&1&0&1&0&0&1&1&1&0&0 \\
1&1&0&0&1&0&0&1&0&0&1&0&0&1&0&1 \\
1&1&0&0&0&1&1&0&0&0&0&1&1&0&1&0 \\
0&0&1&1&0&1&1&0&1&0&0&0&0&1&0&1 \\
0&0&1&1&1&0&0&1&0&1&0&0&1&0&1&0 \\
0&1&1&0&0&0&1&1&0&1&0&1&1&0&0&0 \\
1&0&0&1&0&0&1&1&1&0&1&0&0&1&0&0 \\
1&0&0&1&1&1&0&0&0&1&0&1&0&0&1&0 \\
0&1&1&0&1&1&0&0&1&0&1&0&0&0&0&1
\end{bmatrix}
\cdot
\begin{bmatrix} x_0 \\ x_1 \\ x_2 \\ x_3 \\ x_4 \\ x_5 \\ x_6 \\ x_7 \\ x_8 \\ x_9 \\ x_{10} \\ x_{11} \\ x_{12} \\ x_{13} \\ x_{14} \\ x_{15} \end{bmatrix}
$$

Quantum Resource Estimates for Diffusion Layer (DL). In the implementation of the diffusion layer, we convert the diffusion matrix of 16×16 size into a matrix of 128×128 size by replacing 0 with a zero matrix of 8×8 size and 1 with an identity matrix of 8×8 size. Using the PLU decomposition algorithm, this modified diffusion matrix can be implemented with only 768 CNOT gates, and the circuit depth is 26.

3.4   Key Scheduling Algorithm

ARIA's key scheduling algorithm consists of two parts: initialization and round key generation, which we describe as follows.

In the initialization phase, four 128-bit values W_0, W_1, W_2, W_3 are generated from the master key MK, using a 3-round 256-bit Feistel cipher. MK can be of 128, 192, 256-bit sizes. The 256-bit value input to 256-bit Feistel is defined as

$$KL \| KR = MK \| 00 \ldots 0$$

where KL is a 128-bit value with bits from MK, and the remaining bits of MK are the part of 128-bit value KR by appending zeroes to it.

Let F_o and F_e be odd and even round functions of ARIA round transformation. The round function takes 128-bit predefined constants CK_i to be the rational part of π^{-1} and are given as follows:

$$CK_1 = \text{0x517cc1b727220a94fe12abe8fa9a6ee0}$$
$$CK_2 = \text{0x6db14acc9e21c820ff28b1d5ef5de2b0}$$
$$CK_3 = \text{0xdb92371d2126e970324977504e8c90e0}.$$

The generation of four quantum words is as follows:

$$W_0 = KL, \qquad\qquad W_1 = F_o(W_0, CK_1) \oplus KR,$$
$$W_2 = F_e(W_1, CK_2) \oplus W_0, \qquad W_3 = F_o(W_2, CK_3) \oplus W_1.$$

The initialization process of key schedule of ARIA is shown below in Fig. 8.

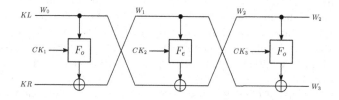

Fig. 8. Initialization phase : 3-round Feistel scheme.

In the round key generation phase, we combine the four values W_0, W_1, W_2, W_3 to obtain the encryption round keys RK_i of 128-bit size each. Note that number of rounds used in ARIA is 12, 14, 16, corresponding to the key sizes 128, 192, 256 of the master key, respectively. Since one extra key is required for the last round key addition, the number of round keys needed is 13, 15, and 17, respectively. The round subkeys are generated as follows:

$$RK_1 = (W_0) \oplus (W_1^{\ggg 19}),$$
$$RK_2 = (W_1) \oplus (W_2^{\ggg 19}),$$
$$RK_3 = (W_2) \oplus (W_3^{\ggg 19}),$$
$$RK_4 = (W_0^{\ggg 19}) \oplus (W_3),$$
$$RK_5 = (W_0) \oplus (W_1^{\ggg 31}),$$
$$RK_6 = (W_1) \oplus (W_2^{\ggg 31}),$$
$$RK_7 = (W_2) \oplus (W_3^{\ggg 31}),$$
$$RK_8 = (W_0^{\ggg 31}) \oplus (W_3),$$
$$RK_9 = (W_0) \oplus (W_1^{\lll 61}),$$
$$RK_{10} = (W_1) \oplus (W_2^{\ggg 61}),$$
$$RK_{11} = (W_2) \oplus (W_3^{\lll 61}),$$
$$RK_{12} = (W_0^{\lll 61}) \oplus (W_3),$$
$$RK_{13} = (W_0) \oplus (W_1^{\lll 31}),$$
$$RK_{14} = (W_1) \oplus (W_2^{\lll 31}),$$
$$RK_{15} = (W_2) \oplus (W_3^{\lll 31}),$$
$$RK_{16} = (W_0^{\lll 31}) \oplus (W_3), \qquad (8)$$
$$RK_{17} = (W_0) \oplus (W_1^{\lll 19}).$$

Quantum Resource Estimates for Round Key Generation. In the implementation of key generation, the main cost comes from the initialization part of the key schedule of ARIA in generating the four quantum words W_0, W_1, W_2, W_3 by using a 256-bit Feistel cipher. The Feistel uses different inner round functions for odd and even rounds, which is one round of ARIA, i.e., AddRoundKey, SubBytes, and Diffusion operations.

1. **Add Round Key (ARK):** We simply XOR the 128-bit key with the current state. Thus, only 128 CNOT gates are required to implement this operation.

2. **Substitution Layer (SL):** Four S-boxes $S_1, S_1^{-1}, S_2, S_2^{-1}$ are used in two different substitution layers for odd and even rounds. Each layer uses four times $S_1, S_1^{-1}, S_2, S_2^{-1}$, i.e., 16 S-boxes. We count the required quantum gates to implement each of these S-boxes.

   – Computing S_1 : To find the multiplication inverse of input α, we require 33 squarings and 7 multiplications, including the uncomputing wires (see Fig. 3). Squaring operation requires 12 CNOT gates (see Fig. 1), and multiplication operation requires 64 Toffoli gates plus 21 CNOT gates (see Fig. 2). To apply affine transformation, we require 26 CNOT gates and 4 Pauli-X gates (see Fig. 4). Thus, the total cost is given as:
     • Number of Toffoli gates = $64 \times 7 = 448$
     • Number of CNOT gates = $12 \times 33 + 21 \times 7 + 26 = 569$
     • Number of Pauli-X gates = 4.

   To compute S-boxes S_1^{-1}, S_2, S_2^{-1}, we use the same circuit to find the inverse as given in Fig. 3. However, the affine functions used in S_1^{-1}, S_2, S_2^{-1} are different from S_1. Therefore, we discuss the cost of affine functions separately while other costs remain same.

- Computing S_1^{-1} : Here, applying affine transformation requires only 18 CNOT gates and 4 Pauli-X gates (see Fig. 5). Thus, the total cost is given as:
  - Number of Toffoli gates = $64 \times 7 = 448$
  - Number of CNOT gates = $12 \times 33 + 21 \times 7 + 18 = 561$
  - Number of Pauli-X gates = 4.

- Computing S_2 : Here, applying affine transformation requires only 35 CNOT gates and 4 Pauli-X gates (see Fig. 6). Thus, the total cost is given as:
  - Number of Toffoli gates = $64 \times 7 = 448$
  - Number of CNOT gates = $12 \times 33 + 21 \times 7 + 35 = 578$
  - Number of Pauli-X gates = 4.

- Computing S_2^{-1} : Here, applying affine transformation requires only 27 CNOT gates and 4 Pauli-X gates (see Fig. 7). Thus, the total cost is given as:
  - Number of Toffoli gates = $64 \times 7 = 448$
  - Number of CNOT gates = $12 \times 33 + 21 \times 7 + 27 = 570$
  - Number of Pauli-X gates = 4.

Therefore, the total number of quantum gates needed to implement the substitution layer are as follows.
- Total number of Toffoli gates = $448 \times (4 \times 4) = 7,168$
- Total number of CNOT gates = $(569 + 561 + 578 + 570) \times 4 = 9,112$
- Total number of Pauli-X gates = $4 \times (4 \times 4) = 64$.

3. **Diffusion Layer (DL):** It is a linear operation and implementing it requires only 768 CNOT gates.

Therefore, one round of ARIA requires the following number of gates:

- Total number of Toffoli gates = $7,168$
- Total number of CNOT gates = $128 + 9,112 + 768 = 10,008$
- Total number of Pauli-X gates = 64.

The round subkeys RK_i are generated using four quantum keywords W_0, W_1, W_2, W_3 as given in the expression (8). It consists of only left or right circular rotation and XOR operations. The circular rotations of words are implemented for free because it is just a particular permutation of the state of the quantum keywords W_0, W_1, W_2, W_3. The only gates required for subkeys generation RK_i are CNOT gates. The number of CNOT gates required for each round subkey is 512 since we are using only one qubit state $|W_4\rangle$ to compute the round subkeys and uncompute the states to save the qubits. For counting of CNOT gates, one can refer to Fig. 9 for the generation of subkey RK_1 working on the state $|W_4\rangle$.

Table 2 demonstrates the estimated cost of generating W_0, W_1, W_2, W_3 in the initialization phase, and the round subkeys RK_i. Some extra Pauli-X gates are also used to generate the round constants CK_1, CK_2, CK_3 of 3-round Feistel.

Table 2. Quantum cost of generating four quantum words and round subkeys for the key schedule of ARIA-{128, 192, 256}.

KeyWords (W_i)	# Pauli-X	# CNOT	# Toffoli
W_0	0	128	0
W_1	$64 + 65 = 129$	$10,008 + 128 = 10,136$	7,168
W_2	$64 + 65 = 129$	$10,008 + 128 = 10,136$	7,168
W_3	$64 + 57 = 121$	$10,008 + 128 = 10,136$	7,168
Total	379	30,536	21,504
Round Subkeys	# Pauli-X	# CNOT	# Toffoli
RK_i for each i	0	$128 \times 4 = 512$	0

4   Resource Estimates: Reversible ARIA Implementation

In this section, we provide the quantum resource estimates to implement the ARIA-{128, 192, 256} for the number of qubits and the number of Pauli-X gates, CNOT gates, and Toffoli gates. We present the full quantum reversible circuit of ARIA-128, as shown in Fig. 9. Note that arranging 12 encryption rounds of ARIA-128 in pipeline fashion requires $12 \times 128 = 1536$ qubits. In order to save qubits, we, therefore, rearrange the encryption rounds in a "zigzag" fashion as adopted by Grassl et al. [10] and Almazrooie et al. [1], to design the reversible circuit of ARIA-128, which requires only 640 qubits of storage. Using the "zigzag" strategy of designing the reversible circuit, we are able to reduce the width but at the cost of increasing depth of the circuit.

The entire circuit of ARIA-128 in Fig. 9 makes use of 1408 qubits (number of qubits required for both key generation and encryption algorithms) and 24 ancilla qubits, which have been used to calculate the multiplicative inverse in the SubBytes function. These 24 ancilla qubits can be placed in between the subkeys generation and the encryption rounds. Every vertical line represents one quantum word of 128-qubits, and every horizontal line indicates 128 connections of the corresponding gates or subroutines. The words KL and KR are assigned for the master key, and the words CK_1, CK_2, CK_3 are assigned to Feistel round constants, which are used to generate four quantum keywords W_0, W_1, W_2, W_3 that are further used for subkeys generation. We also use the extra workspace W_4 of 128-qubits size for generating round subkeys. Each subkey needs only 4 CNOT and few left or right circular rotations, which are considered to be free to implement. The words W_5 to W_9 are devoted to the encryption rounds of ARIA.

Note that ARIA-128 and ARIA-192 require 640 qubits of storage since we need to reverse the encryption rounds on 640 qubits, and the reversing process

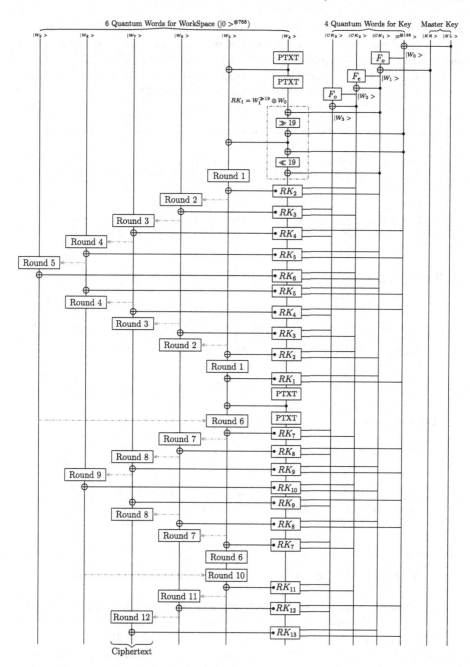

Fig. 9. Quantum circuit of ARIA-128. Each vertical line (wire) constitutes 128 qubits. The wires $|KL\rangle$ and $|KR\rangle$ represent the master key, next four wires are used for generating keywords $|W_0\rangle, |W_1\rangle, |W_2\rangle, |W_3\rangle$, the wire $|w_4\rangle$ is used as ancillas for round key generation, and the wires from $|w_5\rangle$ to $|w_9\rangle$ are used for main round operations. The dark-red colored dash-lines represent the outputs from one round to another. (Color figure online)

is performed after rounds 5, 9, and 12. However, ARIA-256 requires 768 bits of storage for reversing the rounds, and the reversing process is performed after rounds 6, 11, and 15, requiring only 128 qubits more than ARIA-128.

In Tables 3, 4, 5, we provide the overall cost of quantum resource estimates needed to implement full reversible circuits of ARIA-{128, 192, 256}.

Table 3. Quantum resource estimates for the implementation of ARIA-128.

Phase	#Quantum Gates			Depth		#Qubits	
	#Pauli-X	#CNOT	#Toffoli	Toffoli	Overall	Storage	Ancilla
Initial	0	0	0	0	0	256	0
Key Gen	379	41,228	21,504	588	1,342	512	128
Encryption	1,216	189,896	136,192	3,724	7,918	640	24
Total	1,595	231,124	157,696	4,312	9,260	1,408	152

Table 4. Quantum resource estimates for the implementation of ARIA-192.

Phase	#Quantum Gates			Depth		#Qubits	
	#Pauli-X	#CNOT	#Toffoli	Toffoli	Overall	Storage	Ancilla
Initial	0	0	0	0	0	256	0
Key Gen	379	43,336	21,504	588	1,358	512	128
Encryption	1,472	229,928	164,864	4,508	9,590	640	24
Total	1,851	273,264	183,368	5,096	10,948	1,408	152

Table 5. Quantum resource estimates for the implementation of ARIA-256.

Phase	#Quantum Gates			Depth		#Qubits	
	#Pauli-X	#CNOT	#Toffoli	Toffoli	Overall	Storage	Ancilla
Initial	0	0	0	0	0	256	0
Key Gen	379	45,384	21,504	588	1,374	512	128
Encryption	1,792	279,968	200,704	5,488	11,680	768	24
Total	2,171	325,352	222,208	6,076	13,054	1,536	152

5   Grover Oracle and Key Search Resource Estimates

Assume that we have a quantum adversary who makes the use of Grover's algorithm to find a key on given a small number of plaintext-ciphertext pairs. To apply Grover's algorithm for an exhaustive key search on ARIA, we need a circuit to implement unitary operator U_f based on ARIA. Since ARIA works as a PRF, it is possible that multiple keys leads to the same ciphertext,

$$\mathsf{ARIA}(k_0, m) = \mathsf{ARIA}(k_1, m) = \dots,$$

where $k_0, k_1 \in \{0, 1\}^{128}$ are different keys and m is given plaintext. To ensure key uniqueness among other desirable solutions, more than a single pair of plaintext and ciphertext are required. Grassl et al. [10] proposed a method to calculate the required number of pairs (r_k) such that $r_k > \lceil 2k/n \rceil$, where k and n denote the length of the key and plaintext respectively. Thus, to implement ARIA-128, one needs 3 pairs of plaintext-ciphertext, and $(3 \times 1560 = 4680)$ qubits. However, following the work by Langenberg et al. [17], we assume that $r_k = \lceil k/n \rceil$ known plaintext-ciphertext pairs are sufficient to avoid false positives in an exhaustive key search for ARIA-k ($k \in \{128, 192, 256\}$). Thus, taking into account "cleaning up" of wires, we need to implement:

- 2 ARIA instances (for $r_{128} = 1$ plaintext-ciphertext pair) for ARIA-128
- 4 ARIA instances (for $r_{192} = 2$ plaintext-ciphertext pairs) for ARIA-192
- 4 ARIA instances (for $r_{256} = 2$ plaintext-ciphertext pairs) for ARIA-256

5.1   Number of Qubits

As adopted in [10,17], to make the smaller T-depth, we can test the multiple plaintext-ciphertext pairs in parallel. The total number of qubits needed is $r_k.q_k + 1$, where q_k is the number of qubits needed to implement ARIA.

- ARIA-128: $1 \cdot 1,560 + 1 = 1,561$ qubits for a Grover-based key search.
- ARIA-192: $2 \cdot 1,560 + 1 = 3,121$ qubits for a Grover-based key search.
- ARIA-256: $2 \cdot 1,688 + 1 = 3,377$ qubits for a Grover-based key search.

5.2   Gate Counts

Operator U_f. Inside the operator U_f, we need to compare the 128-bit outputs of ARIA instances with r_k given ciphertexts. We use a $128 \cdot r_k$-controlled NOT gates. We can also budget $2 \cdot (r_k - 1) \cdot k$ CNOT gates to make the input key available to all r_k parallel ARIA instances (and uncomputing this operation at the end). However, we need to implement the actual ARIA instances. From Tables 3, 4, 5, we obtain the following resource estimates:

- ARIA-128 : Two ARIA instances require $2 \cdot 157,696 = 315,392$ Toffoli gates with a Toffoli depth of $2 \cdot 4,312 = 8,624$. Additionally, we need $2 \cdot 1,595 = 3,190$ Pauli-X gates and $2 \cdot 231,124 = 462,248$ CNOT gates.
- ARIA-192 : Four ARIA instances require $4 \cdot 183,368 = 733,472$ Toffoli gates with a Toffoli depth of $4 \cdot 5,096 = 20,384$. Additionally, we need $4 \cdot 1,851 = 7,404$ Pauli-X gates and $4 \cdot 273,264 = 1,093,056$ CNOT gates.
- ARIA-256 : Four ARIA instances require $4 \cdot 222,208 = 888,832$ Toffoli gates with a Toffoli depth of $4 \cdot 6,076 = 24,304$. Additionally, we need $4 \cdot 2,171 = 8,684$ Pauli-X gates and $4 \cdot 325,352 = 1,301,408$ CNOT gates.

Grover Operator G. Grover's algorithm repeatedly applies the operator

$$G = U_f \left(\left(H^{\otimes k} \left(2 \left| 0 \right\rangle \left\langle 0 \right| - \mathbf{1}_{2^k} \right) H^{\otimes k} \right) \otimes \mathbf{1}_2 \right)$$

where $|0\rangle$ is the all-zero basis state of appropriate size. So in addition to U_f, further gates are needed. Following [10], for the operator $(2 |0\rangle \langle 0| - \mathbf{1}_{2^k})$, we also budget a k-fold controlled-NOT gate. With $\lfloor \frac{\pi}{4} \cdot \sqrt{2^k} \rfloor$ number of Grover iterations for ARIA-k, we can now give estimates in the Clifford+T model (Fig. 10).

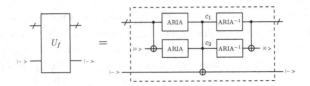

Fig. 10. The reversible implementation of the function U_f for ARIA-128 is shown for which $r = 2$ invocations of ARIA-128 suffice in order to make the target key unique.

5.3 Overall Cost

Here, we provide the overall quantum resource estimates for Grover's based key search in the Clifford+T model. We use the following results/observations:

- By Amy et al. [3], one Toffoli gate requires 7 T-gates and 8 Clifford gates, a T-depth of 4, and a total depth of 8.
- By Wiebe and Roetteler [23], the number of T-gates to realize an ℓ-fold controlled-NOT gate ($\ell \geq 5$) is estimated as $(32 \cdot \ell - 84)$.
- To estimate the total number of Clifford gates, we count only the Clifford gates in the ARIA instances, plus the $2 \cdot (r_k - 1) \cdot k$ CNOT gates inside U_f for the parallel processing of plaintext-ciphertext pairs.
- To estimate the T-depth and overall circuit depth, we take into account only T-depth and circuit depth of ARIA-k. For the S-box used in ARIA, the circuit depth is 391. However, when we represent Toffoli gates in Clifford+T model, the S-box circuit depth is 1,692.

Therefore, the estimated total cost for a Grover-based attack against ARIA-k for $k \in \{128, 192, 256\}$ is as follows.

1. **ARIA-128:**
   - T-gates: $\lfloor \frac{\pi}{4} \cdot 2^{64} \rfloor \cdot (7 \cdot 315, 392 + 32 \cdot 128 - 84 + 32 \cdot 128 - 84) \approx 1.65 \cdot 2^{84}$ T-gates with a T-depth of $\lfloor \frac{\pi}{4} \cdot 2^{64} \rfloor \cdot 4 \cdot 8, 624 \approx 1.65 \cdot 2^{78}$.
   - Clifford gates: $\lfloor \frac{\pi}{4} \cdot 2^{64} \rfloor \cdot (8 \cdot 315, 392 + 3, 190 + 462, 248) \approx 1.11 \cdot 2^{85}$.
   - Circuit depth: $\lfloor \frac{\pi}{4} \cdot 2^{64} \rfloor \cdot 2 \cdot (22 \cdot 1, 692 + 21 \cdot 26 + 112) \approx 1.81 \cdot 2^{79}$.

2. **ARIA-192:**
   - T-gates: $\lfloor \frac{\pi}{4} \cdot 2^{96} \rfloor \cdot (7 \cdot 733, 472 + 32 \cdot 192 - 84 + 32 \cdot 192 - 84) \approx 1.92 \cdot 2^{117}$ T-gates with a T-depth of $\lfloor \frac{\pi}{4} \cdot 2^{96} \rfloor \cdot 4 \cdot 20, 384 \approx 1.95 \cdot 2^{111}$.
   - Clifford gates: $\lfloor \frac{\pi}{4} \cdot 2^{96} \rfloor \cdot (8 \cdot 733, 472 + 7, 404 + 1, 093, 056) \approx 1.30 \cdot 2^{118}$.
   - Circuit depth: $\lfloor \frac{\pi}{4} \cdot 2^{96} \rfloor \cdot 2 \cdot (26 \cdot 1, 692 + 25 \cdot 26 + 132) \approx 1.07 \cdot 2^{112}$.

3. **ARIA-256:**
   - T-gates: $\lfloor \frac{\pi}{4} \cdot 2^{128} \rfloor \cdot (7 \cdot 888, 832 + 32 \cdot 256 - 84 + 32 \cdot 256 - 84) \approx 1.16 \cdot 2^{150}$ T-gates with a T-depth of $\lfloor \frac{\pi}{4} \cdot 2^{128} \rfloor \cdot 4 \cdot 24, 304 \approx 1.16 \cdot 2^{144}$.
   - Clifford gates: $\lfloor \frac{\pi}{4} \cdot 2^{128} \rfloor \cdot (8 \cdot 888, 832 + 8, 684 + 1, 301, 408) \approx 1.57 \cdot 2^{150}$.
   - Circuit depth: $\lfloor \frac{\pi}{4} \cdot 2^{128} \rfloor \cdot 2 \cdot (30 \cdot 1, 692 + 29 \cdot 26 + 152) \approx 1.23 \cdot 2^{144}$.

6   Cost Comparison of ARIA and AES

For fairness and correctness, we choose the block cipher AES as a reference point because of a well-studied quantum resource estimates for Grover's search on AES. In addition, ARIA and AES share many resemblances like SPN structure, similar S-Box computations defined over the same irreducible polynomial, albeit different mixcolumn operations and key-scheduling algorithm.

In Table 6, we compare the results on S-box computations for the number of qubits, squaring, and multiplication operations to compute the multiplicative inverse. The number of Toffoli gates is directly proportional to the required number of multiplications in a multiplier circuit. For ARIA, one S-box computation requires 7 multiplications (see Fig. 3), which leads to 448 Toffoli gates. We also compare the total number of S-box computations needed in the reversible implementations of AES-128 and ARIA-128.

Table 6. Comparison of S-Box computations for AES and ARIA.

Block ciphers	Single S-box (Multiplicative Inverse)			Total S-box computations
	#Qubits	#Multiplication	#Squaring	
AES-128 (Grassl et al. [10])	40	8	23	320
AES-128 (Almazrooie et al. [1])	48	7	14	320
ARIA-128 (this work)	40	7	33	304

Next, we consider the G-cost and DW-cost (the metrics proposed by Jaques and Schanck [14]) for AES and ARIA. By G-cost, we mean the total number of gates, and by DW-cost, we mean the product of circuit depth and width. Finally, we compare overall cost estimates of quantum resources needed for Grover's algorithm with $\lfloor \frac{\pi}{4} \cdot \sqrt{2^k} \rfloor$ AES and ARIA oracles iterations for exhaustive key search attacks, without a depth restriction. On a lighter note, it is clear from the comparison that the G-cost of ARIA and AES is almost the same, but the DW-cost of ARIA is lower than the AES.

Jaques et al.'s work [13]									
Scheme	r_k	#Clifford	#T	T-depth	full depth	width	G-cost	DW-cost	p_s
AES-128	1	$1.03 \cdot 2^{85}$	$1.59 \cdot 2^{84}$	$1.06 \cdot 2^{80}$	$1.16 \cdot 2^{81}$	984	$1.83 \cdot 2^{85}$	$1.11 \cdot 2^{91}$	$1/e$
AES-192	2	$1.17 \cdot 2^{118}$	$1.81 \cdot 2^{117}$	$1.21 \cdot 2^{112}$	$1.33 \cdot 2^{113}$	2224	$1.04 \cdot 2^{119}$	$1.44 \cdot 2^{124}$	1
AES-256	2	$1.46 \cdot 2^{150}$	$1.13 \cdot 2^{150}$	$1.44 \cdot 2^{144}$	$1.57 \cdot 2^{145}$	2672	$1.30 \cdot 2^{151}$	$1.02 \cdot 2^{157}$	$1/e$

This Work									
Scheme	r_k	#Clifford	#T	T-depth	full depth	width	G-cost	DW-cost	p_s
ARIA-128	1	$1.11 \cdot 2^{85}$	$1.65 \cdot 2^{84}$	$1.65 \cdot 2^{78}$	$1.81 \cdot 2^{79}$	1561	$1.93 \cdot 2^{85}$	$1.37 \cdot 2^{90}$	$1/e$
ARIA-192	2	$1.30 \cdot 2^{118}$	$1.92 \cdot 2^{117}$	$1.95 \cdot 2^{111}$	$1.07 \cdot 2^{112}$	3121	$1.13 \cdot 2^{119}$	$1.63 \cdot 2^{123}$	1
ARIA-256	2	$1.57 \cdot 2^{150}$	$1.16 \cdot 2^{150}$	$1.16 \cdot 2^{144}$	$1.23 \cdot 2^{144}$	3377	$1.36 \cdot 2^{151}$	$1.01 \cdot 2^{156}$	$1/e$

7   Conclusion

We investigated the security of the block cipher ARIA-{128, 192, 256} against Grover's search algorithm. Firstly, we estimated the cost of quantum resources needed to implement different components of ARIA such as S-box computations (multiplicative inverse, squaring, multiplication operations), diffusion layer by analyzing theoretically for the number of qubits and the number of Pauli-X gates, CNOT gates, and Toffoli gates. We also estimated the T-depth and the overall circuit depth. We then evaluated the overall cost of one Round of ARIA and key expansion mechanism. We finally constructed a full quantum circuit of ARIA-128, and provided the cost of quantum resources for full quantum circuits of ARIA-{128, 192, 256}. We also provided the cost of Grover's key search attack against ARIA-{128, 192, 256} in the Clifford+T model. However, the established quantum resource estimates remain far beyond the currently available technology and resources. As a future research work, it might be interesting to reduce Grover's key search attack complexity against ARIA by introducing more optimizations to the circuit, in particular the S-box circuit optimization technique by Boyer and Peralta [6]. It would also be interesting to implement the Grover oracle for ARIA in any quantum programming language for automatic resource estimation like the works [13,20]. Another interesting open problem remains to evaluate the cost of block ciphers like AES, ARIA by implementing them against the multi-target attacks [4].

Acknowledgment. We would like to thank the anonymous reviewers of SPACE 2020 for their insightful comments and suggestions, which has significantly improved the presentation and technical quality of this work. The second author would also like to thank MATRICS grant 2019/1514 by the Science and Engineering Research Board (SERB), Dept. of Science and Technology, Govt. of India for supporting the research carried out in this work. We would also like to thank Dr. Kai-Min Chung for initial discussions on quantum computing.

References

1. Almazrooie, M., Samsudin, A., Abdullah, R., Mutter, K.N.: Quantum reversible circuit of AES-128. Quantum Inf. Process. **17**(5), 1–30 (2018). https://doi.org/10.1007/s11128-018-1864-3
2. Amy, M., Maslov, D., Mosca, M., Roetteler, M.: A meet-in-the-middle algorithm for fast synthesis of depth-optimal quantum circuits. IEEE Trans. Comput.-Aided Design Integr. Circu. Syst. **32**(6), 818-830 (2013)
3. Amy, M., Di Matteo, O., Gheorghiu, V., Mosca, M., Parent, A., Schanck, J.: Estimating the cost of generic quantum pre-image attacks on SHA-2 and SHA-3. In: Avanzi, R., Heys, H. (eds.) SAC 2016. LNCS, vol. 10532, pp. 317–337. Springer, Cham (2017). https://doi.org/10.1007/978-3-319-69453-5_18
4. Banegas, G., Bernstein, D.J.: Low-communication parallel quantum multi-target preimage search. In: Adams, C., Camenisch, J. (eds.) SAC 2017. LNCS, vol. 10719, pp. 325–335. Springer, Cham (2018). https://doi.org/10.1007/978-3-319-72565-9_16

5. Bonnetain, X., Naya-Plasencia, M., Schrottenloher, A.: Quantum security analysis of AES. IACR Trans. Symmetric Cryptol. **2**, 2019 (2019)
6. Boyar, J., Peralta, R.: A small depth-16 circuit for the AES S-Box. In: Gritzalis, D., Furnell, S., Theoharidou, M. (eds.) SEC 2012. IAICT, vol. 376, pp. 287–298. Springer, Heidelberg (2012). https://doi.org/10.1007/978-3-642-30436-1_24
7. Boyer, M., Brassard, G., Hoeyer, P., Tapp, A.: Tight bounds on quantum searching (1996). arXiv:quant-ph/9605034
8. Cheung, D., Maslov, D., Mathew, J., Pradhan, D.K.: On the design and optimization of a quantum polynomial-time attack on elliptic curve cryptography. In: Kawano, Y., Mosca, M. (eds.) TQC 2008. LNCS, vol. 5106, pp. 96–104. Springer, Heidelberg (2008). https://doi.org/10.1007/978-3-540-89304-2_9
9. Abraham, H., et al.: Qiskit: An open-source framework for quantum computing (2019. https://qiskit.org
10. Grassl, M., Langenberg, B., Roetteler, M., Steinwandt, R.: Applying Grover's algorithm to AES: quantum resource estimates. In: Takagi, T. (ed.) PQCrypto 2016. LNCS, vol. 9606, pp. 29–43. Springer, Cham (2016). https://doi.org/10.1007/978-3-319-29360-8_3
11. Grover, L.K.: A fast quantum mechanical algorithm for database search. In: ACM Symposium on the Theory of Computing (1996)
12. Guajardo, J., Paar, C.: Itoh-Tsujii inversion in standard basis and its application in cryptography and codes. Design Codes Cryptogr. **25**(2), 207–216 (2002). https://doi.org/10.1023/A:1013860532636
13. Jaques, S., Naehrig, M., Roetteler, M., Virdia, F.: Implementing Grover oracles for quantum key search on AES and LowMC. In: Canteaut, A., Ishai, Y. (eds.) EUROCRYPT 2020. LNCS, vol. 12106, pp. 280–310. Springer, Cham (2020). https://doi.org/10.1007/978-3-030-45724-2_10
14. Jaques, S., Schanck, J.M.: Quantum cryptanalysis in the RAM Model: claw-finding attacks on SIKE. In: Boldyreva, A., Micciancio, D. (eds.) CRYPTO 2019. LNCS, vol. 11692, pp. 32–61. Springer, Cham (2019). https://doi.org/10.1007/978-3-030-26948-7_2
15. Kim, P., Han, D., Jeong, K.C.: Time–space complexity of quantum search algorithms in symmetric cryptanalysis: applying to AES and SHA-2. Quantum Inf. Process. **17**(12), 1–39 (2018). https://doi.org/10.1007/s11128-018-2107-3
16. Kwon, D., et al.: New block cipher ARIA. In: Information Security and Cryptology - ICISC (2003)
17. Langenberg, B., Pham, H., Steinwandt, R.: Reducing the cost of implementing the advanced encryption standard as a quantum circuit. IEEE Trans. Quantum Eng. **1**, 1–12 (2020)
18. Nielsen, M.A., Chuang, I.L.: Quantum Computation and Quantum Information. 10th, Anniversary edn. Cambridge Univ, Press (2011)
19. NIST. Submission requirements and evaluation criteria for the post-quantum cryptography standardization process (2017). https://csrc.nist.gov/CSRC/media/Projects/Post-Quantum-Cryptography/documents/call-for-proposals-final-dec-2016.pdf/
20. Ramos-Calderer, S., Bellini, E., Latorre, J.I., Manzano, M., Mateu, V.: Quantum search for scaled hash function preimages. IACR Cryptol. ePrint Arch. 1062 (2020). https://eprint.iacr.org/2020/1062
21. Selinger, P.: Quantum circuits of T-depth one. Phys. Rev. A **87**, 042302 (2013)

22. Shor, P.W.: Polynomial time algorithms for discrete logarithms and factoring on a quantum computer. In: Adleman, L.M., Huang, M.-D. (eds.) ANTS 1994. LNCS, vol. 877, pp. 289–289. Springer, Heidelberg (1994). https://doi.org/10.1007/3-540-58691-1_68

23. Wiebe, N., Roetteler, M.: Quantum arithmetic and numerical analysis using repeat-until-success circuits. Quantum Inf. Comput. **16**(1&2) (2016)

24. William, S., et al.: Sagemath, the Sage Mathematics Software System Version 8.1 (2017). https://www.sagemath.org

Author Index

Printed in the United States
By Bookmasters